Luther on Faith and Love

Luther on Faith and Love

Christ and the Law in the 1535 Galatians Commentary

Sun-young Kim

Fortress Press
Minneapolis

LUTHER ON FAITH AND LOVE

Christ and the Law in the 1535 Galatians Commentary

Cover design: Alisha Lofgren

Library of Congress Cataloging-in-Publication Data

Print ISBN: 978-1-4514-8772-5

eBook ISBN: 978-1-4514-8976-7

The paper used in this publication meets the minimum requirements of American National Standard for Information Sciences — Permanence of Paper for Printed Library Materials, ANSI Z329.48-1984.

Manufactured in the U.S.A.

This book was produced using PressBooks.com, and PDF rendering was done by PrinceXML.

Contents

Acknowledgments

Conceiving of and effecting this volume demanded more than I could do by myself. The whole process has led me to a deeper appreciation of the presence of God and God's people in my life. Their kind gestures and smiles, thoughtful and encouraging remarks, loving hugs, and warm and attentive hearts carried me through challenges and trials. I want to take this opportunity to thank all those who have walked with me throughout the conception, writing, and finishing of this volume. All of them will be remembered in my heart with genuine appreciation and I regret that, due to space, only a few can be named here.

I would like to express my sincere gratitude to Professor George Hunsinger, who offered pointers on how to go about the writing task and motivated me to work to my full capacity. His challenging questions and comments always impelled me to aim higher in the quality of my research and writing. I am also greatly indebted to Emeritus Professor Scott Hendrix, who, with his scholarly expertise in Luther studies, imbued me with the spirit of Luther's theology. He counseled me on how to hone my thesis and helped me remain focused on its significance and ramifications. He also arranged for me to converse with Professor Timothy Wengert concerning my research interests. I truly appreciate the thought-provoking conversations I had with both of them. I am also greatly thankful to Professor Ellen Charry for her demonstration of Christian love and care. She enriched and refined the content of my dissertation by raising critical questions. The efforts and generosity of these three members of my dissertation committee made it possible for me to pass the oral defense of my dissertation magna cum laude.

It is also a great pleasure to acknowledge my debt to Professor Paul E. Rorem. In my MDiv program at Princeton Theological Seminary, he sparked my interest in St. Augustine's theology, which eventually led me to develop a comparative study between Augustine and Luther. Professor Elsie McKee's academic virtuosity and spiritual virtues also require special thanks. In addition, Professor Bruce L. McCormack's academic advice and friendly encouragement will always be remembered. I would like to offer a special word of thanks to Dr. Eberhard Jüngel and Dr. Oswald Bayer who welcomed me when I was at the University of Tübingen as an exchange student. My deepest appreciation is due to the late Dr. James E. Loder, my spiritual father, academic mentor, counselor, and friend. I will greatly miss the listening ears of my academic advisors and their critical comments. I also benefited tremendously from the use of the Princeton Theological Seminary Speer and Luce Libraries, Firestone Library at Princeton University, the library of the University of Tübingen, and the Institut für Spätmittelalter und Reformation. I wish to credit Dr. Kimberly A. Bresler and Jennifer Adams-Massmann, who, along with being valued conversation partners, proofread my dissertation. Thanks are also due to Rebecca Langley, who carefully proofread the revised version of the dissertation for publication.

I would like to recognize my mother and late father's demonstration of Christian faith, hope, and love towards me. I am exceedingly obliged to them for giving their blessing to my academic and spiritual journey and displaying their confidence in me. In appreciation for their inspirational witness to Christian faith and love, I dedicate this volume to them. Special acknowledgement is also due to my brothers, sisters-in-law, and nephews, who always fill my heart with joy and wonder. This volume is a revised edition of my original dissertation. The main argument remains the same as it is in the original, but an endeavor has been made to improve its presentation.

Above all, I am grateful to God who has trained me to kneel down and keep in mind that God is the sole fountain of wisdom, knowledge, and strength. *Soli Deo gloria*!

Sun-young Kim
South Korea
February 2014

Abbreviations

LW
Luther's Works, American Edition. 75 vols. Edited by Jaroslav Pelikan, Helmut T. Lehmann, and Christopher Boyd Brown. Saint Louis: Concordia Publishing House, 1955ff.; Philadelphia: Fortress Press, 1955–86.

STh
Aquinas, Thomas. *Summa Theologiæ: Complete Set*. Latin-English Edition, vols. 13–20. Translated by Fr. Laurence Shapcote, O.P. Edited by John Mortensen and Enrique Alarcón. Lander, WY: Aquinas Institute, 2012.

WA
D. Martin Luthers Werke, Kritische Gesamtausgabe. 72 vols. Edited by J. K. F. Knaake et al. Weimar: Hermann Böhlau, 1883–2009.

WA, TR
Luthers Werke, Kritische Gesamtausgabe, *Tischreden*. 6 vols. Edited by J. F. K. Knaake et al. Weimar: Hermann Böhlau, 1912–21.

Introduction

Thesis and Choice of Topic

This dissertation will undertake a long-overdue inquiry into the teaching on faith and love in Martin Luther (1483–1546), zeroing in on his commentary on St. Paul's Epistle to the Galatians (1535). My thesis is that faith and love operate as the overriding thematic pair, structurally and conceptually undergirding the Galatians commentary, and that this can especially be seen in dynamic interaction with his outlook on the functions of Christ and the law.[1] To substantiate the thesis, this dissertation brings to the fore

---

1. When I use "Christ," it must be construed in the context of Luther's notion of Christ as the core of the gospel. Viewing Christ as the quintessence of the gospel will help readers recognize that the title of this dissertation can also be rephrased as Luther's doctrine of faith and love in relation to his understanding of the gospel and the law. The reason I chose "Christ" rather than "the gospel" is to feature Christ himself, who is present in Christian faith and active in Christian love, as I will explain. Even though God brings about faith in one's heart only through God's word, written or proclaimed, what is grasped by faith is not merely the written or proclaimed word, but Christ himself. The title of this dissertation signals my intention to underscore this.

   With respect to the word of God preached and the word of God written, Luther always preferred the former to the latter. See David C. Steinmetz, *Luther in Context*, 2nd ed. (Grand Rapids: Baker Academic, 2002), 132–35. Regarding a difference between the Word that became flesh [John 1:14] and the Word that is proclaimed by Christ or by a minister, Luther makes a clear distinction: "The former is the incarnate Word, who was true God from the beginning, and the latter is the Word that's proclaimed. The former Word is in substance God; the latter Word is in its effect the power of God, but isn't God in substance, for it has a man's nature, whether it's spoken by Christ or by a minister." Martin Luther, *Table Talk*, in *Luther's Works*, American edition, 75 vols., ed. Jaroslav Pelikan, Helmut T. Lehmann, and Christopher Boyd Brown (Saint Louis: Concordia Publishing House, 1955ff.; Philadelphia:

an interpretive framework that Luther himself provides, by which to understand his teaching on faith and love. This framework is comprised of two dimensions—alien, passive, and perfect righteousness and holiness vis-à-vis proper, active, and progressing righteousness and holiness. In these two dimensions, Luther reconceptualizes faith and love, and deliberately presents them as a structurally and conceptually interlocked thematic pair. In Luther's reconceptualization of faith and love, Christ, whom he sees as the essence of the gospel, occupies a central position. Furthermore, Luther's contemplations of the person and functions of Christ in relation to the law reveal the dynamics between faith and love, and law and gospel, which all hinge on Jesus Christ.

Indeed, it may not be an exaggeration to say that the Achilles' heel of existing Luther scholarship is its failure to delve into his teaching on love in conjunction with his teaching on justification by faith. The journey that has led me to this scrutiny of Luther's concepts of faith and love in connection with his notions of the functions of Christ and the law has been long and meandering. In my earlier studies, the theology of love in St. Augustine (354–430) was one of my main theological foci. I was particularly interested in his notions of the *ordo amoris* (most explicitly delineated in his *De doctrina christiana*),[2] of the Holy Spirit as the love that binds

---

Fortress Press, 1955–86), 54:395 (no. 5177, dated 7–24 August 1540, hereafter cited as *LW* 54:395); *D. Martin Luthers Werke, Kritische Gesamtausgabe, Tischreden,* 6 vols. (Weimar: Hermann Böhlau, 1912–21), 4. 695. 16–21 (hereafter cited as *WA, TR* 4. 695. 16–21). Unless indicated as "my translation," translations of Luther in this dissertation are based for the most part on the American edition of Luther's Works.

2. With regard to the four different objects of love that must be loved in a right order, St. Augustine states that "quatuor sint diligenda, unum quod supra nos est, alterum quod nos sumus, tertium quod juxta nos est, quartum quod infra nos est." St. Augustine, *De doctrina Christiana,* 1. 23. 22, *Patrologiae cursus completes,* Series Latina, 34–35, ed. Jacques-Paul Migne (Paris, 1865); English Translation (ET) *Teaching Christianity,* trans. Edmund Hill, O.P., ed. John E. Rotelle, O.S.A. (Brooklyn, NY: New City Press, 1997), 1. 23. 22: "[T]here are four kinds of things to be loved: one which is above us, the second which we are ourselves, the third which is on a level with us, the fourth which is beneath us . . . ." See also ibid., 1. 26. 27.

the lover and the beloved together, and of the Christian's spiritual journey in love.[3] These theological explorations left an indelible mark on my mind.[4] As I pursued Augustine's theology of love, an oversimplified general formula of comparison between Augustine and Luther caught my attention: Augustine, the theologian of love, and Luther, the theologian of faith.

My theological curiosity compelled me to probe Augustine and Luther's teachings on faith and love in order to investigate whether this comparison was accurate and, if so, what conceptual variance might explain it. While pressing on with this research, two findings attracted my special interest. First, Augustine was a theologian of faith no less than of love, and Luther was a theologian of love no less than of faith. Second, whereas Augustine employs love as the preeminent—but not exclusive—theological concept for the Christian's relation to God, Luther uses faith. These two discoveries induced me to look more specifically into Luther's teaching on faith and love against the backdrop of Augustine's, with the prevailing question being, what prompted Luther to choose faith rather than love as the primarily sanctioned theological concept defining the Christian's relation to God? I attempted to approach this question sensitively, bearing in mind the danger of casting Luther as a theologian of faith and Augustine as a theologian of love, which I had already found to be potentially misleading.

---

3. Tarsicius J. van Bavel, "Love," in *Augustine through the Ages: An Encyclopedia*, ed. Allan D. Fitzgerald, O.S.A. (Grand Rapids: Eerdmans, 1999), 509–16.

4. For instance, R. D. Crouse raises the question: "What are the phases, or moments, of the soul's ascent to God?" He finds an answer in the "triformal scheme of ascent—*exteriora, interiora (inferior), superiora.*" Crouse, "*Recurrens in te unum:* The Pattern of St. Augustine's *Confessions,*" *Studia Patristica* 14 (1976): 390. Crouse perceives this scheme in his analysis of the structure and unity of St. Augustine's *Confessions* as a triformal scheme of ascent. This triformal scheme constitutes the structure of the *Confessions* and defines the major divisions of the work, according to Crouse.

Over the course of my writing, I have faced several challenges in narrowing my research to a manageable scope for my dissertation. I decided to concentrate on Luther, as I considered that finding plausible answers to the question of his use of faith, in principle—rather than love in determining the Christian's relation to God—might be a key to further comparative study between Augustine and Luther's teachings on faith and love. On this restricted scale, my research has focused on Luther's treatment of faith and love and the import of the dynamic relationship between the two, especially in interconnection with his ideas of the functions of Christ and the law. An assiduous exploration of these dynamics has dragged me straight into the center of the polemical turmoil of Luther's Reformation theology. I have been able to glimpse, though never exhaustively, the rich content of the dynamics among these concepts in Luther's theology, and I will endeavor to share what I have learned in this dissertation.

Problems Diagnosed

Appraising the divergent forms of these dynamics only fragmentarily or inattentively might yield the following misconceptions on the subject of faith and love in Luther's theology. First, Luther's theology has little or no teaching on love or sanctification.[5] Second, Luther's

---

5. John Wesley's reaction to Luther, for example, illustrates this criticism. Luther certainly influenced Wesley's conversion experience through his doctrine of justification by faith in Christ alone. While listening to a Moravian brother's reading of Luther's preface to Romans on May 24, 1738, Wesley received assurance of salvation. Thereafter, Wesley showed an increased appreciation of Luther, praising his doctrine of justification. On June 18, 1738, Wesley preached a sermon on "Salvation by Faith." *The Works of John Wesley*, vol. 1, *Sermons I: 1–33*, ed. Albert C. Outler (Nashville: Abingdon, 1984), 117–30. Wishing to learn more about the teaching on justification, Wesley even visited Hernhut, the Moravian headquarters in Germany. Even though he learned many things from this visit, afterwards Wesley became skeptical of the inclination of the Moravians, especially the Moravians in London, toward quietism, solafideism, and antinomianism. To Wesley, who regarded very highly the means of grace, this kind of inclination was unacceptable. Less than a year later, on April 4, 1739, Wesley recorded his first negative impression of Luther. *The Works of John Wesley*, vol. 19, *Journal*

idea of love or sanctification is reducible to his teaching on justification by faith.[6] Third, Luther's thoughts on faith and love are self-contradictory. These three feasible, though fallacious, judgments on Luther's teaching on faith and love have been available in general evaluations of Luther's theology.

One of the critical reasons the vitality of his teaching on love has not been properly appreciated may be the prevalent assumption that faith and love are unqualifiedly at odds with each other in the whole of Luther's theology. The traditional one-sided emphasis on Luther's teaching on justification by faith alone has certainly exceeded attention to his teaching on love. This inclination has entailed, for instance, a predictable reaction: Luther's theology is deficient in teaching on love or works or sanctification, so that his theology inevitably undermines morality, engendering moral delinquency or dereliction of socio-ethical responsibilities. With regard to such a charge against Luther, William H. Lazareth surveys four representative twentieth-century Protestant misinterpreters of Lutheran theological ethics subsequent to nineteenth-century

and Diaries II (1738–1743), ed. W. Reginald Ward and Richard P. Heitzenrater (Nashville: Abingdon, 1990), 47.

Although he worked together with the Moravians in London and organized the Fetter Lane Society, he left it on July 18, 1740. In his journal entries of June 15–16, 1741, he sharply dissented from Luther's Galatians lectures. Ibid., 200–10. In his sermon "On God's Vineyard," written in about 1787, Wesley stated, "Who has wrote [sic] more ably than Martin Luther on justification by faith alone? And who was more ignorant of the doctrine of sanctification, or more confused in his conceptions of it? In order to be thoroughly convinced of this, of his total ignorance with regard to sanctification, there needs no more than to read over, without prejudice, his celebrated comment on the Epistle to the Galatians." *The Works of John Wesley*, vol. 3, *Sermons III: 71–114*, ed. Albert C. Outler (Nashville: Abingdon, 1986), 505. Wesley's approach to Luther was mediated by his experience with Nicolaus Ludwig von Zinzendorf, the Moravians, and their appropriation of Luther. Therefore, Wesley's criticism on Luther must not be literally accepted but cautiously reevaluated.

6. See Oswald Bayer, *Aus Glauben leben: Über Rechtfertigung und Heiligung* (Stuttgart: Calver Verlag, 1990), esp. 65–66; ET *Living by Faith: Justification and Sanctification*, trans. Geoffrey W. Bromiley (Grand Rapids: Eerdmans, 2003), esp. 58–59; Gerhard O. Forde, "The Lutheran View of Sanctification," in *The Preached God: Proclamation in Word and Sacrament*, ed. Mark C. Mattes and Steven D. Paulson (Grand Rapids: Eerdmans, 2007), 226–44.

dualistic and quietistic German Lutheranism: Ernst Troeltsch ("Conservatism"), Karl Barth ("Quietism"), Johannes Heckel ("Dualism"), and Reinhold Niebuhr ("Defeatism").[7]

According to Lazareth, Troeltsch is most accountable for tenacious faulty presentations of Luther's theological ethics. Mistakenly envisaging Luther from the perspective of nineteenth-century quietistic and dualistic German Lutheranism, Troeltsch, in *The Social Teaching of the Christian Churches*,[8] made a frontal attack against Luther for the "social conservatism" of the German Lutheran church. Troeltsch railed against the Lutheran church's inability to contend with the new social crisis in Germany at the end of the nineteenth century. This censure found an ally in Max Weber, whose reckoning of Calvinist activism as a necessary alternative to Lutheran quietism has had a long-lasting influence.[9]

In the wake of the First World War, however, Karl Holl took up Troeltsch's allegation, avowing that Troeltsch had hardly ever seen the true sixteenth-century Luther, because he had availed himself of the distorted spectacles of nineteenth-century Lutheranism. In Lazareth's opinion, Holl intelligibly exhibited the interrelatedness of Luther's theology and ethics. According to Lazareth, Holl attributed Luther's original contribution to Christian thought and social ethics

7. William H. Lazareth, *Christians in Society: Luther, the Bible, and Social Ethics* (Minneapolis: Fortress Press, 2001), 3. As to controversies on Luther's social or socio-ethical teachings, see also George Wolfgang Forell, *Faith Active in Love: An Investigation of the Principles Underlying Luther's Social Ethics* (Eugene, OR: Wipf & Stock, 1999; Augsburg Publishing House, 1954), 16–25; Eberhard Jüngel, *Zur Freiheit eines Christenmenschen: eine Erinnerung an Luthers Schrift* (Munich: Kaiser, 1991), 59–69; ET *The Freedom of a Christian: Luther's Significance for Contemporary Theology*, trans. Roy A. Harrisville (Minneapolis: Augsburg Publishing House, 1988), 50–56; Martin Marty, "Luther on Ethics: Man Free and Slave," in *Accents in Luther's Theology: Essays in Commemoration of the 450th Anniversary of the Reformation*, ed. Heino O. Kadai (Saint Louis: Concordia Publishing House, 1967), 209–14.

8. For a detailed description of this, see Ernst Troeltsch, *The Social Teaching of the Christian Churches*, vol. 2, trans. Olive Wyon (Louisville: Westminster John Knox, 1992), 472, 508–11.

9. For more on this argument, see Max Weber, *The Protestant Ethic and the Spirit of Capitalism*, trans. Talcott Parsons (London: Routledge, 2002), 39–80.

to the reformer's argument for the close relation between conscience and community. In the Christian life, faithful fellowship with God elicits just and loving fellowship with one's fellow humans.[10]

Next, Lazareth reviews Karl Barth's criticism of Luther's "Law-Gospel Quietism," which, Barth protests, separates law from gospel, creation from redemption, and society from church. This theology was thrown into question for its potential role of engendering a politically and ethically impotent "bourgeois ghetto" that was helpless to check the whims of the demonic Nazi dictatorship.[11]

Third, Lazareth notes the critical response to Johannes Heckel made by Paul Althaus, who underwent a major reversal in his own theological and political ethics dating from the mid-1930s. Heckel declares that Luther's theology of justice and society, in its consistency with his governing doctrine of justification by faith in Christ alone, raises a question about whether Luther ever understood the consequences of the problem of justice for his theology. Heckel's Luther speaks in tones reminiscent of both Troeltsch and Barth.

Heckel argues that Luther spiritually divides humanity between Christians and non-Christians, who live in two kingdoms under two corresponding governments—the former internally by the Word, and the latter externally by the sword. In this framework, Heckel's Luther resorts to an exclusively christological foundation for Christian justice (Christ or Caesar). In contrast, Althaus's Luther is of the view that Christians are citizens as well as saints. They, accordingly, under law and gospel, practice both civil and Christian righteousness. The Creator's "left-hand rule" against injustice, corruption, and oppression governs Christians and non-Christians alike. As public citizens, Christians obeying Christ can and should

---

10. Lazareth, *Christians in Society*, 6.
11. Ibid., 10. Lazareth enumerates Barth's articles and tracts criticizing the public ethics of Luther in general and of German Lutheranism in particular. See ibid., 11.

also render to Caesar what belongs to Caesar without thereby making themselves guilty of serving Satan as well.[12]

Fourth, Lazareth introduces Reinhold Niebuhr's critique of Luther's "Cultural Defeatism."[13] Lazareth endeavors to show that Niebuhr's charge against Luther was determined predominantly by the evaluation of Ernst Troeltsch. Niebuhr faulted Luther for a kind of quietistic tendency and cultural defeatism, as if Luther had failed to articulate the ethical, and particularly the socio-ethical, implications of faith.[14]

An overview of Luther scholarship reveals not only a long history of misinterpretation but also an underappreciation of the gravity of faith and love as a thematic pair for Luther's theology as a whole. For instance, among the well-accepted texts frequently used as an extended introduction to Luther's theology, it is hard to find faith and love paired as a theme, as in Paul Althaus and Bernhard Lohse.[15] In his very valuable book *The Theology of Martin Luther*, Althaus seems to be cognizant of the significance of Luther's teaching on love in its connection to faith, since he brings up the subject of faith and love. Furthermore, he integrates two essays pertinent to the discourse of faith and love in Luther. However, he touches on the subject only sporadically, not intensively under a fixed subtitle of faith and love.

---

12. Ibid., 24–25.
13. Ibid., 25.
14. For further details, see Reinhold Niebuhr, *The Nature and Destiny of Man*, vol. 2, *Human Destiny* (Louisville: Westminster John Knox, 1964), 185–98; Niebuhr, "Love and Law in Protestantism and Catholicism," in *Christian Realism and Political Problems: Essays on Political, Social, Ethical and Theological Themes* (New York: Charles Scribner's Sons, 1953), 162–63.
15. Paul Althaus, *Die Theologie Martin Luthers*, 4th ed. (Gütersloh: Gerd Mohn, 1975); ET *The Theology of Martin Luther*, trans. Robert C. Schultz (Philadelphia: Fortress Press, 1966); Bernhard Lohse, *Luthers Theologie in ihrer historischen Entwicklung und in ihrem systematischen Zusammenhang* (Göttingen: Vandenhoeck & Ruprecht, 1995); ET *Martin Luther's Theology: Its Historical and Systematic Development*, trans. and ed. Roy A. Harrisville (Minneapolis: Fortress Press, 1999). See also Bernhard Lohse, *Martin Luther: Eine Einführung in sein Leben und sein Werk* (Munich: C. H. Beck, 1981); ET *Martin Luther: An Introduction to His Life and Work*, trans. Robert C. Schultz (Philadelphia: Fortress Press, 1986).

On that account, the subject of faith and love does not catch the eye as a paired theme but remains inconspicuous. In addition, the two essays are only added as appendices and certainly are not earmarked for fathoming out the weight of faith and love as a thematic pair.[16]

Althaus's other book entitled *Die Ethik Martin Luthers* contains the first chapter on "Ethos auf dem Boden der Rechtfertigung," which, indeed, could have incorporated subtitles reflecting faith and love as a thematic pair.[17] Two of its subtitles, "Das Leben als Übung des Glaubens" and "Das Leben des Christen als Kampf mit sich selbst" might better have been named "Die Liebe: das Leben als Übung des Glaubens" and "Die Liebe: das Leben des Christen als Kampf mit sich selbst."[18]

Although dealing with the issue of faith and works, Lohse also fails to present the substance of the relationship between faith and love in Luther's theology. Among many things that could be mentioned in the section on "Faith and Works" in his very profitable book, *Martin Luther's Theology*, the following passage deserves special notice:

> Compared with the tradition, but also with some New Testament writings, Luther seldom spoke of 'works.' Characteristically, he preached only once on the periscope of the world judgment in Matthew 25:31-46, dealing, of course, with the point of the text regarding the inquiry into deeds of love for the neighbor at the last judgment, and for his part stressing that works should never be isolated from faith.[19]

---

16. Althaus, *Die Theologie Martin Luthers*, 357–85; ET *The Theology of Martin Luther*, 429–58. The footnotes 61 and 62 in the English translation (p. 456) must refer to *WA* 20, not *WA* 36.

17. "Ethos on the Basis of Justification." Paul Althaus, *Die Ethik Martin Luthers* (Gütersloh: Gerd Mohn, 1965), 11; ET *The Ethics of Martin Luther*, trans. Robert C. Schultz (Philadelphia: Fortress Press, 1972), 3.

18. "Life as the Exercise of Faith." "The Life of the Christian as a Struggle with Himself." "Love: Life as the Exercise of Faith." "Love: The Life of the Christian as a Struggle with Himself." Althaus, *Die Ethik Martin Luthers*, 23, 26; ET *The Ethics of Martin Luther*, 16, 19.

19. Lohse, *Luthers Theologie*, 281; ET *Martin Luther's Theology*, 264.

Lohse continues, "In fact, Luther always claimed that where one's status before God is involved, works are not decisive: here, only justification *sola fide* applies. Only in a very limited sense did he hold to the 'necessity' of works."[20] While perusing Lohse's handling of the issues of faith, love, and works, we might sense his reluctance to expatiate on the topics of love and works. Even when he does not disprove the presence of love and works in Luther's theology, the length and significance of those topics are kept to a minimum. He might be concerned about the prospect that any serious account of love and works in Luther might compromise the profundity of his doctrine of justification by faith. Christians might even relapse into their reliance upon works- or self-righteousness in pursuit of a modern version of pietism, such as the holiness movement. Irrespective of those potential explanations, I am of the opinion that he sounds too cautionary and hesitant to advance a fair presentation of Luther's teaching on faith and love as a thematic pair.

Rationale

In venturing to write this dissertation, I strive to demonstrate that the aforementioned misrepresentations or underestimations of the gravity of Luther's teaching on faith and love as a thematic pair do not do justice to Luther and his theology. This dissertation presses home Luther's own affirmation that the whole of the Christian life consists in both faith and love. On this basis, I call into question an interpretive paradigm that overemphasizes or concentrates exclusively on his doctrine of justification, consequently overlooking his teaching on love or relegating it to the margins. Such a defective paradigm falls far short of appropriately demonstrating the intrinsic dynamics between faith and love as a paired theme, let alone as a

---

20. Lohse, *Luthers Theologie*, 281; ET *Martin Luther's Theology*, 264.

comprehensive theological thematic pair, in Luther's theology. It has produced an unwarranted dichotomy between theology and moral-social ethics and a propensity for losing sight of the moral or socio-ethical implications in his theology. Such a paradigm has also precipitated the contestable opinion that Luther's theology fosters an individualistic piety disjoined from communal-social involvement as validated by his teachings on the law and the gospel or the two kingdoms.

A careful reassessment is demanded regarding how to interpret the assertion that the doctrine of justification by faith is the center of Luther's theology. When a center is isolated in the middle of a circle and not interconnected to the whole circle, then it stops being a center. It becomes only a solitary dot. In fact, an unbalanced overplaying of Luther's doctrine of justification has been unwarrantedly supported by the oft-cited phrase *articulus stantis et cadentis ecclesiae* ("the article, by which the church stands or falls"). However, the exact wording cannot be traced to Luther himself.[21]

---

21. T. Mahlmann explains that the expression "articulus stantis et cadentis ecclesiae" is traceable to Franz Turrettini. Mahlmann also mentions that the spread of the expression was contributed to by Friedrich Loofs's "failed attempt at finding the origin of this expression." T. Mahlmann, "Articulus stantis et [vel] cadentis ecclesiae," in *Die Religion in Geschichte und Gegenwart*, vol. 1, 4th ed. (Tübingen: Mohr Siebeck, 1998), 799. Referring to Mahlmann, Eberhard Jüngel also points out in discreet words that, although similar formulae are found in Luther and this phrasing has indeed been employed to signify a high view of this doctrine, the exact phrasing does not appear in Luther. Eberhard Jüngel, *Das Evangelium von der Rechtfertigung des Gottlosen als Zentrum des christlichen Glaubens: Eine theologische Studie in ökumenischer Absicht* (Tübingen: J. C. B. Mohr (Paul Siebeck), 1998), 13–14; ET in *Justification: The Heart of the Christian Faith—A Theological Study with an Ecumenical Purpose*, 3rd ed., trans. Jeffrey F. Cayzer (Edinburgh: T & T Clark, 2001), 16–17. See Friedrich Loofs, "Der 'articulus stantis et cadentis ecclesiae,'" *Theologische Studien und Kritiken* 90 (1917): 323–420, esp. 344.

Carter Lindberg draws attention to the usage of this formula by an eighteenth-century Lutheran orthodoxy: "In 1712, Valentin Löscher, the champion of Lutheran orthodoxy, termed the doctrine of justification the *articulus stantis et cadentis ecclesiae*." Carter Lindberg, "Do Lutherans Shout Justification but Whisper Sanctification? Justification and Sanctification in the Lutheran Tradition," in *Justification and Sanctification: In the Traditions of the Reformation*. The Fifth Consultation on the First and Second Reformations Geneva, 13 to 17 February 1998, ed. Milan Opočenský and Páraic Réamonn (Geneva: World Alliance of Reformed Churches, 1999), 100–101. Lindberg comments that Löscher's context differs from that of Luther's.

Such a narrowly focused perspective will find it difficult to come up with proper answers to seemingly self-contradictory statements of Luther, such as his categorical rebuff of the law and works of love vis-à-vis his unreserved endorsement of them. When faith and love are appositely considered together as a thematic pair, Luther's theology becomes more perspicuously nuanced. This outlook heightens an interpretive insight of Luther's theology, which is, in fact, repeatedly urged by Luther himself: there is a time to talk only about justification by faith; there is a time to talk only about love; and there is a time to talk about both faith and love. Instead of paying heed to this aspect of the art of Luther's rhetoric (proper time and proper place), many people rush to judgment: either denying his doctrine of love or insisting on an apparent self-contradiction in Luther's theology.[22]

It is no surprise when we confront the same question by Luther scholars who expand their interest into Luther's teaching on love in relation to his teaching on faith: how can Luther's concept of love be brought into harmony with his doctrine of justification by faith alone?[23] How can Luther's plea that where faith operates, the law, works of the law, and love must entirely vanish be harmonized

Consequently, although Löscher's formula is "comparable in intent to Luther's position," since Löscher was speaking in the wake of the period of confessionalization, the church to which he referred in his formula was "the *Lutheran* church as a denomination." Ibid., 101 (italics original). See Gerhard Sauter, "Rechtfertigung," in *Theologische Realenzyklopädie*, vol. 28 (Berlin: Walter de Gruyter, 1997), 315; ET "God Creating Faith: The Doctrine of Justification from the Reformation to the Present," trans. Arthur Sutherland and Stephan Kläs, *Lutheran Quarterly* 11, no. 1 (1997): 17–102, esp. 44.

22. For instance, Luther states, "We concede that good works and love must also be taught; but this must be in its proper time and place, that is, when the question has to do with works, apart from this chief doctrine. But here the point at issue is how we are justified and attain eternal life." *LW* 26:137; *D. Martin Luthers Werke*, Kritische Gesamtausgabe, 72 vols., ed. J. F. K. Knaake et al. (Weimar: Hermann Böhlau, 1883–2009), 40/1. 240. 17–20 (hereafter cited as *WA* 40/1. 240. 17–20): "Concedimus, docendum quoque esse de bonis operibus et charitate, Sed suo tempore et loco, quando scilicet quaestio est de operibus extra hunc capitalem articulum. Hic autem Status caussae est, Qua re iustificemur et vitam aeternam consequamur."

23. Regarding this form of the question, see, for instance, Helmar Junghans, "Martin Luther über die Nächstenliebe: Auszug aus seiner Auslegung der Epistel zum 4. Sonntag nach Epiphanias

with his contention that love is the fruit of faith and the fulfillment of the law?[24] These questions center around Luther's exegeses of biblical passages such as Romans 1:17 and 3:28 (justification by faith alone apart from works prescribed by the law) and Galatians 2:15-16 (justification by faith in Jesus Christ) vis-à-vis Matthew 7:12 (the Golden Rule), 22:36-40 (love your God and love your neighbor as yourself), Romans 13:10 (love as the fulfillment of the law), Galatians 5:6 (faith working through love), 1 Corinthians 13:13 (love as the greatest of faith, hope, and love),[25] Matthew 5:17-18 (Christ has not come to abolish the law but to fulfill it), and Romans 3:31 (not overthrowing the law by faith but upholding it).

Method

An ideal method for dealing with misinterpretations or underestimations of the importance of Luther's teaching on love might be to demonstrate his teaching on faith and love as an inclusive thematic pair in his theology as a whole. In reality, however, a formidable obstacle to this method is the fact that Luther is one of the most prolific theological authors in the history of world Christianity. Considering the sheer volume of Luther's works, it would be a lifelong work to consult all his texts in order to accomplish the task. Furthermore, his works are handed down to us in various literary genres, such as commentaries, lectures, treatises, disputations,

---

(Röm. 13, 8–10) in der 'Fastenpostille' von 1525," *Luther: Zeitschrift der Luther-Gesellschaft* 62, no. 1 (1991): 4.

24. Luther's stance on this issue will be expounded in chapter 4.

25. Apropos this issue, see, for instance, Rainer Vinke, "'. . . aber die Liebe ist die größte unter ihnen' Zu Luthers Auslegung von 1. Korinther 13," in *Freiheit als Liebe bei Martin Luther, Freedom as Love in Martin Luther: 8th International Congress for Luther Research in St. Paul, Minnesota, 1993, Seminar 1 Referate/Papers*, eds. Dennis D. Bielfeldt and Klaus Schwarzwäller (Frankfurt am Main: Peter Lang, 1995), 167–80. Vinke examines Luther's position on Paul's prioritization of love over faith in 1 Cor. 13.

sermons, letters, prefaces, liturgical comments, prayer books, catechisms, and table talks.

After deep meditation, I elected to focus on his 1535 Galatians commentary as the main text of analysis, in consultation with a restricted number of his other texts to substantiate and complement some of the major arguments. Selecting the 1535 Galatians commentary and additional texts from among those different literary genres, though only in a confined scope, should provide a decent opportunity to let Luther speak for himself regarding his teaching on faith and love. The 1535 Galatians commentary was chosen as the primary text because it is deemed as representing Luther's mature theology, and Luther himself esteems it as the masterpiece among his many works.[26] Showing the central role of Luther's teaching on faith and love in this commentary, thus, should yield good evidence toward establishing the noteworthiness of this teaching in his theology as a whole.

Indeed, *The Freedom of a Christian* has been reckoned as the classical locus for Luther's teaching on faith and love. Nonetheless, the 1535 Galatians commentary displays his teaching on faith and love in full measure, since it is expounded in its interdependence with his ideas on the functions of Christ and the law. Furthermore, *The Freedom of a Christian* is usually treated as an isolated tractate to discuss his teaching on faith and love as merely one of his many other teachings on diverse theological themes. However, showing the central role of Luther's teaching on faith and love in this Galatians commentary would entail far-reaching ramifications on how to view

26. In one of his table talks, Luther mentions that "The Epistle to the Galatians is my dear epistle. I have put my confidence in it. It is my Katy von Bora." *LW* 54:20 (no. 146, dated 14 December, 1531–22 January 1532); *WA, TR* 1:69. In another talk, Luther states that whoever wishes to become a theologian needs to read the Bible and Philip Melanchthon's *Loci Communes*, and afterward if he wishes, he can read Melanchthon's *Romans* and his [Luther's] *Galatians* and *Deuteronomy*. *LW* 54:439–40 (no. 5511, dated Winter of 1542–1543); *WA, TR* 5:204.

and value this teaching in his theology as a whole. Investigating faith and love in this commentary should serve as a good point of departure for a more extensive study on faith and love in the whole of his theology and set up a paradigm.

This dissertation also makes reference in footnotes to the lectures on Romans (1515–16), *Treatise on Good Works* (1520), *The Freedom of a Christian* (1520), *Table Talk*, and several sermons. The Romans lectures are pivotal in inquiring into Luther's teaching on faith and love because they disclose the way Luther learns from Paul the art of thinking and speaking about faith and love and their relationship.[27] Hence, they furnish us with the embryonic context, both conceptual and historical, for the further development of Luther's teaching on faith and love. In particular, Luther assimilates Paul's way of speaking about faith first (Romans 1–11) and then love (Romans 12–16), which certainly made a long-lasting impact upon Luther.

The *Treatise on Good Works* is crucial in comprehending Luther's teaching on faith and love, especially since Luther wrote it on realizing that he could not bypass the battlefield, namely, the clarification of his position on love or works of love. Since *The Freedom of a Christian* has been a classic for the treatment of Luther's concepts of faith and love, it certainly deserves mention in this dissertation. The *Table Talks* also offer useful statements for Luther's teaching on faith and love in his plain and everyday words throughout his Reformation career. The several sermons referred to cover a good scope of Luther's Reformation career (between 1515

---

27. "When I was a monk I was a master in the use of allegories. I allegorized everything. Afterward through the Epistle to the Romans I came to some knowledge of Christ. I recognized then that allegories are nothing, that it's not what Christ signifies but what Christ is that counts." *LW* 54:46 (no. 335, dated Summer or Fall 1532); *WA, TR* 1:136. Luther's acknowledgement of St. Paul's significance for him is also detected in the statement he made when a son was born in 1533: "[H]e was named Paul. I've had him named Paul because St. Paul furnished me with many a good passage and argument, and so I wish to honor him by naming a son after him." *LW* 54:184 (no. 2946a, dated 29 January 1533); *WA, TR* 3:111.

and 1546). Therefore, they allow us to gain some perspective on how Luther consistently deals with faith and love as the overriding thematic pair in those sermons throughout his Reformation career. The sermons, differently oriented in their purpose and writing style from his polemical disputations, commentaries, and lectures, make their own contribution to the broad picture of Luther's teaching on faith and love.

In analyzing the Galatians commentary and other texts, this dissertation fundamentally adopts a theological-ideological-structural (versus historical-genetic) approach to Luther's teaching on faith and love. At the same time, this dissertation guards against fabricating a speculative interpretation of Luther's teaching on faith and love. Bearing this danger in mind, it also strives to read Luther with concern for the contexts of his time and the various polemical debates out of which his teaching on faith and love have had their developmental formation.[28] However, since the main goal of this dissertation does not lie in a historical-genetic exploration, it will not attend to the minutest details of Luther's historical context or aim at distinguishing Luther's stance from those of his predecessors or contemporaries. Nor does it attempt to prove that he understands

---

28. A historical-genetic approach puts into perspective historical-contextual necessities, showing that the relationship between faith and love must not be marginalized in Luther's theology. On the methodological issue in Luther studies, see Lohse, *Luthers Theologie*, 17–21; ET *Martin Luther's Theology*, 6–10. Markus Wriedt strongly emphasizes that Luther's theology grew out of a concrete situation and that the "lively, situation-centered and context-related style of Martin Luther's Scripture interpretation cannot and could not be pressed into a Procrustian bed of orthodox confessional and doctrinal writings." Markus Wriedt, "Luther's Theology," in *The Cambridge Companion to Martin Luther*, ed. Donald K. McKim (Cambridge: Cambridge University Press, 2003), 87. Helmar Junghans also illustrates some advantages and disadvantages of depicting Luther's theology from a developmental versus a systematic perspective. Helmar Junghans, "The Center of the Theology of Martin Luther," in *And Every Tongue Confess: Essays in Honor of Norman Nagel on the Occasion of His Sixty-fifth Birthday*, trans. Gerald S. Krispin, ed. Gerald S. Krispin and Jon D. Vieker (Dearborn, MI: Nagel Festschrift Committee, 1990), 179–94, esp. 180–81.

his opponents' arguments accurately or trace the development of his thoughts on faith and love from one text to another.

Plan of the Dissertation

A survey of recent secondary literature on Luther's teaching on faith and love is laid out in chapter 1. In this chapter, I endeavor to present previous research pertinent to Luther's teaching on faith and love. To elucidate the slightly divergent emphases and perspectives among the studies, I have categorized the research in varying subthemes and spotlighted their characteristics. In particular, taking into account the current exchange of views with regard to Finnish Luther scholarship, I furnish chapter 1 with a special space to look into its core arguments. Against the backdrop of the previous research, I then describe features that distinguish my research. These traits will also serve as a rationale for my undertaking of this dissertation.

In terms of the general arrangement of the remaining chapters, which are intended to give Luther opportunities to express his own voice as much as possible, chapters 2 and 3 examine faith and love as two conflicting theses in the dimension of alien, passive, and perfect righteousness and holiness. Chapters 4 and 5, on the other hand, address faith and love as two harmonious theses in the dimension of proper, active, and progressing righteousness and holiness.

Chapter 2 dwells, at the outset, on the literary structure and logical cohesion of the commentary hinging on faith and love on the basis of Luther's exegesis of Paul's Epistle to the Galatians. This depiction will expose the two dynamic dimensions to tackle the paradoxical relationship between faith and love, establishing an interpretive framework for Luther's teaching on faith and love. This chapter then proceeds to probe his notion of faith as antithetical to love, especially in the context of his polemical disputes with both his medieval Roman Catholic and intra-Reformation opponents. The controversy with his Roman Catholic disputants, in particular, revolves around Luther's attack on Thomas Aquinas's ideas of merit and *fides caritate formata* and Gabriel Biel's notion of congruous merit (*meritum de congruo*). The debate with his intra-Reformation opponents progresses on the issues of the place of work or sanctification in a Christian life and on the sacramental controversy.

The polemical controversies pinpoint the marrow of Luther's problem with his adversaries: the law competes with Christ in a duel over justification of the unrighteous. This chapter, accordingly, puts stress on Luther's reconceptualization of faith as the only means of grasping Christ, the sole savior, in one's heart. Faith is not only necessary but also sufficient for justification. Drawing on Paul, Luther advocates *fides Christo formata* as an alternative to the philosophically fashioned scholastic formula *fides caritate formata*. The chapter concludes with Luther's reaffirmation of his stance regarding justification by faith in Christ alone in his campaign against the internal opponents.

Chapter 3, in continuation of our investigation of Luther's concept of faith as an opposing thesis to love in the dimension of alien, passive, and perfect righteousness and holiness, lays bare three cardinal facets of Luther's reconceptualization of faith, namely, justifying faith. They are designated as follows: (1) faith as knowing the truth of the heart about God, Christ, and self; (2) faith as trusting in God and Christ; and (3) faith as being active in love. This chapter also calls attention to Luther's presentation of a theological or spiritual function of the law. Luther's reconceptualization of faith unreservedly excludes the entire law as long as it claims its jurisdiction over sinners for their justification. Nevertheless, Luther holds that, insofar as the law does not transgress Christ's jurisdiction in the matter of justification, the law can stimulate faith in Christ. On the grounds of this theological function of the law, Luther's reconceptualization of faith incorporates the law into its duly qualified role in the dimension of alien, passive, and perfect righteousness and holiness.

Chapter 4 delves into Luther's reintroduction of love in harmony with faith. Luther's reconceptualization of love is essentially sketched as fruits of faith authenticating its genuineness; so Luther labels this love as incarnate faith. Concentrating on Luther's re-conceptualization of love in conjunction with his re-conceptualization of faith, this chapter accentuates his scrupulous and deliberate reconstruction of the relationship of faith to love. Chapter 4 especially inquires into Luther's perceptions of the twofold direction of Christian freedom, the Christ-given law of love, the twofold way of fulfilling the law, and christological terminologies and concepts as logical rationale for his reintroduction of love compatible with faith.

This chapter puts forward the relationship between the two dimensions of righteousness and holiness—alien, passive, and perfect vis-à-vis proper, active, and progressing. As a consequence, this chapter plays up the complexity of the relationship between faith and love, which cannot be properly appreciated if approached as the mere juxtaposition between two things of equal level and weight or as parallel lines that never intersect each other. To confirm this relationship, a simile (Christians like Christ) and two metaphors (doer with deeds and tree with fruits) that epitomize Luther's position on the relationship between faith and love are illustrated at the end of the chapter.

Chapter 5 gives prominence to the three paramount relations, in which the fruits of faith are borne in performance of love—to God, to others, and to self. This chapter also endeavors to clarify that the theological or spiritual function of the law does not entirely vanish in the dimension of proper, active, and progressing righteousness and holiness. In chapters 2–5, Luther's teaching on faith and love is, thus, continuously scrutinized in the dynamics of his conceptions of the functions of Christ and the law. These four chapters are designed to enrich our comprehension of Luther's teaching on faith and love in those dynamics. The conclusion recapitulates the main arguments of each chapter. It also contains my reflections on the issues of the third use of the law and *theosis*, which are relevant to Luther's teaching on faith and love.

1

Research on Faith and Love in Luther

Previous Research

Although the literature on Luther's teaching on faith and love is sparse in comparison with that on his teaching on justification by faith alone (and on other topics), some valuable research is available.[1]

---

1. Though I cannot expound upon the contents in detail, the books, articles, and essays that aided me in my research on Luther's teaching on faith and justification can be selectively illustrated as follows: Virgil Thompson, ed., *Justification is for Preaching: Essays by Oswald Bayer, Gerhard O. Forde, and Others* (Eugene, OR: Pickwick, 2012), 15–119; Timo Laato, "Justification: The Stumbling Block of the Finnish Luther School," *Concordia Theological Quarterly* 72 (2008): 327–46; Piotr J. Malysz, "*Nemo iudex in causa sua* as the Basis of Law, Justice, and Justification in Luther's Thought," *Harvard Theological Review* 100, no. 3 (2007): 363–86; Veli-Matti Kärkkäinen, "Drinking from the Same Wells with Orthodox and Catholics': Insights from the Finnish Interpretation of Luther's Theology," *Currents in Theology and Mission* 34, no. 2 (2007): 85–96; Bruce L. McCormack, ed., *Justification in Perspective: Historical Developments and Contemporary Challenges* (Grand Rapids: Baker Academic, 2006); R. Scott Clark, "*Iustitia Imputata Christi*: Alien or Proper to Luther's Doctrine of Justification," *Concordia Theological Quarterly* 70 (2006): 269–301; Alister E. McGrath, *Iustitia Dei: A History of the Christian Doctrine of Justification*, 3rd ed. (Cambridge: Cambridge University Press, 2005); Joseph A. Burgess and Marc Kolden, eds., *By Faith Alone: Essays on Justification in Honor of Gerhard O. Forde* (Grand Rapids: Eerdmans, 2004); Mark C. Mattes, *The Role of Justification in Contemporary Theology* (Grand Rapids: Eerdmans, 2004); David A. Brondos, "*Sola fide* and Luther's 'Analytic' Understanding of Justification: A Fresh Look at Some Old Questions," *Pro Ecclesia* 13, no. 1

I will unearth secondary literature on this subject by classifying it in accordance with the assorted foci of research. In this section on previous research, special space will also be allotted to salient arguments of the modern Finnish Lutheran scholars, which are germane to our discussion on Luther's teaching on faith and love. Whether they receive a sympathetic hearing or opprobrium from other Luther scholars, it is certain that their unconventional contentions have sparked an interest in reexamining Luther's theology. The first part of this section, therefore, explores facets that characterize the interpretation of the Finns—or, more precisely, of Tuomo Mannermaa, founder of the Finnish school—from the vantage point of Luther's teaching on faith and love. In the second part of this section, research on Luther's teaching on faith and love is enumerated according to the diversely emphasized themes and angles.

Tuomo Mannermaa and Modern Finnish Luther Scholarship

The research model of the Finnish scholars was developed in the course of Finnish Lutheran-Russian Orthodox ecumenical dialogues (especially the implications of Luther's theology) conducted by scholars in the Department of Systematic Theology at the University of Helsinki since the mid-1970s.[2] The main topics of research thus

(2004): 39–57; William G. Rusch, ed., *Justification and the Future of the Ecumenical Movement: The Joint Declaration on the Doctrine of Justification* (Collegeville, MN: Liturgical Press, 2003); Eberhard Jüngel, *Das Evangelium von der Rechtfertigung des Gottlosen als Zentrum des christlichen Glaubens: Eine theologische Studie in ökumenischer Absicht* (Tübingen: J. C. B. Mohr (Paul Siebeck), 1998); ET *Justification: The Heart of the Christian Faith—A Theological Study with an Ecumenical Purpose*, 3rd ed., trans. Jeffrey F. Cayzer (Edinburgh: T & T Clark, 2001); Gerhard O. Forde, *Justification by Faith—A Matter of Death and Life* (Mifflintown, PA: Sigler, 1999); Jared Wicks, "Justification and Faith in Luther's Theology," *Theological Studies* 44, no. 1 (1983): 3–29; Heiko A. Oberman, "'Iustitia Christi' and 'Isutitia Dei': Luther and the Scholastic Doctrine of Justification," *Harvard Theological Review* 59, no. 1 (1966): 1–26.

2. Concerning its history, consequences, and unresolved tasks, see Risto Saarinen, *Faith and Holiness: Lutheran-Orthodox Dialogue, 1959–1994 (Kirche und Konfession)*, (Vandenhoeck & Ruprecht, 1997), esp. 20–83, 232–69.

far have been the relation of Luther's doctrine of justification to the Eastern Orthodox doctrine of *theosis*, *theosis* in Luther, and the meaning of the Golden Rule in Luther. Other projects underway include Luther's pneumatology and the doctrine of the Trinity. This research model, stemming from an ecumenical endeavor, puts on the table an interesting new approach to Luther's teaching on faith and love.[3]

Their quintessential contention is that Christ's presence in faith itself, the idea of which they draw from Luther's own statement that "the One [Christ] who is present in the faith itself" (*in ipsa fide Christus adest*), is the structuring principle of Luther's theology.[4] This claim is most pointedly expressed in Tuomo Mannermaa's *Der im Glauben gegenwärtige Christus: Rechtfertigung und Vergottung*.[5]

On the basis of this structuring principle, the Finnish scholars underscore "participation" as a hallmark of Luther's doctrine of faith and love, arguing that Luther's view of justification can also be called *theosis* according to the ancient doctrine of the fathers, with whom Luther agreed.[6] According to the ancient doctrine of the fathers,

---

3. For further information, see the Finish Luther Studies websites at http://blogs.helsinki.fi/ ristosaarinen/luther-studies-in-finland/ and http://blogs.helsinki.fi/luther-studies/. A recent brief introduction to the methodological orientations and the main results of the Mannermaa School can be found in Tuomo Mannermaa, "Why Is Luther So Fascinating? Modern Finnish Luther Research," in *Union with Christ: The New Finnish Interpretation of Luther*, ed. Carl E. Braaten and Robert W. Jenson (Grand Rapids: Eerdmans, 1998), 1–20. This collection of essays by Finnish Luther scholars is the first attempt to give an overview in English of this new Luther paradigm.

4. A classic formulation of this view that the Finnish scholars frequently employ is found, for example, in Luther's *Lectures on Galatians* (1535): "It takes hold of Christ in such a way that Christ is the object of faith, or rather not the object, but so to speak, the One who is present in the faith itself." *LW* 26:129; *WA* 40/1. 228. 34–229. 15: "quo Christus apprehenditur, Sic ut Christus sit obiectum fidei, imo non obiectum, sed, ut ita dicam, in ipsa fide Christus adest."

5. Tuomo Mannermaa, *Der im Glauben gegenwärtige Christus: Rechtfertigung und Vergottung. Zum ökumenischen Dialog*, Arbeiten zur Geschichte und Theologie des Luthertums, Neue Folge, Band 8 (Hannover: Lutherisches Verlagshaus, 1989).

6. With regard to the historical background of the Finnish scholars' research on their main themes, see Anna Briskina, "An Orthodox View of Finnish Luther Research," trans. Dennis Bielfeldt, *Lutheran Quarterly* 22, no. 1 (2008): 16–18. She mentions that "[w]ith its publications on the

deification means a believer's participation in or union with God. Luther says that Christ is present in faith itself. For that reason, a believer participates in Christ through faith. Christ is God; hence, a believer participates in God through faith.[7]

According to Mannermaa, deification is fundamentally the result of God's love. Human beings cannot participate in God on the basis of their own love; rather, only God's love can effect their deification. A Christian's participation in Christ is thus the result of the divine presence acting in her as love.[8] What is noticeable in this argument is that Mannermaa sees this participation as a participation in the very *ousia* of God.[9] There is, then, a "real-ontic"[10] unity between Christ

teaching of *theosis* in Luther, the Mannermaa School thus became linked to an already well-established Scandinavian tradition of Luther research." Ibid., 17.

7. For a synopsis in English of *theosis*, see Tuomo Mannermaa, "Theosis as a Subject of Finnish Luther Research," *Pro Ecclesia* 4 (1995): 37–48. For further references, see also Mannermaa, "Theosis als Thema der finnischen Lutherforschung," in *Luther und Theosis: Vergöttlichung als Thema der abendländischen Theologie*. Referate der Fachtagung der Luther-Akademie Ratzeburg in Helsinki 30.3–2.4. 1989. Schriften der Luther-Agricola-Gesellschaft A 25, ed. Simo Peura and Antti Raunio (Helsinki: Luther-Agricola-Gesellschaft; Erlangen: Luther-Akademie Ratzeburg, 1990), 11–26; Mannermaa, "Justification and *Theosis* in Lutheran-Orthodox Perspective," in *Union with Christ*, 25–41; Mannermaa, *Der im Glauben gegenwärtige Christus*; Mannermaa, "Hat Luther eine trinitarische Ontologie?" in *Luther und Ontology: Das Sein Christi im Glauben als strukturierendes Prinzip der Theologie Luthers*. Schriften der Luther-Agricola-Gesellschaft 31. Referate der Fachtagung des Instituts für Systematische Theologie der Universität Helsinki in Zusammenarbeit mit der Luther-Akademie Ratzeburg in Helsinki 1.–5.4. 1992, ed. Anja Ghiselli, Kari Kopperi, and Rainer Vinke (Helsinki: Luther-Agricola-Gesellschaft, 1993), 9–27; Mannermaa, "Hat Luther eine trinitarische Ontologie?" in *Luther und die trinitarische Tradition. Ökumenische und philosophische Perspektiven*, Veröffentlichungen der Luther-Akademie Ratzeburg, Bd. 23, ed. Joachim Heubach (Erlangen: Martin-Luther-Verlag, 1994), 43–60; Mannermaa, "Doctrine of Justification and Trinitarian Ontology," in *Trinity, Time, and Church* (Grand Rapids: Eerdmans, 2000), 139–45; Simo Peura, *Mehr als ein Mensch? Die Vergöttlichung als Thema der Theologie Martin Luthers von 1513 bis 1519* (*More than a Human Person? Deification as a Theme of Luther's Theology from 1513 to 1519*), Veröffentlichungen des Instituts für Europäische Geschichte Mainz, Band 152 (Mainz: Philipp von Zabern, 1994); Peura, "Die Teilhabe an Christus bei Luther," in *Luther und Theosis*, 121–61.

8. Tuomo Mannermaa, "Grundlagenforschung der Theologie Martin Luthers und die Ökumene," in *Der im Glauben gegenwärtige Christus*, 200.

9. Tuomo Mannermaa, "Das Verhältnis von Glaube und Liebe in der Theologie Luthers," in *Luther in Finnland—Der Einfluß der Theologie Martin Luthers in Finnland und finnische Beiträge zur Lutherforschung*, ed. Miikka Ruokanen, Schriften der Luther-Agricola-Gesellschaft A 23 (Helsinki: Luther-Agricola-Gesellschaft, 1986), 99–110. This essay originally appeared in

and the Christian, though the substance of each does not change into anything else.[11]

Finnish in *Teologinen Aikakauskirja/Teologisk Tidskrift* (1979), 329–40. See also Mannermaa, "Freiheit als Liebe: Einführung in das Thema," in *Freiheit als Liebe bei Martin Luther, Freedom as Love in Martin Luther: 8th International Congress for Luther Research in St. Paul, Minnesota, 1993, Seminar 1 Referate/Papers*, eds. Dennis D. Bielfeldt and Klaus Schwarzwäller (Frankfurt am Main: Peter Lang, 1995), 9–18. In this paper, Mannermaa cites a passage from Luther expressing his teaching on Christian participation in the divine nature (or in the name of God) through faith: "Das haben wyr (sagt er) durch die krafft des glawbens, das wyr teylhafftig sind und geselschafft odder gemeynschafft mit der Göttlichen natur haben . . . . Was ist aber Gottes natur? Es ist ewige wahrheyt, gerechtigkeyt, weyssheyt, ewig leben, fryd, freude und lust und was man gutt nennen kan. Wer nu Gottes natur teylhafftig wird, der uberkompt das alles." (*WA* 14/1. 19. 3–15), citation from ibid., 10. The same train of argument also appears in Eeva Martikainen, "Die Unio im Brennpunkt der theologischen Forschung," in *Unio: Gott und Mensch in der nachreformatorischen Theologie*, ed. Eeva Martikainen (Helsinki: Luther-Agricola-Gesellschaft, 1996), 13–18.

10. What makes Mannermaa's claim unique—and controversial, especially within the established canons of German Luther interpretation—is the idea that Christ's presence is "real-ontic," not just a subjective experience (*Erlebnis*) or God's effect (*Wirkung*) on the believer, as the neo-Protestant school has held. Mannermaa's student Risto Saarinen in his philosophical-methodological work, *Gottes Wirken auf uns*, demonstrated how the "transcendental effect" orientation, originated by the nineteenth-century German philosopher Hermann Lotze, obscured the meaning of the real presence of Christ in Luther research, whether neo-Protestant, Luther renaissance, or even dialectical theology. Wilhelm Herrman, Otto Ritschl, and especially Albrecht Ritschl understood Luther's theology as a new kind of *theologisches Erkenntnisprinzip*: They argued that Luther was moving beyond the old scholastic metaphysical idea of "essence" toward a more relational view of knowledge of God. Based on neo-Kantian philosophy, these scholars argued that theology cannot know anything about the "essence" (ontology) of God—only God's "effects" in us. Risto Saarinen, *Gottes Wirken auf uns: Die transzendentale Deutung des Gegenwart-Christ-Motivs in der Lutherforschung (God's Work on Us: The Transcendent Meaning of the Presence of Christ Motif in Luther Research)*, (Stuttgart: Franz Steiner, 1989). For an English synopsis, see Risto Saarinen, "The Presence of God in Luther's Theology," *Lutheran Quarterly* 3 (1994): 3–13.

11. The Finnish school also emphasizes "the happy exchange" between Christ and Christians and that Luther himself, unlike later Lutheranism, does not differentiate between the person and the work of Christ. Christ—his person and his work—is the righteousness of a Christian. In the language of the doctrine of justification, this means that Christ is both *donum* and *favor* (not only *favor*, as subsequent Lutheranism teaches). Tuomo Mannermaa, "In ipsa fide Christus adest: Der Schnittpunkt zwischen lutherischer und orthodoxer Theologie," in *Der im Glauben gegenwärtige Christus: Rechtfertigung und Vergottung. Zum ökumenischen Dialog*, ed. Tuomo Mannermaa, trans. Hans-Christian Daniel and Juhani Forsberg (Hannover: Lutherisches Verlagshaus, 1989), 11–93. The essay was originally published in Finnish as *In ipsa fide Christus adest: Luterilaisen ja ortodoksisen kristinuskonkäsityksen leikkauspiste (In Faith Itself Christ Is Really Present: The Point of Intersection between Lutheran and Orthodox Theology)*, Missiologian ja Ekumeniikan Seura R.Y., Missiologian ja Ekumeniikan Seuran julkaisuja, vol. 30 (Vammala: Vammalan Kirjapaino, 1979). It is available in English as *Christ Present in Faith: Luther's View of Justification*, ed. Kirsi Stjerna (Minneapolis: Fortress Press, 2005). For a recent overview, see Simo Peura,

Advancing Christ's presence in faith itself as the structuring principle of Luther's theology, Mannermaa accents the relationship between faith and love expressed in Luther's claim that the whole of the Christian life consists in faith and love. He also asserts that the theme of love has not been treated as it deserves in Luther scholarship. He also mentions the former president of the Lutheran World Federation, Mikko Juva, who believed that attempts to solve the central problem of world Lutheranism—the relation between the vertical and the horizontal dimension of Christian faith—have been unsuccessful so far. Mannermaa himself reformulates this relation as between faith and love. Faith defines the vertical relation to God; love, the horizontal relation to neighbors.[12]

Mannermaa insists that the main interpretations of Luther's theology deviate from one another exactly on this point.[13] He contends that the relation between faith and love and the essence of love itself in Luther's theology can be understood only on the basis of *"dem im Glauben real gegenwärtigen Christus"* [Christ who is really present in faith].[14] The missing joint between faith and love and the center that holds them together is the idea that *"in ipsa fide Christus adest"* [in faith itself Christ is present].[15] This argument of Mannermaa is intriguing and persuasive, while the idea of deification seems to be controversial.[16]

"Christus als Gunst und Gabe: Luthers Verständnis der Rechtfertigung als Herausforderung an den ökumenischen Dialog mit der Römisch-katholischen Kirche," in *Caritas Dei: Beiträge zum Verständnis Luthers und der gegenwärtigen Ökumene, Festschrift für Tuomo Mannermaa zum 60. Geburtstag*, ed. Oswald Bayer, Robert W. Jenson, and Simo Knuuttila (Helsinki: Luther-Agricola-Gesellschaft, 1997), 340–63; Peura, "Christ as Favor and Gift: The Challenge of Luther's Understanding of Justification," in *Union with Christ*, 42–69.

12. Tuomo Mannermaa, "Das Verhältnis von Glaube und Liebe in der Theologie Luthers," in *Luther in Finnland*, 99.

13. Ibid.

14. Ibid.

15. Ibid.

16. I will touch on this topic of *theosis* in the Conclusion.

In seeking the basis of the analogous relation between Christ and Christians, Mannermaa argues that there have been three false interpretations of the parallel characteristics of Christ and Christians. The first false view expresses the relation as an ethical one—one of the main trends in Lutheran studies and one heavily dependent on neo-Kantian metaphysical presuppositions since the end of the nineteenth century, especially after Albrecht Ritschl. This position highlights not the ontic or ontological relation between Christ and Christians but a personal-ethical relation. Focusing on the union between the divine and the human will, this position fails to grasp Luther's understanding that Christians in union with God participate in the divine nature and become gods.[17]

The second fallacious interpretation comes from the so-called dialectical theologians who rely on the Word-relation. This position errs in viewing the Word of God merely in terms of the relation between God and human beings rather than in terms of the presence of Christ in Christians through faith and, thereby, the effectiveness of Christ in Christians. The third defective interpretation contains a one-sided consideration of the forensic aspect of the doctrine of justification, which has prevailed in Lutheranism since Philip Melanchthon. This forensic interpretation severs justification from the presence of Christ in Christians.[18]

---

17. Mannermaa, "Das Verhältnis von Glaube und Nächstenliebe in der Theologie Luthers," in *Der im Glauben gegenwärtige Christus*, 97–98. See also Mannermaa, "Why Is Luther So Fascinating?" in *Union with Christ*, 4–9.

18. Mannermaa points out that Melanchthon's "outside us" (*extra nos*) view of justification as reckoned, forensic, and juridical is severed from sanctification. Mannermaa attempts instead to emphasize the interwoven relation between justification and sanctification on the basis of Christ, who is present in a believer through faith. Mannermaa argues that the principle of the presence of Christ in a believer through faith overcomes Melanchthon's bifurcation of forensic justification and effective sanctification—between being *declared* righteous and being *made* righteous, which has invited caricature as a forensic fiction with its overemphasis on an exclusively external justification. Mannermaa, "Das Verhältnis von Glaube und Nächstenliebe in der Theologie Luthers," in *Der im Glauben gegenwärtige Christus*, 98.

Opposing these three traditional misinterpretations, Mannermaa insists on a different way of defining the relationship between Christ and Christians, offering four reasons to substantiate his argument.[19] First, Luther, unlike later Lutheranism, does not differentiate the person from the work of Christ. Christ himself, both his work and his person, is the justification of human beings by God. Faith signifies justification because the person of Christ is present: *in ipsa fide Christus adest*.[20] Second, unlike the scholastic theologians who argue that love is the form of faith, Luther's conception of Christ present in faith finds its expression also in his idea of *Christus forma fidei*. Christ is the divine reality (form) that forms faith.

Third, Christ is not only the favor of God—the forgiveness of sins and abolition of God's wrath—but also the gift of God—God's presence in the fullness of God's nature and essence. On this account, in faith, a person participates in the divine nature of God through union with Christ.[21] Fourth, the properties of God are construed as God's nature according to what Luther calls "a Hebrew way of speaking." On that account, when Christians participate in Christ by faith, they participate at the same time in God's properties and nature, because Christ is none other than God.[22]

---

19. Ibid., 98–100.

20. Mannermaa quotes from *WA* 40/1. 229. 28–30: "Ergo fide apprehensus et in corde habitans Christus est iustitia Christiana propter quam Deus nos reputat iustos et donat vitam aeternam." ("Therefore, being grasped by faith and dwelling in our hearts, Christ is the Christian righteousness because of which God imputes righteousness to us and gives eternal life.") Ibid., 98 (my translation).

21. See *WA* 21. 458. 11–24.

22. See *WA* 17/1. 438. 14–28; *WA* 10¹/1. 157. 14. The same argument also appears in Mannermaa, "Why is Luther So Fascinating?" in *Union with Christ*, 15. The property/essence identity thesis is developed by many of the Finnish commentators. Peura points to *WA* 3. 189. 13–14: "In hiis laudatur Deus, ut quando veritatem, sapientiam, bonitatem loquimur, quia hec omnia est deus," and to *WA* 3. 303. 20–21: "Nomen domini non dat sanctis bonum aliud quam est ipsummet: sed ipsummet est bonum eorum." Peura, *Mehr als ein Mensch*, 51ff. See also Mannermaa, "Das Verhältnis von Glaube und Nächstenliebe in der Theologie Luthers," in *Der im Glauben gegenwärtige Christus*, 99–100; Peura, "Participation and Love in the Theology of Martin Luther," in *Philosophical Studies in Religion, Metaphysics, and Ethics: Essays in Honour*

Mannermaa suggests a resolution of the relation between faith and love in the following formulation: love is the fulfillment of the law; faith offers the fulfillment of the law. One of the properties of God's nature, in which Christians can participate by faith, according to Mannermaa, is love. Christ, who is present in faith, brings love with himself because Christ is God in his nature and God is love. Mannermaa makes a similar point on the basis of a different Luther text, a 1525 sermon on Ephesians 3:14-21, which is printed under the title "Ein Sermon von Stärke und Zunehmen des Glaubens und der Liebe."[23] According to Mannermaa, this text displays that faith entails participation in the being and the properties of God and, since love is one of the properties that Christ brings with himself as *donum*, the believer participates in the love of God as well.[24]

The same argument reappears in Mannermaa's "Participation and Love in the Theology of Martin Luther," where he mentions Luther's recognition of the notion of love as agapē in its relation to participation in God. According to Mannermaa, Christ Himself is the incarnate agapē. Here Mannermaa emphasizes Christ as both favor of God (forgiveness of sins, atonement, abolition of wrath) and donum (gift, God Himself present), and also as the form of faith (*Christus forma fidei*).

Mannermaa's interpretation of the relationship between faith and love in connection with the theme of participation in Luther's theology can be summarized in the following three ways: (1) Christ is the incarnate agapē. Christians are united with Christ by faith. Therefore, Christians participate in the divine agapē through their

of Heikki Kirjavainen, Schriften der Luther-Agricola-Gesellschaft 38, ed. Timo Koistinen and Tommi Lehtonen (Helsinki: Luther-Agricola-Society, 1997), 308–309.

23. See *WA* 17/1. 428–38.

24. Mannermaa, "Why Is Luther So Fascinating?" in *Union with Christ*, 16. Mannermaa claims that "[t]he idea of participation in Christ and in his divine properties was thus the content of his so-called reformatory insight and at the same time the foundation of his criticism of scholastic theology." Ibid., 17.

participation in Christ, the incarnate agapē, by faith. (2) Christ is God. Christians are united with Christ by faith. Their being united with Christ who is God means their participation in God. Christians participate in God's being and properties. Love is one of the divine properties. Therefore, Christians participate in the divine love through their being united with Christ by faith. (3) Christ is present in faith. Christ in his divine nature and properties is God. God is love. Christ who is present in faith brings love with him.[25] Therefore, Christians participate in the divine love through their participation in Christ by faith. As a consequence, even though faith itself is not the fulfillment of the law, it brings the love that is the fulfillment of the law.[26]

On the basis of this relation between faith and love, Mannermaa also finds a solution to the problem of the analogous relation between Christ and Christians, which he depicts as a real analogy involving the two natures of a Christian. According to Mannermaa, just as Christ has two natures, human and divine, so a Christian has, in a certain sense, two natures through participation in Christ by faith. The divine nature of a Christian is Christ himself. It is no longer merely a Christian who lives in her, but Christ. In Christ or in his divine nature, a Christian has all the treasure and goods of the divine nature. She does not need anything else for salvation. Really and ontically/ontologically she becomes like God (*conformis Deo*).[27]

---

25. Mannermaa, "Participation and Love in the Theology of Martin Luther," in *Philosophical Studies in Religion, Metaphysics, and Ethics*, 303–11.

26. See *WA* 17/2. 98. 13–24.

27. Mannermaa, "Das Verhältnis von Glaube und Nächstenliebe in der Theologie Luthers," in *Der im Glauben gegenwärtige Christus*, 101. Luther's exegesis (*WA* 17/2. 74. 20–75. 11) of Psalm 81 (82) is one of the most frequently cited biblical passages in discussions of the Finnish scholars' concept of divinization—being divine by participating in the divine nature and being a god to others. For instance, see Mannermaa, "Participation and Love in the Theology of Martin Luther," in *Philosophical Studies in Religion, Metaphysics, and Ethics*, 306–307.
Also citing Psalm 82:6, Antti Raunio shows that, for Luther, love is not an extrinsic human quality of the Christian that fulfills the Golden Rule by external acts alone. Rather, love is God's own love, which is received by faith and in which Christians participate by cooperating with

At the same time, by means of this divine love, a Christian gives herself to her neighbor and takes upon herself the neighbor's burden, misery, sins, poverty, and weakness as if they were hers. In this way, a Christian takes on, figuratively speaking, a human nature, namely, the misery and burden of a neighbor. A Christian lives not in or for herself but in Christ and for her neighbor. Conversely, it is Christ and the neighbor (not she herself) who live the life that a Christian lives; hence, Christians are to become Christs to their neighbors.[28]

Taking the parallelism between Christ and a Christian as real, Mannermaa analogically explicates the relationship between the relation of Christ to Christian and that of faith to love in Luther's theology as follows: (1) Christ is begotten by the Father continuously in eternity as true God. In a like manner, Christians are also born in faith as "God's children and gods, lords and kings." (2) Christ has "broken out" through pure love and stepped into the position of human beings in all their miseries. Likewise, Christians, who participate in the divine and human nature of Christ, must step into the position of their neighbors and take their burdens on themselves. (3) Just as Christ did not earn his divinity out of his works of love, so Christians do not gain their justification or righteousness as the result of their works of love. They are justified only through faith.

God as God loves the neighbor through them. Raunio, "Natural Law and Faith: The Forgotten Foundations of Ethics in Luther's Theology," in *Union with Christ*, 96–124. See *WA* 10¹/1. 100. 16–19: "da geht den der spruch ps. 81: Ich habe gesagt, yhr seyt Gotter und kinder des allerhochsten allesampt. Gottis kinder sind wyr durch den glawben, der unsz erben macht aller gottelichen gutter. Aber gotte synd wyr durch die liebe, die unsz gegen unszernn nehisten wolthettig macht . . . ."

In similar fashion, Simo Peura points to Luther's comment on Romans 5:5 from the Romans lectures, which argues that love or charity is the only gift of God that requires that the giver Himself, the Holy Spirit, be present as the gift is made. To have love, therefore, means that Christians give not only of themselves but also of the Spirit and love of Christ which is in them. Peura, "Christ as Favor and Gift (*donum*): The Challenge of Luther's Understanding of Justification," in *Union with Christ*, 48–49. See also, *WA* 56. 308. 15–309. 5.

28. Mannermaa, "Das Verhältnis von Glaube und Nächstenliebe in der Theologie Luthers," in *Der im Glauben gegenwärtige Christus*, 102.

For this reason, the relation of faith to God is understood as an analogy of the relation of divine Logos to God the Father before His incarnation. The Logos is continuously born of the Father. Christians, likewise, are continuously born in their faith as "gods and children." As the Logos takes on human nature and becomes incarnate in human flesh out of pure love, so Christians out of love step into the position of their neighbor and become like the poorest of the poor. However, as the Logos does not need to be incarnate in order to be God, so Christians do not need to perform works of love in order to be justified.[29]

Mannermaa also explains that a Christian confronts the commandment of love in two forms: one in the example of Christ; the other in the example of a Christian herself, namely, the Golden Rule. First, just as there is a joyful exchange between Christ and a Christian, so there should be a joyful exchange between a Christian and her neighbor. Everything that a Christian possesses on grounds of faith must become properties of her neighbor, while all the sins, condemnation, death, weakness, and brokenness of her neighbor must become her properties.[30]

Second, the commandment of love is materialized not only in the example of Christ but also in the example of a Christian's own heart. All people have the capacity to put themselves in another's place,

---

29. In reference to both *Operationes in Psalmos* (Ps 1: 2–3 in *WA* 5. 38. 27–39. 12) and *Von der Freiheit eines Christenmenschen*, Mannermaa treats this issue again in "Freiheit als Liebe: *Einführung in das Thema*," in *Freiheit als Liebe bei Martin Luther*, 17–18. This relation between Christ and the Christian in light of the relation between faith and love appears also in Mannermaa's "Participation and Love in the Theology of Martin Luther," in *Philosophical Studies in Religion, Metaphysics, and Ethics*, 307–309. Citing the same passage from Luther (*WA* 17/2. 74. 20–75. 11), Mannermaa argues that it shows a paradigmatic model of Luther's understanding of participation (*theosis*) and love. According to Mannermaa, the relation between faith and love in this text is determined christologically. Perceiving that Luther portrays Christ and the Christian as having exactly parallel characteristics, Mannermaa claims that Christ and Christians seem to have analogous constitutions. Ibid., 307.

30. Mannermaa, "Das Verhältnis von Glaube und Nächstenliebe in der Theologie Luthers," in *Der im Glauben gegenwärtige Christus*, 102–103.

knowing what that person would want to be done. By using this capacity, a Christian ought to love her neighbor. This is the principle of the Golden Rule. According to Mannermaa, Luther connects this principle of the Golden Rule to the way he interprets Jesus Christ's commandment to "love your neighbor as yourself." This principle is observed in the nature of Christ's love for human beings, because when God the Son became a human person, he followed the principle of the Golden Rule. A Christian also complies with the Golden Rule when she takes the place of her neighbor. Mannermaa emphasizes that this idea is crystallized in Luther's view that a Christian is a Christ to her neighbor.[31]

In sum, Mannermaa claims that faith and love are not merely a special theme in Luther's theology, but rather "the total main-content of the Christian belief" (den gesamten Hauptinhalt des christlichen Glaubens).[32] Christ has two natures and so does a Christian through participation in Christ by faith. Mannermaa explains these two natures of a Christian in terms of faith and love.[33] This means that Christian teaching has two main points: faith and love.

Consequently, Mannermaa insists that the traditional view that justifying faith is the center of Luther's thought requires revision. Justifying faith is, according to Luther, an abstract faith (fides abstracta). It is not the content of the whole of a Christian life and teaching. It finds its expression in concrete faith (fides concreta) or incarnate faith (fides incarnata) through love. Only fides concreta is the center of Christian belief. Fides concreta, in which faith and love are united by virtue of Christ who is present in faith, has been neglected, Mannermaa argues, as the presence of Christ was separated

31. Ibid., 103–104.
32. Ibid., 104.
33. Ibid., 101–102.

from justifying faith, and faith was viewed only as the reception of forgiveness through the merits of Christ.[34]

Other Researches

In addition to the insights that the Finns have brought into the discussion of Luther's teaching on love and the relation of faith to love, other studies enrich the discourse with a wide range of research subjects and emphases. First, Anders Nygren's *Agape and Eros* deserves attention, though his treatment of St. Augustine needs to be critically approached.[35] Nygren, a leading representative of the so-called Lundensian school of theology, properly recognizes and appreciates the radical nature of Luther's teaching on love as agapē.

Utilizing "motif-research," Nygren claims that Christianity, Hellenism, and Judaism differently express characteristic motifs in their thought and cultus: the motif of Judaism is the law; of Hellenism, *eros* (an acquisitive and egocentric love); of Christianity, *agapē* (a self-sacrificing and unconditional love). This motif-research induces Nygren to declare that St. Augustine synthesized agapē and eros into *caritas*, a divinely inspired love for God. According to

34. Mannermaa, "In ipsa fide Christus adest," in *Der im Glauben gegenwärtige Christus*, 55; *Christ Present in Faith: Luther's View of Justification*, 46.
35. Anders Nygren, *Agape and Eros*, trans. Philip S. Watson (New York: Harper & Row, 1969). When we read Nygren's *Agape and Eros*, it becomes obvious that Nygren's labor to make Luther a hero led him to make some overstatements and an overly stark contrast between the medieval church's teaching on love and Luther's. Nygren's view that Augustinian *caritas* is a combination of self-sacrificing *agapē* and self-seeking *eros* has been critically reassessed and replaced by new interpretations. Concerning critical evaluations and new interpretations of St. Augustine's conception of love, see, among many, Raymond Canning, *The Unity of Love for God and Neighbour in St. Augustine* (Heverlee-Leuven: Augustinian Historical Institute, 1993); John Burnaby, *Amor Dei: A Study of the Religion of St. Augustine* (Norwich: Canterbury, 1991); Oliver O'Donovan, *The Problem of Self-Love in St. Augustine* (New Haven, CT: Yale University Press, 1980).

For an analysis of the history of the concepts of love, see Irving Singer, *The Nature of Love: Plato to Luther*, vol. 1 (New York: Random House, 1966). See also Pierre Rousselot, *The Problem of Love in the Middle Ages: A Historical Contribution*, trans. Alan Vincelette, reviewed and corrected by Pol Vandevelde (Milwaukee: Marquette University Press, 2001; 1908).

Nygren, the Augustinian idea of caritas was the predominant Christian idea of love for more than a thousand years, until Luther finally rejected this synthesized notion of caritas allegedly because of its egocentrism and returned to the pure New Testament idea of agapē.[36]

Agapē has the following features, according to Nygren: (1) it is a sacrificial and unconditional divine love; (2) it is not motivated by the value of the object of its love; (3) it is creative, in that it does not recognize a value or worth in the object it loves but creates the worth or value in it; and (4) it initiates fellowship with God, that is, agapē is God's way to human beings. In contrast, Platonic eros is characterized as follows: (1) it is an egocentric and acquisitive love; (2) it is motivated by the value of its object; (3) it seeks the possession of an object that is recognized as valuable and good to have; and (4) it is a human way to God. Nygren certainly exaggerates Luther as a hero who reintroduced a purified, biblical conception of agapē. Furthermore, he does not do justice to St. Augustine's teaching on love. Nonetheless, Nygren provides a rare study of Luther's concept of love in detail.

At the core of Nygren's explication of Luther's view of love is the contention that, in opposition to all egocentric forms of religion, Luther insists on a purely theocentric relation to God.[37] Nygren elaborates on this argument as follows:

> What is to be broken down and destroyed is everything 'that is in us,' all our righteousness and wisdom, absolutely everything in which we take a selfish delight. What is to be built up and planted is 'everything that is outside us and in Christ.' The righteousness by which God wills to save

36. It is true, as Nygren admits, that "Luther himself did not use these terms [eros and agapē], nor does he consciously seem to have considered the problem of love from this point of view." Anders Nygren, *Agape and Eros*, 692. Notwithstanding, Nygren is determined to employ eros and agapē to probe Luther's stance on love because he is convinced that this is the problem with which Luther is essentially wrestling.
37. Ibid., 681 (italics original).

us, is not produced by us, but has come to us from elsewhere; it is not derived from our earth, but has come to us from heaven.[38]

Nygren underscores that there is "an inner connection and an exact correspondence between Luther's doctrine of justification and his thinking on love. *The very same thing which made him a reformer in the matter of justification, made him also the reformer of the Christian idea of love.*"[39] In reference to Luther's depiction of his exegetical discovery of Romans 1:17 in *Table Talk*, Nygren contends, "Just as justification is not a question of the 'iustitia' in virtue of which God makes His demands upon us, but of the 'iustitia' which He bestows, so Christian love is strictly not concerned with the love with which we love God, but essentially with the love with which God Himself loves. Luther himself clearly saw this parallel between his view of justification and of love."[40]

Nygren stresses that Luther's idea of love is to be set apart from a moralistic love because Luther's idea of love is fundamentally construed in terms of God's love for us, not our love for God. Likewise, it is differentiated from a eudaemonistic inclination that is not unconnected with an egocentric, acquisitive love. Nygren illustrates how Luther's idea of love can be designated as a theocentric love. In Luther's model, fellowship with God is not conceived of as fellowship on the level of God's holiness but as fellowship on our human level, namely on the basis of sin, not of holiness.[41] When Christ came from heaven to earth, he was given for sinners.[42] When a person toils to become holy and godly to gain standing for herself

---

38. Ibid., 682.
39. Ibid., 683 (italics original). Nygren claims that when Luther realizes that the righteousness involved in the justification of sinners is not a righteousness from us or in us, but righteousness from God, this puts Luther on an "entirely new Way of salvation, for 'righteousness from God' is equivalent to God's Agape." Ibid., 693.
40. Ibid., 683–84.
41. Ibid., 684.
42. Ibid., 686.

before God, this aspiration instead makes her yet more insusceptible to God's grace and leads her even further away from God. In opposition to human endeavor, God's will teaches differently. God wants us to entirely rely on God's free bestowal of the divine love—God's agapē in Christ—and become its beneficiary without any merit on our part.[43] Thus, "every attempt to make one's way to God by self-sanctification runs counter to the message of Christ's self-offering."[44] Every attempt rooted in works- or self-righteousness is rejected. Such an attempt or even the natural disposition towards it is not godly but godless.

Nygren proceeds to demonstrate how Luther breaks down the caritas-synthesis and builds up agapē-love. According to Nygren, Luther finds it necessary to deconstruct the union of the two motifs of eros and agapē and put in its place a doctrine of love that Nygren reckons to be wholly determined by the agapē motif. Nygren sets forth three features that mark the medieval caritas-synthesis. The first feature is the notion of heavenly ladders, that is, the upward tendency. This tendency asserts itself no less in the moralistic piety of popular Catholicism (works-righteousness based on the system of merit through works) than in the rational theology of Scholasticism and the ecstatic religiosity of Mysticism. Despite all dissimilarities, Nygren detects an upward tendency as a common feature among them.[45]

In contrast to this upward tendency, Nygren distinguishes a descending movement in his understanding of the agapē motif in Luther's view of love, claiming that "if Christ is *our way to God*, that is only because He is first and foremost *God's way to us*."[46] Hence,

---

43. Ibid., 685.
44. Ibid., 688.
45. Ibid., 700. "They all know a Way by which man can work his way up to God, whether it is the Way of merit known to practical piety, the ἀναγωγή of mysticism, or the Way of speculative thought according to the 'analogy of being' (*analogia entis*)." Ibid.

God's way of salvation is not our ascent to God in heaven but God's descent to us on earth in Christ.[47] According to Nygren, the sharp contrast between the upward and downward movements is what differentiates eros from agapē, namely, "the Platonic, Hellenistic" from "the specifically Christian Way of salvation. Eros is man's way to God, Agape is God's way to man. Eros is egocentric, Agape theocentric fellowship with God. Luther himself was fully aware that his ultimate concern was with these opposites."[48]

The second feature is laid bare in Luther's battle against self-love, which the medieval tradition interpreted as a separate commandment of love. Nygren pays attention to Luther's disapproval of any kind of self-love and his divergence from the traditional interpretation of

---

46. Ibid., 708 (italics original).
47. Nygren indicates that Luther's serious problem concerns the idea of caritas and the tension it involves. He considers how this issue is bound up with Luther's personal development and illustrates its significance for Luther's thought with an example—that of the Sacrifice of the Mass and the Lord's Supper. Nygren claims that it was "the refinement of the Caritas doctrine by Mediæval theology, which brought Luther to the point where this doctrine had to be broken down. He found this sublimated idea of caritas in Occam and Biel, with their demand for a penitence and contrition based not merely on fear and acquisitive love, but on a pure and unselfish love of God. This demand becomes the more pointed when the authors mentioned affirm that man is able 'ex puris naturalibus,' by his natural powers alone, to love God above all things. It was this theory which Luther in the monastery tried to put into practice in his own life." Ibid., 694.

   However, as Nygren points out, the more seriously Luther takes the commandment to love God and the demand that his love for God should be pure and unselfish, the more impossible it becomes. Ibid. By realizing that human beings cannot fulfill the commandment of love, Luther holds that we are justified not by ascending to God in caritas, but solely by receiving in faith God's love, which has descended to us in Christ. According to Nygren, this is one of the ways in which the caritas-synthesis falls to pieces, vanquished by God's agapē. Ibid., 695.

   Nygren finds the same pattern in the Lord's Supper. Primarily designating Luther's approach to the Lord's Supper as receiving Christ's gift and the Catholic approach to it as our giving a sacrifice to God, Nygren contrasts the two: The former comes from God to us, the latter comes from us to God. In the Lord's Supper, Christ has instituted his testament and it is God who in Christ descends to us. In it, there is given to us the forgiveness of sins; there we are met by God's self-giving love, God's agapē. In the Sacrifice of the Mass, we strive to ascend to God; hence, it gives expression to the false way of salvation. The same logic is applied when Luther criticizes the spiritualizing idea of the Lord's Supper. Nygren focuses on the question of what is it that impels them to deny the real presence of Christ in the Lord's Supper. It is chiefly the idea that this would conflict with the glory of Christ. At the celebration, they strive for a fellowship with the glorified Christ, while also seeking to mount up to God in His majesty. Ibid., 697.
48. Ibid., 708.

self-love with the conviction that even one's seeking fellowship with God is polluted by this inborn egocentricity. The third feature is identified in Luther's campaign against the scholastic formula *fides caritate formata*, which Nygren reckons as the "culmination of Luther's attack on the caritas-synthesis."[49] In this campaign, Luther removes love and places it outside the locus of justification, declaring that justification takes place *sola fide*, by faith alone.

Focusing on this position of Luther, Nygren puts forward a compelling argument that the "contrast between Luther and Catholicism, which at first appears to be the contrast between faith and love, is just as much a contrast between two fundamentally different conceptions of love."[50] Nygren asserts that "'fides caritate formata' constitutes a threat not only to faith, but equally to the purity of Christian love."[51] Luther had no intention to dismiss or depreciate love itself. The reason Luther was so anxious to keep love apart from the matter of the justification of sinners was that "*to do the contrary would mean a depreciation of love, a denial of Christian love*. To speak of love *in loco iustificationis* is to preach another and lower kind of love than the Christian."[52] Accordingly, it can be said that Luther's intention was not to banish or minimize love in his theology but to retrieve what he believed to be the pure Christian love that is nothing other than God.

After affirming that Luther succeeded in building up the theocentric agapē-love, Nygren handles the question of whether or not this idea of agapē is merely an ideal picture drawn from God's love, having no relation whatever to human life as it actually is. Nygren's answer is that, while the subject of Christian love,

49. Ibid., 716.
50. Ibid., 719.
51. Ibid.
52. Ibid., 720 (italics original).

according to Luther, is not a human person but the very God, divine love employs a Christian as its instrument and organ. Being placed between God and her neighbor, in faith she receives God's love and in love she passes it on to her neighbor; hence, Christian love is the extension of God's love.[53]

Second, instead of dealing with individual topics, Gerhard Ebeling concentrates on the inner dynamic of Luther's thought or the process of his thinking and calls our attention to this inner dynamic by selecting and treating ten thematic pairs. Ebeling's ten thematic pairs are: "theology and philosophy, the letter and the Spirit, the law and the gospel, the double use of the law, person and works, faith and love, the kingdom of Christ and the kingdom of the world, man as a Christian and man in the world, freedom and bondage, God hidden and God revealed."[54] These ten thematic pairs, Ebeling asserts, should not be studied separately from one another, since a true appreciation of the structure of Luther's thinking can be grasped only when all these themes are put into perspective together. They originate from a single pattern of thinking but are presented in different forms; thus, they are organically related to one another by an integrated thinking process.

Ebeling's deliberate selection of faith and love as one of the ten complementary thematic pairs in Luther's theology deserves special attention.[55] Ebeling's explicit pairing of faith and love is quite valuable, since it visibly demonstrates the importance of faith and

53. Ibid., 737.
54. Gerhard Ebeling, *Luther—Einführung in sein Denken*, 2nd ed. (Tübingen: Mohr Siebeck, 2006; 1964), 16; ET *Luther: An Introduction to His Thought*, trans. R. A. Wilson (Philadelphia: Fortress Press, 1977), 25.
55. Ebeling, *Luther—Einführung in sein Denken*, 178–97; ET *Luther: An Introduction to His Thought*, 159–74. The chapter on "Glaube und Liebe" was reproduced as "Faith and Love" in *Martinus Luther: 450th Anniversary of the Reformation*, ed. Helmut Gollwitzer (Bad Godesberg: Inter Nationes, 1967), 69–79. See also Ebeling, "Einfalt des Glaubens und Vielfalt der Liebe: Das Herz von Luthers Theologie," in *Lutherstudien III* (Tübingen: J. C. B. Mohr (Paul Siebeck), 1985), 126–53.

love as a thematic pair in Luther's theology. However, Ebeling's intentional focus on faith and love turns out to carry even more weight in his scrutiny of the underlying dynamics between faith and love than in his presentation of faith and love as a thematic pair because of his method of interpreting the dynamics.

This method examines "the tension that runs through the whole of Luther's thought, the play between the harsh opposition of opposing theses and the spirit of compromise which reconciles both sides of an issue,"[56] namely, "an antithesis, tension between strongly opposed but related polarities."[57] Accordingly, the relationship between faith and love is characterized by the tension that emerges from both the opposition and the connection between them; faith and love are both opposed and related. Ebeling perceives this paradoxical relationship between faith and love especially in the relationship between the doer and the deed.

In Ebeling's understanding of Luther's doctrine, the Word of God or the proclamation of the Word, by which a Christian is confronted, plays a crucial role. The Word, which has created the universe *ex nihilo*, has the power to lead sinners to justification and justified Christians effectively to works of love. The direct address of the gospel, the essence of which is the proclamation of the forgiveness of sins available by reason of Christ's merit, sets a sinner free from anguish of conscience and motivates loving service. It is the active, deed-generating power of the word of faith, as it initiates a new personal existence in assurance and freedom, which connects faith

---

56. Ebeling, *Luther—Einführung in sein Denken*, v: "der durchgehenden Spannung in Luthers Denken nachzugehen, die zwischen schroffer Gegensätzlichkeit und beruhigendem Kompromiß, zwischen Entweder-Oder und Sowohl-Als-Auch zu schillern scheint."; ET *Luther: An Introduction to His Thought*, 11.

57. Ebeling, *Luther—Einführung in sein Denken*, 16: "in antithetischer Spannung, in sehr verschiedenartigen, aber doch zueinander in Beziehung stehenden Polaritäten."; ET *Luther: An Introduction to His Thought*, 25. See also *Luther-Einführung in sein Denken*, 157–58, 161–62; ET *Luther: An Introduction to His Thought*, 141–42, 144–48.

to love. The certainty of faith sets Christians free to serve their neighbors without any trace of calculating, self-interested piety.

Third, in addition to the treatment of faith and love in Luther by the modern Finnish Luther scholars, Nygren, and Ebeling, Luther interpreters also have focused on freedom as love and love as freedom, undoubtedly inspired by Luther's well-known tractate *The Freedom of a Christian*. Rudolf Mau's article, "Liebe als gelebte Freiheit der Christen," is very helpful in exploring Luther's teaching on love as the lived freedom of a Christian in Luther's 1519 Galatians commentaries.[58]

In *Freiheit als Liebe bei Martin Luther*, Mannermaa reclaims Luther's understanding that freedom is never to be attributed to human beings but only to God.[59] In Luther's *De servo arbitrio*, for instance, freedom is exclusively a divine property (Eigenschaft).[60] Here again applying his argument that Christ is present in a Christian through faith, Mannermaa claims that freedom, as the name or property of God, is identical with the divine nature and that a Christian can participate in this divine nature of freedom through union with Christ in justifying faith. Only by acknowledging and confessing their lack of freedom, and by emptying themselves, can sinners participate in Christ and thereby in God, through the word of the gospel. According to Mannermaa, when Luther treats the problem of free will, it is a matter of a person's capability of fulfilling the divine commandments—the twofold commandment of love of God and love of neighbor. Only through participation in the divine love that is freedom can a person fulfill the commandments.[61]

---

58. Rudolf Mau, "Liebe als gelebte Freiheit der Christen," *Lutherjahrbuch* 59 (1992): 11–37.

59. Tuomo Mannermaa, "Freiheit als Liebe: *Einführung in das Thema*," in *Freiheit als Liebe bei Martin Luther*, 9–18.

60. See *WA* 18. 636. 27–637. 1.

61. His explication of Luther's concept of freedom as love in this essay, though very insightful, focuses on "freedom to" not "freedom from," which is primarily connected to Luther's doctrine of justification by faith in Christ alone. Furthermore, Luther's concept of freedom as love is

A fourth classification of research on faith and love in Luther focuses on Luther's teaching on neighbor-love, which highlights the Christian's metaphorically paradoxical roles as simultaneously a lord and a servant, and also as a Christ to her neighbors. This research also deals with the role of the Golden Rule in Luther's concept of love, especially as the principle of neighbor-love. Donald C. Ziemke's *Love for the Neighbor in Luther's Theology: The Development of His Thought 1512–1529* is one example.[62] Ziemke aims to clarify Luther's understanding of love for the neighbor by tracing his work on it during the years 1512–1529. Bearing in mind that theology and ethics are closely tied to each other in Luther's cogitation, Ziemke explores Luther's understanding of the biblical concept of neighbor-love and its relation to his theological ethics.

Gustaf Wingren treats the nonmeritorious nature of horizontal Christian love in Luther's theology in light of his concept of vocation.[63] Helmar Junghans inquires into the relationship of love as the content and the fulfillment of the law, and faith as the condition of making such love available to Christians.[64] He explicates Luther's notions of the person who performs works of love, the way to perform works of love, the object (field or area) of love, and the example of the works of love.

delineated in three relational dimensions: to God, to neighbors, and to oneself. Mannermaa's explanation highlights only two of these: to God and to neighbors.

62. Donald C. Ziemke, *Love for the Neighbor in Luther's Theology: The Development of His Thought 1512–1529* (Minneapolis: Augsburg Publishing House, 1963). See also Ziemke, *The Hermeneutical Basis for Luther's Doctrine of Love for the Neighbor* (PhD diss., Princeton Theological Seminary, 1960).

63. Gustaf Wingren, *Luther on Vocation*, trans. C. C. Rasmussen (Eugene, OR: Wipf & Stock, 2004; 1957), esp. 37–50. See also Eberhard Jüngel, *Zur Freiheit eines Christenmenschen: eine Erinnerung an Luthers Schrift* (Munich: Kaiser, 1991), 91–115; ET *The Freedom of a Christian: Luther's Significance for Contemporary Theology*, trans. Roy A. Harrisville (Minneapolis: Augsburg Publishing House, 1988), 68–87.

64. Helmar Junghans, "Martin Luther über die Nächstenliebe," *Luther: Zeitschrift der Luther-Gesellschaft* 62, no. 1 (1991): 3–11.

Mannermaa also treats the issue of neighbor-love in relation to Luther's concept of faith.[65] Many of Mannermaa's arguments are taken up by Veli-Matti Kärkkäinen.[66] Drawing on modern Finnish Luther studies, Kärkkäinen also brings to the fore the meaning of Christ's real presence in Christians as the gateway for expressing Christ's love toward neighbor and the Christian's role as Christ to neighbors. He finds the Golden Rule to be Luther's guiding principle for understanding the Christian's relationships to both God and neighbor.

He also underscores important ecclesiological implications of Luther's ideas about God's love and neighbor-love: church members as Christs to each other and the church as a hospital. For Luther, human love is no less valuable than divine love. The relationship between faith and love is integral and necessary in Luther's doctrine of justification.[67] Kärkkäinen holds that faith is the reception of God's gifts—primarily the greatest gift, love. Christ as gift inhabits the Christian and makes the believer act as Christ acts, loving and caring. The works of the Christian are in a sense not the believer's own but rather the works of Christ present in faith. This is the fulfillment of the law.[68]

Another Finnish scholar, Antti Raunio, scrutinizes Luther's teaching on love, especially from the vantage point of the Golden Rule and its theological and ethical implications.[69] His research offers

---

65. Tuomo Mannermaa, "Das Verhältnis von Glaube und Liebe in der Theologie Luthers," in *Luther in Finnland*, 99–110; Mannermaa, "Das Verhältnis von Glaube und Nächstenliebe in der Theologie Luthers," in *Der im Glauben gegenwärtige Christus*, 95–105.

66. Veli-Matti Kärkkäinen, "'The Christian as Christ to the Neighbor': On Luther's Theology of Love," *International Journal of Systematic Theology* 6, no. 2 (2004): 101–17.

67. Ibid., 103.

68. Ibid., 116.

69. Antti Raunio, *Summe des christlichen Lebens: die "Goldene Regel" als Gesetz der Liebe in der Theologie Martin Luthers von 1510–1527* (Mainz: Verlag Philipp von Zabern, 2001). Originally published in *Helsingin yliopiston systemaattisen teologian laitoksen julkaisuja* 13 (Helsinki: Yliopistopaino, 1993). See also idem, "Die 'Goldene Regel' als theologisches Prinzip beim jungen Luther," in *Thesaurus Lutheri* (Helsinki: Suomalainen Teologinen Kirjallisuusseura,

an elaborate treatment of Luther's idea of God's love as formulated in the Golden Rule, its relationship to human love and neighbor-love, and its implications for Luther's theology of the cross and of suffering.

Fifth, as previously sketched research already discloses, the Golden Rule plays an important role in Luther's teaching on faith and love. However, in terms of Luther's concept of the role of the law for justified Christians, the Ten Commandments, in particular, play a role no less significant. Considering that the Decalogue is encapsulated in Christ's two ultimate love commandments (Matthew 22:37-40), it is no surprise to find research on the issue of the law—or, more precisely, the Decalogue—in Luther's teaching on faith and love, which can be classified as a fifth area of scholarship on faith and love in Luther. For instance, there are studies on this issue by Klaus Schwarzwäller, George W. Forell, and Christoph Burger.[70] Bernhard Erling treats the question of how to understand freedom within the context of Anders Nygren's agapē-motif.[71] Placing Luther's concept of the role of law within the agapē-motif, Erling contends that, before coming to faith, one does not have freedom to obey the law, according to Luther. Yet once Christians receive a new heart through the Holy Spirit's gift of divine love, they do have freedom to obey the law of love.

In a sixth classification of research on faith and love in Luther, many recent works have examined the socio-ethical implications

---

1987), 309–27; Raunio, "Die Goldene Regel als Gesetz der göttlichen Natur: Das natürliche Gesetz und das göttliche Gesetz in Luthers Theologie 1522–1523," in *Luther und Theosis*, 163–86.

70. Klaus Schwarzwäller, "Verantwortung des Glaubens Freiheit und Liebe nach der Dekalogauslegung Martin Luthers," in *Freiheit als Liebe bei Martin Luther*, 133–58; George W. Forell, "Freedom as Love: Luther's *Treatise on Good Works*," in *Freiheit als Liebe bei Martin Luther*, 79–83; Christoph Burger, "Gottesliebe, Erstes Gebot und menschliche Autonomie bei spätmittelalterlichen Theologen und bei Martin Luther," *Zeitschrift für Theologie und Kirche* 89, no. 3 (1992): 280–301.

71. Bernhard Erling, "The Role of Law in How a Christian Becomes What He/She Is," in *Freiheit als Liebe bei Martin Luther*, 63–78.

of Luther's teaching on faith and love. For instance, Bernd Wannenwetsch treats Luther's concepts of faith and love in terms of Luther's moral theology,[72] and William H. Lazareth focuses on the biblical norms of Luther's theological ethics in order to argue that the chief features of Luther's theological ethics are determined by his christocentric reading of Scripture.[73] He accents the dramatic and dialectical twofold rule of the Triune God against Satan through Caesar and Christ. God preserves creation and renews redemption by the intersecting functions of the law and the gospel for Christian salvation and service. The law has not only a judging function before God but also a corollary preserving function within society. This strange work of God is also complemented by the two interpenetrating functions of the gospel: carrying out Christ's proper work by effecting his justification of sinners before God and the Holy Spirit's accompanying sanctification of Christians within society.

Svend Andersen argues that Luther's ethics is an ethics of neighbor-love.[74] Pointing to Luther's view that the world cannot be governed by the gospel, Andersen claims that this remark has too often been misunderstood. Andersen interprets Luther's concept of love first and foremost as neighbor-love. It is a spontaneous expression of the Christian's joy and gratitude for the beneficence

72. Bernd Wannenwetsch, "Luther's Moral Theology," in *The Cambridge Companion to Martin Luther*, 120–35, esp. 128–29. See also, David Wright, "The Ethical Use of the Old Testament in Luther and Calvin: A Comparison," *Scottish Journal of Theology* 36 (1983): 463–85, esp. 467–68; Mark T. Totten, "*Luther on unio cum Christo*: Toward a Model for Integrating Faith and Ethics," *Journal of Religious Ethics* 31, no. 3 (2003): 443–62; Bayer, *Living by Faith*.

73. William H. Lazareth, *Christians in Society: Luther, the Bible, and Social Ethics* (Minneapolis: Fortress Press, 2001). Lazareth clearly indicates his strong interest in prompting and contributing to unprecedented ecumenical developments that have been taking place since the end of the twentieth-century, such as the *Joint Declaration on the Doctrine of Justification* (1999) and the Evangelical Lutheran Church in America's affirmation of a relation of full communion with the Episcopal Church USA in 1998 and with three churches of the Reformed tradition: the Presbyterian Church (USA), the Reformed Church in America, and the United Church of Christ in 1997. Ibid., viii–ix.

74. Svend Andersen, "Lutheran Ethics and Political Liberalism," in *Philosophical Studies in Religion, Metaphysics, and Ethics*, 292–302.

bestowed by Christ, namely, freely granted salvation. Luther's teaching on neighbor-love, according to Andersen, opens a door to the notion that the world can be governed on the basis of Christian neighbor-love. This neighbor-love sends Christians into the secular domain, that is, the socio-political sphere; hence, neighbor-love can be practiced in the exercise of political power and can assume the nature of justice.

In addition to these studies, a classic examination of Luther's teaching on faith and love and its socio-ethical ramifications is detected in George W. Forell's *Faith Active in Love*. Forell opposes the assertion that Luther had no social ethics because he placed society outside the influence of the Christian gospel. He also disapproves of the claim that Luther's social ethics was purely pragmatic, accepting the social order of his day and consequently promoting the growth of capitalism and nationalism. Suspending any judgment that Luther's utterances about social ethics sound meaningless or contradictory, Forell maintains that there is a framework for Luther on social ethics, comprising four principles: methodological, ethical, practical, and limiting.

In the interest of probing Luther's teaching on faith and love, Forell's perception of "faith active in love" as the bedrock of Luther's social ethics is no less engaging than his advancing of the four principles themselves. According to Forell, Luther's ethical stance proceeds from his theological method, the kernel of which is the forgiveness of sins by God's gracious justification through Christ.[75] Luther's ethical treatment is built upon his doctrine of justification by faith in Christ alone. For Luther, "justification is the basis for all Christian ethics."[76] With this view of justifying faith, Luther

---

75. George Wolfgang Forell, *Faith Active in Love: An Investigation of the Principles Underlying Luther's Social Ethics* (Eugene, OR: Wipf & Stock, 1999; Minneapolis: Augsburg Publishing House, 1954), 47–48.
76. Ibid., 84.

postulates that actions are measured as good or evil commensurate with the function they fulfill in helping or hindering the establishment of the saving relation between God and human beings.[77] Forell designates Luther's implementation of his theological core to his social ethics as its methodological principle.

On the basis of this methodological principle, a claim ensues: faith guarantees ethical action, not actions motivated toward self-righteousness, rewards, or happiness.[78] More fundamentally, the motivating force springing from faith for Christian ethics is God's love. The one justified receives God's love in faith and passes it on to her neighbor; therefore, the Christian life is a life of faith and love.[79] Here Forell puts forward an apposite formulation: "If the principle of Luther's ethics can be defined in relation to its source in God as 'justification by faith,' it can be described in relation to its outlet as 'faith active in love.'"[80] According to Luther, Forell contends, "all ethics, individual as well as social, must be understood from the key-principle of love."[81] This principle of love is bound to have widespread social-ethical implications: the works of love must benefit fellow individuals, especially those in greatest need, and society.[82] The Christian service resulting from faith is to be rendered to not only individuals but also the world.

Luther's concern for society as reflected in the service of Christians through faith active in love leads to Forell's understanding of the practical principle of Luther's social ethics, which is characterized by its pragmatic approach to the problems of society. For Luther, Forell

77. Ibid., 62–65, 69.
78. Ibid., 79–81, 83.
79. Ibid., 89.
80. Ibid., 90. Forell features Luther's concept of Christian love as diametrically opposed to all human acquisitive desire. Love, insofar as it is truly Christian, is modeled after the love of Christ. Ibid., 95. This Christian love as a gift of God is self-giving, spontaneous, overflowing as the love of God, and does not ask after the worthiness of the object. Ibid., 98–99.
81. Ibid., 101.
82. Ibid., 103.

argues, the natural orders are "the practical realm of social ethics."[83] Although Luther differentiates the secular from the spiritual realm, the secular realm is also God's realm. On that account, social ethics is practiced within the framework of the natural orders that are divinely ordained and have their source in the preserving will of God.[84] Forell finds in Luther's social ethics a point of contact between the secular and the spiritual realms in the justified Christian living in society:

> A point of contact between the secular realm and the spiritual realm exists in the person of the individual Christian. In this point the spiritual realm penetrates the secular, without, however, abolishing it. The Gospel itself cannot be used to rule the world, because it is the Gospel and demands a voluntary response from man. It would cease to be the Gospel if it became a new law. But through the person of the believer, who is related to Christ through the Gospel and who is at the same time a member of the natural orders, the faith active in love penetrates the social order."[85]

Through the justified Christian, the ethical principle penetrates the practical principle in Luther's social ethics, and the Christian faith finds its social relevancy.[86]

---

83. Ibid., 145.
84. Ibid., 146. A person as a member of society is a part of certain orders or collectivities such as the family, the state, the empirical church, and her calling. This membership in the natural orders is part of God's design to preserve the world and to contain the creative forces within a person that, under the influence of sin, might lead to disorder and destruction. Ibid., 113. See also ibid., 123, 127, 153.
85. Ibid., 148–49.
86. Ibid., 154. This point of view is also well expressed in Martin Marty's "Luther on Ethics: Man Free and Slave," in *Accents in Luther's Theology: Essays in Commemoration of the 450th Anniversary of the Reformation*, ed. Heino O. Kadai (Saint Louis: Concordia Publishing House, 1967), 199–227. Marty denounces the allegation that Luther's ethics and Lutheran ethics teach that the secular order is abandoned because the gospel is irrelevant to it, or that it is autonomous because God's law alone is operative in it, which has nothing—except in its theological function—to do with Christian salvation and freedom. This opinion falsely accuses Luther of severing the temporal and spiritual spheres and generating a dichotomy between personal ethics and participation in public and official life. Marty criticizes this dualistic interpretation for viewing Luther's two-kingdom approach too statically, isolating the temporal order from the spiritual one. This way of thinking obscures the dynamics constituting Luther's and Lutheran social ethics.

On the other hand, Forell also claims that this very concept of faith active in love, which functions as the underpinning of Luther's social ethics, curbs the desire for any drastic or thoroughgoing social revolutions or changes. Faith "made it impossible for Luther to take any social reform ultimately seriously. Faith was the 'motive' and the 'quietive' of his social ethics," Forell articulates.[87] An indispensible characteristic of Luther's faith is the expectation of the immediate advent of the Kingdom of God. All the problems of individual and social existence can ultimately be solved only with the coming of God's kingdom. Until that time, all human efforts are merely attempts to eliminate "proximate evils."[88] Forell construes this eschatological outlook or "this firm belief in God's impending solution of all human problems" as "the limiting principle of Luther's social ethics."[89] However, "this practical conservatism does not imply a principle of static acceptance of all existing orders," Forell clarifies.[90]

Finally, due to its limited scope, this dissertation does not analyze Luther's lectures on Genesis as a whole. These lectures were written between 1535 and 1545 (one year before Luther's death) and can certainly be claimed as representative of the so-called "older" Luther.[91] Nevertheless, the sheer volume of the lectures covering

Marty then claims, "Given the 'water over the dam' of Troeltsch-Holl and the many sad historical episodes by Lutherans who misused the [two-kingdom] teaching, it seems more advantageous to begin with the concrete view of love and the neighbor on the part of the free and serving Christian as the first word in Lutheran ethics. After it is understood, a discussion of the spheres or orbits or situation-complexes of ethics can be expounded as regulative so that no word of ethics keeps 'the Gospel from being heard as Gospel.'" Ibid., 214. Luther's ethics and Lutheran ethics were "born in faith" and "Faith-ethics does not remain idle." Ibid., 224. Faith bears fruit in love for neighbors who await the Christian's service, not only in the spiritual sphere but also in the temporal sphere. Christian freedom is inextricably connected with Christian servanthood in Luther's and Lutheran ethics, which, Marty contends, can be recapitulated as neighbor-oriented ethics of freedom. Ibid., 202.

87. Forell, *Faith Active in Love*, 162.
88. Ibid., 176.
89. Ibid., 182.
90. Ibid., 135–36.
91. For the young Luther's notions of faith and love, see Reinhard Schwarz, *Fides, spes und caritas beim jungen Luther, unter besonderer Berücksichtigung der mittelalterlichen Tradition* (Berlin:

a span of over ten years has necessitated postponing their close examination from this particular angle. Indeed, a good resource already exists, addressing Luther's concepts of faith and love in the Genesis lectures, which is Scott Hendrix's "The Reformer of Faith and Love: Luther's Lectures on Genesis."[92] According to Hendrix, faith and love are constitutive of the Christian life,[93] and Christian love is always united to faith in Christ.[94] He concludes that, "[a]lthough it is not dominant as an explicit theme, the references to faith and love in the Genesis lectures show that the so-called older Luther is just as much a theologian of faith and love as the young reformer."[95]

Walter de Gruyter, 1962). In this book, Schwarz investigates Luther's ideas of faith, hope, and love in his early career in three distinctive periods: the first period, between 1509 and 1510, when he delivered Peter Lombard's *Four Books of Sentences* (*Libri Quatuor Sententiarum*); the second period, between 1513 and 1515, when he offered his first Psalm lectures; the third period, between 1515 and 1518, when he lectured on Paul's Epistles to the Romans and the Galatians, and Hebrews. According to Schwarz, one of the critical changes in Luther's thoughts on faith and love by the time he was engaged in glossing Paul's Epistle to the Romans was the abandonment of the Aristotelian-scholastic conception of virtue as a habitual quality ontologically inhering in one's soul. This change already had begun to appear in Luther's first Psalm lectures. Ibid., 241–44. See also Arthur S. Wood, "Theology of Luther's Lectures on Romans, I," *Scottish Journal of Theology* 3, no. 1 (1950): 1–18.

As to Luther's teaching on faith and love in his 1519 Galatians lectures, see Rudolf Mau, "Liebe als gelebte Freiheit der Christen: Luthers Auslegung von G 5, 13–24 im Kommentar von 1519" *Lutherjahrbuch* 59 (1992): 11–37; Eric W. Gritsch, "Martin Luther's Commentary on Gal 5, 2–24, 1519 (WA 2, 574–597) and Sermon on Gal 4, 1–7, 1522 (WA 10 I 1, 325–378)," in *Freiheit als Liebe bei Martin Luther*, 105–11.

92. Scott Hendrix, "The Reformer of Faith and Love: Luther's Lectures on Genesis" ("Luther als Theologe des Glaubens und der Liebe," Helsinki, September 2000) This paper was delivered at a conference celebrating the retirement of Tuomo Mannermaa. In the following discussion, this hitherto unpublished document is quoted according to its numbered paragraphs.

For a summary of the arguments for authenticity and reliability, Hendrix refers to Ulrich Asendorf, *Lectura in Biblia: Luthers Genesisvorlesung (1535–1545)*, (Göttingen: Vandenhoeck & Ruprecht, 1998), 33–39. Hendrix also states (endnote, 33) that texts dealing with faith and love are not explicitly mentioned by Peter Meinhold in the section of his study that distinguishes the theological emphases of Luther from those of his editors. However, Hendrix continues to say that related themes dealt with in his paper—the kingdom of Christ and the Christian life as continual purgation and sanctification—are judged by Meinhold to belong to the authentic thought of Luther. For a further reference, see Peter Meinhold, *Die Genesisvorlesung Luthers und ihre Herausgeber* (Stuttgart: W. Kohlhammer, 1936), 370–428, esp. 413–15

93. Hendrix, "The Reformer of Faith and Love," par. 6.

94. Ibid., par. 45.

To inquire into Luther's treatment of faith and love in the Genesis lectures, Hendrix aptly pays attention to Genesis 15:6, where Luther discusses the justification of Abraham.[96] The figure of Abraham plays a central role, according to Hendrix, in Luther's elaboration of faith and love in the Genesis lectures. Abraham is extolled not only as the example of justifying faith but also as the model of faith and love in Christian life. The Genesis lectures contain a continual polemic against monasticism, while Abraham is portrayed as a true monk and a genuine saint who practices faith and love in the correct way.[97]

Hendrix highlights that the "liberated Christian lives in what Luther calls the kingdom of promise"[98] that is wrought by union with Christ, declaring that the goal of Luther's theology (Luther's "Reformation agenda") is "to describe, recover and install this new reality in the society of his day."[99] This "focus on real change in the kingdom of Christ gives Luther's theology of faith and love a dynamic, historical quality which it would not otherwise have if it were understood only as *Tugendlehre* or as one locus in a system of doctrine."[100] For this reason, Hendrix argues that both faith and love belong not only to the heart of Luther's theology in analytical terms but also to the center of his agenda of reform in practical terms.[101]

This survey of recent Luther research on the subject of faith and love exhibits some changes, though as yet insufficient, of landmarks in Luther scholarship. Behind these changes, the contributions of the

95. Ibid., par. 30. Hendrix acutely perceives that most of the main texts cited by the modern Finnish Luther scholars in support of their interpretation of Luther's doctrine of faith and love come from Luther's writings of 1525 and before. Considering this, Hendrix's treatment of Luther's doctrine of faith and love in the Genesis lectures certainly extends the scope of research on faith and love in Luther.
96. Ibid., pars. 25–26. See *LW* 2:399; *WA* 42. 549. 21–23, *LW* 3:24; *WA* 42. 565. 32–34, *LW* 3:25; *WA* 42. 566. 35–40, *LW* 4:38; *WA* 43. 162. 28–31, *LW* 4:41; *WA* 43. 165. 8–14.
97. Hendrix, "The Reformer of Faith and Love," par. 27.
98. Ibid., par. 32.
99. Ibid., par. 41.
100. Ibid.
101. Ibid., par. 31.

modern Finnish Luther scholars need to be acknowledged, though not all of their arguments are accepted. Luther's teaching on love or sanctification is beginning to be appreciated more appropriately in relation to his teaching on faith or justification. This growing cognizance of the significance of Luther's teaching on faith and love has led Luther scholars into divergent areas of research on the subject, as sketched above, producing research with various foci and results and thereby enriching and widening the scope of this subject.

My Research

This dissertation shares many of the concerns of previous research on Luther, but it also has distinctive features, which will be illustrated in the following.

1. While other research focuses primarily on the specific aspects of Luther's teachings on faith and love, this dissertation strives to achieve a macroscopic perspective by advancing faith and love as the overriding theological thematic pair in his major commentary on Galatians (1535). Although the main analysis is confined to the Galatians commentary, I labor to put into perspective the extent of these teachings in Luther's theology by drawing on other texts in the footnotes.

Among the existing studies on this subject, George Forell insightfully elucidates how faith and love uphold Luther's social ethics. However, in my understanding, Luther does not draw a clear division between Christian social ethics and Christian theology proper. Rather, Luther's teachings on faith and love seem to undergird the whole of his theology, not merely his social ethics or, more precisely, a reading of his theology through the projection of the modern category of social ethics. Forell himself seems to be aware of this aspect when, in his treatment of the methodological principle of Luther's social ethics, he contends that Luther's ethical methodology corresponds to his theological methodology. Still, this argument might be more accurate if we say that our reading of Luther's ethical methodology corresponds to his theological methodology. This is because his ethical methodology is already integrated into his theological methodology, not because his ethical methodology is distinct from but fortuitously correlative to his theological methodology.

So my desideratum is that a reader would not approach Luther's teaching on faith and love with the prejudice that this topic is primarily pertinent to his social ethics and not to his theology as a whole. I would also suggest that, even while dealing with Luther's teaching on faith and love in individual texts, a reader apply a broad perspective in order to consider it in the context of his whole theology, not merely as isolated incidents.

2. This dissertation pays attention to certain personal, exegetical, ministerial, and polemical contexts that impelled Luther to develop and elaborate on his concept of love in relation to faith. Among many others, the following facets can be illustrated: his own spiritual disquietude (especially centering on the concept of the righteousness of God), his exegesis of the Pauline Epistles, his ministerial sense of accountability to God concerning his sheep's spiritual and material well-being, and his polemical disputes.[102] My introduction already touched on some of these elements under "Method" and "Plan of the Dissertation."

Here the following observation is apposite: some conceptual and structural traits of Luther's teaching on faith and love in the 1535 Galatians commentary reflect the decisive impact Paul had upon him, starting with his lectures on Paul's Epistle to the Romans. The

---

102. Luther often mentions that his opponents helped him cogitate more intensively and deeply, enabling him to articulate and clarify his positions on various issues under fervent debate. See *LW* 54:273–74 (no. 3793, dated 25 March 1538); *WA, TR* 3:617–18.

Romans lectures (1515–1516) already show Luther applying his critical acumen to the church's excessive legalism reflected in the sale of indulgences and his gradual appropriation of a prophetic role against the abuse of the penitential system by the Roman Church in Europe. In 1517, deeply sympathetic toward the incremental complaints of the poor in an era of escalating poverty, Luther made public his ninety-five theses, intending to provoke scholarly discussion on the ongoing and highly controversial indulgence sales. Going beyond mere appearances, Luther began to intuit what was fundamentally wrong in the whole nexus of underlying systems—theological, ecclesiastical, and practical. This 1517 event is one example that implies that the spirit of Luther's teaching on faith and love cannot be fully appreciated without grasping the ethos of his ministerial service in doing theology.

3. While the categories of justification and sanctification are conventionally well established, this dissertation finds that a rigid application of these two categories without clear qualification is not very effective in accurately analyzing Luther's theology. I have come to have the firm conviction that the categories of faith and love are much more suitable than those of justification and sanctification to discuss Luther's thoughts on what are usually germane to justification and sanctification. Furthermore, Luther's doctrine of faith is about receiving not only alien, passive, and perfect righteousness but also alien, passive, and perfect holiness. On the other hand, his doctrine of love is about increasing proper, active, and progressing righteousness and holiness. Luther unveils his teaching on faith and love, utilizing the two dimensions of righteousness and holiness (alien, passive, and perfect vis-à-vis proper, active, and progressing).

4. To give prominence to the two dimensions as an interpretive framework for Luther's teaching on faith and love, this dissertation calls attention to Luther's treatment of Paul's topical shift from faith

to love in his Epistle to the Galatians. This will be set out at the beginning of chapter 2.

5. This dissertation argues that Luther's reconceptualization of faith and love entails an exploration of his thought about the law and exposes its functions revolving around faith and love. In the dimension of alien, passive, and perfect righteousness and holiness, the law is handled in two ways. In the matter of justification of the unrighteous, the function of the law, insofar as it claims its jurisdiction over sinners, is completely nullified because of Christ. Nevertheless, Luther ascribes a theological or spiritual function to it, in which it stimulates sinners to faith in Christ as an asylum from the menacing and conscience-binding reign of the law. Luther, in fact, deems this as the primary function of the law, making it an indispensable component of his reconceptualization of faith in Christ.

Yet, if the theological or spiritual function of the law absorbs all the attention and outshines the function of the law that enters the picture in Luther's reconceptualization of love, then the picture of Luther's notion of the law is only partially puzzled out. In the dimension of proper, active, and progressing righteousness and holiness, the law is portrayed as having a different function. The spirit of the whole law contained in the Decalogue is redefined in light of the Christ-given law of love. Luther proclaims that those who consider themselves followers of Christ should not fail to keep the Christ-given law of love. Accordingly, the law or the Decalogue—or, more precisely, the Christ-given law of love—surfaces as divine instruction for justified Christians in the exercising and strengthening of their faith.

At the same time, Luther does not lose sight of the fluctuations of human effort in faithfully observing the law of love. He knows that even justified Christians, whom he calls saints, undergo spiritual temptations and afflictions owing to the residual sin clinging tenaciously to the flesh. In this account, Luther affirms that the theological or spiritual function of the law in the dimension of alien, passive, and perfect righteousness and holiness still has an impact in the dimension of proper, active, and progressing righteousness and holiness. However, the theological function of the law in the latter dimension needs to be carefully distinguished, in principle, from that in the former dimension. It is no longer for the unjustified sinners; it is for the justified Christians. It is no longer to inspire unjustified sinners to faith in Christ; it is to motivate justified Christians to stay in their faith in Christ, always and entirely, reflecting their imperfection in the unrelenting battle between flesh and spirit.

6. This dissertation also highlights that Luther's notion of the relationship of faith to love is strongly analogous to his understanding of the relationship of Christ's proper function to his accidental function. Here, what draws our special attention is Luther's tendency to stress Christ's divinity in relation to his proper function and Christ's humanity in relation to his accidental function. In this context, Luther puts faith in analogous correspondence to Christ's divinity and love to his humanity. As a matter of fact, this dual correlation can lead us to the hasty judgment that Luther's Christology and teaching on faith and love hint at docetism. Thus, in handling this analogous parallel between the relationship of Christ's proper function to his accidental function and that of faith to love, we need to guard against such a misjudgment.

Being aware of the potential for such a misunderstanding, I accentuate that Luther's emphasis on the divinity of Christ is never severed from the expression of that divinity in human flesh. On the other hand, his notion of Christ's humanity is always tied to divinity in an inseparable but distinguishable relation. I additionally underscore Luther's salient point that only a divine power can conquer the opposing power of Satan for the justification of sinners and bring about new creation in justified Christians. Only in that context can we suitably appreciate the reason Luther envisages faith as analogically corresponding to the divinity of Christ.

Bearing these agendas in mind, I carefully differentiate my interpretation of this analogous parallel from Mannermaa's, which does not point to Luther's treatment of Christ's proper and accidental functions but narrowly focuses on Luther's remarks about Christ's divinity and humanity. First, I put into perspective Luther's view of Christ's proper and accidental functions, both of which are tied to the incarnate, eternal Son. Only then do I zero in on his use of an analogical parallel between faith and love on the one hand, and Christ's divinity and humanity on the other.

This christologically analogous parallel between the relations of Christ's divine and human natures and those of faith and love in a Christian can be further elaborated in the following way. Just as there is a union in Christ's divinity and humanity, so there is a unity of faith and love in a Christian, because Christ is the content of both faith and love. However, just as the union of Christ's divinity and humanity is not a mingling or confusion between them, so faith and love are not to be mingled or confused with each other. Christ's divinity and humanity are distinguished from each other. Faith and love, likewise, are characterized by their distinctiveness, but they are not separate from each other. Furthermore, just as Christ's divinity always takes priority over his humanity, so does faith over love. On this basis, in Luther's christologically analogous parallel between the relation of Christ's two natures and that of faith and love, the Chalcedonian formula defines the relation of faith and love by analogy. This christological analogy, however, is not to be decoded literally.

7. While many studies of Luther's concept of love feature his notion of neighbor-love, this dissertation undertakes to demonstrate that love, as the pure and tangible fruits of faith, in accordance with

Luther's redefinition, is practiced in three relations: to God, neighbor, and self. Luther portrays loving and honoring God as the supreme fruits of faith, the signs of which are evinced in concrete ways in the relations of justified Christians to their neighbors and themselves. Crucial to the trichotomous direction of love is the dynamic interrelatedness among them.

This dissertation also aims to underscore Christ not only as the source of Christian love but also as the example of how to bear fruits in this three-dimensional love. Luther's love is neither an erotic or romantic love nor a love that strives to climb up a ladder to God. Neither does it yearn for selfish happiness. Luther's love is about the whole of the Christian life that manifests through faith the presence of Christ, who sets free and empowers a Christian to bear fruits of faith in those three relations: to God, neighbor, and self.

8. To capture the essence of Luther's redefined relationship between faith and love, this dissertation elucidates a simile and metaphors, such as the illustrious horticultural metaphor of a tree bearing fruits, and the theologically reformulated metaphor of the relation of a craftsperson to her work, namely, the relation of doer to deed.

9. Finally, this dissertation endeavors to appropriate strengths found especially in Ebeling's model and the work of modern Finnish Luther scholars in their distinctive approaches to Luther's teaching on faith and love.

The strength of Ebeling's model lies in his definition of the relationship between faith and love as an "antithesis, tension between strongly opposed but related polarities."[103] Explicating the relationship between faith and love in terms of "the harsh opposition of opposing theses"[104] and the spirit of compromise that reconciles

---

103. Ebeling, *Luther—Einführung in sein Denken*, 16; ET *Luther: An Introduction to His Thought*, 25.
104. Ebeling, *Luther—Einführung in sein Denken*, v; ET *Luther: An Introduction to His Thought*, 11.

faith and love, Ebeling's model appropriately brings into relief the tension between faith and love. Thereby, the model does not lose its balance in either direction: between faith and love as two inevitably clashing, opposing theses and faith and love as two harmoniously interlocked theses. On this account, Ebeling's model does not slip into a denial of the existence or import of the teaching on love in Luther's theology, especially in conjunction with his teaching on justification by faith in Christ alone.[105]

Notwithstanding this strength, one shortfall in Ebeling's model is that Luther's notion of the presence of Christ in faith or in a Christian through faith is not clearly delineated. On that account, even though Ebeling's model describes the relationship between faith and love both as two opposing theses and two compatible theses, it seems to place more weight on the former. From this perspective, the Finnish scholars' interpretation, which sheds light on Luther's thoughts on Christ present in faith and Christ present in a Christian by faith, is worthy of special note. Their interpretation, however, has its own drawback in that it does not sufficiently bring out the tension between faith and love. In addition, the arguments of the Finnish scholars with respect to *theosis* and participation could lead to misapprehension of Luther's intention.

By carefully comparing and contemplating both models, I endeavor to press home the dynamic relation between faith and love in conjunction with the functions of Christ and the law in the two dimensions. In the matter of an unrighteous sinner's becoming

---

105. Ebeling's model can be contrasted with Albrecht Ritschl's view that separates faith and love as two different centers in an ellipse. Ritschl declares that his theological aim is "to discover the conceptions originally held of the religious relation of Christians to God," which turn out to have two foci in an ellipse: spiritual and ethical. He placed the ethical dimension as an independent center alongside the spiritual center in his elliptical theological system: "Christianity in its genus is religion, in its species it is the perfect spiritual and moral religion." Ritschl, *The Christian Doctrine of Justification and Reconciliation*, ed. H. R. Mackintosh and A. B. Macaulay (Eugene, OR: Wipf & Stock, 2002; 1966), 80.

a righteous person in the dimension of alien, passive, and perfect righteousness and holiness, faith unreservedly shuts out any cooperation from or contribution of love. Luther firmly rejects a love that claims its own collaborative role in the matter of justification. Christ, who is present in a Christian through faith, takes sole credit for the justification of sinners. In this context, the keen opposition between faith, which accepts Christ as the only savior for justification, and love, which insists on its synergistic cooperation for the justification of sinners, remains irreducible to any form of compromise. This is true even if love is already present in faith. Luther makes it quite clear that faith always contains love in its concept, but he never views love as causing justification in addition to faith, let alone on its own. Luther consistently declares that Christ is the sole cause and faith is the sole instrument in the matter of a sinner's justification.

However, in the dimension of proper, active, and progressing righteousness and holiness, while faith is still operating as the foundation of a Christian life, love blooms as a seed originally contained in faith, bearing fruits in every area of a Christian's life. In this dimension, the law or, more precisely, the Christ-given law of love is embraced as having a guiding function for justified Christians. Christ is related to Christians not only as the sole justifier but also as the very example to be imitated. Here, by virtue of Christ's presence in Christians as savior and as example, faith and love, which were in rigid opposition in the dimension of alien, passive, and perfect righteousness and holiness, are brought together in reconciliation and harmony in the dimension of proper, active, and progressing righteousness and holiness. Now I invite the reader to study the primary source with me in the following chapters to investigate these matters.

2

Faith and Love in the Dimension of Passive Righteousness and Holiness

As mentioned in chapter 1, this dissertation situates Luther's teaching on faith and love in two dimensions—alien, passive, and perfect righteousness and holiness vis-à-vis proper, active, and progressing righteousness and holiness. Grasping the nexus of these two dimensions is decisive for delving into the dynamics of Luther's discussion of faith and love. This chapter concentrates on Luther's thoughts on faith, love, and their relationship in the dimension of alien, passive, and perfect righteousness and holiness. In this dimension, the salient point is that faith in Christ does everything for the justification of sinners to the utter exclusion of love.

This dimension involves several interrelated questions: who are human beings in the sight of God (*coram Deo*), as opposed to in the sight of the world or other human beings (*coram mundo*)? How can human beings stand justified before God? How does God alone work to justify sinners through and in Christ? What has Christ achieved for humanity? How can this work of God be personally made efficacious only by faith in Christ? Why should sinners rely completely on God's promise, and not their own power and calculations for justification and the attainment of eternal life? Where does the hope for the salvation of sinners lie?

On the other hand, in the matter of a Christian's being and life in the dimension of proper, active, and progressing righteousness and holiness, Luther's main point is that love is the incarnation and fruit of faith. This dimension primarily concerns itself with the following questions: how does a justified Christian existentially and socially live a Christian life in relation to God, neighbor, and self? How does God work through justified Christians? How does Christ relate to Christians? What does it mean for a justified Christian to bear fruit in works of love in lieu of being idle or sterile? Why are Christians held accountable for bearing fruit in every estate of life?

How then do these two dimensions exist with each other? Are they mutually exclusive? Is the relationship between them asymmetrical? Is one reducible to the other? Is there an internal connection between them?

Two Dimensions: Interpretive Framework

Although the six concise chapters of Paul's Epistle to the Galatians expand into several hundred pages in Luther's commentary on the epistle, Luther indicates that both proclaim the same fundamental message, namely, faith and love. Luther discerns faith and love in the Epistle as the two cardinal theological themes in terms of its literary structure as well as its contents. Accordingly, Luther reflects this prioritization of faith and love in his own commentary. Luther's assessment emphasizes faith and love as a paired theme that constitutes the whole structure and contents of the Epistle.

The paired theme defines the major division of the letter: the guiding topic of the first part is faith and that of the second part is love. According to Luther, specifically Galatians 4:8-9 signals the transition point in Paul's two main concerns: from faith, Christ, righteousness, and justification (or more precisely, alien, passive, and perfect righteousness and holiness) to love, works of the law, and sanctification (or more precisely, proper, active, and progressing righteousness and holiness). Touching on this transition-point, Luther states, "This is the conclusion of Paul's argument. From here until the end of the Epistle he will not argue very much but will set forth commandments about morality."[1]

In his comment on Galatians 5:12, Luther again articulates that

> there follow exhortations and commandments about good morals. For *the Apostle makes it a habit*, after the teaching of faith and the instruction of consciences, to introduce some commandments about morals, by which he exhorts the believers to practice the duties of godliness toward one another.[2]

In fact, these statements seem to be insufficient evidence that Luther assesses Paul's teaching according to two paramount theological themes, faith and love, because of the absence of the exact word "love." To resolve this problem, George Rörer's original lecture notes (1531) are useful. For Luther's exposition of Galatians 5:12, the original lecture notes contain a succinct and valuable sentence for our claim: "He will exhort the duties of *love* after the doctrine of *faith*."[3]

---

1. *LW* 26:394; *WA* 40/1. 600. 25–26: "Haec conclusio est disputationis Paulinae. Deinceps usque ad finem Epistolae non multum disputabit, sed praecepta de moribus tradet."
2. *LW* 27:47 (italics mine); *WA* 40/2. 59. 20–24: "Sequuntur nunc exhortationes et praecepta de bonis moribus. *Apostolus enim in more habet*, post doctrinam fidei et instructionem conscientiarum subiicere praecepta morum, quibus exhortatur credentes ad officia pietatis inter se mutuo exercenda. Et eam partem doctrinae aliquo modo intelligit et docet etiam ratio, de doctrina fidei prorsus vero nihil novit."
3. The passage in the original lecture notes (George Rörer's 1531 notes) reads: "Iam incipiunt exhortationes, Iam veniunt Pareneses. Et exhortabitur ad officia *charitatis* post doctrinam *fidei*, et stabilitam conscientiam per fidem sequuntur exhortationes ad praestanda officia invicem. Das

What draws our further attention in Luther's exegesis of the same passage (as cited above) is his contention that Paul habitually repeats the identical pattern of teaching faith and then love.

When it is understood that Luther holds faith and love as the key to Paul's epistles, including his Epistle to the Galatians, a question arises: what does this have to do with our contention that faith and love is the interpretive key to Luther's commentary on Paul's Epistle to the Galatians? Some might protest that Luther's faithful following of the sequence of Paul's message is one thing and Luther's own theology as revealed in his exegesis is another. Therefore, Luther's remark on Paul's teaching on faith and love may not carry any substantial weight in an investigation of the substance of Luther's theology in this commentary. Yet this suspicion needs to be reappraised if we have appropriately perceived Luther's deliberation in dwelling on Paul's shift from faith to love:

> Therefore to avoid the impression that *Christian teaching* undermines good morals and conflicts with political order, *the apostle [Paul]* also admonishes about good morals and about honest outward conduct, the observance of love and harmony, etc. Thus *the world* has no right to accuse *Christians* of undermining good morals or of disturbing public peace and respectability; for they teach morals and all the virtues better than any philosophers or teachers, because they add faith.[4]

What is intriguing in this exegesis is that it expresses no less Luther's description of his own theology and context than his elucidation of Paul's theology and context. This perception is substantiated, for

---

find moralia. De 1. articulo nihil scit mundus, de 2. utcunque et ratio etiam docet." *WA* 40/2. 59. 4–8 (italics mine; my translation).

4. *LW* 27:47; *WA* 40/2. 59. 24–30 (italics mine): "Ne igitur videatur doctrina *Christiana* dissolvere bonos mores et pugnare contra politicas ordinationes, admonet *Apostolus* etiam de bonis moribus et honesta externa conversatione, de servanda charitate, concordia etc. Non potest igitur *mundus* iure accusare *Christianos*, quod dissolvant bonos mores, quod publicam pacem, honestatem etc. perturbent, quia melius tradunt mores et omnes virtutes quam ulli aut Philosophi aut Magistratus, quia fidem addunt. "

instance, by a comparison between George Rörer's notes on Luther's lectures and the published lectures on the same passage. "Nostra," "nos," and "docemus" in the original lecture notes (1531) are become "Christiana" and "Christianos," and the name of the Apostle Paul is integrated into the passage in the published commentary (1535).[5]

A juxtaposition of these two versions alludes to a convergence in Luther's exegesis of two worlds—those of Paul and Luther.[6] There are understandable dissimilarities between the two worlds, considering the almost fifteen-hundred-year gap between them; nonetheless, there are similarities as well. So Luther draws on the hermeneutical imagination of his readers to place themselves in Paul's circumstances and see how he handles the theological and practical agendas he confronts in the matter of faith and love. In this way, Luther generates a clear parallel between his own polemical milieu and Paul's and prompts his readers to follow him in heeding the authoritative instruction of Paul. Soliciting Paul and his way of teaching on faith and love, Luther is arming himself with the best equipment to defend his own teaching on faith and love against his polemical opponents.

Hence, we need to unearth three layers of significance for this convergence of two worlds in Luther's exegesis from the vantage point of his teaching on faith and love: (1) his explication of Paul's context and theology at the surface level, (2) the implications of his own context and theology at the underlying level, and (3) his

---

5. The passage in the original lecture notes reads: "Ne videatur doctrina *nostra* dissolvere bonos mores et dissolvere publicas ordinationes, Ideo melius docet bonos mores quam ulli gentium philosophi. Ideo non possunt *nos* accusare contra mores bonos et ordinationes publicas. Sed haec ratio, quod mundus turbatur, quod *docemus* Christum." *WA* 40/2. 59. 8–12 (italics mine).

6. Timothy Maschke explains this aspect of Luther's biblical interpretation in terms of "hermeneutic of contemporaneity." Maschke, "Contemporaneity: A Hermeneutical Perspective in Martin Luther's Work," in *Ad Fontes Lutheri: Toward the Recovery of the Real Luther-Essays in Honor of Kenneth Hagen's Sixty-Birthday*, ed. Timothy Maschke, Franz Posset, and Joan Skocir (Milwaukee: Marquette University Press, 2001), 165–82, esp. 174–79.

intention to borrow Paul's authority to defend himself against his contemporary opponents.

Accordingly, when we decipher Luther's above-quoted exegesis against the backdrop of his own polemical context, it becomes apparent that "Christian teaching" in this exposition does not stand for a general Christian teaching vis-à-vis other non-Christian teachings but for Luther's teaching in contrast to other theological teachings in his own polemical context. "The world" connotes not the world in contrast to Christendom, but Luther's own adversaries—not only the scholastic theologians, to whom he frequently refers as "sophists" or "papists" but also the intra-Reformation Radicals who accuse him and his followers of undermining "good morals" or of "disturbing public peace and respectability." Bearing in mind that Luther intends to bring these two worlds together for the sake of his message, it is not surprising when he makes an explicit comparison between the Galatians and the Germans: "Some people think that we Germans are descended from the Galatians, and there may be some truth in this. For we Germans do resemble them in nature."[7] If the Germans are compared with the Galatians, Luther is playing the role of Paul.

In this context, Luther's argument that Paul thought out the design of his letter in advance—to remark on faith first and then love—becomes momentous, since it directs attention to the heart of his own message in the Galatians commentary. When Luther thus stresses that Paul's contemporaries misunderstood him because of his proclamation on justification by faith in Christ alone and criticized him concerning the deficiency of his teaching on love, Luther betrays his own circumstances. Just as Luther understands Paul, Luther is claiming that he likewise teaches not only justification

---

7. *LW* 26:47; *WA* 40/1. 105. 13–14: "Quidam putant nos Germanos oriundos esse ex Galatis, neque vana est forsan ea divinatio. Non enim valde dissimili ingenio sumus Germani."

by faith in Christ alone but also love. Furthermore, Luther claims that his teaching on love is better than that of his opponents because it has a solid foundation in faith, as with Paul.

Consequently, by reading Luther's exegesis of Paul's Epistle to the Galatians, we can interpret that Luther himself (re-)employs faith and love as the overriding thematic pair in his Galatians commentary. This is not a mere coincidence resulting from Luther's literary exegetical procedure following Paul's way of writing the letter. Rather, it can be construed as Luther's carefully thought-out structural and conceptual device to disseminate his teaching on faith and love.[8]

---

8. Considering the following texts, it may not be incorrect to claim that Luther makes it his own habit to use faith and love as the overarching theme throughout his writings. Luther's utilization of faith and love as a thematic pair is not confined to his Galatians commentary. While the classic locus for Luther's use of faith and love as a thematic duo is found in *The Freedom of a Christian*, 1520 (*LW* 31:327–77; *WA* 7. 49–73), Luther also highlights how faith and love constitute the whole structure of Paul's Epistle to the Romans and thereby define its major division (*Lectures on Romans*, 1515/16). He further draws attention to the way Paul shifts from the first division on faith in rejection of love in chapters one through eleven to the second on love flowing out of faith in chapters twelve through the end (*LW* 25:444–45; *WA* 56. 452. 1–10).

That Luther is deliberately underscoring this transition is confirmed by his repeated mentioning of this structural feature in his last sermon, which was delivered in Wittenberg on January 17, 1546. The sermon text came from Romans 12:3. Luther says that "St. Paul, as was his custom, taught first the great chief articles of Christian doctrine—the law, sin, and faith, how we are to be justified before God and live eternally. As you have often heard and still hear every day, namely, that there are two points to be taught and preached: first, we must see to it that faith in Christ is rightly preached, and second, that the fruits and good works are rightly taught and practiced . . . . This is the way Paul teaches in all his epistles; first concerning faith in Christ . . . . This he has been describing up to this point in the twelfth chapter. From here to the end of the epistle he teaches the fruits of faith, in order that we may not be false Christians, who have only the name of Christian, but rather real, true believers. This is the preaching concerning good works, which God commands, especially in the first and second table [i.e., of the Ten Commandments]." *LW* 51:372; *WA* 51. 123. 8–124. 27. The way Luther employs faith and love as the interpretive key to Paul's Epistle to the Romans is also perceptible in his Preface to Paul's Epistle to the Romans. *Luthers Werke*, Kritische Gesamtausgabe, *Die Deutsche Bibel*, 15 vols., ed. Paul Pietsch et al. (Weimar: Hermann Böhlau, 1906–1961), 7. 27. 15–24; *LW* 35:380. See Arthur S. Wood, "Theology of Luther's Lectures on Romans, I," *Scottish Journal of Theology* 3, no. 1(1950): 1–18; Wood, "Theology of Luther's Lectures on Romans, II," *Scottish Journal of Theology* 3, no. 1(1950): 113–26. On the basis of his analysis of Luther's commentary on Romans, Wood explores Luther's teaching on justification in his first article and Luther's teaching on sanctification in his second article.

See also *Treatise on Good Works* where Luther exegetes the Ten Commandments from the perspective of his teaching on faith and love. *LW* 44:15–114; *WA* 6. 202–76. Intriguingly, Luther makes an excursus in the middle of this treatise by inserting an engaging paragraph on the Lord's Prayer between his expositions of the first and second table of the law. Luther's intention is unambiguous: The Lord's Prayer is to be expounded in light of his gloss of the Decalogue in this treatise, namely, from the standpoint of faith and love as the overriding thematic pair. *LW* 44:80; *WA* 6. 250. 1–16.

Other representative writings that also reveal Luther's deployment of faith and love as the overriding structural and thematic pair are as follows: "The Blessed Sacrament of the Holy and True Body of Christ, and the Brotherhoods, 1519," *LW* 35:49–73; *WA* 2. 742–58; "A Sermon on the Strength and Increase of Faith and Love, October 1, 1525 (?) Sixteenth Sunday after Trinity," in *Sermons of Martin Luther*, ed. John Nicholas Lenker, vol. 8 (Grand Rapids: Baker Book House, 1988), 259–80. This sermon can also be found in *Early Protestant Spirituality*, ed. Scott H. Hendrix (Mahwah, NJ: Paulist, 2009), 168–75. "Sermon on the Sum of the Christian Life, I Tim. 1:5-7, preached in Wörlitz, November 24, 1532," *LW* 51:256–87; *WA* 36. 352–75; "Sermon at the Dedication of the Castle Church in Torgau, Luke 14:1-11, October 5, 1544," *LW* 51:331–54; *WA* 49:588–615.

Luther's eight "Invocavit Sermons" are also noteworthy: "Eight Sermons by Dr. M. Luther, preached by him at Wittenberg in Lent, dealing briefly with the masses, images, both kinds in the sacrament, eating [of meats], and private confession, and so on," *LW* 51:67–100; *WA* 10/3. 1-64. In "The Second Sermon, March 10, 1522, Monday after Invocavit," Luther insists that "the chief characteristics of a Christian man," namely, "his whole life and being is faith and love." *LW* 51:75; *WA* 10/3. 13. 16–17: "Lieben freünd, yr habt gestern gehort die haüptstuck eins Christenlichen menschen, wie das ganze leben und wesen sei glauben und lieben." These sermons are known as "Invocavit Sermons" because the first sermon was preached on Invocavit Sunday, namely, the first Sunday during the Lent, and continued until the next Sunday, March 16, 1522.

These sermons are worthy of special note because Luther teaches not only faith and love but also introduces the themes of "müssen sein" (must) and "frei sein" (free) as the reformulated themes of faith and love. *LW* 51:74; *WA* 10/3. 11. 4-9. A more frequently used term for "free" is *adiaphoron/adiaphora*. As to studies on these sermons, see Neil R. Leroux, *Luther's Rhetoric: Strategies and Style from the Invocavit Sermons* (Saint Louis: Concordia Publishing House, 2002); Jane E. Strohl, "Luther's Invocavit Sermons," in *Freiheit als Liebe bei Martin Luther, Freedom as Love in Martin Luther: 8th International Congress for Luther Research in St. Paul, Minnesota, 1993, Seminar 1 Referate/Papers*, eds. Dennis D. Bielfeldt and Klaus Schwarzwäller (Frankfurt am Main: Peter Lang, 1995), 159–66.

In a sermon preached at Weimar in 1522, Luther also contends that "in the whole gospel nothing is more clearly emphasized than faith and love." "The Second Sermon, Matt. 22:37-39, the Afternoon of October 19, 1522," *LW* 51:111; *WA* 10/3. 352. 16-17: "ym ganczen Euangelio wurt nichts anders am meisten angezeigt dan der glaub und die lieb."

In *The German Mass and Order of Service* (*Deudsche Messe und Ordnung Gottis Diensts*, 1526), Luther states, "One may take these questions from our *Betbüchlein* where the three parts [the Ten Commandments, the Creed, and the Our Father] are briefly explained, or make others, until the heart may grasp the whole sum of Christian truth under two headings or, as it were, in two pouches, namely, *faith and love*. *LW* 53:66 (italics mine); *WA* 19. 77. 10–15: "Solche fragen mag man nemen aus dem unsern betbuchlin, da die drey stuck kurz ausgelegt sind, odder selbs anders machen, bis das man die ganze summa des Christlichen verstands ynn zwey stucke als ynn zwey secklin fasse ym herzen, wilchs sind *glaube und liebe*."

When I claim that Luther's teaching on faith and love operate as the overriding thematic pair in his Galatians commentary, this claim can be analyzed from two distinctive but complementary angles: (1) in the whole of the commentary, Luther's reconceptualization of faith prevails in the first part and that of love in the second part, and (2) in each of the two subsections, Luther's reconceptualization of faith is depicted in tension with love in the first part and in harmony in the second part. The first part is the dimension of alien, passive, and perfect righteousness and holiness, which principally concerns the matter of a sinner's becoming a righteous person.[9] The second part is the dimension of proper, active, and progressing righteousness and holiness, which principally concerns the matter of a Christian's active living.[10]

Some of Luther's expositions and sermons on the catechism also display that his teaching on faith and love frame the general structure of each component of the catechism. See in particular the third series of sermons on the Catechism delivered between November 30 and December 18, 1528, before the publication of the Small and Large Catechisms. The first series, comprising eleven sermons, was preached from May 18 to May 30 and the second series of ten sermons from September 14 to September 25, 1528. The text of all three series may be found in *LW* 51:133–93; *WA* 30/1. 1–122. The following sermons also present Luther's teaching on faith and love. "The Holy and Blessed Sacrament of Baptism, 1519," *LW* 35:29–43; *WA* 2. 727–37; "The Gospel for the Festival of the Epiphany, Matthew 2 [:1–12]," *LW* 52:159–286; *WA* 10^1/1. 555–728; "Sermon on Matt. 3:13-17 at the Baptism of Bernhard von Anhalt, Preached in Dessau, April 2, 1540," *LW* 51:315–29; *WA* 49. 124–35.

I have inquired into other important topics that Luther explicates from the perspective of the paired theme of faith and love. See Sun-young Kim, "Faith and Love as the Overriding Thematic Pair in Luther's Exposition of the Lord's Prayer," *Korean Journal of Christian Studies* 72 (2010): 87–107; "The Third Use of the Law in Luther?" *Korean Journal of Christian Studies* 73 (2011): 119–51; "Faith and Love in Luther's Sacramental Theology: Its Theological Significance and Ethical Ramifications," *Korean Journal of Christian Studies* 84 (2012): 127–47; "Luther on 'Sabbatical Observance': Faith and Love," *Korean Journal of Christian Studies* 87 (2013): 81–102; "Luther's Principles of Biblical Interpretation: Jesus Christ, Law & Gospel, and Faith & Love," (paper presented at the Conference of Korea Association of Christian Studies, Asan, South Korea, October 18, 2013), *Source Book*, 99–116; "Luther on Women: The Dualism of Flesh and Spirit versus the Logic of Faith and Love," (paper presented at the Conference of the Church History Society in Korea, Pyungtaek, South Korea, May 24, 2014), *Source Book*, 90–108.

9. Luther mentions that Jesus Christ grants "eternal righteousness and holiness." *LW* 27:83; *WA* 40/2. 104. 23–24.

10. For instance, Luther emphasizes the significance of drawing a distinction between the active righteousness and the passive righteousness, although both of them are necessary: "This is our

Hence, the nature of Luther's teaching on faith and love as an overarching thematic duo can be properly appreciated by putting these two angles together. This is the reason Luther's scrupulous attention to Paul's transition of discourse from faith to love is so crucial. It will guide us to analyze Luther's teaching on faith and love in two dimensions corresponding to the first and second parts of Paul's Epistle to the Galatians. Grasping this division as Luther's interpretive key to Paul's Epistle to the Galatians, this dissertation also faithfully appropriates it as our interpretive framework for Luther's teaching on faith and love in his Galatians commentary. Keeping in perspective these two dimensions, I now proceed to scrutinize faith and love as two incompatible theses in interdependence with the functions of Christ and the law in the dimension of alien, passive, and perfect righteousness and holiness.

Fides Caritate Formata

What, then, is a good entry point to understanding Luther's reconceptualization of faith and love, especially in the dimension of alien, passive, and perfect righteousness and holiness? One of the most convenient places to begin is with the well-known Reformation catchphrase "justification by faith alone." Hence, this inquiry will commence with the following question: what compels Luther to attach the qualifier "alone" (*sola*) to Paul's "justification by faith"?[11]

---

theology, by which we teach a precise distinction between these two kinds of righteousness, the active and the passive, so that morality and faith, works and grace, secular society and religion may not be confused." *LW* 26:7; *WA* 40/1. 45. 24–26: "Haec est nostra theologia qua docemus accurate distinguere has duas iustitias, activam et passivam, ne confundantur mores et fides, opera et gratia, politia et religio." A basic scheme for this two-dimensional interpretive framework can also be found in Luther's "Two Kinds of Righteousness" (1519). *LW* 31:293–306; *WA* 2. 145–52. See Robert Kolb, "Luther on the Two Kinds of Righteousness; Reflections on His Two-Dimensional Definition of Humanity at the Heart of His Theology," *Lutheran Quarterly* 13, no. 4 (1999): 449–66.

11. Luther's own explanation can be found in his "On Translating: An Open Letter." *LW* 35:181–98; *WA* 30/2. 632–43.

From a semantic and logical point of view, one reason for this qualification could be to refute the contention that, although sinners are justified by faith, this faith is insufficient in itself; something else must be added to attain justification. To this assertion, Luther's addition of "alone" itself declares a fervid "No!" He zealously affirms the sufficiency as well as the necessity of faith for justification. The opponents who predominate in the controversy on faith and love are the scholastic theologians. Hence, a rudimentary knowledge of Thomas Aquinas's instructions on merit and *fides caritate formata* and Gabriel Biel's adjustment of Thomas's outlook on merit are foundational to fathoming Luther's teaching on faith and love. On this account, I will point out some principal aspects of those instructions and then proceed to Luther's refutation thereof.

Thomas on Merit and *Fides Caritate Formata* and Biel

Thomas defines "the justification of the ungodly" as "a movement whereby the soul is moved by God from a state of sin to a state of justice."[12] Every sin implies "the disorder of a mind not subject to God" and thereby "may be called injustice."[13] In contrast, justice signifies "a certain rectitude of order in the interior disposition of a man, insofar as what is highest in man is subject to God, and the inferior powers of the soul are subject to the superior, i.e., to the reason."[14] This justice may be brought about in a person "by a movement from one contrary to the other," that is, by the movement

---

12. Thomas Aquinas, *Summa Theologiæ: Complete Set*, Latin-English Edition, vols. 13–20, trans. Fr. Laurence Shapcote, O.P., ed. John Mortensen and Enrique Alarcón (Lander, WY: Aquinas Institute, 2012), Part 1a2æ, Question 113, Article 6 (hereafter cited as *STh* 1a2æ. 113. 6): "iustificatio est quidam motus quo anima movetur a Deo a statu culpae in statum iustitiae."

13. *STh* 1a2æ. 113. 1: "omne peccatum, secundum quod importat quandam inordinationem mentis non subditae Deo, iniustitia potest dici, praedictae iustitiae contraria."

14. *STh* 1a2æ. 113. 1: "rectitudinem quandam ordinis in ipsa interiori dispositione hominis, prout scilicet supremum hominis subditur Deo, et inferiores vires animae subduntur supremae, scilicet rationi."

from the state of injustice to the state of justice, which is the justification of the unrighteous (*justificatio impii*).[15]

For this justification, Thomas esteems four components as constitutional: "the infusion of grace, the movement of the free-will towards God by faith, the movement of the free-will towards sin, and the remission of sins."[16] The rationale behind this definition of justification is not difficult to detect. Adapting Aristotle's teleologically oriented conception of motion as the actualization of potency, Thomas utilizes the following concepts to frame his teaching on justification: the motion of the mover, the movements—of departure from the term *whence* and of approach to the term *whereto*—and the end of the movement.

In this philosophical theological enterprise, the motion of God the Mover corresponds to the infusion of grace. The movement or disposition of the moved corresponds to the free will's double movement—the movement of the free will towards God by faith and the movement of the free will towards sin for the free will's suitable handling of it. The term or end of the movement corresponds to the forgiveness of sin.[17] More specifically, the logic behind these four requisites for justification is recapitulated in the following way:

Now in the movement whereby one thing is moved by another, three things are required: first, the motion of the mover; second, the

15. *STh* 1a2æ. 113. 1: "Alio modo potest fieri huiusmodi iustitia in homine secundum rationem motus qui est de contrario in contrarium. Et secundum hoc, iustificatio importat transmutationem quandam de statu iniustitiae ad statum iustitiae praedictae." "And because movement is named after its term *whereto* rather than from its term *whence*, the transmutation whereby anyone is changed by the remission of sins from the state of ungodliness to the state of justice, borrows its name from its term *whereto*, and is called *justification of the ungodly*." (italics original) *STh* 1a2æ. 113. 1: "Et quia motus magis denominatur a termino ad quem quam a termino a quo, ideo huiusmodi transmutatio, qua aliquis transmutatur a statu iniustitiae per remissionem peccati, sortitur nomen a termino ad quem, et vocatur iustificatio impii."

16. *STh* 1a2æ. 113. 6: "gratiae infusio; motus liberi arbitrii in Deum per fidem; et motus liberi arbitrii in peccatum; et remissio culpae." In fact, *liber arbitrium* is better translated as free choice than as free will.

17. *STh* 1a2æ. 113. 9.

movement of the moved; third, the consummation of the movement, or the attainment of the end. On the part of the Divine motion, there is the infusion of grace; on the part of the free-will which is moved, there are two movements—of departure from the term whence, and of approach to the term whereto; but the consummation of the movement or the attainment of the end of the movement is implied in the remission of sins; for in this is the justification of the ungodly completed.[18]

Thomas underscores that the aforesaid four things are instantaneous in time, since "the justification of the ungodly is not successive."[19] Nonetheless, "in the order of nature, one is prior to another."[20] In every movement the motion of the mover comes first; the disposition of the matter, or the movement of the moved, is second; the end or term of the movement, at which the motion of the mover terminates, is last.[21] So strictly in the sense of the natural order of the four elements, it can be attested: "the first is the infusion of grace; the second, the free-will's movement towards God; the third, the free-will's movement towards sin; the fourth, the remission of sin."[22]

What must be noticed here is that the necessity of the infusion of grace as the first of the four is an indication that the turning of the free will towards God and away from sin is not connatural to

18. *STh* 1a2æ. 113. 6: "In quolibet autem motu quo aliquid ab altero movetur, tria requiruntur, primo quidem, motio ipsius moventis; secundo, motus mobilis; et tertio, consummatio motus, sive perventio ad finem. Ex parte igitur motionis divinae, accipitur gratiae infusio; ex parte vero liberi arbitrii moti, accipiuntur duo motus ipsius, secundum recessum a termino a quo, et accessum ad terminum ad quem; consummatio autem, sive perventio ad terminum huius motus, importatur per remissionem culpae, in hoc enim iustificatio consummatur."

19. *STh* 1a2æ. 113. 7: "Ergo iustificatio impii non est successiva, sed instantanea." See also 1a2æ. 113. 8: "quatuor quae requiruntur ad iustificationem impii, tempore quidem sunt simul, quia iustificatio impii non est successiva."

20. *STh* 1a2æ. 113. 8: "ordine naturae unum eorum est prius altero."

21. *STh* 1a2æ. 113. 8.

22. *STh* 1a2æ. 113. 8: "inter ea naturali ordine primum est gratiae infusio; secundum, motus liberi arbitrii in Deum; tertium est motus liberi arbitrii in peccatum; quartum vero est remissio culpae." With regard to the double movement of the free will, Thomas further expounds: "for he who is being justified detests sin because it is against God, and thus the free-will's movement towards God naturally precedes the free-will's movement towards sin, since it is its cause and reason." *STh* 1a2æ. 113. 8.

the ungodly in their fallen condition. The turning around per se can be operated only by the infusion of God's supernatural gift, namely, grace. In any event, God does not make it happen by external force against the nature of human beings. On the contrary, God moves everything according to its own nature. That being so, God moves human beings to justice in compliance with the condition of their human nature. The movement of human free will is involved in the justification of the ungodly. Since it is a human being's proper nature to have free will, God's motion to justice takes place with a movement of the free will. God so infuses the gift of justifying grace that God simultaneously moves the free will to accept the gift and become capable of being moved as a consequence. Based on this, the following statement is vindicated: "Hence, no one comes to the Father by justifying grace without a movement of the free-will."[23]

Another way to enunciate the necessity for justification of the infusion of God's supernatural gift, namely grace as a quality and habit in one's soul, is that no one can earn the first grace. Thomas puts forward two reasons for this. The gift of justifying grace cannot be merited by a person who does not have it, because it exceeds the proportion of his human nature and because prior to receiving justifying grace a person is in a state of sin that hinders him from meriting it. Additionally, if anyone merits a further gratuitous gift by virtue of the receipt of a preceding grace, then this merit already presumes the first grace. As a corollary, no one can earn for himself the first grace.[24]

Thomas proceeds from treating the four prerequisites for the justification of the ungodly to dealing with the attainment of eternal life, which is construed as a good exceeding the proportion of the

23. *STh* 1a2æ. 113. 3: "Ergo nullus venit ad Deum per gratiam iustificantem absque motu liberi arbitrii."
24. *STh* 1a2æ. 114. 5.

created nature, since it exceeds its knowledge and desire. Here we have to understand Thomas's treatment of merit, which makes a distinction between congruous merit (*meritum de congruo*) and condign merit (*meritum de condigno*).

Thomas explains that a person's meritorious work can be calculated in two ways: first, insofar as it proceeds from free choice; second, insofar as it proceeds from the Holy Spirit's supernatural gift of grace. Works in the first way are considered acquiring congruous merit; works in the second way, condign merit. Congruous merit stands for the merit or reward of a work insofar as it proceeds from a person's own free choice or natural power. Since there is no intrinsic proportion between work and merit but a great inequality between them, this merit is not based on the rule of equivalence. Instead, congruous merit is built on the idea of "congruity, on account of an equality of proportion: for it would seem congruous that, if a man does what he can, God should reward him according to the excellence of his own power."[25] Hence, congruous merit signifies merit that is granted to a person by God gratuitously as something fitting, not obligatory. If a person does what he can out of his own free will, God should reward him commensurately with the excellence of his power.[26]

On the other hand, merit of condignity denotes merit or reward that is bestowed for certain human works on the basis of an equation of accomplishment and recompense. Accordingly, the entitlement to reward is legitimate and the reward must be granted. Thomas's thought on the attainment of the eternal life by the one justified

25. *STh* 1a2æ. 114. 3: "dicendum quod opus meritorium hominis dupliciter considerari potest: uno modo, secundum quod procedit ex libero arbitrio; alio modo, secundum quod procedit ex gratia Spiritus sancti. Si consideretur secundum substantiam operis, et secundum quod procedit ex libero arbitrio, sic non potest ibi esse condignitas, propter maximam inaequalitatem. Sed est ibi congruitas, propter quandam aequalitatem proportionis, videtur enim congruum ut homini operanti secundum suam virtutem, Deus recompenset secundum excellentiam suae virtutis."
26. *STh* 1a2æ. 114. 3.

through the first grace is substantially elaborated in this notion of merit of condignity. When the one justified performs good works in cooperation with the assistance of the Holy Spirit through the infused grace of God, his works are worthy of eternal life.

Notwithstanding, we should not misunderstand Thomas's conception of the merit of condignity and think that it rests on an idea of absolute equation between the dignity of human works and God's reward in the form of eternal life. In lieu of this view of intrinsic equation, Thomas contends that the system of merit of condignity is predicated on God's prior ordination of a system of merit and reward.

Making allowances for the great inequality between God and human beings, Thomas affirms that a human being cannot merit eternal life, even with grace, on the basis of a rule of absolute equation. Human beings can earn merit before God only "on the presupposition of the Divine ordination, so that man obtains from God, as a reward of his operation, what God gave him the power of operation for."[27] Thomas writes that "God ordained human nature to attain the end of eternal life, not by its own strength, but by the help of grace; and in this way its act can be meritorious of eternal life."[28]

Thomas further elucidates that the merit of the works of the one justified by the first grace is worth eternal life as a merit of condignity only because the value of the merit is assessed in compliance with the power of the Holy Spirit moving him to eternal life. The merit of work is evaluated by the worth of the grace of the Spirit infused in the soul.[29] Therefore, the remark that a merit of condignity involves

---

27. *STh* 1a2æ. 114. 1: "Et ideo meritum hominis apud Deum esse non potest nisi secundum praesuppositionem divinae ordinationis: ita scilicet ut id homo consequatur a Deo per suam operationem quasi mercedem, ad quod Deus ei virtutem operandi deputavit."
28. *STh* 1a2æ. 114. 2: "Deus ordinavit humanam naturam ad finem vitae aeternae consequendum non propria virtute, sed per auxilium gratiae. Et hoc modo ejus actus potest esse meritorius vitae aeternae."

an obligation on the part of God to reward must always be made with due qualification, for the rule of equivalence between work and merit is implemented only under the condition of a prior divine ordination. Thomas understands the idea of divine obligation not in the sense that God becomes indebted to human beings, but rather, since their action has "the character of merit, only on the presupposition of the Divine ordination, God becomes indebted to Himself "inasmuch as it is right that His will should be carried out."[30]

In this scheme of the Aristotelian primary cause (*causa prima* or *movens*) and the secondary cause (*causa secunda* or *motum*), Thomas envisions a person's progress in merit—a person's acquisition of eternal life by a merit of condignity through God's ordination. In this framework, human works are designated as "secondary [subsequent] cause" for eternal life,[31] whereas the first grace—the mercy of God—from which every good work proceeds is "the primary cause of our reaching eternal life"[32] or the "principle."[33] When it is said that God's own mercy leads human beings to life everlasting, then, this saying is to be understood, Thomas claims, only with regard to the primary cause of our reaching eternal life.[34]

Thomas's stance on the cooperation between God and the one justified in the attainment of life everlasting through the merit of

---

29. *STh* 1a2æ. 114. 3: "Si autem loquamur de opere meritorio secundum quod procedit ex gratia spiritus sancti, sic est meritorium vitæ æternæ ex condigno. Sic enim valor meriti attenditur secundum virtutem spiritus sancti moventis nos in vitam æternam . . . . Attenditur etiam pretium operis secundum dignitatem gratiæ."

30. *STh* 1a2æ. 114. 1: "quia actio nostra non habet rationem meriti nisi ex præsuppositione divinæ ordinationis, non sequitur quod Deus efficiatur simpliciter debitor nobis, sed sibi ipsi, inquantum debitum est ut sua ordinatio impleatur."

31. *STh* 1a2æ. 114. 3: "Meritum autem nostrum est causa subsequens."

32. *STh* 1a2æ. 114. 3: "primam causam perveniendi ad vitam æternam, quæ est miseratio Dei." Thomas also states, "By grace the Holy Spirit dwells in a person; and the Holy Spirit is "the sufficient cause of eternal life." *STh* 1a2æ. 114, 3: "per gratiam inhabitat hominem Spiritus Sanctus, qui est sufficiens causa vitæ æternæ."

33. *STh* 1a2æ. 114. 5: "omne bonum opus hominis procedit a prima gratia sicut a principio."

34. *STh* 1a2æ. 114. 3.

condignity takes on additional complexity through his idea of meriting an increase of grace or charity. While the justification of the ungodly takes place at once and the ungodly cannot merit justifying grace, after this justification, the one justified goes through constant movement toward the end term, namely, eternal life. The end term of movement as reward is specifically explained in two ways: the final end (eternal life) and an intermediary one that is both beginning and end. The latter kind is "the reward of increase."[35]

A person merits growth in grace by meritorious acts, in the same way that she merits the consummation of grace—eternal life. Just as eternal life is not granted at once, but in its proper time, so too grace does not grow greater at once, but in its proper time: when someone is "sufficiently disposed for the increase of grace."[36] Accordingly, growth in grace falls under the merit of condignity [equivalence] in two senses: first, the motion of grace extends to the final term of the movement—eternal life; second, it extends to the whole progress in this movement that occurs by "the increase of charity or grace."[37]

A question ensues: what, then, does charity have to do with the merit of condignity? Why charity and not any other kind of virtue? Thomas has the idea that human beings need supernaturally bestowed virtues to propel their movement toward God since God

---

35. *STh* 1a2æ. 114. 8: "praemium est terminus meriti. Est autem duplex terminus motus, scilicet ultimus; et medius, qui est et principium et terminus. Et talis terminus est merces augmenti."

36. *STh* 1a2æ. 114. 8: "quolibet actu meritorio meretur homo augmentum gratiae, sicut et gratiae consummationem, quae est vita aeerna. Sed sicut vita aeterna non statim redditur, sed suo tempore; ita nec gratia statim augetur, sed suo tempore; cum scilicet aliquis sufficienter fuerit dispositus ad gratiae augmentum."

37. *STh* 1a2æ. 114. 8: "illud cadit sub merito condign, ad quod motio gratiae se extendit. Motio autem alicuius moventis non solum se extendit ad ultimum terminum motus, sed etiam ad totum progressum in motu. Terminus autem motus gratiae est vita aeterna, progressus autem in hoc motu est secundum augmentum caritatis vel gratiae . . . . Sic igitur augmentum gratiae cadit sub merito condigni." With regard to the notion of growth, Thomas clarifies, "The increase of grace is not above the virtuality of the pre-existing grace, although it is above its quantity, even as a tree is not above the virtuality of the seed, although above its quantity." *STh* 1a2æ. 114. 8: "augmentum gratiae non est supra virtutem praeexistentis gratiae, licet sti supra quantitatem ipsius, sicut arbor, etsi sit supra quantitatem seminis, non est tamen supra virtutem ipsius."

as the object of human movement surpasses a human soul's capacity. These supernaturally granted virtues are classified as theological virtues, as distinct from connatural virtues, and they are faith, hope, and charity. The "theological virtues direct man to supernatural happiness in the same way as by the natural inclination man is directed to his connatural end."[38]

Among the three, charity is yet the greatest, and the merit of consistent growth and eternal life rests chiefly with charity.[39] The rationale is that human "actions are meritorious insofar as they proceed from the free-will moved with grace by God. Therefore every human act proceeding from the free-will, if it be referred to God, can be meritorious."[40] Now "inasmuch as merit depends on voluntariness," it is principally accredited to charity, since what we do out of love, we do with the utmost willingness.[41] Likewise, the merit of eternal life "pertains first to charity, and second, to the other

---

38. *STh* 1a2æ. 62. 3: "virtutes theologicæ hoc modo ordinant hominem ad beatitudinem supernaturalem, sicut per naturalem inclinationem ordinatur homo in finem sibi connaturalem." Thomas advances three reasons for calling faith, hope, and love theological virtues: "Such like principles are called *theological virtues*: first, because their object is God, inasmuch as they direct us aright to God: second, because they are infused in us by God alone: third, because these virtues are not made known to us, save by Divine revelation, contained in Holy Writ." *STh* 1a2æ. 62. 1. Thomas points to the limitation of human reason and will in directing us to God, the object of supernatural happiness: "The reason and will are naturally directed to God, inasmuch as He is the beginning and end of nature, but in proportion to nature. But the reason and will, according to their nature, are not sufficiently directed to Him insofar as He is the object of supernatural happiness." *STh* 1a2æ. 62. 1.

39. According to Thomas, none of the theological virtues is greater than another by reason of its having a greater object, since all of them have God as their proper object. Nevertheless, because charity approaches nearer than the others to that object, charity is greater than the others: "Because the others, in their very nature, imply a certain distance from the object: since faith is of what is not seen, and hope is of what is not possessed. But the love of charity is of what which is already possessed: since the beloved is, in a manner, in the lover, and, again, the lover is drawn by desire to union with the beloved." *STh* 1a2æ. 66. 6: "Nam aliæ [virtutes] important in sui ratione quandam distantiam ab objecto, est enim fides de non visis, spes autem de non habitis. Sed amor caritatis est de eo quod jam habetur, est enim amatum quodammodo in amante, et etiam amans per affectum trahitur ad unionem amati."

40. *STh* 2a2æ. 2. 9: "actus nostri sunt meritorii inquantum procedunt ex libero arbitrio moto a Deo per gratiam. Unde omnis actus humanus qui subiicitur libero arbitrio, si sit relatus in Deum, potest meritorius esse."

virtues, inasmuch as their acts are commanded by charity," since the movement of the human mind toward the enjoyment of the good—God—is the proper act of charity.[42]

Only by charity are all the acts of the other virtues ordered to this end. Charity fuels all other virtues; so faith is also in need of being directed by charity. Here enters the contentious scholastic premise: *fides caritate formata*—faith formed by love.[43] For Thomas, faith is "a habit of the mind, *whereby eternal life is begun in us, making the intellect assent to what is non-apparent.*"[44] The "first turning to God is by faith" and so "a movement of faith is required for the justification of the ungodly."[45]

Faith as an assent to the divine truth involves an act of the mind, insofar as the mind is brought to its decision owing to the command of the free will as it is moved by God through grace. In this way, the act of faith is "subject to the free-will in relation to God" and consequently it can be "meritorious."[46] In this sense, charity perfects

41. *STh* 1a2æ. 114. 4: "Similiter etiam manifestum est quod id quod ex amore facimus, maxime voluntarie facimus. Unde etiam secundum quod ad rationem meriti requiritur quod sit voluntarium, principaliter meritum caritati attribuitur."

42. *STh* 1a2æ. 114. 4: "Et ideo meritum vitae aeternae primo pertinet ad caritatem, ad alias autem virtutes secundario, secundum quod eorum actus a caritate imperantur."

43. See Carter Lindberg, *Love: A Brief History through Western Christianity* (Malden, MA: Blackwell, 2008), 103–17.

44. *STh* 2a2æ. 4. 1 (italics original): "fides est habitus mentis, qua inchoatur vita æterna in nobis, faciens intellectum assentire non apparentibus."

45. *STh* 1a2æ. 113. 4: "Prima autem conversio in Deum fit per fidem . . . . Et ideo motus fidei requiritur ad justificationem impii." "But if we suppose . . . that the beginning of faith is in us from God, the first act must flow from grace; and thus it cannot be meritorious of the first grace. Therefore man is justified by faith, not as though man, by believing, were to merit justification, but that, he believes, whilst he is being justified; inasmuch as a movement of faith is required for the justification of the ungodly. *STh* 1a2æ. 114. 5: "Sed si supponamus . . . quod initium fidei sit in nobis a Deo, iam etiam ipse actus fide fidei consequitur primam gratiam, et ita non potest esse meritorius primæ gratiæ. Per fidem igitur iustificatur homo, non quasi homo credendo mereatur justificationem, sed quia, dum iustificatur credit; eo quod motus fidei requiritur ad iustificationem impii, ut supra dictum est."

46. *STh* 2a2æ. 2. 9: "Ipsum autem credere est actus intellectus assentientis veritati divinae ex imperio voluntatis a Deo motae per gratiam, et sic subjacet libero arbitrio in ordine ad Deum. Unde actus fidei potest esse meritorius." See also *STh* 2a2æ. 2. 2.

the movement of faith by forming it to be voluntary and destined for God.[47] Charity is called *"the form of faith* insofar as the act of faith is perfected and formed by charity."[48] "Charity is called the form of faith because it quickens the act of faith."[49] For this reason, "in the justification of the ungodly, a movement of charity is infused together with the movement of faith."[50]

Faith without charity lacks the perfect character of virtue. Virtue is directed to the doing of good works; perfect virtue is that which gives the faculty of doing a perfectly good work, and this consists in not only doing what is good, but also in doing it well.[51] Now, the act of faith is to believe in God, and to believe is to assent to someone

---

47. Thomas affirms that charity perfects not only faith but also hope: "Charity is the root of faith and hope, insofar as it gives them the perfection of virtue." *STh* 1a2æ. 65. 5: "caritas est radix fidei et spei, inquantum dat eis perfectionem virtutis." Thomas views the order among the three theological virtues in two ways: the order of generation and that of perfection. "By order of generation, in respect of which matter precedes form, and the imperfect precedes the perfect, in one same subject faith precedes hope, and hope charity, as to their acts: because habits are all infused together. For the movement of the appetite cannot tend to anything, either by hoping or loving, unless that thing be apprehended by the sense or by the intellect. Now it is by faith that the intellect apprehends the object of hope and love. Hence in the order of generation, faith precedes hope and charity. In like manner a man loves a thing because he apprehends it as his good. Now from the very fact that a man hopes to be able to obtain some good through someone, he looks on the man in whom he hopes as a good of his own. Hence for the very reason that a man hopes in someone, he proceeds to love him: so that in the order of generation, hope precedes charity as regards their respective acts. But in the order of perfection, charity precedes faith and hope: because both faith and hope are quickened by charity, and receive from charity their full complement as virtues. For thus charity is the mother and the root of all the virtues, inasmuch as it is the form of them all." *STh* 1a2æ. 62. 4.
48. *STh* 2a2æ. 4. 3 (italics mine): "Et ideo *caritas* dicitur *forma fidei,* inquantum per caritatem actus fidei perficitur et formatur." While charity perfects faith, an act of charity presupposes faith, since the will can respond to God in perfect love only if the intellect possesses right faith about God. *STh* 2a2æ. 4. 7: "sed talis acuts [actus voluntatis caritate informatus] praesupponit fidem, quia non potest voluntas perfecto amore in Deum tendere nisi intellectus rectam fidem habeat circa ipsum."
49. *STh* 2a2æ. 4. 3: "caritas dicitur esse forma fidei inquantum informat actum ipsius."
50. *STh* 1a2æ. 113. 4: "motus fidei non est perfectus nisi sit caritate informatus, unde simul in iustificatione impii cum motu fidei, est etiam motus caritatis."
51. See Aristotle, *Nicomachean Ethics,* in *The Basic Works of Aristotle,* ed. Richard McKeon (New York: Modern Library, 2001), Book 2, Ch. 6 (pp. 957-959). This idea clearly indicates the influence of Aristotelian philosophy. See also Theodor Dieter, *Der junge Luther und Aristoteles: Eine historisch-systematische Untersuchung zum Verhältnis von Theologie und Philosophie* (Berlin: Walter de Gruyter, 2001).

or something out of one's own free will. To will as one ought is a perfect act of faith, and it is the outcome of charity, which perfects the will, since every right movement of the will proceeds from a right love.[52]

Yet Thomas also qualifies the meaning of charity as the form of faith. A form and the thing of which it is the form are in one subject. Faith is in the intellect, while charity is in the will. So, charity is not the form of faith in the strict sense of the word. Nonetheless, since charity informs faith as described above, charity is called the form of faith. Accordingly, Thomas avers that what makes faith living or lifeless is determined not by different types of faith but by the presence or absence of charity: "When living faith becomes lifeless, faith is not changed, but its subject, the soul, which at one time has faith without charity, and at another time, with charity."[53]

In addition to Thomas's delineation on merit and *fides caritate formata*, Gabriel Biel's view on merit is also critical, in that it was one of the factors that impelled Luther to develop his teaching on faith and love as a counterargument. Gabriel Biel (c. 1425–1495), a nominalist, modifies Thomas's belief that the unrighteous person cannot merit the first justifying grace out of his own natural power. Biel incorporates the merit of congruity into the *ordo salutis*: the moral good works of the unjustified fittingly merit justification. God gives grace to those who are as yet unjustified but do their best with what lies within their natural powers. Human beings without grace can love God above all else and detest sin above all other evils with their purely natural capacity.[54] To those who do this, God fittingly

---

52. *STh* 1a2æ. 65. 4.

53. *STh* 2a2æ. 4. 4: "per hoc quod fides formata fit informis non mutatur ipsa fides, sed mutatur subiectum fidei, quod est anima, quod quandoque quidem habet fidem sine caritate, quandoque autem cum caritate."

54. See Heiko A. Oberman, *The Harvest of Medieval Theology: Gabriel Biel and Late Medieval Nominalism* (Grand Rapids: Baker Academic, 2000), 132–34.

grants grace (*meritum de congruo*). The good works of the justified, then, justly merit eternal life (*meritum de condigno*).[55]

Luther's Refutation

These two representative varieties—Thomas's and Biel's—of the medieval teachings on merit and the premise of *fides caritate formata* are frequently referred to in the Galatians commentary. It is indeed no surprise that, from the vantage point of Luther's reconceptualization of faith and love, his criticisms of the medieval notions of merit and the idea of *fides caritate formata* specifically and predominantly address these two varieties.[56]

---

55. Concerning the history of the slightly changing usages of the merit of congruity and condignity, see Johann Heinz, *Justification and Merit: Luther vs. Catholicism* (Eugene, OR: Wipf & Stock, 2002), 136–53.

56. Markus Wriedt points to a very important aspect of scholasticism in the late medieval period, namely, its diversity. He states, "New studies have shown that the evaluation of Luther is in desperate need of correction. It is true that scholasticism was the dominant thought and knowledge system at the universities in Luther's time, especially at the universities known to him. Yet the term 'scholasticism' is a question in itself. Over the course of the late Middle Ages numerous and highly different ways of scholastic thought had developed that denied one another's authorization . . . . Yet an overview summarizing the diversity of these movements did not exist—until now." See Markus Wriedt, "Luther's Theology," in *The Cambridge Companion to Martin Luther*, ed. Donald K. McKim (Cambridge: Cambridge University Press, 2003), 115–16, n. 13.

On the issue of the diversity of the scholasticism, Oberman calls attention to Luther's clear awareness of the varieties of scholastic positions: "When, after a study of the schools and school opinions in the later middle ages, one arrives at a study of Luther, for instance, of his early (1517) disputation against scholastic theology, one is struck by the fact that the reformer does not by any means identify the whole scholastic theological tradition with nominalism but rather, acutely aware of the varieties of positions, takes up each point separately in order to direct his attack especially and precisely against that theologian whom he regards as responsible for each particular thesis. From this basis, then, he directs himself several times 'contra communes,' against all scholastic theologians together." Heiko Oberman, *The Dawn of the Reformation: Essays in Late Medieval and Early Reformation Thought* (Grand Rapids: Eerdmans, 1992), 108. Oberman also points to Luther's Preface to the second Disputation against the Antinomians (1538), where Luther clearly differentiates "between the earlier tradition, approximately from Lombard to Scotus, and the succeeding school of Occam and his disciples. It is only these last ones whom he assails on the grounds of their shameless teaching that reason without the illumination by the Holy Spirit can love God above everything else and secondly because of their teaching that Christ would have earned for the Christians only the first grace." Ibid., 109. This explication indicates that it is not Luther himself but Luther

Luther recapitulates the Thomistic notion of *fides caritate formata* in his own words:[57] "They [the scholastics] say that we must believe in Christ and that faith is the foundation of salvation, but they say that this faith does not justify unless it is 'formed by love.'"[58] As this depiction of Luther discloses, he notices that, with this postulation, scholastic theologians in line with Thomistic tradition do not entirely invalidate the soteriological function of faith in the justification of sinners.

Hence, when Luther adds the qualifier "alone" to "justification by faith," the backbone of his contention surfaces: are we acknowledging the sufficiency as well as the necessity of faith for justification without reservation? He is redirecting the discourse on faith: what kind of faith are we discussing in relation to the justification of the ungodly and the attainment of everlasting life?

The Thomistic notion of "unformed faith" (*fides informis*), in particular, is a stumbling block to Luther, in terms of not only theological and spiritual teaching but also religious practice or piety.[59] Luther detects in this combination of two tiny words the point of division between life and death and between hope and despair in the matter of a soul's eternal destiny.

researchers who have fallen victim to generalizing the scholasticism of Luther's day in their research on Luther.

57. Once Luther even says that the "papists" are much worse than those false apostles who distracted the Galatians: "The false apostles taught that in addition to faith in Christ, the works of the Law of God were also necessary for salvation. But our opponents skipped faith altogether and taught human traditions and works not commanded by God but invented by them without and against the Word of God." *LW* 26:52; *WA* 40/1. 112. 16–19. Luther regards this kind of unformed faith as not even faith.

58. *LW* 26:88; *WA* 40/1. 164. 15–17: "Sophistae nostri idem docuerunt Quod scilicet in Christum sit credendum fidemque salutis, sed eam non iustificare, nisi formata sit charitate." See also "The sophists, ready as they are to evade the Scriptures, carp at this passage as follows: 'The righteous shall live by faith,' that is, by a faith that is active, working, or 'formed' by love. But if it is an unformed faith, it does not justify.'" *LW* 26:268; *WA* 40/1. 421. 15–16: "Sophistae, ut parati sunt ad eludendum Scripturas, hunc locum sic cavillantur: Iustus vivit ex fide, scilicet efficaci, operante vel formata charitate. Si vero est fides informis, non iustificat."

59. *LW* 26:268; *WA* 40/1. 421. 16. See also *LW* 54:289–90 (no. 3895, dated 20 June 1538); *WA*, *TR* 3:691–92.

As Luther recounts it, the Thomistic position teaches that when a person performs a good work, God accepts it and infuses charity into the heart of that person in virtue of the work.[60] This infused charity is a quality that is attached to the heart as the actor's formal righteousness. A person is viewed as righteous by means of this formal righteousness, which is called grace or love. This grace in the form of love makes a person pleasing in the sight of God.[61] A person is righteous because she is performing good works of love and therefore eternal life is obtainable by virtue of her performance of good works. So "they [the Thomists] attribute formal righteousness to an attitude and 'form' inherent in the soul, namely, to love, which is a work and gift according to the Law; for the Law says: 'You shall love the Lord' (Matt 22:37)."[62]

In fact, the teaching on merit becomes more repugnant to Luther when he comes across the late scholastic handling of merit, especially the merit of congruity, as part of the *ordo salutis*: The moral good works of the unjustified fittingly merit justification. As representatives of this group, Luther refers to John Duns Scotus (1265/66–1308) and William of Ockham (c. 1287–1347);[63] but his

---

60. Luther states that his opponents teach that "'infused faith,' which they properly call faith in Christ, does not free from sin, but that only 'faith formed by love,' does so. From this it follows that faith in Christ by itself, without the Law and works, does not save . . . . On the other hand, if you perform the Law and works, then faith justifies, because it has works, without which faith is useless. Therfore works justify, not faith . . . . For if faith justifies because of works, then works justify more than faith." *LW* 26:146; *WA* 40/1. 254. 27–35: "Quia fides, inquiunt [adversarii], infusa (quam proprie vocant fidem in Christum) non liberat a peccatis, sed fides formata charitate. Ex hoc sequitur, quod sola fides in Christum sine lege et operibus non salvat . . . . Econtra, si feceris legem et opera, tum fides iustificat, quia habet opera sine quibus alioqui fides nihil prodest. Ergo opera iustificant, non fides . . . . Si enim fides propter opera iustificat, ergo opera magis iustificant quam fides."

61. "Man is righteous by means of his formal righteousness, which is grace making him pleasing before God, that is, love." *LW* 26:127; *WA* 40/1. 226. 13–14: "Homo est iustus formali sua iustitia quae est gratia gratum faciens, id est, dilectio."

62. *LW* 26:127–28; *WA* 40/1. 226. 14–15: "Sic isti habitui et formae inhaerenti animae, id est charitati, quae est opus et donum secundum legem,—quia Lex dicit: 'Diliges Dominum' etc."

63. *LW* 26:128; *WA* 40/1. 226. 20–22: "Alii non sunt tam boni, ut Scotus et Occam qui dixerunt non opus esse pro acquirenda gratia Dei charitate illa divinitus donata, sed hominem posse

opposition is especially targeted at Gabriel Biel. Luther contends that those adopting this latter position do not even deem love given by God as necessary to obtain God's grace. By means of one's own natural powers alone, one is able to love God above all things. A person, accordingly, may procure a "merit of congruity"[64] by doing what lies in her natural power (*facientibus quod in se est*) without any assisting grace.[65]

Luther condemns this teaching on the "merit of congruity" along with its accompanying concept of grace. "A man obtains forgiveness of sins and justification in the following manner: By his works that precede grace, which they call a 'merit of congruity,' he merits grace, which, according to them, is a quality that inheres in the will, granted by God over and above the love we have by our natural powers. They say that when a man has this quality, he is formally righteous and a true Christian."[66] Luther continues to depict the scholastic outlook on

ex naturalibus viribus elicere charitatem Dei super omnia." The editors point to the passages from Duns Scotus quoted by Parthenius Minges, *Ioannis Duns Scoti doctrina philosophica et theologica* (Quaracchi: Collegii S. Bonaventurae, 1930), 1:506 and 2:444–45. There is a table talk regarding Luther's comments on Gabriel Biel, the German disciple of Ockahm, Duns Scotus, William of Ockham, and Thomas Aquinas. *LW* 54:263–64 (no. 3722, dated 2 February 1538); *WA, TR* 3:563–64.

64. "They [the papists] say that a good work performed before grace can earn a 'merit of congruity.'" *LW* 26:124; *WA* 40/1. 220. 5–6: "Opus bonum ante gratiam valere ad impetrandam gratiam de Congruo."

65. "Scholastic theology agrees on this point, that man can merit grace *de congruo* by his purely natural powers, and all the schoolmen taught at least this: 'Do what lies in your strength.' But Occam, though he was superior to all the others in mental acumen and refuted all the rest of the positions, expressly said and taught that it isn't to be found in the Scriptures that the Holy Spirit is necessary for good works." *LW* 54:391–92 (no. 5135, dated 7–24 August 1540); *WA, TR* 4:679–80. See Heiko A. Oberman, "*Facientibus quod in se est Deus non denegat gratiam*," *Harvard Theological Review* 75 (1962): 317–42. Oberman explains that the nominalistic doctrine of *facere quod in se est* had implications in two aspects—moral and intellectual—in Luther. Oberman argues that, at least as to the moral implications of the doctrine, "between the comments on Psalm 113:1 (c. 1515) and Rom. 14:1 (c. 1516), Luther has radically revised his position on a doctrine [the doctrine of the *facere quod in se est*] which in 1515 he espoused but which in 1516 he attacks as responsible for perverting the Church." Oberman, *The Dawn of the Reformation*, 99–100.

66. *LW* 26:130; *WA* 40/1. 230. 18–22: "Scholastici Theologi docuerunt hominem hac ratione consequi remissionem peccatorum et iustificationem, Si operibus praecedentibus quae appellant

merit: the "sophists" instruct that "once grace has been obtained, the work that follows deserves eternal life by the 'merit of condignity.'"[67]

This late scholastic or nominalistic position on merit or, more exactly, the merit of congruity, scandalizes Luther more than the Thomistic view. Luther's assessment is apparent in the following pronouncement:

> They [the sophists] go on to say that the works that follow have the power to merit eternal life 'by condignity,' because God accepts the work that follows and applies it to eternal life, on account of the love that He has infused into man's will. Thus they say that God 'accepts' a good work for eternal life but 'disaccepts' an evil work for damnation and eternal punishment.... Nevertheless, they do not all speak even this well; but some, as we have said, have taught that by our purely natural powers we are able to love God above all things [merit of congruity].[68]

Luther aptly points out that even the scholastics are divided over the merits of congruity and condignity. Luther further recounts how the medieval church dealt with these two disparate opinions in order to avoid the appearance of contradiction.

Luther describes that the scholastics find a solution by speaking about the fulfillment of the law in two ways: according to the content

merita congrui, mereatur gratiam, Quae ipsis est qualitas inhaerens voluntati, divinitus donata supra illam dilectionem quam viribus naturalibus habemus. Hac habita dicunt hominem esse iustum formaliter et vere Christianum."

67. *LW* 26:124; *WA* 40/1. 220. 6–7: "Impetrata vero iam gratia sequens opus mereri vitam aeternam de Congidgno."

68. *LW* 26:131; *WA* 40/1. 230. 28–231. 18: "Sequentia autem opera dixerunt valere ad promerendam vitam aeternam de condigno, Ita, quod Deus propter charitatem quam infudit voluntati hominis, acceptet illud opus sequens ad vitam aeternam. Sic enim loquuntur Deum acceptare bonum opus ad vitam aeternam, malum autem opus deacceptare ad damnationem et poenam aeternam.... Quanquam non omnes tam bene loquuntur, sed quidam, ut diximus, docuerunt nos ex puris naturalibus posse Deum supra omnia diligere." Also see, among other places, *LW* 2:123; *WA* 42. 348. 37–349. 9. On the subject of "*ex puris naturalibus*" ("purely natural endowments"), see *LW* 2:121, n. 37; *WA* 42. 347. 35–39. The scholastic idea of the unimpaired natural endowments (*integra naturalia*) is that when Adam was created, the added gift of grace was superimposed upon his natural endowments; his fall cost him the superadded gift, but he retained his natural endowments unimpaired. These were not sufficient to save him so grace had to be restored for that. Nonetheless, they did make him good in his essence.

of the act or the intention of the One who gave the commandment.[69] From the standpoint of the content of the act, human beings can fulfill everything that the law commands. From the perspective of the fulfillment of the law in compliance with the intention of God, the scholastics argue that God additionally requires the law to be kept "in love—not the natural love that human beings have but a supernatural and divine love that He Himself confers."[70] This love is designated as "a supernatural quality infused into us from heaven" and called "the formal righteousness that informs and adorns faith and makes it justify us."[71]

Luther finds this solution straying far away from Scripture. Scripture never declares that human beings are able to love God above all things by their own natural powers. Nor does it aver that human beings are able to incur grace and eternal life by the mere performance of good deeds. The insistence that God demands love as a supernatural quality infused into human beings from heaven is certainly not biblical but philosophical.

Luther inveighs against these notions of love because they place too much stock in human merit for justification. Worse, they construe Christian faith as a useless and formless material. Luther subjects those who engage in this attempt at philosophizing the theological concepts of Christian faith and love to biting criticism. They "make God a tyrant and a tormentor who demands of us what we cannot produce," which is equal to declaring that, "if we are damned, the fault is not so much in us as in God, who requires us to keep His Law in this fashion."[72]

---

69. *LW* 26:128–29; *WA* 40/1. 227. 21–23: "dicunt Legem dupliciter impleri, Primo secundum substantiam facti, Deinde secundum intentionem praecipientes."
70. *LW* 26:129; *WA* 40/1. 227. 27–29: "in charitate legem facias, non naturali quam habes, sed supernaturali et divina quam ipse dat."
71. *LW* 26:129; *WA* 40/1. 228. 23–25: "habitum supernaturalem, e coelo infusum, qui est charitas, Quam dixerunt esse formalem iustitiam, formantem et ornantem fidem facientemque, ut ea iustificet."

In discarding this conception of forming love and instead advocating faith alone, Luther does not, of course, intend to set up a competition between the two theological virtues of faith and love. A deeper investigation of this issue uncovers that it is just the tip of the iceberg.

Duel between the Law and Christ

In his argument with the scholastics, the question of greatest urgency for Luther is: if love (whether a supernatural quality infused into human beings from heaven or a natural human quality) forms faith and attains merits for justification through works of the law, then what is the significance of the incarnation of the Son? What is his soteriological function? What has happened to God's promise for human salvation—the promise that is "the very inheritance or blessing promised to Abraham, that is, deliverance from the Law, sin, death, and the devil; and the gift of grace, righteousness, salvation, and eternal life" through a blessed offspring, Christ?[73]

What Luther detects in the idea that faith is formed and completed by love is not merely a question of superiority between the theological virtues, namely, faith and love. In what appears to be a rivalry between faith and love on the surface, Luther perceives grave antagonism between Christ and the law, which concerns the matter of life and death for human beings. Luther delineates this antagonism by way of powerful imagery, which is the "duel between the Law and Christ."[74] Christ asserts his exclusive patent for justification and

---

72. *LW* 26:129; *WA* 40/1. 227. 29–228. 17: "Quid hoc aliud est, quam ex Deo facere tyrannum et carnificem, qui hoc exigit a nobis, quod praestare non possumus? Et parum abfuit, quin manifeste dicerent non fieri nostra culpa, quod damnemur, sed Dei qui ista circumstantia exigit legem suam a nobis impleri."

73. *LW* 26:334; *WA* 40/1. 515. 25–27: "Promissio autem est hereditas ipsa, seu benedictio Abrahae promissa, hoc est, liberatio a lege, peccato, morte et diabolo Et donatio gratiae, iustitiae, salutis et vitae aeternae."

74. *LW* 26:371; *WA* 40/1. 567. 14: "Hoc duellum *gestum est* inter Legem et Christum."

the law alleges its collaborative validity alongside God's grace for justification. This duel takes place because the law puts itself in competition with Christ over the justification of human sinners. This competition is also a rivalry between Christ and a sinner striving in vain for self- or works-righteousness under the law. In this rivalry, the sinner, who denies that Christ has already attained justification and freely gives it to whoever believes in him, vies with Christ for justification.

However, in order to discern the real issue surrounding this duel between Christ and the law, Luther declares that Christ's two functions must be carefully differentiated. Luther expressly describes a twofold function of "Christ, the divine and human Person": the proper and the accidental function. It is precisely Christ's proper function on which the justification of sinners hinges. Though the following statement is lengthy, it is worth reproducing here:

> When Christ issues commandments in the Gospel and teaches, or rather interprets, the Law, this belongs, not to the doctrine of justification but to the doctrine of good works. Besides, teaching the Law is not the proper function of Christ on account of which He came into the world; it is an accidental function, just as when He healed the sick, raised the dead, helped the poor, and comforted the afflicted. These are glorious and divine works, of course; but they are not peculiar to Christ. For the prophets taught the Law too, and performed miracles. But Christ is true God and man . . . . Therefore it is Christ's true and proper function to struggle with the Law, sin, and death of the entire world, and to struggle in such a way that He undergoes them, but, by undergoing them, conquers them and abolishes them in Himself, thus liberating us from the Law and from every evil. Therefore teaching the Law and performing miracles are special benefits of Christ, which were not the chief reason for His coming.[75]

---

75. *LW* 26:372–73; *WA* 40/1. 568. 25–569. 23: "Quod autem Christus in Evangelio praecepta tradit et legem docet seu potius interpretatur, hoc non ad locum de iustificatione, sed ad locum de bonis operibus pertinet. Deinde etiam non est proprium Christi officium, propter quod praecipue venit in mundum, docere legem, sed accidentale, Cuiusmodi erat et hoc, quod sanabat infirmos, excitabat mortuos, benefaciebat indignis, consolabatur afflictos etc. Ea quidem

The reason Luther emphasizes that a sinner's justification exclusively belongs to the proper function of Christ, the Savior, is to stress that only Christ, who is not only truly human but also truly God, can deal with the matter. According to Luther, if someone only sees the historical Jesus who performed works that other great prophets or teachers also did, that person is missing the point of the divine work of human salvation.

Drawing on Paul, Luther states that only God can exonerate human beings of their sins. That Christ is the victor over sin, death, and the eternal curse testifies that Christ is very God by nature, that is, true deity.[76] This implies that Christ, as the savior, cannot

gloriosa ac divina opera et beneficia sunt, sed non propria Christi. Nam Prophetae docuerunt etiam legem, et miracula aediderunt. Christus vero est Deus et homo, qui pugnans cum lege passus est extremam ipsius saevitiam ac tyrannidem, et hoc ipso, quod fecit et sustinuit legem, vicit eam in Semetipso Ac postea resurgens a more Legem, infestissimum hostem nostrum, damnavit et e medio sustulit, ut amplius damnare et occidere nos non possit. Quare Christi verum et proprium officium est, luctari cum lege, peccato et morte totius mundi, et sic luctari, ut ista sustineat et sustinendo in Semetipso vincat et aboleat et hoc modo nos a lege et omnibus malis liberet. Itaque particularia beneficia Christi sunt legem docere et miracula aedere, propter quae praecipue non venit." See also *LW* 26:38: "Christ also interprets the Law, to be sure; but this is not His proper and chief work."; *WA* 40/1. 91. 28–29: "Interpretatur quidem legem Christus, sed hoc non est proprium et principale ipsius officium."

76. In his exposition of Galatians 1:3 ("Grace to you and peace from God the Father and our Lord Jesus Christ"), Luther states as follows: "The second thing that Paul teaches us here is a substantiation of our faith that Christ is true God. Statements like these about the divinity of Christ should be assembled and carefully noted, not only against the Arians and other sectarians past or future but also for the substantiation of our own faith." *LW* 26:30–31; *WA* 40/1. 80. 17–21. Luther continues to say as follows: "The true deity of Christ is proved by this conclusion: Paul attributes to Him the ability to grant the very same things that the Father does—grace, peace of conscience, the forgiveness of sins, life, and victory over sin, death, the devil, and hell. This would be illegitimate, in fact, sacrilegious, if Christ were not true God . . . . The Father creates and gives life, grace, peace, etc.; the Son creates and gives the very same things. To give grace, peace, eternal life, the forgiveness of sins, justification, life, and deliverance from death and the devil—these are the works, not of any creature but only of the Divine Majesty. The angels can neither create these things nor grant them. Therefore these works belong only to the glory of the sovereign Majesty, the Maker of all things. And since Paul attributes the very same power to create and give all this to Christ just as much as to the Father, it follows necessarily that Christ is truly God by nature." *LW* 26:31; *WA* 40/1. 80. 25–81. 22.

Luther also states, "many of such arguments appear in John, where it is proved and concluded from the works ascribed to the Son as well as to the Father that the deity of the Father and of the Son is one. Therefore the gifts we receive from the Father are none other than those we receive from the Son; the same things come both from the Father and the Son." *LW* 26:31;

be imitated, supplemented, or replaced by any creature.[77] So Luther insists that "Christ who blesses and redeems" in light of his proper function "is vastly different from Christ the example" who is tied to his accidental function.[78] In conjunction with these two functions of Christ, Luther also points to how Scripture presents Christ in a twofold way: "Scripture presents Christ in two ways. First, as a gift . . . . Secondly, Scripture presents Him as an example for us to imitate."[79] Christ the example has nothing to do with the justification of sinners; human beings can but passively receive as gift the blessing and redeeming Christ who is given for justification.[80]

WA 40/1. 81. 23–26. "I am warning you about this matter so earnestly on account of the danger that, amid the many errors and various sects today, some Arians, Eunomians, Macedonians, and other such heretics might arise and damage the churches with their subtlety. The Arians were truly sharp. They conceded that Christ has a double nature and that He is called 'God of true God'—but only in name. Christ, they said, is a most noble and perfect creature, higher than the angels; through Him God then created heaven and earth and everything else . . . . But all this is nothing but fallacious reasoning and words that are pleasant and reasonable, by which the fanatics deceive men unless they are careful. But Paul speaks of Christ differently." *LW* 26:31–32; *WA* 40/1. 82. 14–23.

77. "Therefore when we teach that men are justified through Christ and that Christ is the victor over sin, death, and the eternal curse, we are testifying at the same time that He is God by nature." *LW* 26:283; *WA* 40/1. 441. 31–33: "Quare cum docemus hominess per Christum iustificari, Christum esse victorem peccati, mortis et aeternae maledictionis, testificamur simul eum esse natura Deum." See also *LW* 26:282; *WA* 40/1. 441. 19, 27, *LW* 26:30–32; *WA* 40/1. 80. 18, 25, 81. 20–22, 82. 28–29.

78. *LW* 26:247; *WA* 40/1. 390. 17–18: "longe aliud est Christus benedicens et redimens quam exemplum."

79. *LW* 27:34; *WA* 40/2. 42. 19–25: "Scriptura proponit Christum dupliciter, Primum ut donum . . . . Deinde scriptura proponit etiam eum ut exemplum nobis imitandum." This twofold way of Christ's being given to human beings will be elaborated in detail in chapter 4.

80. *LW* 26:246–47: "Here [in the discussion of justification] nothing but Christ dying for sins and rising again for our righteousness should be set forth. He must be grasped by faith as a gift, not as an example."; *WA* 40/1. 389. 19–20: "Ibi solus Christus proponendus est moriens pro peccatis et resurgens pro iustitia nostra, et fide apprehendendus est [Christus] ut donum, non ut exemplum."

On human beings' passivity in terms of their justification, Luther says, "Therefore we come to these eternal goods—the forgiveness of sins, righteousness, the glory of the resurrection, and eternal life—not actively but passively." *LW* 26:392; *WA* 40/1. 597. 20–21: "Itaque passive, non active pervenimus ad ista aeterna bona, remissionem peccatorum, iustitiam, resurrectionis gloriam et ad vitam aeternam."

Considering this twofold function of Christ, Luther's objection to the scholastic teaching of unformed faith and forming love reveals a deeper concern. Luther dismisses the ideas of *fides caritate formata*, merit of congruity and condignity, and love (no matter how it is described—naturally inherent or supernaturally infused) because the issue at stake is one of divine affairs: the death of the Son of God, the truthfulness of God, and God's promise for human salvation in Christ. Accordingly, Luther declares,

> By this wicked and blasphemous teaching they have not only obscured the Gospel but have removed it altogether and have buried Christ completely. For if in a state of mortal sin I can do any tiny work that is not only pleasing before God externally and of itself but can even deserve grace "by congruity"; and if, once I have received grace, I am able to perform works according to grace, that is, according to love, and receive eternal life by a right—then what need do I have of the grace of God, the forgiveness of sins, the promise, and the death and victory of Christ? Then Christ has become altogether useless to me; for I have free will and the power to perform good works, and through this I merit grace "by congruity" and eventually eternal life "by condignity."[81]

Indeed, the ideas of unformed faith, forming love, and the merits of congruity and condignity are spurious, since they attribute what properly belongs to God and Christ to love, the law, and human performances.[82] As a consequence, love, the law, and human performances transgress their own proper jurisdiction. The

---

81. *LW* 26:124–25; *WA* 40/1. 220. 20–29: "Ista sua impia et blasphema doctrina non solum obscuraverint, sed simpliciter sustulerint Evangelium et Christum obruerint. Si enim ego exsistens in peccato mortali possum facere aliquod opusculum quod non solum secundum substantiam sit gratum Deo, sed etiam possit mereri gratiam de congruo; Et ubi habuero gratiam, possum facere opera secundum gratiam, id est dilectionem, et acquirere de iure vitam aeternam: Quid iam opus est mihi gratia Dei, remissione peccatorum, promissione, morte et victoria Christi? Christus plane iam mihi otiosus est. Habeo enim liberum arbitrium et vires faciendi bonum opus per quod gratiam mereor de congruo et postea vitam aeternam de condigno."

82. *LW* 26:142; *WA* 40/1. 248. 20–30, *LW* 26:258–59; *WA* 40/1. 406. 17–26, *LW* 26:283; *WA* 40/1. 441. 34–442. 30.

crucifixion of Christ is the "sublime crucifixion by which sin, the devil, and death are crucified in Christ, not in me. Here Christ does everything alone. But I, as a believer, am crucified with Christ through faith."[83] As long as the law confines its role to keeping order, it is highly encouraged and applauded; but if the law takes the credit for the justification of sinners, then the law and works of the law are exceeding their own domain. Moreover, Christ's unique, proper, non-imitative, and unrepeatable function is usurped and mistakenly attributed to the law as if the proper function of Christ could be shared, imitated, or repeated by human creatures.

In addition, the ideas of unformed faith, forming love, and the merits of congruity and condignity are grounded on a false assessment of the requirements of the law for justification and of the seriousness of sin and its power, now hardwired into human nature. The scope of the law to be observed for the justification of the unrighteous is not confined to a part but is the entirety of the whole law. Luther assiduously stresses, "for Paul 'works of the Law' means the works of the entire Law. Therefore one should not make a distinction between the Decalog and ceremonial laws."[84] We must "take 'works of the Law' generally, to mean whatever is opposed to grace: Whatever is not grace is Law, whether it be the Civil Law, the Ceremonial Law, or the Decalog."[85]

Even when human beings strive to do the works of the law "according to the commandment, 'You shall love the Lord your God

83. *LW* 26:165; *WA* 40/1. 281. 18–20: "de illa sublimi concrucifixione qua peccatum, Diabolus, mors crucifigitur in Christo, non in me. Hic Christus solus omnia facit; sed credens concrucifigor Christo per fidem, ut et mihi illa sint mortua et crucifixa."

84. *LW* 26:122; *WA* 40/1. 218. 12–13: "Significat ergo 'Opus legis' Paulo opus totius legis. Ideo non est faciendum discrimen inter decalogum et leges ceremoniarum." See also *LW* 26:156; *WA* 40/1. 268. 26, *LW* 26:181; *WA* 40/1. 302. 26, *LW* 26:203; *WA* 40/1. 329. 26–29, *LW* 26:447; *WA* 40/1. 671. 30–672. 12.

85. *LW* 26:122; *WA* 40/1. 218. 6–8: "Opus ergo legis accipe simpliciter per Antithesim contra gratiam: Quidquid non est gratia, Lex est, sive sit Iudicialis, Ceremonialis, sive Decalogus."

with all your heart, etc. (Matt. 22:37),'" this strain is of no avail for justification in the sight of God.[86] When Paul says that a person is not justified by the law or by the works of the law, he is "contrasting the righteousness of faith with the righteousness of the entire Law, with everything that can be done on the basis of the Law, whether by divine power or by human."[87]

The entirety of the law consists not only in the all-inclusiveness of each and every stipulation but also in its internal fulfillment. Luther lambasts the scholastics because they do not seriously meditate on the internal fulfillment of the law. The scholastics "take mortal sin to be only external work committed against the Law" and do not see that "ignorance, hatred, and contempt of God in the heart, ingratitude, murmuring against God, and resistance to the will of God are also mortal sin."[88] They are blinded to the fact that "these huge plagues are rooted in the nature of man" and that no amount of rationalization can justify the invention of such ideas as the merit of congruity and condignity.[89] A sinner cannot thoroughly observe the entire requirement of the law externally, let alone internally, owing to the seriousness of sin and its power over human nature.

When the profundity of sin and its ubiquitous power over human nature is grasped in its full measure, any mention of the capacity of

---

86. *LW* 26:122; *WA* 40/1. 218. 8–11: "Ideo si etiam feceris opus legis secundum hoc praeceptum; 'Diliges Dominum Deum tuum ex toto corde tuo' etc. tamen non iustificaberis coram Deo, Quia ex operibus legis non iustificatur homo."

87. *LW* 26:122; *WA* 40/1. 218. 17–18: "opponens per Antithesin iustitiam fidei iustitiae totius legis quae potest parari sive virtute divina, sive humana ex lege." Especially, in respect to the issue of making humanly invented laws—the laws of the Roman pontiff—necessary for salvation, which Luther vehemently criticizes, see *LW* 26:87; *WA* 40/1. 162. 19–25, *LW* 26:225–26; *WA* 40/1. 358. 17–359. 13, *LW* 26:407–08; *WA* 40/1. 618. 29–619. 31.

88. *LW* 26:125; *WA* 40/1. 221. 15–19: "Ipsi peccatum mortale tantum intellexerunt de opere externo, commisso contra legem . . . . Non viderunt peccatum mortale esse Ignorantiam, odium, contemptum Dei in corde, ingratitudinem, murmurationem contra Deum, aversari voluntatem Dei."

89. *LW* 26:125; *WA* 40/1. 221. 20–22: "Si istas maximas pestes in natura hominis haerentes vidissent, non tam impie nugati fuissent de merito congrui et condigni etc." See also *LW* 26:291; *WA* 40/1. 453. 22–454. 17.

human sinners to merit God's grace and justification is preposterous. There is no exception to this universal human fate, because "all men are the captives and slaves of sin" and no one has free will to serve and love God above all things.[90] For Luther, in the matter of salvation, the free will of human beings is as good as useless because of its depraved nature. It is not free at all in its own volition to know or to do good. By this reason, Luther urges people to turn away from false self-confidence and from vainly seeking self- or works-righteousness.[91] When an unclean heart despising God and seeking self-righteousness tries to perform the law, it is "hypocritical" and "a double sin" because it is not truly keeping the law but only pretending to do so outwardly.[92] Such a pretense is "a double wickedness in the sight of God."[93]

One of the contentious issues revolving around free will is: if we cannot observe the law, why has God given it to us, especially the commandment to love God? When God gives us this commandment, does God not expect us to observe it? If God gives us this commandment, does this not imply that we are capable of observing it? If we are incapable of observing the commandment, why does God give it to us? To these questions, Luther responds that,

---

90. *LW* 26:33; *WA* 40/1. 84. 25–26: "omnes homines captivi et servi sint Peccati."

91. The issue of free will and the justification of the unrighteous are tightly interwoven with each other. Luther had some opponents who declared that we have "a free will; do as much as in you lies, God will do his part." *LW* 51:58; *WA* 2. 247. 29–30. The free will issue is connected with the issue of works- or self-righteousness. "It follows from this that the free will of man, praise and extol it as you will, can do absolutely nothing of itself and is not free in its own volition to know or to do good, but only in the grace of God, which makes it free and without which it lies bound in sin and error and cannot get loose by itself." *LW* 51:57; *WA* 2. 247. 3–7. "One never speaks of the free will or understands it aright unless it be adorned with God's grace, without which it should rather be called one's own will than free will; for without grace it does not do God's will, but its own will, which is never good. It is true that it was free in Adam, but now through his fall it is corrupted and bound in sin. However, it has retained the name of free will because it was once free and, through grace, is to become free again." *LW* 51:57; *WA* 2. 247. 15–21.

92. *LW* 27:131; *WA* 40/2. 168. 18: "hypocriticum est et duplex peccatum."

93. *LW* 27:132; *WA* 40/2. 168. 31–32: "Simulatio autem coram Deo duplex iniquitas est."

although we are given this commandment as an ideal, the depravity of human nature means that we simply cannot fulfill it. Accordingly, Luther notes,

> Of course, we should keep the Law and be justified by keeping it; but sin gets in the way. The Law prescribes and commands that we love God with all our heart, etc., and our neighbor as ourselves (Matt. 22:37-39); but from this it does not follow: "This is written, and therefore it is done; the Law commands love, and therefore we love." You cannot produce anyone on earth who loves God and his neighbor as the Law requires.[94]

This citation contains Luther's critical attack on Gabriel Biel's idea that human beings can love God by their own nature above all other things. To Luther, because of the total depravity of human nature, human love is not pure. Even when it loves God, it seeks its own benefits. It loves not out of purity but out of fear of punishment or expectation of reward. Given this view of fallen human love, Luther is very reluctant to employ "love" to define the character of the disposition of human sinners towards God. To Luther, there is no way whatsoever for sinners to climb the ladder to God by their own natural capacities. Humans can truly love God only on one condition: that they receive Christ in faith, who came down from God the Father to reconcile them to God and make them children of God. It is nothing but faith that unites them with Christ, the Savior. Only after this faith in Christ has correctly established the right relationship of human beings toward God and made them children of God can Luther now cautiously say that Christ in faith enables them to love God rightly out of a pure heart. The commandment to love God is

---

94. *LW* 27:63–64; *WA* 40/2. 79. 22–26: "Deberemus quidem implere legem et impletione eius iustificari, sed peccatum obstat. Praescribit et praecipit quidem lex, ut 'Deum ex toto corde etc. et proximum ut nos ipsos diligamus', sed ideo non sequitur: 'Hoc scriptum est, ergo fit, Lex praecipit dilectionem, ergo diligimus. Non dabis aliquem in terris, qui ita diligat Deum et proximum, ut lex requirit."

fulfilled only because they have Christ in themselves through faith. Only then can they love God with purity.

In the scholastics' assertion about the uselessness of faith without love for justification, Luther discerns the perversity "of confusing the Law and grace and of changing Christ into Moses."[95] By this confusion, "the Law becomes Christ; for they attribute to the Law what properly belongs to Christ."[96] They make the mistake of attributing to love what properly belongs to faith, to the law what properly belongs to Christ. Luther goes further, arguing that this thought amounts to the proposition: "Moses is Christ and Christ is Moses."[97]

By the same token, they confuse the law and grace. Though the scholastics formally distinguish grace from the law, in practice they call grace "love" (*dilectionem*), because the church says that faith (whether acquired or infused) must be followed by love (*dilectio*) and consequently adds works to faith.[98] This is nothing other than a perverse confusion of grace with the law, because "Christ or faith is neither the Law nor the work of the Law."[99] The redemption of Christ, conversely, is "altogether different from my merit based on works of the Law," for "Christ is something altogether different from a work that we do."[100] So, with the opinion that their own works are contributing to justification, people are making their own work Christ—Christ, the divine Son.[101]

---

95. *LW* 26:144; *WA* 40/1. 251. 15: "legem et gratiam confundant [Papistas et Phanaticos] et Christum in Mosen transforment."

96. *LW* 26:144; *WA* 40/1. 248. 23–24: "Sic Lex fit Christus perversitate intolerabili, quia legi tribuitur quod proprie Christo competit."

97. *LW* 26:143; *WA* 40/1. 250. 15: "Mosen esse Christum et Christum esse Mosen."

98. *LW* 26:144; *WA* 40/1. 251. 24: "Revera tamen Gratiam vocat [Papa] dilectionem."

99. *LW* 26:130; *WA* 40/1. 229. 32: "Christus enim vel fides non est Lex nec opus legis."

100. *LW* 26:286; *WA* 40/1. 446. 25–29: "redemptio Christi longe aliud est quam meum meritum ex operibus legis . . . . Christus enim longe aliud quiddam est quam opus quod nos facimus."

101. "No papist, no matter how insane he is, will have the audacity to say that the alms he grants to someone in need or the obedience that a monk yields is a Christ." *LW* 26:286; *WA* 40/1. 446.

Fides Christo Formata

Rebuking the scholastics—whether they are following Thomas Aquinas or Gabriel Biel in their notions of human merits—Luther proclaims that "Christ alone is our merit of congruity and condignity."[102] If the law and works of love are chosen, Christ has died in vain, God's grace is blasphemed, and God's promise for human salvation becomes empty and nullified.[103] Those who seek to be justified by the law are "not only deniers and the murderers but the guiltiest crucifiers of Christ."[104] If Christ has accomplished everything for justification, then no human works of love are necessary for justification, and God has kept God's promise for human salvation. In the matter of justification, human beings need to let God work alone, which is to let God be God and let Christ be God.[105] God does not work synergistically with sinners for their justification. God is the sole agent. Luther presents this argument by employing the expression, the "duel between the Law and Christ."[106] In this duel between Christ and the law, there is no neutral place: "Either Christ

---

30–31: "Nullus Papista, quantumvis insanus, audebit dicere Eleemosynam quam ipse largitur egenti, Obedientiam quam Monachus praestat, Christum esse."

102. *LW* 26:375; *WA* 40/1. 572. 33–573. 11: "solum Christum esse meritum nostrum congrui et condigni." See also *LW* 26:132: "By the true definition Christ is not a lawgiver; He is a Propitiator and a Savior. Faith takes hold of this and believes without doubting that He has performed a superabundance of works and merits of congruity and condignity."; *WA* 40/1. 232. 29–31: "Christus autem definitive non est Legislator, sed Propitiator et Salvator. Hoc fides apprehendit et sine dubio credit eum opera et merita congrui et condigni fecisse superabundanter."

103. *LW* 26:179–83; *WA* 40/1. 300. 23–305. 13, *LW* 26:185; *WA* 40/1. 307. 22–308. 18, *LW* 26:279; *WA* 40/1. 436. 24–437. 17, *LW* 27:10; *WA* 40/2. 11. 22–26.

104. *LW* 26:199; *WA* 40/1. 324. 37–325. 12: "cum audit Paulum hic dicere eos etiam qui ex lege divina iustificari quearunt, non solum esse abnegatores et homicidas, sed etiam sceleratissimos crucifixores Christo."

105. Philip Watson's choice of *Let God Be God!* as the title for his book interpreting Luther's theology reflects the magnitude of this argument in Luther's theology. Watson's claim strongly resonates with readers. Philip S. Watson, *Let God Be God!: An Interpretation of the Theology of Martin Luther* (Eugene, OR: Wipf & Stock, 2000).

106. *LW* 26:371; *WA* 40/1. 567. See also *LW* 26:164; *WA* 40/1. 279, *LW* 26:282; *WA* 40/1. 440.

must abide, and the Law perish; or the Law must abide, and Christ perish."[107]

It cannot be underscored enough that it is only along this argument that we can launch an accurate inquiry into Luther's conception of faith. Categorically opposing the scholastic formula *fides caritate formata*, Luther clings to what he deems to be Paul's conception of faith. In his treatment of the scholastic formula *fides caritate formata*, Luther finds (in reference to Galatians 3:11: "the righteous shall live by faith") that Paul is employing a general statement (in Habbakuk 2:4) for a specific purpose, applying it to a peculiar situation (as he did in Romans 1:17 and Galatians 3:11).[108]

Paul is interpreting the term "faith" as used by the prophet Habakkuk "in its exclusive and antithetical sense," that is, faith that excludes the law and works of love for righteousness.[109] From this point of view, the exegesis of the scholastics does not correctly comprehend this exclusivity and antithesis in Paul's use of the term "faith" because they read the passage as follows: "'The righteous shall live by faith,' that is, by a faith that is active, working, or 'formed' by love. But if it is an unformed faith, it does not justify."[110] Luther understands the faith that Paul is teaching to have nothing in common with the scholastic notion of unformed faith that must first be formed by love or be supplemented by works of the law, namely, by the works of supernaturally infused love.

On the contrary, faith in Christ is both necessary and sufficient for justification, for faith is the sole means of grasping Christ in one's heart and, thereby, the only way to salvation.[111] Joining hands not

---

107. *LW* 26:54; *WA* 40/1. 114. 13–14: "Aut enim Christus stabit et Lex peribit, aut Lex stabit et Chrsitus peribit." See also *LW* 26:445; *WA* 40/1. 669. 15–16.

108. See *LW* 17:307; *WA* 31/2. 497. 8–34.

109. *LW* 26:268; *WA* 40/1. 421. 13: "Paulus fidei vocabulum exclusive et per contrarium accipit."

110. *LW* 26:268; *WA* 40/1. 421. 15–16: "Iustus vivit ex fide, scilicet efficaci, operante vel formata charitate. Si vero est fides informis, non iustificat."

with scholasticism but with Paul, Luther declares that any faith that must be completed by works of the law or love is not faith at all because such a "faith" would deny Christ's own unique and proper soteriological work. True faith is completely free of works and solely receptive to Christ. Only Christ constitutes true faith, and Christ is grasped and embraced only by faith.[112]

Luther's formula for this reciprocal relationship between faith and Christ is: faith in Christ and, in inverted form, Christ in faith. As to faith in Christ, Luther also specifies, "That promise . . . is not obtained by any merit, Law, or work; but it is given. To whom? To believers. Believers in whom? In Jesus Christ, the Blessed Offspring."[113] Luther's confession below reveals the significance of his thought on faith in Christ: "in my heart there rules *this one doctrine, namely, faith in Christ. From it, through it, and to it all my theological thought flows and returns, day and night.*"[114]

---

111. *LW* 26:146–47; *WA* 40/1. 255. 15–35. According to Luther, this is the purpose of Paul's writing this epistle: "His [Paul's] purpose in this epistle is to discuss and to defend the righteousness that comes by faith, and to refute the Law and the righteousness that comes by works." *LW* 26:21; *WA* 40/1. 64. 16–17: "Vult enim in hac Epistola de iustitia fidei agere et eam defendere et legem ac iustitiam operum evertere."

112. *LW* 26:177; *WA* 40/1. 297. 30–31: "Sic fides, ut dixi [Luther], apprehendit et involvit Christum filium Dei pro nobis traditum."

113. *LW* 26:334; *WA* 40/1. 515. 27–30: "Illa promissio, inquit, nullo merito, nulla lege, nullis operibus impetratur, sed donatur. Quibus? Credentibus. In quem? In Iesum Christum qui est Semen benedictum."

114. *LW* 27:145 (italics mine); *WA* 40/1. 33. 7–9: "Nam in corde meo *iste unus* regnat *articulus*, scilicet *Fides Christi, ex quo, per quem et in quem omnes meae diu noctuque fluunt et refluunt theologicae cogitationes.*"

This aspect displays Luther's christologically centered concept of faith and soteriologically oriented Christology. Luther declares that Christ and faith must be the center: "Faith is, as it were, the center of a circle. If anybody strays from the center, it is impossible for him to have the circle around him, and he must blunder. The center is Christ." *LW* 54:45 (no. 327, dated Summer or Fall 1532); *WA, TR* 1:135: "Fides autem est sicut centrum circuli. Quando quis aberrat a centro, so ists unmuglich, das man den cirkel hab, so mus man fehlen. Centrum est Christus." Luther also mentions: "Everything circles around the center, and that is Christ." *LW* 54:61 (no. 388, dated 30 November 1532); *WA, TR* 1:169. According to Luther, "[t]here is only one article and one rule of theology, and this is true faith or trust in Christ. Whoever doesn't hold this article and this rule is no theologian. All other articles flow into and out of this one; without it the others are meaningless." *LW* 54:157 (no. 1583, dated 20–27 May 1532); *WA,*

Christ, or more precisely, the proper function of Christ, is the point of departure and simultaneously the destination for Luther's conception of faith. Accordingly, an approach to Luther's conception of faith will be widely off target if it does not start and end up with Christ. Christ in his proper function is the sole demand, object, content, and form of faith. Such faith is genuine and living faith. Otherwise, it is counterfeit and dead.

This conceptual circularity—the steadfast interconnection between faith and Christ—is the nucleus of Luther's reconceptualization of faith. True faith is both necessary and sufficient for justification because Christ is the only one who is promised by God as justifier and redeemer, and faith is the only means of grasping and being cemented to this Christ. For this reason, Luther protests that the idea of *fides caritate formata* adulterates the genuine faith that "takes hold of Christ in such a way that Christ is the object of faith, or rather not the object but, so to speak, *the One who is present in the faith itself*."[115]

The scholastics maintain that both infused faith—a gift of the Holy Spirit—and acquired faith—produced by Christians through their many acts of believing—are unformed. They must be formed by love.[116] The scholastics allegedly argue that "faith is the body, the shell, or the color; but love is the life, the kernel, or the form."[117] So

---

TR 2:140–41. Bernhard Lohse also emphasizes that "the goal of Christology is soteriology, as conversely soteriology has its basis in Christology." Bernhard Lohse, *Luthers Theologie in ihrer historischen Entwicklung und in ihrem systematischen Zusammenhang* (Göttingen: Vandenhoeck & Ruprecht, 1995), 241; ET *Martin Luther's Theology: Its Historical and Systematic Development*, trans. and ed. Roy A. Harrisville (Minneapolis: Fortress Press, 1999), 224.

115. *LW* 26:129 (italics mine); *WA* 40/1. 228. 34–229. 15: "Sed si est vera fides, est quaedam certa fiducia cordis et firmus assensus quo Christus apprehenditur, Sic ut Christus sit obiectum fidei, imo non obiectum, sed, ut ita dicam, *in ipsa fide Christus adest*." See also *LW* 26:239–40; *WA* 40/1. 378. 29–379. 17.

116. *LW* 26:269; *WA* 40/1. 422. 14–16: "Quamvis . . . adsit fides infusa quae donum Spiritus sancti est, et acquisita quam nos ipsi parimus nobis multis actionibus credendi, tamen utraque est informis et formatur charitate."

117. *LW* 26:129; *WA* 40/1. 228. 25–26: "fides est corpus, siliqua, color, charitas vero est vita, nucleus, forma."

"love is the form of faith, and faith is merely the 'matter' of love. In this way they prefer love to faith and attribute righteousness, not to faith but to love."[118]

Contrariwise, Luther avers that Christ, not love, is the form of faith: "In short, just as the sophists say that love forms and trains faith, so we say that *it is Christ* who forms and trains faith or *who is the form of faith*. Therefore the Christ who is grasped by faith and who lives in the heart is the true Christian righteousness, on account of which God counts us righteous and grants us eternal life."[119] Luther

---

118. *LW* 26:269; *WA* 40/1. 422. 18–20: "Itaque charitas est forma fidei et fides pura materia charitatis. Hoc modo praeferunt charitatem fidei et tribuunt iustitiam non fidei, sed charitati."

119. *LW* 26:130 (italics mine); *WA* 40/1. 229. 26–30: "Summa: Sicut Sophistae dicunt charitatem formare et imbuere fidem, Sic nos dicimus *Christum* formare et imbuere fidem vel *formam esse fidei*. Ergo fide apprehensus et in corde habitans Christus est iustitia Christiana propter quam Deus nos reputat iustos et donat vitam aeternam." See George Hunsinger, "*Fides Christo Formata*: Luther, Barth and the Joint Declaration," in *The Gospel of Justification in Christ: Where Does the Church Stand Today?*, ed. Wayne C. Stumme (Grand Rapids: Eerdmans, 2006), 69–84, esp. 73–79.

Regarding the issue of Christ's righteousness, Heiko Oberman provides a very helpful explanation. Oberman says that, according to the whole medieval tradition, in the justification of the sinner the *iustitia Christi* is bestowed as *gratia* or *caritas*. The *iustitia Dei*, however, is not granted along with or attached to the *iustitia Christi*, which is conveyed in the process of justification. The *iustitia Dei* remains the *finis*, the ultimate goal, or "the 'Gegenüber' of the viator who is propelled on his way to the eternal Jerusalem by the *iustitia Christi*." As "the eternal immutable Law of God," the *iustitia Dei* functions as the standard according to which "the degree of appropriation and the effects of the *iustitia Christi* are measured and will be measured in the Last Judgment." Oberman states that, attacking this whole medieval tradition—which was later confirmed at the Council of Trent—Luther disputes that the *iustitia Christi* and the *iustitia Dei* coincide and are granted simultaneously. According to Oberman, the significance of this contention is that "it is not the task of those who are justified to implement the iustitia Christi by relating themselves in an optimal fashion to the iustitia Dei. The Pauline message is the Gospel exactly because the iustitia Dei—revealed at the Cross as the iustitia Christi—is given to the faithful per fidem. The 'fides Christo formata' replaces the medieval 'fides charitate formata'. Oberman, *The Dawn of the Reformation*, 120.

Steven Ozment adds something more to this point. In "*Homo Viator*: Luther and Late Medieval Theology," Ozment assesses certain traditional assumptions about the originality of Luther's Reformation discovery. It has been argued that medieval theology made the believer an uncertain pilgrim, suspended between present hope and fear of future judgment, and that Luther, having discovered the unity of God's judgment and mercy in Christ, overcame this anxious pilgrim status. Concerning this position, Ozment illustrates the following explanations with particular terminologies: "'Judgment [=*iudicium Dei*] and righteousness [=*misericordia Dei*] occur in the *existentiell* Now of the Word'; 'God sends righteousness [=*iudicium Dei*]

complains that the scholastics "deprive faith of its task and give this to love, so that faith amounts to nothing at all unless the 'form,' namely, love, is added to it . . . . [F]aith, that miserable virtue, would be a sort of unformed chaos, without any work, efficacy, or life, a purely passive material."[120] Now, Luther declares, whereas the scholastics

simultaneously with peace [=*misericordia Dei*]'; the gospel is the 'Word from Christ' as 'judgment' and 'righteousness'; there is a 'realized eschatology'; 'the heart of the gospel [as Luther discovered] is that the *iustitia Christi* [=*misericordia Dei*] and the *iustitia Dei* [=*iudicium Dei*] coincide and are granted simultaneously'." Steven E. Ozment, "*Homo Viator:* Luther and Late Medieval Theology," in *The Reformation in Medieval Perspective,* ed. Steven E. Ozment (Chicago: Quadrangle Books, 1971), 144. See also Heiko A. Oberman, "'Iustitia Christi' and 'Iustitia Dei': Luther and the Scholastic Doctrines of Justification," *Harvard Theological Review* 59 (1966): 19.

Ozment explains that each of these descriptions, in fact, is materially heir to Erich Vogelsang's conclusions in his analysis of the *scholia* to Psalm 70/71 of Luther's *Dictata super Psalterium* (1513–1516). Ozment cites the following statements from Vogelsang: "'God's heart is not divided: once in the past, mercy; once in the future, wrath. No, God's will is from eternity to eternity united and unchangeable'; 'What is new lies in the fact that Luther now says that *iudicium Dei est Christus in persona sua,* i.e., that Christ has Himself borne the judgment, which He now executes upon [the believer] in faith'; 'Here lies the heartbeat of Luther's doctrine of justification and his Christology: two focal points, justification and the forgiveness of sins, *iustitia et iudicium, opus proprium et opus alienum Dei,* are held together by Christ as their midpoint.'" Eric Vogelsang, *Die Anfänge von Luthers Christologie nach der ersten Psalmenvorlesung* (Berlin, 1929), 64, 103, 119. Quoted in Ozment, "*Homo Viator,*" 144.

Ozment elucidates that this description oversimplifies both medieval and Reformation theology. Especially in the medieval mystical traditions, one finds not only a reconciliation of divine judgment and mercy, but also a reconciliation strikingly similar to that which supposedly characterizes the uniqueness of Luther's discovery. This suggests, on the one hand, a motive for Luther's early preoccupation with and praise of mystical writings. On the other hand, it indicates that the most important distinction between Luther and medieval theology may not be found in the problem of divine judgment and mercy. Ozment advances that the decisive differences do not lie in the suspension of the pilgrim status (since Luther and medieval theology can both do that easily enough), but in the way in which that status is overcome. For the medieval theologian, the pilgrim status could be suspended only in direct proportion to the degree to which man himself was no longer human and sinful. The medieval mystical traditions go furthest in overcoming man's pilgrim status precisely because they go furthest in "deifying" man. Luther, on the other hand, overcomes the pilgrim status "by faith alone"—a feat theologically impossible for every medieval theologian, since such faith leaves man fully human and sinful in himself. Ozment, "*Homo Viator:* Luther and Late Medieval Theology," in *The Reformation in Medieval Perspective,* 145–52. Ozment's essay is also available in *Harvard Theological Review* 62 (1969): 275–87.

120. *LW* 26:270; *WA* 40/1. 422. 27–423. 18: "Ita auferunt fidei omne suum officium et tradunt charitati, Ut fides prorsus nihil valeat, nisi accesserit forma, id est charitas. Ergo iuxta hoc pestilens figmentum Sophistarum fides illa, misera virtus, erit quoddam informe chaos, nullius operis, efficaciae et vitae, sed tantum passiva material . . . . ut diligam, et venio in facere morale."

term love as the formal righteousness of Christians,[121] he pronounces faith as the formal righteousness of Christians.[122] Hence, "where they speak of love, we speak of faith," Luther affirms.[123]

This faith in Christ, in fact, freely grants not only justification but also sanctification, which is bestowed once and for all in perfect and complete form. Luther explains this in his definition of "saints." Saints are not those who perform works that appear to be spectacular in the sight of other human beings but those who, "being called by the Gospel and baptized, believe that they have been sanctified and cleansed by the blood and death of Christ."[124] Luther continues, "Therefore saints are all those who believe in Christ . . . whether men or women, whether slaves or free. And they are saints, on the basis, not of their own works but of the works of God, which they accept by faith . . . . In other words, they are saints, not by active holiness but by passive holiness."[125] For Christians, *being* is predicated upon *believing*. Nothing else defines or constitutes their identity as Christians. As a corollary, if faith in Christ is lost, then everything that establishes the foundation for the identity of a Christian collapses, that is, perfect and complete righteousness and holiness.

This is the rationale that makes Luther proclaim that, "[i]f faith yields on this point, the death of the Son of God will be in vain. Then it is only a fable that Christ is the Savior of the world. Then God is a liar, for He has not lived up to His promises" and thereby, "[i]f we

---

121. *LW* 26:129; *WA* 40/1. 228. 24: "charitas, Quam dixerunt esse formalem iustitiam."; "Man is righteous by means of his formal righteousness, which is grace . . . that is, love." *LW* 26:127; *WA* 40/1. 226. 13–14: "Homo est iustus formali sua iustitia quae est gratia . . . id est, dilectio."
122. "It [the formal righteousness of Christians] is faith itself." *LW* 26:130; *WA* 40/1. 229. 19: "Sed [formalis nostra iustitia est] ipsa fides."
123. *LW* 26:129; *WA* 40/1. 228. 27–28: "Nos autem loco charitatis istius ponimus fidem."
124. *LW* 27:82; *WA* 40/2. 103. 21–23: "qui vocati per Euangelium et baptisati credunt, se Christi morte et sanguine sanctificatos et mundatos esse."
125. *LW* 27:82; *WA* 40/2. 103. 24–28: "Sancti igitur sunt omnes, quotquot credunt in Christum, sive masculi, sive foeminae, sive servi, sive liberi etc. sint, non ex suis operibus, sed Dei, quae fide accipiunt . . . . In summa, Sancti sunt sanctitate passiva, non activa."

lose this, we lose God, Christ, all the promises, faith, righteousness, and eternal life."[126] Since Luther can never consent to lose Jesus Christ, he instead eliminates what he sees as the opponents of Jesus Christ in the matter of justification—the law, love, and the works of love. This is the premise on which Luther fervently campaigns for justification by faith *alone* or, more strictly, justification by faith *in Christ alone.*

This is the context in which Luther's conception of faith can be correctly approached. Only in this context can the following statements by Luther on love be properly analyzed: "A curse on a love that is observed at the expense of the doctrine of faith, to which everything must yield."[127] "We must not attribute the power of justifying to a 'form' that makes a man pleasing to God; we must attribute it to faith, which takes hold of Christ the Savior Himself and possesses Him in the heart. This faith justifies without love and before love."[128] Christ grasped by faith in the heart is "the true Christian righteousness, on account of which God counts us righteous and grants us eternal life. Here there is no work of the Law, no love [*nulla dilectio*]; but there is an entirely different kind of righteousness [*longe alia iustitia*], a new world above and beyond the Law."[129]

126. *LW* 26:90–91; *WA* 40/1. 167. 30–168. 14: "Si fides hic cedit, illa mors filii Dei inanis est; Item fabula est Christum esse Salvatorem mund; Denique Deus ipse mendax invenitur, quia quod promisit, non servavit . . . . utque veritatem Evangelii retineamus qua amissa amisimus Deum, Christum, omnes promissiones, fidem, iustitiam et vitam aeternam."

127. *LW* 27:38; *WA* 40/2. 47. 26–28: "Maledicta sit charitas, quae servatur cum iactura doctrinae fidei, cui omnia cedere debent."

128. *LW* 26:137; *WA* 40/1. 240. 14–16: "Quare non isti formae gratificanti tribuenda est vis iustificandi, sed fidei quae apprehendit et possidet in corde ipsum Christum Salvatorem. Haec fides sine et ante charitatem iustificat."

129. *LW* 26:130; *WA* 40/1. 229. 29–32: "Christus est iustitia Christiana propter quam Deus nos reputat iustos et donat vitam aeternam. Ibi certe nullum est opus legis, nulla dilectio, sed longe alia iustitia et novus quidam mundus extra et supra legem."

Criticism of Intra-Reformation Opponents

The polemical battle against the scholastics intensifies by the undesired participation of parties from among Luther's own allies. As the Reformation movement evolves, Luther begins to confront challenges from the Zwinglians, the Anabaptists, and other Radical Reformers, whom he used to call brothers and sisters.[130] These former followers of Luther unexpectedly stand up against him, accusing him of not following the work that he started through to the end.[131]

Amidst physical threats and indignant verbal attacks from these divergent opposers, Luther does not give any sign of vacillation in his stance on the issue of justification by faith in Christ alone. Against this intensifying polemical backdrop, Luther, ironically, intuits more acutely that even though he seems to be surrounded by disparate foes, he is in fact campaigning for the same cause: the exclusivity of Christ in the matter of justification, and faith as the sole means of possessing the gratuitously justifying Christ.

There is no difference, according to Luther's categorical assessment, between the "papists" and the "fanatics":

> Therefore it is inevitable that the papists, the Zwinglians, the Anabaptists, and all those who either do not know about the

---

130. "Sacramentarians" is Luther's term for those (especially Anabaptists and Zwinglians) who denied that the sacraments are means of grace. See Roland H. Bainton, *Studies on the Reformation: Collected Papers* (Boston: Beacon, 1963), 119–20.

131. The fanatics call Luther and his followers or the so-called magisterial Reformers "'neopapists,' who are twice as bad as the old papists" (*novos papistas, duplo deteriores veteribus*). *LW* 26:57; *WA* 40/1. 118. 28–29. "Nowadays, when the sectarians cannot condemn us overtly, they say instead: 'These Lutherans have a cowardly spirit. They do not dare speak the truth frankly and freely and draw the consequences from it. We have to draw these consequences. To be sure, they have laid a foundation, that is, faith in Christ. But the beginning, the middle, and the end must be joined together. God has not assigned to them the task of accomplishing this; He has left it to us." *LW* 26:50; *WA* 40/1. 109. 23–26: "Lutherani habent spiritum timoris, non audent libere fateri veritatem et perrumpere. Nos perrumpere oportet. Ipsi quidem iecerunt primum fundamentum, hoc est fidem in Christum. Sed principium, medium et finis coniungenda sunt. Hoc ut efficient, non est illis a Deo datum, sed nobis." See also *LW* 27:107; *WA* 40/2. 136. 8–13, *LW* 26:221; *WA* 40/1. 353. 13–16, *LW* 26:402; *WA* 40/1. 610. 26–611. 25.

righteousness of Christ or who do not believe correctly about it should change Christ into Moses and the Law and change the Law into Christ. For this is what they teach: Faith in Christ does indeed justify, but at the same time observance of the Commandments of God is necessary.[132]

The "papists" and the "fanatics" are like two wolves "joined at the tail, even though they have different heads. They pretend to be fierce enemies publicly; but inwardly they actually believe, teach, and defend the same doctrine, in opposition to Christ, the only Savior, who is our only righteousness."[133] By emphasizing human worthiness and preparation for God's acceptance of human sinners, both groups incur a reprimand from Luther for not giving full and exclusive credit to Christ for justification. The tendency of the Radical Reformers to swing the pendulum back to an emphasis on the sinner's soteriological participation and cooperation is one of the most frustrating experiences for Luther in his arduous campaign for justification.

One occasion that precipitated Luther's avid criticism on the issue of faith is the re-baptism controversy. The Anabaptists teach that baptism is nothing unless the person baptized is a believer.[134] The issue under discussion is that the faith of believers must be proved by their zealous works in conformity with Christ, the example. Faith does not justify without love, that is, the cross, suffering, and bloodshed. In this idea, Luther recognizes the theologically hazardous presupposition that the work of God depends upon the preliminary worthiness of a person.[135] To Luther, although they recite his

---

132. *LW* 26:143; *WA* 40/1. 249. 10–13: "Itaque Papistae, Cingliani, Anabaptistae et omnes qui iustitiam Christi ignorant aut non recte tenent, non possunt non facere ex Christo Mosen et legem et ex lege Christum. Sic enim docent : Fides in Christum iustificat quidem, sed simul servari etiam oportet praecepta Dei." See also *LW* 26:176–77; *WA* 40/1. 296. 23–297. 14.

133. *LW* 27:149; *WA* 40/1. 36. 21–24: "Caudis enim sunt coniunctae istae vulpes, sed capitibus diversae. Fingunt enim sese foris magnos hostes illorum, cum tamen intus vere idem sentiant, doceant ac defendant contra unicum illum salvatorem Christum qui solus est iustitia nostra."

134. *LW* 27:148; *WA* 40/1. 36. 3–4: "Sic enim docent Anabaptistae: Baptisma nihil est, nisi persona sit credens."

teaching on the gospel and faith in Christ, in terms of practice, they are no different from teachers of the law.

When the Anabaptists advocate a faith that requires human works for justification, Luther believes that they confuse Christ the justifier and the redeemer with Christ the example: "For the Anabaptists have nothing in their entire teaching more impressive than the way they emphasize the example of Christ and the bearing of the cross . . . . Therefore we must learn how to resist this Satan when he transforms himself into the appearance of an angel (2 Cor. 11:14), namely, by distinguishing when Christ is proclaimed as a gift and when as an example."[136] They make the same mistake as the "papists," who "do not look at and grasp the Christ who justifies but look at and grasp the Christ who performs works."[137] In this perspective, it is no surprise that Luther identifies the Anabaptists as "Neo-Arians."[138]

Another matter in which a group of Radical Reformers arouses Luther's criticism is the sacramental controversy.[139] Though the occasion is dissimilar, the same ground for criticism applies: their faith is empty because it does not have Christ in it. "The fanatical spirits today speak about faith in Christ in the manner of the sophists. They imagine that faith is a quality that clings to the heart apart from

---

135. *LW* 26:144; *WA* 40/1. 251. 34–37: "Atque ita Christus fide apprehensus non est Iustificator, nihil prodest gratia nec fides vera esse potest sine charitate (Aut ut Anabaptistae dicunt: sine cruce, passione et effusione sanguinis). Si vero adest charitas, opera et crux, fides vera est et iustificat." See also Luther's note on the Waldensians. Luther states that the Waldensians do not have the article of justification in its purity. They confess that human beings are saved by faith and grace, but their understanding of faith as a quality producing regeneration does not ascribe everything to faith in Christ alone. *LW* 54:176 (no. 2864b, dated 2 January 1533); *WA, TR* 3:37.

136. *LW* 27:34–35; *WA* 40/2. 43. 8–13: "Anabaptistae enim nihil habent speciosius in tota doctrina sua, quam quod exemplum Christi et crucem ita urgent . . . . Discendum est igitur, quo modo Satanae huic in speciem Angeli se transformanti resistamus, Nempe hoc modo, ut discernamus inter Christum, qui alias ut donum, alias ut exemplum praedicatur."

137. *LW* 26:247; *WA* 40/1. 389. 22–23: "intuentur [Papistae et omnes Iustitiarii] et apprehendunt Christum non iustificantem sed operantem."

138. *LW* 26:312; *WA* 40/1. 485. 13: "de Anabaptistis, Novis Arrianis."

139. *LW* 27:36–37; *WA* 40/2. 45. 23–28.

Christ."[140] Moreover, according to Luther, faith and Christ are not truly cemented to each other in the view of the Radical Reformers because they teach that Christ is present only spiritually in Christians, while he is really present in heaven. Luther judges that their notion of "spiritual" means no more than "speculative," since they believe that Christ is really present only in heaven.[141]

In bitter denunciation of these sectarian notions of faith and Christ's presence in Christians, Luther seeks to safeguard a faith that has Christ's real presence in the believer's heart: "He [Christ] is not sitting idle in heaven but is completely present with us, active and living in us."[142] Luther is convinced that "Christ and faith must be completely joined . . . . He lives and works in us, not speculatively but really, with presence and with power."[143]

Still more, the fanatics "deal with God apart from this Man [Jesus Christ],"[144] which Luther finds incongruent with a Christian faith in which Christ is really present. Going back to the fundamental issue of Christian faith, Luther submits that, in the matter of justification and struggling with the Law, sin, death, and the devil, people must look at "no other God than this incarnate and human God"[145] who "presents Himself to us as the Mediator."[146] Hence, faith without this

---

140. *LW* 26:356; *WA* 40/1. 545. 24–25: "Phanatici spiritus hodie loquuntur more Sophistarum de fide in Chrsitum somniantes eam esse qualitatem haerentem in corde, excluso Christo."

141. "The speculation of the sectarians is vain when they imagine that Christ is present in us 'spiritually,' that is, speculatively, but is present really in heaven." *LW* 26:357; *WA* 40/1. 546. 23–25: "Ideo vana est Sectariorum speculatio de fide qui somniant Christum spiritualiter, hoc est, speculative in nobis esse, realiter vero in coelis."

142. *LW* 26:356; *WA* 40/1. 545. 27–29: "Non enim sedet ociosus in coelis, sed praesentissimus est nobis, operans et vivens in nobis."

143. *LW* 26:357; *WA* 40/1. 546. 25–28: "Oportet Christum et fidem omnino coniungi . . . ; vivit autem et operatur in nobis non speculative, sed realiter, praesentissime et efficacissime."

144. *LW* 26:29; *WA* 40/1. 78. 19–20 : "Verum phanatici isti spiritus qui extra hunc hominem cum Deo agunt . . . ."

145. *LW* 26:29; *WA* 40/1. 78. 24–26: "Quare diligenter memineris, in causa Iustificationis seu Gratiae, ubi nobis omnibus res est cum Lege, Peccato, Morte, Diabolo, nullum Deum cognoscendum esse praeter hunc incarnatum et humanum Deum."

146. *LW* 26:30; *WA* 40/1. 79. 16–17: "qui [Christus] sese nobis Mediatorem proponit."

incarnate and human God, Jesus Christ, is an empty faith, namely, not a justifying faith.

Just as Luther remains resolutely opposed to the medieval Roman church despite its threat of excommunication in the matter of justification by faith in Christ alone, his determination is likewise unshaken when he earns the name and reputation among the sectarians of being "seditious," a "schismatic," and a "troublemaker."[147] "Today the name of Luther is completely contemptible to the world. Whoever praises me sins more gravely than any idolater, blasphemer, perjurer, fornicator, adulterer, murderer, or thief,"[148] Luther sighs. Notwithstanding, throughout these ordeals, he never wavers in his belief, in order to let God be God and to let Christ be God.

Indeed, Luther's cardinal argument always flows from and returns to justification by faith in Christ alone. He attributes this pattern of disputing with his opponents to his teacher, Paul: "As a very good teacher of faith, Paul always has these words on his lips: through faith, in faith, on the basis of faith in Christ Jesus, etc."[149] Elaborating on this theme, he states,

> Paul always has Christ on his lips and cannot forget Him. For he foresaw that in the world, even among those who claimed to be Christians, nothing would be less well known than Christ and His Gospel. Therefore he continually inculcates Him and presents Him to our view. Whenever he speaks about grace, righteousness, the promise, sonship, and the inheritance, he always makes a practice of adding "in" or "through" Christ, at the same time taking a sidelong look at the Law, as though he were saying: "We do not obtain these things through the

---

147. *LW* 26:450; *WA* 40/1. 676. 21–23: "quod pios hoc nomen et titulum in mundo oporteat gerere, quod seditiosi et schismatici ac infinitorum malorum autores sint."

148. *LW* 26:423; *WA* 40/1. 640. 26–28 : "Ita hodie nomen Lutheri est invisissimum mundo: qui me laudat, gravius peccat quam ullus idolatra, blasphemus, periurus, scortator, adulter, homicida, fur etc."

149. *LW* 26:351; *WA* 40/1. 539. 14–15: "Paulus ut optimus fidei doctor simper in ore habet istas voces: 'Per fidem,' 'in fide,' 'ex fide, quae est in Christo Iesu' etc."

Law and its works, much less through our own abilities or the works of human tradition, but through Christ alone."[150]

To this exposition, he adds, "It is as though he [Paul] were saying: 'Even though you have been troubled, humbled, and killed by the Law, the Law has not made you righteous. It has not made you sons of God, but faith has. Which faith? Faith in Christ. Thus, faith in Christ, not the law, creates sons of God.'"[151] As a consequence, there is only one demand for justification, which is faith, and "there is only one demand of faith, which is to believe in Jesus Christ."[152] Luther cannot compromise this faith with anything in this world because any compromise means denying and losing Christ, especially in his proper function.[153] That being so, Luther argues that "here

150. *LW* 26:394; *WA* 40/1. 600. 13–20: "Paulus semper in ore habet Christum, non potest eum oblivisci. Praevidit enim nihil minus notum fore in mundo, etiam apud eos, qui professuri essent se esse Christianos, quam Christum et eius Evangelium. Ideo perpetuo inculcat et ob oculos eum nobis ponit. Et quoties loquitur de gratia, iustitia, promissione, filiatione et haereditate, semper addere solet : 'In,' vel : 'per Christum', oblique per hoc etiam petens legem, Quasi dicat: Ista neque per legem aut opera ipsius (multominus per vires nostras aut opera humanarum traditionum), sed per solum Christum contingunt nobis."

151. *LW* 26:351; *WA* 40/1. 539. 22–25: "Quasi dicat [Paulus]: Etiamsi per legem sitis vexati, humiliati et occisi, tamen lex non fecit vos iustos, non fecit vos filios Dei, sed fides. Quae ? In Christum. Fides ergo in Christum efficit filios Dei, non lex."

152. *LW* 26:86; *WA* 40/1. 160. 19–20: "Unicum tantum fidei exemplum sit, scilicet credere in Iesum Christum."

153. Concerning this Christocentrism of Luther, we can agree with Carter Lindberg when he states that "according to Luther and the Lutheran Confessions the emphasis of the doctrine of justification lies upon Jesus Christ and his saving act, not upon a formalistic doctrine that is one part of a theological system." Lindberg, "Do Lutherans Shout Justification but Whisper Sanctification? Justification and Sanctification in the Lutheran Tradition," in *Justification and Sanctification: In the Traditions of the Reformation*. The Fifth Consultation on the First and Second Reformations Geneva, 13 to 17 February 1998, ed. Milan Opočenský and Páraic Réamonn (Geneva: World Alliance of Reformed Churches, 1999), 101. Lindberg insists that, as a "metalinguistic stipulation" of proclamation, justification by faith alone, without works of the law, presents the proclamation of Christ as unconditional promise and that, in this sense, "justification by faith alone is *the* Lutheran ecumenical proposal to the churches." Ibid. Dwelling on this issue, Lindberg contends that, "in the face of the current theological forgetfulness of the doctrine of justification, this cannot be overstated." Ibid. Carl Braaten also mentions as follows: "The doctrine of justification seems to be eclipsed in most current academic trends of theology, including the various liberationist and feminist models of theology, as well as the theologies of process and theologies of religious pluralism. The cumulative impact of these theologies has relegated theologies normed by the article of justification to a relatively marginal existence."

we are perfectly willing to have ourselves called 'solafideists' by our opponents."[154] Insofar as justification by faith in Christ alone is kept, Luther states that he is willing to make peace with his adversaries.[155]

To inquire into Luther's teaching on faith and love, this chapter started by demonstrating how Luther contemplates Paul's transition from faith to love in his Galatians commentary. Drawing attention to Luther's intentionality in dwelling on this shift, I sought to put into perspective Luther's teaching on faith and love as the overriding thematic pair in the whole of his commentary in the two dimensions—the dimensions of alien, passive, and perfect righteousness and holiness and of proper, active, and progressing righteousness and holiness. I then proceeded to examine his teaching on faith and love in the first dimension as the foundation of our further investigation.

This chapter, in particular, concentrated on delving into the polemical milieu in the Galatians commentary, out of which faith and love emerge as two incompatible theses. More specifically, Luther's astringent critical reflections on the doctrines of merit and *fides caritate formata* of the scholastic theologians, especially of Thomas Aquinas and Gabriel Biel, reveal the impetus behind Luther's designation of faith as antithetical to love. In addition, Luther's clash with the intra-Reformation Radicals intensifies his campaign to teach justification by faith in Christ alone. The Radical Reformers tend to return to the concept and practice of love that Luther criticizes in light of his teaching on justification by faith in Christ alone. Denouncing this inclination, Luther reaffirms the incompatibility of

---

Braaten, *Justification: The Article by Which the Church Stands or Falls* (Minneapolis: Fortress Press, 1990), 10.

154. The editors remark, "For the Latin *solarii*, used by Luther's detractors, we have borrowed the Wesleyan term 'solafideists.'" *LW* 26:138, n. 57. See *WA* 40/1. 241. 24–26: "Victoria peccati et mortis non est in opribus legis nec in voluntate nostra etc. Ergo est in solo Iesu Christo. Ibi libenter patiemur nos vocari Solarios ab adversariis."

155. *LW* 27:108; *WA* 40/2. 137. 11–14. See also *LW* 26:90–91; *WA* 40/1. 167. 18–168. 14.

faith with love in the matter of the justification of the unrighteous. Against this polemical backdrop, we will now move on to scrutinize the concrete content of Luther's reconceptualization of faith in chapter 3.

3

Faith: Sole Means of Grasping Christ

Faith in Christ: Three Major Features

With faith suitably comprehended as the only means of grasping the sole savior, Jesus Christ, for the justification of the unrighteous, let us now inquire into the specifics of Luther's reconceptualization of this justifying faith in Christ. Luther's reconceptualization of faith can be investigated in light of three primary traits: faith as knowing the truth of the heart about God, Christ, and self; faith as trusting God and Christ; and faith as being active in love. This chapter will then show how Luther's reconceptualization of faith assigns a redefined function to the law in the dimension of alien, passive, and perfect righteousness and holiness.

Faith as Knowing the Truth about God, Christ, and Self

Knowledge of God

Luther's use of the term "faith in Christ" includes some distinct features. First, indispensable to Luther's concept of faith is its sound intellectual underpinning. Faith as genuine knowledge of God and Christ—*fides quam credimus*—plays a pivotal role in the believer's grasping of Christ in the heart. The prevalent presumption that Luther's faith is mostly about trust is unfounded. Unfortunately, this misconception can lead to the idea of faith as a form of passionate conviction without substantial conceptual content. As far as the east is from the west, so far is Luther's faith from a merely subjective, personal, and psychological fervor or confidence. In lieu of such a fallacious notion, Luther professes that "faith is nothing else but the truth of the heart, that is, the right knowledge of the heart about God."[1]

This genuine knowledge of the heart about God is not reached by natural human reason, whereby sinners vainly invent distorted and idolatrous opinions about God. Faith comes to those who listen and respond to God's word about Jesus Christ. Faith is God's gift bestowed through the Holy Spirit.[2] In this sense, faith contrasts with natural human reason: "Reason cannot think correctly about God; only faith can do so."[3] Nonetheless, Luther does not intend to nullify

---

1. *LW* 26:238; *WA* 40/1. 376. 23–24: "Fidem nihil aliud esse quam veritatem cordis, hoc est, rectam cogitationem cordis de Deo."

2. "The knowledge of Christ and of faith is not a human work but utterly a divine gift." *LW* 26:64; *WA* 40/1. 130. 12–13: "Quare perpetuo inculcamus cognitionem Christi et fidem non esse rem aut opus humanum, sed simpliciter donum Dei."

3. *LW* 26:238; *WA* 40/1. 376. 24–25: "Recte autem de Deo cogitare non ratio, sed sola fides potest." With regard to this, Paul Althaus mentions as follows: "For Luther, there is a contrast between man's attempt to find and know God on his own and the knowledge and encounter which God gives through His word, and this contrast is of decisive importance. This theme runs through Luther's entire theology, in all phases of its development, and Luther repeatedly discusses it." Paul Althaus, *Die Theologie Martin Luthers*, 4th ed. (Gütersloh: Gerd Mohn, 1975),

human reason *per sebut* to emphasize that, unless it is illumined by faith, reason can never grasp Christ: "Christ is grasped, not by the Law or by works but by a reason or an intellect that has been illuminated by faith."[4]

Luther divides this intellectual feature of faith into the general (*generalis*) and the proper (*propria*) knowledge of God. The former knows that God is; the latter knows what God holds us to be and what exactly God intends to redeem the unrighteous:

> There is a twofold knowledge of God: the general and the particular. All men have the general knowledge, namely, that God is, that He has created heaven and earth, that He is just, that He punishes the wicked, etc. But what God thinks of us, what He wants to give and to do to deliver us from sin and death and to save us—which is the particular and the true knowledge of God—this men do not know.[5]

The intellectual feature of Luther's faith is essentially characterized as divinely illumined and soteriologically loaded special knowledge revealed in and through Jesus Christ. The knowledge of God and God's soteriological intention for human beings are closely

31; ET *The Theology of Martin Luther*, trans. Robert C. Schultz (Philadelphia: Fortress Press, 1966), 20. Philosophical and scholastic theological speculations about God also belong to this category. Due to the corrupted nature of human beings, this project is destined to fail. Sinners cannot confront the unveiled majesty and glory of God without being terrified. Therefore, the only salvific way to the knowledge of God is through Christ, through whom God revealed God's mercy and goodness and to whom Scripture bears witness. For a variety of expressions used by Luther to convey the antithesis between God in himself and God as he reveals himself, see Althaus, *Die Theologie Martin Luthers*, 33–34; ET *The Theology of Martin Luther*, 23–24. This issue is also related to Luther's understanding of God's hidden and revealed will. See also *LW* 54:377–78 (no. 5015, dated 21 May–11 June 1540); *WA, TR* 4:613–14; *LW* 54:385 (no. 5070, dated 11–19 June 1540); *WA, TR* 4:641–42.

4. *LW* 26:287; *WA* 40/1. 447. 15–16 : "Apprehenditur autem Christus non lege, non operibus, sed ratione seu intellectu illuminato fide."

5. *LW* 26:399; *WA* 40/1. 607. 28–32: "Duplex est cognitio Dei, Generalis et propria. Generalem habent omnes homines, scilicet, quod Deus sit, quod creaverit coelum et terram, quod sit iustus, quod puniat impios etc. Sed quid Deus de nobis cogitet, quid dare et facere velit, ut a peccatis et morte liberemur et salvi fiamus (quae propria et vera est cognitio Dei), homines non noverunt." In respect to this, see Althaus, *Die Theologie Martin Luthers*, 29–30; ET *The Theology of Martin Luther*, 17–19.

interwoven. On that account, to have the right knowledge of the heart about who God is and what God wills in conjunction with human beings is no trivial matter, but one of eternal life and death. Luther contends, for instance, against the devil's strategy of leading people into hell by reminding them of their sin and portraying God as an irate Judge and Christ as lawgiver, judge, and condemner, and thus causing them to lose hope of divine mercy.[6] Christians should be well equipped with "strategy and Christian wisdom, by which alone sin, death, and the devil are vanquished."[7]

Luther's crusade against false knowledge of God and Christ is straightforwardly expressed in his reprimand of the ideas of unformed faith, forming love, and the merits of congruity and condignity. According to these concepts, once a person has obtained grace by congruity, she goes on to perform works that merit eternal life by condignity. God becomes a "debtor" and "obliged by right to grant eternal life."[8] The scholastics assert that "this is not only a work of the free will, carried out externally; but it is performed in the grace that makes a man pleasing before God, that is, in love."[9] If justification is obtained in proportion to human works of love, the relation between human beings and God is that of creditor and

6. Luther's portrayal of the duel between God and the devil for human souls and consciences in the 1535 Galatians commentary makes an indelible impression, though this mental picture should not mislead readers to assume that Luther adopts a dualistic cosmology, as represented by Manichaeism, for instance. Nonetheless, as Heiko Oberman states, "the Reformer can only be understood as a late medieval man for whom Satan is as real as God and mammon." Heiko Oberman, *Luther: Man between God and the Devil*, trans. Eileen Walliser-Schwarzbart (New York: Image Books, 1992), xv. Luther's spiritual temptations and trials in terms of his idea of God's righteousness in conjunction with the justification of the ungodly communicate that every human being, without exception, is standing at the fork of a road leading to eternal life or eternal death and that it is critical for an impotent sinner to submit totally to God for justification.

7. *LW* 26:37; *WA* 40/1. 90. 15–17: "nisi hac arte ac sapientia Chrsitianorum resistat ei [diabolum], Qua sola peccatum, mors, diabolus vincuntur."

8. *LW* 26:124; *WA* 40/1. 220. 13–14: "Post gratiam autem iam factus est debitor et iure cogitur dare vitam aeternam."

9. *LW* 26:124; *WA* 40/1. 220. 15–16: "Quia iam non solum est opus liberi arbitrii, factum secundum substantiam, sed etiam factum in gratia gratificante, hoc est, in dilectione."

debtor, as in a mercantile or mercenary system. What makes this idea more troublesome still is that God is portrayed as "a wrathful Judge who damns sinners."[10]

The righteousness of this judging Father was envisaged as the righteousness by which a Superior Judge finds human beings guilty and condemns them to eternal death. This Judge expects satisfaction from each sinner and rewards each in proportion to her merit. No matter how much effort sinners make, there is no guarantee that the Judge will ever be satisfied. Thereby, human beings must remain endlessly uncertain and anxious about their ultimate destiny. This thought devises a capricious and unreliable God, who is not bound by any definite criteria for justifying one who performs works of love.

Luther can relate to this misconstrual because he himself suffered from such an image of God. His own taxing spiritual battles, which are dramatically depicted in his writings, were belayed by the illumination of a very different idea about the righteousness of God. This is well known as the so-called "tower experience."[11] Before

---

10. *LW* 26:365; *WA* 40/1. 558. 19–20: "ostendit [Lex] Deum iratum iudicem qui damnet peccatores."

11. See his brief autobiography in *Preface to the Complete Edition of Luther's Latin Writings*, 1545, *LW* 34:336–37; *WA* 54. 185. 12–186. 24. Luther also recounts his own experiences of struggling with the image of Christ as the Judge in his early monastic life. *LW* 26:154; *WA* 40/1. 265. 17–18. See also *LW* 26:70; *WA* 40/1. 137. 17–138. 8, *LW* 54:339–40 (no. 4422, dated 20 March 1539); *WA*, *TR* 4:305–306. The "tower experience" of Luther is so called because it occurred in the tower of the Black Cloister in Wittenberg (later Luther's house) at an undetermined date between 1508 and 1518.

As to Luther's own accounts of his "tower experience," namely, the exegetical discovery that propelled his Reformation breakthrough, see *LW* 54:339–40 (no. 4422, dated 20 March 1539); *WA*, *TR* 4:305–306, *LW* 54:193–94 (no. 3232c, dated 9 June–21 July 1532); *WA*, *TR* 3:228–29, *LW* 54:442–43 (no. 5518, dated Winter of 1542–1543); *WA*, *TR* 5:210. With regard to the date and nature of this experience, see Bernhard Lohse, *Luthers Theologie in ihrer historischen Entwicklung und in ihrem systematischen Zusammenhang* (Göttingen: Vandenhoeck & Ruprecht, 1995), 97–110; ET *Martin Luther's Theology: Its Historical and Systematic Development*, trans. and ed. Roy A. Harrisville (Minneapolis: Fortress Press, 1999), 85–95; Gottfried G. Krodel, "The Lord's Supper in the Theology of the Young Luther," *Lutheran Quarterly* 13, no. 1 (1961): 19–24; Alister E. McGrath, *Luther's Theology of the Cross: Martin Luther's Theological Breakthrough* (Malden, MA: Blackwell, 2004), 141–47.

this experience, Luther confesses, he did not want to confront what Paul says in Romans 1:17 ("in the gospel a righteousness of God is revealed"). Furthermore, he admits that his understanding of the righteousness of God revealed in the gospel augmented the feeling of enmity toward God in his heart.

However, after the experience, Luther is set free from the agony he suffered in his relation to God. He is cognizant of a new way of interpreting the righteousness of God. Luther recounts that the text in Romans 1:17 helped him see what righteousness Paul was pondering over. Luther connects the righteousness of God with the righteous and thereby finds himself liberated from the excruciating struggle over the righteousness of God in its absolute and abstract meaning. What is unambiguous in Paul's mention of the righteousness of God is that it is the kind of righteousness that makes sinners righteous. As a corollary, Luther declares that the righteousness of God in Romans 1:17 is not the kind of righteousness by which God judges and punishes each person without exception but the kind of righteousness by which God in his mercy makes sinners righteous.[12]

---

12. In fact, Luther consistently applies the identical interpretive rule for phrases constructed in the same grammatical structure, namely, a Hebrew genitive form. For instance, in his exposition of Rom. 1:16 ("it is the power of God"), Luther comments that "power of God is understood not as the power by which according to His essence He is powerful but the power by virtue of which He makes powerful and strong. As one says 'the gift of God,' 'the creature of God,' or 'the things of God,' so one also says the power of God, that is, the power that comes from God." *LW* 25:149; *WA* 56. 169. 29–170. 1. Luther also mentions as follows: "And here again, by the righteousness of God we must not understand the righteousness by which He is righteous in Himself but the righteousness by which we are made righteous by God." *LW* 25:151; *WA* 56. 172. 3–5. He also remarks that "'glory of God' is used in the same way as righteousness, wisdom, and virtue, that is, something which is given to us by God and because of which we can before Him glory in Him and about Him." *LW* 25:248; *WA* 56. 261. 20–22. See also *LW* 25:201; *WA* 56. 215. 16–17.

Luther accredits this liberating illumination to Paul, adding that it is affirmed by Augustine. Referring to Augustine's *On the Spirit and the Letter*, Luther describes that "therefore blessed Augustine writes in chapter 11 of *On the Spirit and the Letter*: 'It is called the righteousness of God because by imparting it He makes righteous people, just as 'Deliverance belongs to the Lord' [Ps. 3:8] refers to that by which He delivers.' Augustine says the same thing in chapter

The righteousness of God is the righteousness by which God forgives sinners, imputing righteousness to them and, at the same time, making them righteous without demanding any prior merit or works of love.[13] This freely justifying God is a graciously forgiving

9 of the same book." *LW* 25:151–52; *WA* 56. 172. 5–9. See St. Augustine, *De spiritu et littera* in *Patrologiae cursus completes*, Series Latina, 44–45, ed. Jacques-Paul Migne (Paris, 1865), 211. One of Luther's *Table Talks* also reveals that Augustine's concept of the righteousness of God reaffirmed his realization: "'That expression 'righteousness of God' was like a thunderbolt in my heart. When under the papacy I read, 'In thy righteousness deliver me' [Ps. 31:1] and 'in thy truth,' I thought at once that this righteousness was an avenging anger, namely, the wrath of God. I hated Paul with all my heart when I read that the righteousness of God is revealed in the gospel [Rom. 1:16, 17]. Only afterward, when I saw the words that follow—namely, that it's written that the righteous shall live through faith [Rom. 1:17]—and in addition consulted Augustine, was I cheered. When I learned that the righteousness of God is his mercy, and that he makes us righteous through it, a remedy was offered to me in my affliction.'" *LW* 54:308–309 (no. 4007, dated 12 September 1538); *WA, TR* 4:72–73.

In the transitional period of Luther's understanding of the righteousness of God, the role of Johann von Staupitz, vicar general of the German wing of the Augustinian eremites and Luther's father confessor, should not be forgotten. Martin Brecht supposes that Luther met Staupitz for the first time at Erfurt in April 1506. See Martin Brecht, *Martin Luther*, vol. 1, *His Road to Reformation*, trans. James L. Schaaf (Philadelphia: Fortress Press, 1985), 70–71; Heiko A. Oberman, *Forerunners of the Reformation: The Shape of Late Medieval Thought*, trans. Paul L. Nyhus (Cambridge: James Clarke & Co., 2002; Lutterworth, 1967), 138–40, 175–200.

13. Luther's emphasis on the conceptions of *reputare* and *imputare* is found in reference to Romans 3:28—4:25 or, more precisely, Romans 4:5 ("And to one who does not work but trusts him who justifies the ungodly, his faith is reckoned as righteousness."). Regarding Luther's use of the concepts of *reputare* or *imputare*, Lohse elucidates, "The question from where Luther appropriated these concepts has been discussed often. On occasion, Augustine could use them. Since Luther later made repeated reference to Augustine's significance for the origin and formation of his theology, and especially of his doctrine of justification, Augustinian influence is altogether probable. In Occamism as well the concept *reputare* was used, though as a rule the term *acceptare* was employed. This suggests that it was chiefly the biblical text itself that furnished Luther his stimulus. The Vulgate version of Romans 4:5 uses the term *reputare*: 'To the one . . . who trusts in him [God] who justifies the ungodly, his faith is counted as righteousness.' Luther thus interpreted the Greek term *logizetai* in terms of the Latin *reputatur*, reflecting the influence of the tradition of Augustine's and Occam's ideas on the subject. What is new is that Luther furnished the term *reputare/imputare* with its content. At issue is the 'acquittal' of the guilty one, or the promise of the grace of God." Lohse, *Luthers Theologie*, 277–78; ET *Martin Luther's Theology*, 261.

"The statements on justification constitute one of the standard themes of the Romans lecture. In ever-new thrusts Luther took up the Pauline utterances on this theme, always setting forth new aspects. For his theology, *iustificare* was of central importance. At the same time, certain concepts such as *reputare* or *imputare* were from the outset used synonymously. Luther took support from Augustine's treatise *De spiritu et littera*, which referred to God's righteousness not merely in terms of an attribute but also in terms of a divine gift. It may be that in its reference to God's righteousness and our justification, no other treatise of the ancient or

and loving God. With his new understanding of the righteousness of God, Luther perceives an image of God that is diametrically opposite to the image of God as the great Judge brandishing a righteousness that no human being could fathom nor satisfy. Luther embraces God who mercifully forgives, loves, and freely justifies.

The righteousness of God is not retributive or punitive but salutary. Instead of requiring works of love and merits, this God wants to bless; instead of sentencing sinners with the death penalty, this God wants to give life. The only thing a person needs to do to be justified is to believe and receive the gift of God, which is Christ. Exclaiming that "the righteousness of God" became the sweetest words to him, Luther underscores out of his own experience the significance of accurate knowledge of God.

This true knowledge of God is necessary, especially since human beings must remember that they are sinners, not reprobates eternally forsaken by God. Insofar as human beings acknowledge themselves as sinners, they respond correctly to God's initial outreach towards them. Hence, this true knowledge of God precludes both lifelong despair on account of the gravity of sins and overconfidence in one's own goodness. Instead, it rests on a hope firmly rooted in God's promise, as the gospel teaches that Christian hope is built "on the promises of God and on nothing else"—certainly not on one's own merits.[14]

---

medieval church comes as close to Luther's Reformation theology as this anti-Pelagian treatise. Yet in citing it Luther at important points characteristically went beyond what Augustine intended: he interpreted Augustine in line with his own new theological position . . . . As for his caution, Luther's statements on Romans 2:13 are particularly instructive. He described 'to justify' (*iustificare*) and 'to declare' or 'reckon as righteous' (*reputare*) as synonymous. In addition, he construed *declarare* or *decernere* ['adjudge'] as parallel concepts. Through such identification Luther accented God's sole authorship as well as the nature of justification as gift: it can only be received in faith." Lohse, *Luthers Theologie*, 87–88; ET *Martin Luther's Theology*, 75. Lohse describes how Luther further developed these ideas in particularly detailed and thorough fashion in his exposition of Romans 4:7.

14. *LW* 52:243; *WA* 10^1/1. 672. 7–10.

Knowledge of Christ

Just as the true knowledge of God is crucial in Luther's reconceptualized faith, so is "the true and correct definition of Christ,"[15] as opposed to "a false idea of Christ."[16] In fact, the true knowledge of God and the true knowledge of Christ are not separated, because the former is revealed only through Christ.

> God does not want to be known except through Christ; nor . . . can He be known any other way. Christ is the Offspring promised to Abraham; on Him God founded all His promises. Therefore Christ alone is the means, the life, and the mirror through which we see God and know His will.[17]

Christ reveals who God really is when Christ is correctly presented as the sole redeemer and justifier: "Through Christ God announced His favor and mercy to us. In Christ we see that God is not a wrathful taskmaster and judge but a gracious and kind Father, who blesses us."[18]

Consequentially, Luther's concern for the genuine knowledge of Christ in light of God's will for human salvation is no less important than his concern for the true knowledge of God the Father.[19] If

---

15. *LW* 26:39; *WA* 40/1. 93. 18–19: "Atque ea est causa, cur tam vehementer urgeam, ut bene et proprie Christum definire discatis." Luther also continuously uses "the genuine Christ" (*verus Christus*) or "genuine knowledge of Christ" (*vera cognitio Christi*). See also *LW* 27:17; *WA* 40/2. 19. 30, 31–32.

16. *LW* 27:33; *WA* 40/2. 41. 29: "falsam opinionem de Christo."

17. *LW* 26:396; *WA* 40/1. 602. 18–21: "Quia Deus non vult (neque enim aliter potest Ioh. 1.) cognosci nisi per Christum. Is semen est Abrahae promissum, in quod fundavit Deus omnes suas promissiones. Quare solus Christus medium, vita et speculum est, per quod videmus Deum et cognoscimus eius voluntatem."

18. *LW* 26:396; *WA* 40/1. 602. 22–24: "Per Christum annunciat nobis Deus suum favorem et misericordiam. Videmus in Christo Deum non esse iratum exactorem et iudicem, sed faventem et clementissimum Patrem, qui benedicit."

19. Luther's concern for the genuine knowledge of Christ is primarily soteriologically oriented, as is his concern for the genuine knowledge of God: "Now what is it that we teach? That Christ, the Son of God, redeemed us from our sins and from eternal death by His death on the cross." *LW* 26:453; *WA* 40/1. 679. 30–31: "Quid docemus igitur? Christum, filium Dei, morte crucis redemisse nos a peccatis nostris et morte aeterna."

human beings succumb to the rationalizations of their fallen reason, which speak doubts in their hearts about Christ as their sole savior and oblige them to claim their own works of the law for justification, then they are ruining their chance for salvation.

The ideas of unformed faith, forming love, and the merits of congruity and condignity jeopardize and obscure the true definition of Christ as the sole savior and justifier. When Christ is mixed up with the law, he becomes the minister of sin, wrath, and death. Christ is neither a tyrant nor "a lawgiver, a teacher of the Law, or a taskmaster, who teaches good works and love."[20] Christ is the "sweet Savior and High Priest" and not a "stern Judge."[21] Christ is "the Dispenser of righteousness and of eternal life" and "the Lord of the Law, sin, and death."[22]

Faith must further know that, for the justification of sinners, Christ, the most righteous one, became "a curse and a sinner of sinners," so that sinners may become righteous.[23] If this twofold paradox is not accepted by faith, the knowledge of God and Christ and the knowledge of self are as good as useless.

Only by taking over the totality of human sin could Christ become "Law to the Law, sin to sin, and death to death, in order that He might redeem me from the curse of the Law, justify me, and make me alive. And so Christ is both: While He is the Law, He is liberty; while He is sin, He is righteousness; and while He is death, He is life."[24]

---

20. *LW* 26:148; *WA* 40/1. 256. 25–26: "Legislator seu Doctor et exactor legis, Hoc est qui docet bona opera et charitatem." See also *LW* 26:367–69; *WA* 40/1. 561. 27–563. 26; *LW* 26:372; *WA* 40/1. 568. 25–29.

21. *LW* 26:38; *WA* 40/1. 92. 12–15: "Qui tum Christum proprie definire posset et eum magnificare ac inspicere ut dulcissimum Salvatorem ac Pontificem, non ut saeverum Iudicem, is iam vicisset omnia mala ac iam esset in regno coelorum."

22. *LW* 26:151; *WA* 40/1. 260. 26–27: "Donator iustitiae et viae aeternae."

23. *LW* 26:278; *WA* 40/1. 434. 35–36: "neque absurdum sit eum [Christum] dicere maledictum et peccatorem peccatorum."

24. *LW* 26:163; *WA* 40/1. 278. 22–25: "Ideo autem factus est [Christus] Lex legi, peccatum peccato, mors morti, ut me a maledicto legis redimeret, iustificaret et vivificaret me. Sic utroque modo Christus dum est Lex, est libertas, dum est peccatum, est iustitia, dum est mors, est vita."

As a result, there is a collision between two antithetical things in one person—Jesus Christ:

> Not only my sins and yours, but the sins of the entire world, past, present, and future, attack Him, try to damn Him, and do in fact damn Him. But because in the same Person, who is the highest, the greatest, and the only sinner, there is also eternal and invincible righteousness, therefore these two converge: the highest, the greatest, and the only sin; and the highest, the greatest, and the only righteousness . . . . In this duel, therefore, it is necessary for sin to be conquered and killed, and for righteousness to prevail and live.[25]

Luther portrays this rivalry as a "very joyous duel" (*iucundissimum duellum*): "The Law battling against the Law, in order to become liberty to me; sin battling against sin, in order to become righteousness to me; death battling against death, in order that I might have life."[26] Christ is "a poison against the Law, sin, and death, and simultaneously a remedy to regain liberty, righteousness, and eternal life."[27] Christ is a conqueror not a minister of sin. God's grace "accuses the accusing Law and damns the damning Law" and brings life to sinners as the "death which kills death."[28]

From this standpoint, Luther recognizes that the emphasis of the scholastics' teaching is reversed: they bring Christ, as the example, to the fore, and, consequently, they portray him as a minister of sin not

---

25. *LW* 26:281; *WA* 40/1. 438. 32–439. 26: "Quo modo in hac persona duo extreme contraria concurrant. Invadunt eam non solum mea, tua, sed totius mundi peccata praeterita, praesentia et futura et conantur eam damnare, sicut etiam damnant. Sed quia in eadem illa persona quae est summus, maximus et solus peccator, est quoque aeterna et invicta iustitia, ideo congrediuntur illa duo: summum, maximum et solum peccatum et summa, maxima et sola iustitia. Hic alterum cedere et vinci necessario oportet . . . . Ideo necesse est in hoc duello vinci et occidi Peccatum et Iustitiam vincere et vivere."

26. *LW* 26:164; *WA* 40/1. 279. 25–27: "lex contra legem pugnet, ut sit mihi libertas peccatum contra peccatum, ut sit mihi iustitia mors contra mortem, ut habeam vitam."

27. *LW* 26:163; *WA* 40/1. 278. 28–29: "Christus simul est venenum contra legem, peccatum et mortem et remedium pro libertate, iustitia et vita aeterna."

28. *LW* 26:156; *WA* 40/1. 267. 18–21. See also *LW* 26:163; *WA* 40/1. 278. 12–14: "Lex enim Decalogi ligabat me. Contra illam nunc habeo aliam legem, scilicet gratiae, quae non est mihi Lex neque ligat, sed liberat me."

a conqueror of sin.[29] They obscure the true knowledge of Christ as the greatest sinner and a curse for all humanity and downplay the joyous duel that points to the deity of Christ in his proper function.[30] Because of this error, it is critical to draw a clear line between the proper and the accidental functions of Christ, since Christ as the example does not redeem humanity of its sins. If people miss this point, they miss salvation; therefore, it is pivotal to accurately conceive of Christ according to his two functions.[31] Against the backdrop of this intellectual facet of Luther's reconceptualized faith, we can correctly capture what he means when he claims that Christ "justifies us by our knowledge of Him."[32]

Knowledge of Self

The other side of this intellectual feature of Luther's conception of faith, knowledge of self, is no less decisive in the matter of eternal life or death. Unless human beings truly know who and what they are in the sight of God, they will choose humanly devised ways of salvation, not God's ways. Cognizant of this human tendency toward overconfidence, self-righteousness, and minimization of sin, Luther reiterates that our natural dispositions and unbelief are the very things that lay bare the gravity of human sinfulness.

Entangled in their own sinfulness, human beings do not even recognize how sinful they are or what degree of redemption they need. Reason does not illumine them with the knowledge of their sin. Therefore, if human beings cannot, on their own, perceive how

29. *LW* 26:278; *WA* 40/1. 434. 21–28.
30. *LW* 26:278; *WA* 40/1. 435. 16–20: "Quaecunque peccata Ego, Tu et nos omnes fecimus et in futurum facimus, tam propria sunt Christi, quam si ea ipse fecisset. In Summa, Oportet peccatum nostrum fieri Christi proprium peccatum, aut in aeternum peribimus. Hanc veram cognitionem Christi quam tradiderunt Paulus et Prophetae, obscurarunt impii Sophistae."
31. *LW* 26:369; *WA* 40/1. 563. 27–28, *LW* 27:27; *WA* 40/2. 25–30.
32. *LW* 26:380; *WA* 40/1. 579. 14: "qui [Christus] primum notitia sui iustificat nos."

sinful they are, they must observe how God has handled human sin. When they look upon Christ on the cross, they will see clearly the magnitude of the ransom paid for their sins, which was none other than God the Son. Christ on the cross exposes the depth of their sins and their desert, which includes the eternal wrath of God and the entire kingdom of Satan.[33] On realizing who and what they truly are, and, at the same time, how greatly God has loved them, human beings readily surrender their will to God and submit themselves to God's way of salvation.

In this way, it becomes obvious that the knowledge of God and Christ and the knowledge of self compose the core of the intellectual facet of Luther's faith. Or, more precisely, Christ stands at the midpoint between God and human beings, revealing who and what God is to them as reflected in a mirror, which is Christ himself. He likewise displays who and what human beings were originally created to be and how far away they (as sinners) have gone astray from their original condition.

Faith as Trusting in God and Christ

Faith requires exact knowledge of God, Christ, and self. Nonetheless, this is not everything Luther has in mind concerning true faith. Another trait of true faith is trust of heart (*fiducia cordis*), about which Luther says that "if it is true faith, it is a sure trust and firm acceptance in the heart."[34] According to Luther, faith as mere understanding and assent to what we hear needs to be differentiated from faith as an inner conviction and "a sure confidence that takes hold of Christ."[35]

---

33. *LW* 26:33; *WA* 40/1. 84. 12–24.
34. *LW* 26:129; *WA* 40/1. 228. 33–34: "Sed si est vera fides, est quaedam certa fiducia cordis et firmus assensus quo Christus apprehenditur."
35. *LW* 26:348; *WA* 40/1. 533. 30: "certa fiducia quae apprehendit Christum." In his exposition of the Creed in the *Betbüchlein* (*Personal Prayer Book*), Luther also draws a distinction between faith as intellectual assent and faith as trust in God: "Faith is exercised in two ways. First, a faith about

Luther insists that even the devil has faith in the form of assent to propositions or articles of belief, yet this faith certainly does not save the devil but instead brings condemnation.[36] "Therefore when I take hold of Christ as I have been taught by faith in the Word of God, and when I believe in Him with the full confidence of my heart—something that cannot happen without the will—then I am righteous through this knowledge."[37]

This aspect of trust in Luther's conception of faith (*fides qua credimus*) accentuates the fact that sinners are justified neither solely by their subjective faith (faith without Christ) nor merely by virtue of the objective fact of Christ's death and resurrection itself—which, without question, has a universal soteriological efficacy—apart from faith. For Luther, trust of the heart signifies that no one is justified vicariously by the faith of someone else, and no one is justified without personally appropriating Christ's universally valid soteriological work and merit.

For this reason, in his conception of faith as trust in Christ, Luther calls attention to the notion of *pro me* or *pro nobis*.[38] This aspect has

---

God meaning that I believe that what is said about God is true . . . . This kind of believing is more an item of knowledge or an observation than a creed. The second kind of faith means believing in God—not just that I believe that what is said about God is true, but that I put my trust in him, that I make the venture and take the risk to deal with him, believing beyond doubt that what he will be toward me or do with me will be just as they [the Scriptures] say." *LW* 43:24; *WA* 10/2. 389. 1–8. Luther goes on to say: "So that little word *in* is well chosen and should be noted carefully; we do not say, I believe God the Father, or I believe about the Father, but rather, I believe *in* God the Father, *in* Jesus Christ, *in* the Holy Spirit. And this faith is given only by God himself and through it we confess the deity of Christ and of the Holy Spirit." *LW* 43:25 (italics original); *WA* 10/2. 389. 16–20.

36. "Faith justifies not as a work, or as a quality, or as knowledge, but as assent of the will and firm confidence in the mercy of God. For if faith were only knowledge, then the devil would certainly be saved because he possesses the greatest knowledge of God and of all the works and wonders of God from the creation of the world. Accordingly faith must be understood otherwise than as knowledge. In part, however, it is assent." *LW* 54:359–60 (no. 4655, dated 16 June 1539); *WA, TR* 4:420.

37. *LW* 27:23; *WA* 40/2. 27. 14–16: "Quando igitur fide in verbum Dei edoctus apprehendo Christum et tota fiducia cordis (quod tamen sine voluntate fieri non potest) credo in eum, hac noticia iustus sum."

been misunderstood by those who submit that Luther's doctrine of justification by faith is to blame for generating "a salvation-egoistical isolated I," thus engendering a Christian faith that works privately and individualistically in seclusion from society or community.[39] Such an interpretation reflects a misunderstanding of Luther.

Luther's point is that Christian faith is not vicarious, but dependent on a person's own trust in God's promise and faithfulness in keeping it. This aspect of trust is vital because the content of God's promise is not revealed in its fullness, and Christ who is grasped in the heart through faith is invisible to human eyes.[40] Even more, it is about God's being available for me as well as for others and about God's solicitous attentiveness toward me, not by my request but on God's own initiative. It also delivers the message that the universal God is God for each person, including me. God is not an object for speculative inquiry but a Being who approaches with a personal, soteriological concern for me.

It is easy to envision others' salvation, but when it comes to the issue of my salvation, it is very difficult for me to believe that Christ will save me without my own contribution of good works. It seems

---

38. *LW* 26:179; *WA* 40/1. 299. 29–30 (emphasis original): "Lege igitur cum magna Emphasi has voces: 'ME', 'PRO ME', et assuefacias te, ut illud, 'ME' possis certa fide concipere et applicare tibi."

39. Oswald Bayer, "The Being of Christ in Faith," *Lutheran Quarterly* 10, no. 2 (1996): 144. Bayer also stresses that interpreting *pro me* as an "epistemological problem" is intrinsic to the modern question of subjectivity that has occurred "under the considerable influence of Kantian philosophy." According to Bayer, in the neo-Protestantism stamped by Kant, the Reformation *pro me* has been misused as a methodological principle. In this misuse, every objectivity concerning the object that faith narrates is diminished; instead, one's holding fast to one's own certainty is amplified. Denouncing this misinterpretation, Bayer reads Luther's faith as that by which one holds onto *God's promise*. Ibid. See also Jaroslav Pelikan, "Luther Comes to the New World," in *Luther and the Dawn of the Modern Era: Papers for the Fourth International Congress for Luther Research*, ed. Heiko A. Oberman (Leiden: Brill, 1974), 4–7.

40. "But it [the formal righteousness of Christians] is faith itself, a cloud in our hearts, that is, trust in a thing we do not see, in Christ, who is present especially when He cannot be seen." *LW* 26:130; *WA* 40/1. 229. 19–21: "Sed [formalis nostra iustitia est] ipsa fides et nebula cordis, hoc est, fiducia in rem quam non videmus, hoc est, in Christum qui, ut maxime non videatur, tamen praesens est."

too good to be true, so people easily generalize about this good news but critically fail to personalize it. On that account, Luther states that he applies *pro nobis* or *pro me* to himself, declaring that "this applying is the true power of faith."[41] The phrase "for me" is surely comforting and produces assurance that God really wants to help me, which gives power to persevere in the tribulations of this life that can seem to contradict God's promise.

Just as a ring encases a gem, when faith embraces Christ and secures his presence in the heart, then God's acceptance of sinners and imputation of Christ's righteousness become effective.[42] Therefore, faith, Christ, and acceptance or imputation must always be joined together. In this sense, faith is never a mechanical device designed to bring about justification by itself. This idea exposes one of the chief features of Luther's faith in Christ, that is, complete Christ-oriented passivity in our submission to God's master plan: "We work nothing, render nothing to God; we only receive and permit someone else to work in us, namely, God."[43]

Even the reception of faith itself is not considered action on our part, since reception is possible only by the Holy Spirit's work in us. The reception of faith is passive. That being so, in answering whether faith is a human work because it is we who assent and trust, Luther is clear: it is the Holy Spirit's work, not ours. "The knowledge of Christ and of faith is not a human work but utterly a divine gift; as God creates faith, so He preserves us in it."[44]

---

41. *LW* 26:177; *WA* 40/1. 297. 21–22: "Istaque applicatio est vera vis fidei."
42. *LW* 26:132; *WA* 40/1. 233. 16–19: "Est et hic notandum, quod ista tria, Fides, Christus, Acceptio vel Reputatio, coniuncta sunt. Fides enim apprehendit Christum et habet eum praesentem includitque eum ut annulus gemmam, Et qui fuerit inventus cum tali fide apprehensi Christi in corde, illum reputat Deus iustum."
43. *LW* 26:5; *WA* 40/1. 41. 18–20: "Ibi enim nihil operamur aut reddimus Deo, sed tantum recipimus et patimur alium operantem in nobis, scilicet Deum."
44. *LW* 26:64; *WA* 40/1. 130. 12–14: "Quare perpetuo inculcamus cognitionem Christi et fidem non esse rem aut opus humanum, sed simpliciter donum Dei. Qui ut creat, ita conservat fidem in nobis."

Accordingly, Christian righteousness is a passive and alien righteousness. This passive righteousness is distinct from political, ceremonial, legal, or works-righteousness. The righteousness of faith—the most excellent righteousness—is imputed to us by God through Christ without works. Hence, it is a merely passive righteousness in contrast to those enumerated above, which are active.[45] To receive the passive divine righteousness, we do nothing but assent and trust: namely, to know and believe that Christ has been made for us wisdom, righteousness, sanctification, and redemption.[46]

Here an important differentiation between two kinds of righteousness comes in: "The righteousness of the Law" or the "earthly and active righteousness" and the "heavenly and passive" or the "Christian" righteousness.[47] We can earn the former through

---

45. *LW* 26:4; *WA* 40/1. 41. 15–18: "Ista autem excellentissima iustitia, nempe fidei, quam Deus per Christum nobis absque operibus imputat, nec est politica nec ceremonialis nec legis divinae iustitia nec versatur in nostris opribus, sed est plane diversa, hoc est mere passiva iustitia (sicut illae superiores activae)."

With regard to the expression "iustitia dei passiva," Oberman emphatically points to a subtle but very critical difference between the two terms of *property* and *possession*, especially in reference to their usages in the history of Roman law and in marriage, though he does not pursue the details. "To summarize the Roman law tradition in one sentence: *aliquid proprium* [proprietatem] *habere est iure possidere.* Possessio stands with ususfructus over against proprietas or dominium." Oberman, *The Dawn of the Reformation: Essays in Late Medieval and Early Reformation Thought* (Grand Rapids: Eerdmans, 1992), 122, n. 47. Oberman clarifies that the righteousness granted is not one's *proprietas* (property) but rather one's *possessio* (possession). Oberman explicates, "Whereas one root of the understanding of the new righteousness as *possessio* rather than as *proprietas* is to be found in Roman civil law, the other root can be discerned more specifically in the application of marriage imagery—*contractus, sponsalia, consummatio*—with the exchange of possession between the partners." Ibid., 121–22; 125, n. 52.

"The meaning of the words 'extra nos' comes through in connection with the term possession . . . . The 'extra nos' is therefore directed against the separation of iustitia Christi in us from the iustitia Dei over against us and thus directed against the fides caritate formata." Oberman, *The Dawn of the Reformation*, 122. Luther explains, "To be outside of us means not to be out of our powers. Righteousness is our possession, to be sure, since it was given to us out of mercy. Nevertheless, it is foreign to us, because we have not merited it." *LW* 34:178; *WA* 39/1. 109. 1–3: "Extra nos esse est ex nostris viribus non esse. Est quidem iustitia possessio nostra, quia nobis donata est ex misericordia, tamen est aliena a nobis, quia non meruimus eam."

46. *LW* 26:8; *WA* 40/1. 47. 19–20.

47. *LW* 26:8; *WA* 40/1. 46. 27–29: "iustitiam legis" or "iustitiam terrenam et activam" vis-à-vis "iustitiam christianam" or "iustitia coelestis et passiva."

good works; we can receive the latter from heaven. We can perform the former by works; we can accept the latter by faith. This passive, divine, heavenly, and eternal righteousness, which is the righteousness of Christ, is not gained through human performance; we simply receive it, if only we have faith.[48] The concepts of passivity and receptivity are intricately tied to the notion that human salvation is all about God's promise, God's power to carry it out, and God's faithfulness in keeping God's promise.

One of the well-known motifs in Luther's theology, the "joyful exchange" (der fröhliche Wechsel), brings to the fore his concept of passive or alien righteousness.[49] This motif is theologically pivotal: it signifies that, when Christ is present in Christians through faith, he brings all his divine blessings—sonship, inheritance of eternal life, righteousness, and everything good—and grants them to Christians without asking for anything in return; Christians lack nothing, but they should not boast, for it is not their own doing.

48. With regard to this issue, the Holl-Ritschl debate on justification as impartation (*sanatio*) versus imputation draws special attention. Whereas Karl Holl perceives an analytical judgment in Luther's idea of God's justification of sinners and views justification as impartation (*sanatio*), Ritschl contends that, at the core of the conception of justification in the Lutheran and Reformed theologians, there lies not an analytical but a *synthetic* judgment. Karl Holl, *Die Rechtfertigungslehre in Licht der Geschichte des Protestantismus* (Tübingen: T. G. B. Mohr (Paul Siebeck), 1906), 9 and Albrecht Ritschl, *The Christian Doctrine of Justification and Reconciliation: The Positive Development of the Doctrine*, trans. and ed. H. R. Mackintosh and A. B. Macaulay (Eugene, OR: Wipf & Stock, 2002), 80. See also Alister E. McGrath, *Iustitia Dei: A History of the Christian Doctrine of Justification*, 3rd ed. (Cambridge: Cambridge University Press, 2005), 224–25; Althaus, *Die Theologie Martin Luthers*, 210; ET *The Theology of Martin Luther*, 241–42.

49. *LW* 26:284; *WA* 40/1. 443. 23: "feliciter commutans" (by happily exchanging). See also *LW* 26:292; *WA* 40/1. 454. 26–455. 14. The locus classicus for the happy exchange between Christ and the Christian is Luther's treatise *The Freedom of the Christian* (1520). *LW* 31:351–52; *WA* 7. 25. 28–26. Having Christ in faith is like allowing no one else into the Bridegroom's chamber except the Bridegroom and the Bride (*LW* 26:137–38; *WA* 40/1. 241. 12–16) or enjoying the fortunate exchange between Christ and a Christian (*LW* 26:167–68; *WA* 40/1. 283. 19–284. 33). Luther goes even further: Having Christ in faith, in fact, creates a relationship between a Christian and Christ that is more intimate than the relation between husband and wife. Faith couples Christ and a Christian as Christ's own flesh and bones more intimately than a husband is coupled to his wife (*LW* 26:168; *WA* 40/1. 285. 27–286. 17). In faith we live "an alien life, that of Christ" in us (*LW* 26:170; *WA* 40/1. 287. 28–29).

Faith as Being Active in Love

In the Galatians commentary, Luther indeed seeks to refute the accusations that he and his followers condemn good works by teaching that pious practices do not add up to forgiveness of sins. He also realizes that even many of his own followers have misunderstood his doctrine of justification by faith in Christ alone.[50] Luther finds himself face to face with a dilemma: to preach or not to preach his doctrine of justification. There is danger on both sides.

> If grace or faith is not preached, no one is saved; for faith alone justifies and saves. On the other hand, if faith is preached, as it must be preached, the majority of men understand the teaching about faith in a fleshly way and transform the freedom of the spirit into the freedom of the flesh.[51]

50. The dilemma Luther already confronted during his lifetime as to different interpretations on his doctrine of justification certainly did not end with his death. His followers argued over what is a correct statement of Luther's doctrine of justification, and the internal debates that almost split Lutheranism in the decades following Luther's death were for the most part debates over details surrounding this doctrine. The settlement that occurred in 1577 in the *Formula of Concord* was achieved only because of the exclusion of one side of the argument—the more radical Philippists—following the so-called Crypto-Calvinist controversy. These intra-Lutheran debates have continued to this day. With regard to the historical sketch of these debates primarily centering on diverse interpretations of justification and sanctification in the Lutheran tradition, see Carter Lindberg, "Do Lutherans Shout Justification but Whisper Sanctification? Justification and Sanctification in the Lutheran Tradition," in *Justification and Sanctification: In the Traditions of the Reformation*. The Fifth Consultation on the First and Second Reformations Geneva, 13 to 17 February 1998, ed. Milan Opočenský and Páraic Réamonn (Geneva: World Alliance of Reformed Churches, 1999), 97–112. Answering "No!" to the question whether Lutherans shout justification but whisper sanctification, Lindberg claims that the tone and substance for centuries of suspicion that Luther preached "cheap grace" is unattested. Ibid., 98, 112.

    With regard to the relation between Luther's teaching on faith and love and Lutheran acceptance of this teaching, on the one hand, and contemporary ecumenical endeavors, on the other, see Michael Root, "The Implications of the *Joint Declaration on Justification* and its Wider Impact for Lutheran Participation in the Ecumenical Movement," in *Justification and the Future of the Ecumenical Movement: The Joint Declaration on the Doctrine of Justification*, ed. William G. Rusch (Collegeville, MN: Liturgical Press, 2003), 47–60, esp. 47–56. On the subject of arguments among Lutherans over how rightly to relate faith and works of love or justification and sanctification, Root points out that they go back at least to the Saxon visitation of the late 1520s. Ibid., 54. See Günther Gassmann and Scott Hendrix, *Fortress Introduction to the Lutheran Confessions* (Minneapolis: Fortress Press, 1999), 173.

51. *LW* 27:48; *WA* 40/2. 60. 27–31: "Itaque utrimque periculum est . . . . Si gratia seu fides non praedicatur, nemo fit salvus, Fides enim sola iustificat et salvat. Contra, si praedicatur Fides,

There are two types of hypocrites: those who are diligent but wrongly seek self-righteousness through the performance of good works in love and those who discard good works in their laziness, idleness, and sluggishness. The latter mistakenly conjecture that since faith without works justifies, they are exempt from all works; they can believe and do as they please.[52]

ut necesse est eam praedicari, maior pars hominum carnaliter intelligit doctrinam de fide et libertatem spiritus in libertatem carnis rapit."

Luther expresses the same concern in his exposition of John 15:12 ("This is my commandment, that you love one another as I have loved you."): "Wherever faith is not preached and is not given primary importance, wherever we do not begin by learning how we are united with Christ and become branches in Him, all the world concentrates only on its works. On the other hand, wherever faith alone is taught, this leads to false Christians, who boast of their faith, are baptized, and are counted among the Christians but give no evidence of fruit and strength. This makes it difficult to preach to people. No matter how one preaches, things go wrong; the people always hedge. If one does not preach on faith, nothing but hypocritical works result. But if one confines one's preaching to faith, no works ensue. In brief, the outcome is either works without faith or faith without works. Therefore the sermon must address itself to those who accept and apprehend both faith and works." *LW* 24:249; *WA* 45. 688. 31–689. 4.

52. *LW* 27:30; *WA* 40/2. 36. 24–37. 23. In fact, the motive for writing *Treatise on Good Works* is a good example that clearly exposes this concern of Luther. When Luther nailed the ninety-five theses on the Castle Church on August 31, 1517, he was ready to publicly criticize the practice of selling indulgences as well as any kind of theological or dogmatic support for this kind of practice, claiming that no works could contribute to one's attainment of justification. By that time, Luther was assured that only by faith in Jesus Christ could a person be justified and saved. Luther's lectures on Paul's Epistle to the Romans between 1515 and 1516 certainly made an impact upon his conviction.

The question here is whether, when Luther berated wrong kinds of works prevalent during his time as religious practices among Christians and stepped forward prophetically to proclaim justification by faith in Christ alone, he stopped there, without presenting any alternative concerning the issue of works. As mentioned above, Luther acknowledges that the situation he faced led him to further development and articulation of his position. In the wake of making public his ninety-five theses, Luther found himself drawn into the middle of an inflamed controversy that he had never expected to induce. He realized that he had no other choice but to confront the external challenges. Criticism and attacks from the Roman Church and its political supporters whirled around him. One of the most pressing issues that instigated such criticism was the question of whether his doctrine of justification by faith alone led to moral insensitivity and delinquency. In other words, how did the doctrine relate to or incorporate love or good works of love? Luther's response to such immanent criticisms and challenges—whether friendly and sympathetic or vehement and antipathetic—appears in the *Treatise on Good Works*. This was supposed to be a sermon, but when he began to write it, it grew into a small booklet and was published in early 1520.

What makes this monograph noticeable is Luther's recourse to none other than the Decalogue as the most fitting expository material for communicating his reconceptualization

Luther witnesses how people abuse their Christian freedom by giving in to evil desires—greed, pride, envy, violence, and destruction—and indulging in debauchery instead of faithfully performing their duties as Christians, serving one another in love, with abstinence, humility, empathy, peace, and tolerance. Luther labels this freedom of the flesh "misbehavior" (*indignitas*). He does not hesitate to heap parental reproaches on those who so misbehave like "swine that trample pearls underfoot (Matt. 7:6)."[53] To them, borrowing from Paul, Luther fiercely proclaims, "'Not so, you wicked men,' says Paul. 'It is true that faith alone justifies, without works; but I am speaking about *genuine faith*, which, after it has justified, will not go to sleep but is *active through love.*'"[54] Christian life is "not the life of the flesh, although it is a life in the flesh; but it is the life of Christ, the Son of God, whom the Christian possesses by faith."[55]

of faith and love. The material speaks for itself in arguing that there is only one kind of good work and that all good works of love derive from the divinely given Ten Commandments, which Luther construes as an elaboration of Jesus Christ's commandment to love. What this implies is that any kinds of humanly invented laws that do not originate out of these Ten Commandments possess no authority over Christians. However, what makes this treatise special is that Luther uses the fact that the Ten Commandments consist in two Tables to present the true good works in light of the relationship between faith and love, which in turn redefines and reorganizes the relationship between the law and the gospel. The well-known *Freedom of a Christian* appeared several months after the *Treatise on Good Works*, in which the conceptual and structural traits of Luther's teaching on faith and love are demonstrated with substantial succinctness. The polemical background of Luther's writing of the *Treatise on Good Works* demands a re-estimation of its significance in his theology, especially from the vantage point of his teaching on faith and love. Furthermore, reading this treatise along with *The Freedom of a Christian* will enrich our understanding of the teaching.

53. *LW* 27:48; *WA* 40/2. 60. 35–37.
54. *LW* 27:30 (italics mine); *WA* 40/2. 37. 23–25: "Non sic, impii, dicit Paulus. Verum est sine operibus solam fidem iustificare, Sed *de fide vera* loquor, *quae*, postquam iustificaverit, non stertet ociosa, Sed est *per Charitatem operosa*." Luther also emphasizes that true faith is "true and living" and "arouses and motivates good works through love." *LW* 27:30; *WA* 40/2. 37. 14–15: "[fides est] vera et vivax. Ea est, quae exercet et urget bona opera per Charitatem." According to Luther, faith is "the impulse and motivation of good works or of love toward one's neighbor." *LW* 27:30; *WA* 40/2. 38. 9–10: "Hic dicit eam [fidem] esse impultricem et effectricem bonorum operum seu Charitatis erga proximum."

Alleging that "it has been a long time since anyone taught a more pious and sound doctrine of good works than we do today,"[56] Luther presents himself as a true advocate of love or good works. Against "Satan's hatred for truly good works," "it is as necessary that faithful preachers urge good works as that they urge the doctrine of faith. For Satan is enraged by both and bitterly resists them."[57] Those who stand upon an accurate doctrine of justification by faith in Christ alone are in a better position to love than those who seek self- or works-righteousness. Vindicating himself as a champion of genuine faith and genuine love, Luther proclaims these as the two constitutive components in a complete Christian life: "the chief characteristics of a Christian man, that his whole life and being is faith and love."[58]

What is noteworthy, however, is Luther's indication (in his exposition of Galatians 5:6) that his identity as the true champion of both faith and love and his conviction that faith and love are the two constituents of a complete Christian life are not self-inventions but represent the authoritative teachings of Paul:

> As I have said, therefore, Paul is describing the whole of the Christian life in this passage: inwardly it is faith toward God, and outwardly it is love or works toward one's neighbor. Thus a man is a Christian in a total sense: inwardly through faith in the sight of God, who does not need our works; outwardly in the sight of men, who do not derive any benefit from faith but do derive benefit from works or from our love.[59]

55. *LW* 26:172; *WA* 40/1. 290. 30–31: "ista vita non est carnis, licet sit in carne, sed *Christi* filii Dei, quem fide possidet Christianus."

56. *LW* 26:84; *WA* 40/1. 157. 30–31: "nemo multis retro saeculis melius ac magis pie de operibus docuit, quam nos hodie etc."

57. *LW* 27:53; *WA* 40/2. 66. 28–33: "aeque necessarium est, ut pii doctores tam diligenter urgeant doctrinam de bonis operibus, quam doctrinam de fide. Satan enim utrique infensus est et acerrime resistit . . . . Quod vero Satan doctrinam etiam vere bonorum operum oderit . . . ."

58. *LW* 51:75; *WA* 10/3. 13. 16–17: "Lieben freünd, ir habt gestern gehört die haüptstuck eins Christenlichen menschen, wie das ganze leben und wesen sei glauben und lieben."

59. *LW* 27:30; *WA* 40/2. 37. 26–30: "Igitur sicut dixi, totam vitam Christianam Paulus hoc loco pingit, scilicet esse Fidem erga Deum intus et Charitatem seu opera erga proximum foris, Ut sic homo absolute sit Christianus, intus coram Deo per fidem, qui operibus nostris non indiget, foris coram hominibus, quibus fides nihil prodest, sed opera seu Charitas."

Here the third pivotal facet of Luther's teaching on faith emerges: faith active in love.[60] It becomes clear that Luther's emphasis on the passive receptivity of faith does not imply any sterility or infecundity of faith. What is critical in the dimension where a sinner becomes a righteous person is that faith passively receives the gift of God, Christ the Savior. However, in the dimension where a righteous person lives out the Christian life, faith that remains passive and receives what is given to it proves itself false. True faith, according to Luther, renews and changes one's heart, creating a new person and producing a new perspective and lifestyle. If faith does not bear its fruits, it is not a genuine faith. Luther asserts that a counterfeit faith damages people and that it is much better not to have such a faith. He describes a counterfeit faith as follows:

> A counterfeit faith is one that hears about God, Christ, and all the mysteries of the incarnation and redemption, one that also grasps what it hears and can speak beautifully about it; and yet only a mere opinion and a vain hearing remain, which leave nothing in the heart but a hollow sound about the Gospel, concerning which there is a great deal of chatter. In fact, this is no faith at all; for it neither renews nor changes the heart. It does not produce a new man, but it leaves him in his former opinion and way of life. This is a very pernicious faith, and it would be better not to have it.[61]

A Christian who has a renewed heart and has become a new person by a true faith is characterized, among many others, by an active life of serving others, since a true faith never stops being active in giving what it receives in absolute passivity from God in and

---

60. See Carter Lindberg, *Love: A Brief History through Western Christianity* (Malden, MA: Blackwell, 2008), 118–32.

61. *LW* 26:269; *WA* 40/1. 421. 21–27: "Inter fidem fictam et veram. Ficta est quae audit de Deo, Christo et omnibus mysteriis incarnationis et redemptionis et apprehendit illas res auditas et pulcherrime de eis novit loqui, et tamen mera opinio et inanis auditus manet qui tantum relinquit bombum in corde de Evangelio, de quo multa garrit, re vera autem non est fides, quia non renovat nec immutat cor, non generat novum hominem, sed relinquit eum in priori sua opinione et conversatione. Estque haec fides valde perniciosa, quam satius esset non habere."

through Christ.[62] Here, Luther does not neglect to further elucidate the fundamental divergence between his stance and that of the scholastics on the claim that faith without works is worthless. He delineates the difference as follows:

> The papists and the fanatics take this to mean that faith without works does not justify, or that if faith does not have works, it is of no avail, no matter how true it is. That is false. However, faith without works—that is, a fantastic idea and mere vanity and a dream of the heart—is a false faith and does not justify.[63]

This remark unequivocally displays Luther's distinction between his interpretation and that of his opponents. The latter interpret "without works" as signifying the insufficiency of faith, which requires love to form it. Faith that is not formed by love is incomplete and insufficient; hence, faith without love is not a justifying faith.

In contrast, Luther's interpretation of "without works" presupposes that true, living faith includes true love. Luther makes it clear that even this love does not function as a causal or collaborative element of justification, nor does it form or complete faith. Rather, love, figuratively speaking, lies dormant and in this sense, faith that justifies

---

62. Luther considers good works as signs of the effectiveness of God's grace and election: "For it is not works that justify a person, but a righteous person does righteous works. Yet the works show that faith is being put into practice and that through them it increases and becomes fat, as it were. For while Abraham carries out this act of obedience, and is circumcised together with his household, faith thinks of God, who gives us His promises and accepts us. Thus Peter (2 Peter 1:10) tells us to certify our election by doing good works, for they bear witness that grace is effective in us and that we have been called and elected. On the other hand, an inactive faith—a faith that is not put into practice—quickly dies and becomes extinct; but when faith has become extinct, it is doubtful whether we have been elected. But he who progresses in the unremitting exercise of his faith concludes: 'I am not in the host that is against Christ; I am for Christ. I do not deny the Word, and I do not persecute the church. Hence I have been called to the kingdom of God and have been elected.'" LW 3:169–70; WA 42. 669. 22–33.

63. LW 26:155; WA 40/1. 266. 15–19: "Quare et nos dicimus fidem sine oepribus nihili esse et inanem. Hoc Papistae et phanatici sic intelligunt: Fidem absque operibus non iustificare Vel fidem quantum vis veram, si opera non habeat, nihil valere. Hoc falsum est, Sed fides sine operibus, id est, phanatica cogitatio et mera vanitas et somnium cordis, falsa est et non iustificat." Luther also states, "The fools don't know what faith is. They suppose it's just a lifeless idea." LW 54:290 (no. 3895, dated 20 June 1538); WA, TR 3:692.

sinners can be said to exclude love and works of love in the dimension of alien, passive, and perfect righteousness and holiness. However, in the dimension of proper, active, and progressing righteousness and holiness, love emerges and must emerge in a Christian's being and life as an activated power and the fruit—visible and tangible—produced out of inner necessity from true faith. In this way, love serves as the criteria for distinguishing true faith from counterfeit faith. Only within the context of this careful semantic and logical analysis, according to Luther, can it be rightly argued that faith without works is useless, since such a faith is not even qualified to be called "faith." It is a counterfeit faith, so it does not justify.[64]

It is striking that Luther makes so little use of the terminology developed to such an extraordinary degree in scholasticism, with its numerous distinctions regarding faith, such as unformed faith, infused faith, acquired faith, and so on. Relinquishing all of these meticulous differentiations, Luther considers only two: genuine faith and counterfeit faith. Genuine faith grasps Christ with illumined reason and a purified heart and bears fruit through love; counterfeit faith does not. A detailed examination of Luther's reconceptualization of love will be the main topic in chapters 4 and 5.

Before we turn to chapter 4, there is one last thing to discuss here: another aspect of the relationship between faith and the law or, more precisely, between Christ and the law. As described above, once Christ properly forms the center of inquiry for Luther's conception of faith, this faith in Christ alone sheds new light on the function of the law. It becomes clear that, for justification itself, no law whatsoever is necessary in the dimension of alien, passive, and perfect righteousness and holiness. When the debate is about righteousness, life, and eternal salvation, the law must, therefore, be removed from sight completely.

---

64. Speaking with Paul, Luther says that not "the fruits of faith make the faith to be faith" but "faith makes the fruit to be fruit." *LW* 54:74 (no. 458, dated early in the year 1533); *WA, TR* 1:199.

No law whatsoever is necessary insofar as it is deemed an effectual cause of justification. However, the previous statement must be properly qualified, because Luther's thought on the law in relation to faith in Christ does not stop here. In his discourse on justification, Luther acknowledges the necessity of the law in its appropriate service to Christ. Insofar as the law no longer competes with Christ over the issue of justification of the ungodly, Luther says that it prompts sinners to flee to and find a haven in Jesus Christ through faith. This will be our next topic.

The Law and Christ in the Dimension of Passive Righteousness and Holiness

What has been emphasized in Luther's idea of the law is "a double use of the law": "the civic use" and "the theological or spiritual" use.[65] Regarding this double use of the law, Luther mentions, "We say that the Law is good and useful, but in its proper use, namely, first, as we have said earlier, to restrain civic transgressions; and secondly, to reveal spiritual transgressions."[66]

Luther's primary concern lies in the theological and spiritual function of the law that produces unadulterated knowledge of the identity of human beings as sinners subject to and worthy of eternal wrath and death. The central message is that human beings are unable

---

65. *LW* 26:308; *WA* 40/1. 479. 17: "duplicem esse legis usum. Alter ciilis est." *LW* 26:309; *WA* 40/1. 480. 32: "Alter legis usus est Theologicus seu Spiritualis." See also *LW* 26:361; *WA* 40/1. 551. 17–552. 15.

66. *LW* 26:312–13; *WA* 40/1. 485. 26–28: "dicimusque legem bonam et utilem, sed in suo usu, scilicet Primum ad cohercendas, ut diximus supra, civiles transgressiones, Deinde ad revelandas spirituales transgressiones." Luther expands on these different uses of the law: "In society, on the other hand, obedience to the law must be strictly required. There let nothing be known about the Gospel, conscience, grace, the forgiveness of sins, heavenly righteousness, or Christ Himself; but let there be knowledge only of Moses, of the Law and its works. When these two topics, the Law and the Gospel, are separated this way, both will remain within their limits. The Law will remain outside heaven, that is, outside the heart and the conscience; and, on the other hand, the freedom of the Gospel will remain outside the earth, that is, outside the body and its members." *LW* 26:116; *WA* 40/1. 208. 14–20.

to carry out their own salvation. Under the law, they come to know who they truly are. This spiritual function or ministry of the law is the primary purpose of the law of Moses. Luther calls it "a ministry of sin" and "a ministry of wrath and death." "Just as the Law reveals sin, so it strikes the wrath of God into a man and threatens him with death."[67] Furthermore, this function includes multiplying and increasing sin, especially in conscience. Once sinners become aware of their own impending eternal death, they want God not to exist. In this way, the law produces subjective hatred of (extreme hate toward) God; hence, through the law, sin is "increased, inflated, inflamed, and magnified."[68]

The "proper and absolute use of the law" is, first of all, to lead sinners to accurate self-knowledge.[69] Like a powerful heavy-duty hammer, the law is used "to break, bruise, crush, and annihilate this beast with its false confidence, wisdom, righteousness, and power," to the point of despair.[70] What then is the value of this effect—this

---

67. *LW* 26:150; *WA* 40/1. 260. 15–17: "Porro si Lex est ministerium peccati, sequitur, quod sit etiam ministerium irae et mortis, Quia Lex, ut revelat peccatum, ita incutit homini iram Dei et minatur ei mortem."

68. *LW* 26:314; *WA* 40/1. 487. 23–27: "Iam autem revelato peccato et morte vellet Deum non esse. Atque ita lex summum odium Dei affert. Et hoc non solum est ostendi et cognosci lege peccatum, sed etiam per ostensionem augeri, inflari, incendi et magnificari peccatum." In his article entitled "The Role of Law in How a Christian Becomes What He/She Is," Bernhard Erling raises the question of how the spiritual/theological function of the law can be understood in relation to children, whose conscience is not mature enough to deal with its theological and spiritual function. He mentions that, according to Luther, children are brought to faith primarily in baptism; however, their coming to conscious faith in compliance with God's predestination and the obedience that faith prompts comes later. When this change is effected, the law will play its indispensable role. To substantiate his argument, Erling cites Luther's comments on Romans 7:8: "The Law revives and sin begins to make its appearance when the Law begins to be recognized; then concupiscence which had lain quiet during infancy breaks forth and becomes manifest. When this concupiscence breaks forth in adolescence, it immediately shows what had been lying hidden in the child." (*LW* 25:337; *WA* 56. 348. 8–10). Erling, "The Role of Law in How a Christian Becomes what He/She is," in *Freiheit als Liebe bei Martin Luther, Freedom as Love in Martin Luther: 8th International Congress for Luther Research in St. Paul, Minnesota, 1993, Seminar 1 Referate/Papers*, eds. Dennis D. Bielfeldt and Klaus Schwarzwäller (Frankfurt am Main: Peter Lang, 1995), 63–78.

69. *LW* 26:310; *WA* 40/1. 482. 12: "proprius et absolutus legis usus."

humiliation, wounding, and crushing of obstinate human overconfidence by the hammer? Luther answers: "Grace can have access to us."[71] In order to subdue and humble the flesh—the entire human nature of a person, with reason and all its powers—God makes use of that hammer, the law, so that human beings learn that they have been destroyed and damned by their fallen nature. In perceiving themselves as sinners, they are then humbled before God.[72] Once humbled, they cry out for the help of the mediator and savior. There comes, then, at the appropriate time, the saving word of the gospel, since it is "the nature of God to exalt the humble, to feed the hungry, to enlighten the blind, to comfort the miserable and afflicted, to justify sinners, to give life to the dead, and to save those who are desperate and damned."[73]

In its theological and spiritual function, therefore, "the Law is a minister and a preparation for grace."[74] The law is "like a stimulus that drives the hungry toward Christ"[75] and "makes us ready for Christ."[76] The sinner is no longer "under the Law" but "under grace."[77] According to Luther, this is "the beginning of salvation."[78] The law

70. *LW* 26:314; *WA* 40/1. 488. 22–24: "Ideo oportet Deum adhibere malleum istum, legem scilicet quae frangat, contundat, conterat et prorsus ad nihilum redigat hanc beluam cum sua vana fiducia, sapientia, iustitia, potentia etc."

71. *LW* 26:314; *WA* 40/1. 488. 13–14: "Ad hoc prodest, ut gratia ad nos possit habere aditum."

72. *LW* 26:131; *WA* 40/1. 231. 21–22: "Ut homo primum erudiatur lege ad cognitionem sui."

73. *LW* 26:314; *WA* 40/1. 488. 16–19: "Estque Dei natura exaltare humiles, cibare esurientes, illuminare caecos, miseros et afflictos consolari, peccatores iustificare, mortuos vivificare, desperatos et damnatos salvare etc."

74. *LW* 26:314; *WA* 40/1. 488. 14: "Sic ergo lex ministra et praeparatrix est ad gratiam."

75. *LW* 26:345; *WA* 40/1. 529. 9–10: "Lex est quasi impulsor quidam qui impellit esurientes ad Christum."

76. *LW* 26:329; *WA* 40/1. 509. 22: "Atque sic nos Christi capaces reddit [lex]."

77. *LW* 26:7; *WA* 40/1. 45. 19–20: "nec amplius est sub lege, sed sub gratia." This aspect of contrition seems to take an indispensable role in Luther's understanding of receiving the righteousness of Christ. Although contrition is not a condition for receiving the righteousness of Christ, it is a necessary forestage to receiving it. Here a question is raised whether contrition is a human work. Luther makes it clear that even to be able to sigh is evidence of the presence of the Holy Spirit in the repentant person. In this sense, contrition, like faith, is God's gift, not a human work.

kills so that God can create new life in sinners: the killing function of the law is in the service of creating new life.[79] The best use of the law is "to employ it to the point that it produces humility and a thirst for Christ."[80] As a corollary, "it is being used correctly; and so, through the Gospel, it serves the cause of justification. This is the best and most perfect use of the Law."[81] Strictly only in this sense, "the Law with its function does contribute to justification—not because it justifies, but because it impels one to the promise of grace and makes it sweet and desirable."[82]

Accordingly, although Luther emphatically affirms that "it is impossible for Law and grace to exist together"[83] and that the four things (the law, the promise, faith, and works) must be distinguished perfectly,[84] he also clarifies that the law does not at all go against the promise of God.[85] Speaking with Paul, Luther endorses not only the usefulness of the law but also its necessity.[86] Clearly, Luther's

---

78. *LW* 26:132; *WA* 40/1. 232. 21: "Hoc initium est salutis." Even though we must be very cautious in specifying any *ordo salutis*, Luther certainly mentions in many places that the proper use of the law is to lead humbled sinners to Christ—the beginning of salvation. See *LW* 26:126–27; 131–32; 208; 215; 260; 380; 389–90; 401; see also the 1519 Galatians Commentary, *LW* 27:371–72; *WA* 2:591.

79. *LW* 26:335; *WA* 40/1. 517. 26: "Legis ergo officium est tantum occidere, sic tamen, ut Deus possit vivificare."

80. *LW* 26:329; *WA* 40/1. 509. 27–28: "Ille ergo usus legis optimus est, eatenus scilicet ea posse uti, quatenus humiliat et facit sitire Christum."

81. *LW* 26:316; *WA* 40/1. 490. 22–24: "tum est [lex] in vero usu, Sicque servit per Evangelium ad iustificationem. Et is est optimus ac perfectissimus legis usus."

82. *LW* 26:315; *WA* 40/1. 489. 27–29: "Lex cum suo officio etiam prodest ad iustificationem, Non quidem iustificans, sed urgens ad promissionem gratiae et faciens eam dulcem ac desiderabilem."

83. *LW* 26:445; *WA* 40/1. 669. 15–16: "impossibile est Legem et Gratiam simul posse existere."

84. "Therefore these four things must be distinguished perfectly. For just as the Law has its proper task, so the promise has its proper task. Refer doing to the Law, believing to the promise. As widely as the Law and the promise are distinct, so far apart are faith and works—even if you understand 'doing works' in a theological sense." *LW* 26:272; *WA* 40/1. 426. 22–26: "Oportet itaque ista quatuor distincta esse perfectissime. Nam sicut Lex habet suum proprium officium, ita et promissio habet suum proprium officium. Ad legem refer facere, ad promissionem credere. Quam late ergo lex et promissio distincta sunt, tam late fides et opera distincta sunt, etiamsi Theologice intelligas operari."

85. *LW* 26:329; *WA* 40/1. 510. 13: "Igitur lex non est contra promissa Dei."

intention is not to abolish the law. He campaigns on behalf of the correct function and use of the law, wherein it is used to impel sinners to Christ and to faith in Christ alone. Luther professes that "the Law is good, holy, useful, and necessary, so long as one uses it in a legitimate way. Its civic use is good and necessary, but its theological use is the most important and the highest."[87]

This law is abused, first, when one attributes to it the power to justify, and second, when one despairs out of the ignorant belief that the law is only a custodian until Christ comes. One should know that "the Law humbles us, not to harm us but to save us. For God wounds in order to heal; He kills in order to make alive."[88] To "sense fear and horror before the wrath of God and at the same time to hope in His steadfast love" must remain firmly joined together so that people are neither overconfident nor despairing.[89]

How long, then, is the dominion of the law to last? It lasts until the coming of "the Offspring," Jesus Christ.[90] Luther takes into consideration the duration of the law in two ways: literal and spiritual.[91] In a literal way, "the Law and the whole Mosaic system of worship came to an end"[92] "through the coming of Christ into the flesh at a time set by the Father."[93] In a spiritual way, the duration

86. *LW* 26:335; *WA* 40/1. 517. 15: "legis utilitatem et necessitatem."

87. *LW* 26:348; *WA* 40/1. 534. 12–14: "Est [lex] igitur bona, sancta, utilis et necessaria, modo ea quis legitime utatur. Civilis usus ipsius bonus est et necessarius, Theologicus vero praecipuus et summus est."

88. *LW* 26:348; *WA* 40/1. 534. 16–17: "legem humiliare non in perniciem sed salutem. Deus enim percutit, ut sanet, occidit, ut vivificet etc." Luther expresses that though God's proper function is to make alive, God first kills to let sinners live. See *LW* 26:345; *WA* 40/1. 528. 35–529. 14.

89. *LW* 26:340; *WA* 40/1. 523. 15–16: "metuere et perhorrescere iram Dei et similiter sperare in misericordia eius."

90. *LW* 26:316–17; *WA* 40/1. 491. 23–24: "Quamdiu ergo dominium legis durare debet? Donec veniat Semen."

91. *LW* 26:316; *WA* 40/1. 492. 11: "Durationem temporis legis vel ad literam vel spiritualiter intellige."

92. *LW* 26:317; *WA* 40/1. 492. 15–16: "ad literam desiit lex et totus ille cultus Mosaicus."

93. *LW* 26:360; *WA* 40/1. 550. 20–21: "per adventum Christi in carnem tempore a Patre praefinito."

of the law is tied to its spiritual or theological function, namely, disclosing the iniquity of sinners, accusing them, revealing the wrath and judgment of God, increasing and intensifying their transgressions, terrifying them and driving them to despair, and thereby impelling them to Christ through the word of the gospel. The law, then, has reached "the prescribed manner, time, and purpose" and the time has come for it to withdraw and let Christ take its place.[94]

So far, chapters 2 and 3 have inquired into Luther's reconceptualization of faith in the dimension of alien, passive, and perfect righteousness and holiness. This faith excludes love—in particular, the scholastic concept of love—in the matter of a sinner's justification. We also have learned that this faith invalidates the law insofar as it trespasses into the jurisdiction of Christ and competes with him in a duel over justification of the unrighteous. Nevertheless, Luther does ascribe a redefined function to the law, namely, a theological or spiritual function, as a stimulus for sinners to flee to Christ. In this function, the law impels sinners to yearn for the gospel containing Christ, thus paving the way to faith in him. We also have explored the polemical contexts in which Luther discredited the scholastic notions of merit and *fides caritate formata* and railed against the intra-Reformation Radicals on their ideas and practices of faith and love.

Inveighing against his antagonistic polemists, Luther consistently underscores the cemented relationship between faith and Jesus Christ effecting God's imputation of righteousness to sinners and God's new creation in them. Chapter 3, in particular, investigated the three cardinal features of Luther's reconceptualized faith: faith as knowing the truth of the heart about God, Christ, and self; faith as trusting in

---

94. *LW* 26:317; *WA* 40/1. 492. 20–21: "praescriptum modum, tempus et finem habet lex."

God and Christ; and faith as being active in love. This last feature will be our guiding theme in the following two chapters.

4

Faith and Love in the Dimension of Active Righteousness and Holiness

The reason faith excludes love in the matter of justification of sinners in the dimension of alien, passive, and perfect righteousness and holiness is that faith in Jesus Christ alone can make sinners righteous. In consequence, even the love that Luther deems biblical and genuine neither contributes to nor collaborates with faith in the matter of justification. That being so, it is not surprising that Luther adamantly renounces the scholastic concept of love, which he reckons as unbiblical and diametrically opposed to true faith.

In the matter of a Christian's daily living in the dimension of proper, active, and progressing righteousness and holiness, Luther now turns to biblical and genuine love. He highlights this love as the fruit of faith and the incarnate faith. What must be kept in mind throughout the discussion on Luther's reconceptualized love is that it is nothing more and nothing less than the fruit of faith in Christ. This is the reason love is operative in a compatible manner with faith in the dimension of proper, active, and progressing righteousness and holiness. Luther's delineation of this new concept of love unveils the dynamics among faith, love, Christ, and the law, which differ from those observed in the dimension of alien, passive, and perfect righteousness and holiness.

In order to examine the features of these new dynamics, chapter 4 will explore Luther's views on Christian freedom, the law of Christ as the law of love, the twofold way of fulfilling the law, and some christological terminologies and concepts that provide the grounds for the reintroduction of love as a thesis in harmony with faith. In addition, chapter 4 will dig into three of Luther's favorite metaphors illustrating the relationship between faith and love and laying bare the deliberateness and delicacy with which Luther correlates faith and love.

From "Freedom From" to "Freedom For"

One of the serious theological challenges that arise as we inquire into Luther's redefined love is: for what purpose did and does Jesus Christ save sinners? This question is legitimate and momentous because Luther's discourse on a sinner's justification by faith in Christ alone and the consequential freedom from sin, the law, and eternal death plainly indicates that this "freedom from" is not the final destination in the freedom of a Christian. Luther believes that the Christian freedom in faith from the law, sin, and death is not the end but rather the impetus for Christian freedom in love for service. These two aspects of the Christian freedom are indissolubly bound to each other. This conviction provides good reason for Luther to redesign faith and love as two compatible theses.

As mentioned in chapter 2, Luther marks Galatians 4:8-9 as a transitional point in Paul's treatment of his two overriding agendas: faith, justification, Christ, and Christians' alien righteousness (Christ's righteousness), on the one hand, and love, works of the law, Christians' proper righteousness, and sanctification, on the other. Dwelling on "faith working through love" (Galatians 5:6), Luther uses the passage to highlight the core of his doctrine of faith and love in the dimension of proper, active, and progressing righteousness and holiness.[1] Explicating Paul in a brief summary, Luther draws "a conclusion about the Christian life," namely, that it is "faith working through love."[2]

What is notable in Luther's explication of this passage is that it resembles a conceptual and structural miniature of his tractate *The Freedom of a Christian*. Moreover, it is one of the biblical passages, whose divergent exposition split Luther from the medieval Roman church in a sharp debate surrounding faith and love. Seizing an opportune moment to articulate his teaching on faith and love, Luther crystallizes it in a way that strongly resonates with *The Freedom of a Christian*.[3] The intended focal point of Luther's concepts of faith, love, and their relationship is clearly revealed in the transition from "freedom from" to "freedom for." The freedom from sin—unbelief, self-centeredness, bound will—through faith in Christ,

---

1. With regard to the relation of faith and love in Paul, Luther states, "Concerning the verse in Galatians [5:6], 'faith working through love,' we also say that faith doesn't exist without works. However, Paul's view is this: Faith is active in love, that is, that faith justifies which expresses itself in acts. Now, it is assumed by some that the fruits of faith make the faith to be faith, although Paul intends something different, namely, that faith makes the fruit to be fruit. Faith comes first and then love follows." *LW* 54:74 (no. 458, dated early in the year 1533); *WA, TR* 1:199.

2. *LW* 27:30; *WA* 40/2. 37. 11–13: "brevi velut Epiphonemate concludit, quid sit ipsa Vita Christiana . . . fides per Charitatem operosa."

3. In this treatise, Luther's salient argument in the matter of the Christian as both "a perfectly free lord of all, subject to none" and "a perfectly dutiful servant of all, subject to all" centers on 1 Cor. 9:19, Rom. 13:8, Gal. 4:4, and Phil. 2:6-7. See *LW* 31:344; *WA* 7. 49. 27–50. 4: Paul states "in I Cor. 9[:19], 'For though I am free from all men, I have made myself a slave to all,' and in Rom. 13[:8], 'Owe no one anything, except to love one another.' Love by its very nature is ready to serve and be subject to him who is loved. So Christ, although he was Lord of all, was 'born of woman, born under the law' [Gal. 4:4], and therefore was at the same time a free man and a servant, 'in the form of God' and 'of a servant' [Phil. 2:6-7]." The whole treatise is aiming to prove that these seemingly contradicting ideas are in fact concordant with each other.

out of the necessity of its inner dynamic, leads to the freedom for bearing fruits of faith in love in relation to God, neighbor, and self with eager willingness and genuine spontaneity. Christian freedom through faith in Christ, according to Luther, is characterized as follows.

First, Christian freedom is freedom from "sin, death, the curse, hell, and the wrath and judgment of God."[4] Second, faith in Christ brings forth freedom from the law because Christ is the fulfillment of the law in its entirety. Explicating this liberating faith, Luther zeroes in on Christ who, breaking into human history through his assumption of human nature, came once for all at a set time to carry out his soteriological mission for sinful human beings. In fulfilling the law through his death and resurrection, Christ has abrogated the law with all its effects and accordingly delivered the entire human race from sin and eternal death as sentenced under the law.[5] Third, the proper function of the law is to make human beings guilty and defendants; Christian freedom sets Christians free from guilt and from the accusations of the plaintiff, the law.[6]

Fourth, faith in Christ engenders freedom from being troubled by a guilty conscience according to the law in the matter of the attainment of justification and salvation. In reference to Galatians 4:7, Luther explains that "to be a slave . . . means to be sentenced and imprisoned under the Law, under the Wrath of God, and under death; it means to acknowledge God, not as God or as Father but as a tormentor, an enemy, a tyrant. This is truly to live in slavery and in a Babylonian captivity, and to be cruelly tormented in it."[7] Again, he writes that "the more someone performs works under the Law, the

---

4. *LW* 26:293; *WA* 40/1. 455. 32–34: "promissus Spiritus. Est autem Spiritus libertas a lege, peccato, morte, maledictione, inferno, ira et iudicio Dei etc." See also *LW* 26:4; *WA* 40/2. 4. 13–14.

5. *LW* 26:349; *WA* 40/1. 534. 35–536. 12.

6. *LW* 26:345; *WA* 40/1. 529. 11: "legis proprium officium est nos reos facere."

more he is oppressed by its slavery."[8] Self-righteous people who seek to be justified and redeemed through the law are not under a physical slavery, which lasts for a time, but "a perpetual slavery."[9] They are never at peace because they are always in doubt about the will of God and afraid of death and of the wrath and judgment of God.[10] Christian freedom is the opposite of this. Therefore, justification by faith in Christ alone is nothing but "an issue between either endless, eternal freedom or slavery."[11]

Fifth, Christians are free from any obligation to observe the law out of the notion of pleasing God for the sake of reward (*merces*) for one's labor[12] or to avoid penalties and fearful punishment.[13] Sixth, even for justified Christians, the law continues to increase a guilty feeling in conscience, which Luther calls harsh "theological slavery."[14]

---

7. *LW* 26:390; *WA* 40/1. 594. 16–19: "servum esse . . . est esse reum et captum sub lege, sub ira Dei et morte, agnoscere Deum non ut deum vel Patrem, sed ut tortorem, hostem, tyrannum. Hoc vere est agere in servitute et Captivitate Babylonica et saevissime torqueri in ea."

8. *LW* 26:390; *WA* 40/1. 594. 19–20: "Quo magis enim quispiam operatur in lege, hoc magis premitur servitute ipsius."

9. *LW* 27:8; *WA* 40/2. 8. 26–28: "servitus peccati, mortis, diaboli . . . non est corporalis, quae ad tempus aliquod durat, sed perpetua."

10. *LW* 27:8; *WA* 40/2. 8. 28–29: "Nam tales iusticiarii . . . nunquam quieti et pacati sunt."

11. *LW* 27:8; *WA* 40/2. 8. 23–24: "vel de infinita et aeterna libertate vel servitute."

12. To the question regarding whether those justified should expect some merit on account of the works that follow justification, Luther points out two things. First, those justified are still sinners; therefore, they live under the grace of the forgiveness of sins. Second, surely God promises reward to those who do works, and therefore they earn something. Yet all of these are under the forgiveness of sins. To explain the relation of grace to justification and love to good works as fruit of faith, Luther employs a metaphor: "As heaven (that is, justification) is under grace, so much the more are the stars. As the stars don't make heaven but only adorn it, so works don't merit heaven but only adorn justifying faith." Christ alone merits everything; we merit nothing. Everything is Christ's; nothing is ours. In Christ there are gifts, not merits. Therefore, those justified have only gifts and, as Augustine claims, God crowns nothing but his own gifts. *LW* 54:328–29 (no. 4331, dated 15–21 January 1539); *WA, TR* 4:227.

13. "Such is the power of the Law and such is righteousness on the basis of the Law that it forces us to be outwardly good so long as it threatens transgressors with penalties and punishment. Then we comply with the Law out of fear of punishment, but we do so unwillingly and with great indignation." *LW* 26:336; *WA* 40/1. 519. 13–15: "Talis est etiam vis legis et iustitia ex lege, cogens nos externe esse bonos, dum minatur poenam et supplicium transgressoribus. Ibi obtemperamus legi quidem timore poenae, sed inviti et maxime indignantes." See also *LW* 26:397; *WA* 40/1. 604. 22–26.

14. *LW* 26:362; *WA* 40/1. 553. 21–22: "Haec Theologica servitus durissima est."

Christian freedom includes a freedom from such feelings of guilt. This Christian freedom from guilt and exhaustive conflict caused by the law cannot be underscored enough.[15] This freedom is not "a political freedom or a freedom of the flesh" but "a theological or spiritual freedom, that is, to make our conscience free and joyful, unafraid of the wrath to come (Matt. 3:7)." It is, for Luther, "the most genuine freedom; it is immeasurable."[16]

Seventh, faith in Christ also signifies freedom for Christians from any abuse of the law, such as obligating Christians to observe laws, especially in the interest of accumulating merits for justification. From this standpoint, the ideas of unformed faith, forming love, and merits of congruity and condignity are immensely erroneous. They take away Christian freedom, which the costly price of Christ's body and blood has secured, only to let Christians relapse into either a meaningless and exhausting effort to earn God's grace or a precipitous and heedless abandonment of divine mercy.

Eighth, Christian freedom is also freedom from idolatry.[17] Where there is a false knowledge of God and Christ, there is "nothing but sheer idolatry, an idol and a false fiction about God."[18] What the self-righteous do with the name and word of God is more damaging than the idolatry of those who are ignorant of God, because this kind of idolatry is spiritual.[19] When the pope requires works of

---

15. *LW* 27:4; *WA* 40/2. 3. 20–21: "Christus nos liberavit . . . ira Dei aeterna. Ubi? In conscientia."

16. *LW* 27:4; *WA* 40/2. 3. 22–25: "Nam Christus nos liberos reddidit non Politice, non carnaliter, sed Theologice seu spiritualiter, hoc est, ut conscientia nostra sit libera et laeta, nihil timens venturam iram. Ea est verissima ac inaestimabilis libertas."

17. "We also wish to have the pure doctrine of faith and justification which banishes all idolatry." *LW* 54:231 (no. 3551, dated 19 March 1537); *WA, TR* 3:402–403. "Ah, if the article on justification hadn't fallen, the brotherhoods, pilgrimages, masses, invocation of saints, etc., would have found no place in the church. If it falls again . . . these idols will return." *LW* 54:340 (no. 4422, dated 20 March 1539); *WA, TR* 4:306.

18. *LW* 26:401; *WA* 40/1. 609. 19: "Nihil est nisi mera idolatria, idolum et falsum figmentum de Deo."

19. *LW* 26:399; *WA* 40/1. 607. 16–17: "Ideo quo sanctior et spiritualior est in speciem idolatria, hoc nocentior est."

the law—in particular, of his laws, as necessary for righteousness and salvation, which bind consciences and are counted as acts of worship—he sanctions lies and wickedness, and engages in idolatry.[20] "To attach righteousness, reverence, confidence in salvation, and the fear of death to such things is to attribute divinity to ceremonies."[21] This is blasphemy and idolatry. This aspect of Christian freedom is tied to freedom from the intellectual arrogance evident in a speculative search for God's nature. It is the freedom to maintain an intellectual humility that finds God and God's will in nothing other than the incarnate man, Jesus Christ. It is also connected to freedom from the vainglory of self-righteousness and freedom for the practical humility that submits oneself to the service of God and neighbor.

Last, but not least, Christian freedom sets Christians free from their inability to observe the divine commandments with a pure heart and free will. Christ has brought freedom from the self-centeredness of their sinful human nature. Through justification as a new creation, Christ creates a new nature that enables them to establish a proper and orderly relationship to God, their neighbors, and themselves, replacing their old disposition to exploit God and neighbors for their own profit. This Christian freedom also signifies freedom from captivity to a debauched will that is bound to sin and from the inability to live in accordance with God's will.[22] Hence, Christian

---

20. *LW* 26:409; *WA* 40/1. 620. 16–22: "Omnino contrarium de lege iudicat [homo], videlicet eam non solum necessariam esse ad salutem . . . . Hac opinione stante . . . statuitur mendacium, impietas, idololatria. Papa autem . . . docuit leges suas ad iustitiam necessarias esse."

21. *LW* 26:92; *WA* 40/1. 170. 18–19: "Ponere iustitiam, reverentiam, fiduciam salutis, timorem mortis in istis, hoc est, tradere cereoniis divinitatem."

22. "For the Law cannot be fulfilled without the Holy Spirit, and the Holy Spirit cannot be received without Christ. Unless He has been received, the human spirit remains unclean; that is, it despises God and seeks its own glory. Therefore whatever part of the Law it may perform is hypocritical and is a double sin. For an unclean heart does not keep the Law but only pretends outwardly to be keeping it; thus it is only confirmed even more deeply in its wickedness and hypocrisy." *LW* 27:131; *WA* 40/2. 168. 15–20: "Lex enim sine Spiritu sancto non potest impleri. Sine Christo autem non accipitur Spiritus sanctus, quo non accepto manet Spiritus immundus, id est, contemnens Deum et quaerens suam gloriam. Ideo quicquid legis facit, hypocriticum

freedom is freedom from the will's captivity to its fallen condition. As a new creation, Christians receive a pure heart, unadulterated motivation, and a renewed capacity to observe the divine commandments and find genuine joy in abiding by them.

Having set the precise groundwork in terms of who and what Christ is, what the law is in relation to sinners for justification, and what Christian freedom signifies, Luther moves to the next stage of building a Christian life on this foundation. He demonstrates how the inner necessity of the movement from "freedom from" to "freedom for" compellingly ushers in a theologically befitting discourse on love and the usefulness and necessity of the law even for Christians:

> When we have taught faith in Christ this way, then we also teach about good works. Because you have taken hold of Christ by faith, through whom you are righteous, you should now go and love God and your neighbor. Call upon God, give thanks to Him, preach Him, praise Him, confess Him. Do good to your neighbor, and serve him; do your duty. These are truly good works, which flow from this faith and

est et duplex peccatum. Immundum enim cor non implet, sed foris tantum simulat se implere legem, atque ita fortius corroboratur in impietate et hypocrisi sua."

It must always be remembered that, while Luther denies human freedom in relation to God (what God requires of us we are unable by ourselves to accomplish), he does grant that we have a free will in a natural way: "But if we are unwilling to let this term [free will] go altogether—though that would be the safest and most God-fearing thing to do—let us at least teach men to use it honestly, so that free choice is allowed to man only with respect to what is beneath him and not what is above him. That is to say, a man should know that with regard to his faculties and possessions he has the right to use, to do, or to leave undone, according to his own free choice, though even this is controlled by the free choice of God alone, who acts in whatever way he pleases. On the other hand in relation to God, or in matters pertaining to salvation or damnation, a man has no free choice, but is a captive, subject and slave either of the will of God or the will of Satan." *LW* 33:70; *WA* 18. 638. 3–11.

"Therefore the first argument, which is also the least important, is this: Man has been given a free will by which he either merits or fails to merit something. The answer: The free will without grace has absolutely no power to achieve righteousness, but of necessity it is in sin. Therefore blessed Augustine is correct in his book *Against Julian* when he calls it 'a bound will rather than a free will.' For when we possess grace, then the will is actually made free, especially with respect to salvation. To be sure it is always free in a natural way, but only with respect to those things which are under its power and lower than itself, but not with respect to the things above it, since it is captive in sin and now cannot choose that which is good in God's eyes." *LW* 25:375; *WA* 56:385. 13–22.

joy conceived in the heart because we have the forgiveness of sins freely through Christ.[23]

Luther also mentions that after Paul establishes the foundation of Christian doctrine, that is, the righteousness of Christ, Paul "builds good works."[24]

Luther accentuates, with reference to Galatians 5:13, that Christians are indeed not set free from the bound will to monopolize and conceal their freedom to satisfy their carnal desire.[25] On the contrary, it is granted by God for them to be free so that they may be of genuine service to God, neighbors, and themselves, that is, to bear fruits of faith in relation to God, their neighbors, and themselves, wherever and whenever opportunities are given. The Christian life is not the life of the flesh, but the life of Christ, who is grasped by faith in the heart. Christians are continuously engaged in tangible and visible acts of love, with Christ in their inmost hearts as the driving force of their lives.[26]

23. *LW* 26:133; *WA* 40/1. 234. 18–23: "Postquam fidem in Christum sic docuimus, docemus etiam de bonis operibus. Quia apprehendisti fide Christum per quem iustus es, nunc eas et diligas Deum et proximum, Invoca, Gratias age, praedica, lauda, confitere Deum, Benefac et servi proximo, fac officium tuum. Haec vere sunt bona opera quae fluunt ex ista fide et hilaritate cordis concepta, quod gratis habemus remissionem peccatorum per Christum." Considering this indissoluble interconnection between "freedom from" and "freedom for," a one-sided emphasis on "freedom from" in Luther's doctrine of justification, in fact, distorts his full doctrine.

24. *LW* 27:51; *WA* 40/2. 64. 26–28: "Fundamentum autem aliud nullum est . . . quam ipse Iesus Christus seu iusticia Christi. Super hoc fundamentum nunc superstruit [Paulus] bona opera et vere bona."

25. "For you were called to freedom, brothers and sisters; only do not use your freedom as an opportunity for self-indulgence, but through love become slaves to one another." (NRSV)

26. Bearing in mind how Luther builds love on the foundation of faith in Christ alone as constitutive of Christian life and practices of piety, we can positively accede to Scott Hendrix's claim that "if spirituality is taken in the sense of piety or living the Christian life, then I am convinced that Luther initiated a reformation of spirituality; or, to say it another way: the Reformation which Luther initiated was also intended to be a Reformation of spirituality." Hendrix, "Martin Luther's Reformation of Spirituality," *Lutheran Quarterly* 13, no. 3 (1999): 250. Hendrix points to one instance in which Luther uses the German equivalent of the Latin term *spiritualitas*. The German word *Geistlichkeit* occurs in Luther's exposition of the Gospel of John and is used in a negative way. Ibid., 251. See *LW* 24:229; *WA* 45. 670. 9–12. Hendrix then refers to a passage in Luther's letters in which Luther talks about a "spiritual life" (*vita spiritualis;*

When we fully appreciate the integral movement from "freedom from" to "freedom for" in Luther's mentality as a basis for his assessment of the compatibility between faith and love, then we encounter another rationale for esteeming love as concordant with faith: the twofold way of fulfilling the law. As was made explicit in chapter 2, the jurisdiction of the law over human beings in terms of justification has been terminated, since Jesus Christ completed it. By grasping Christ through faith in one's heart, the one justified also fulfills the law. With regard to fulfilling the law, however, Luther unfolds yet another way that may be taken as the justified person's own accomplishment. In order to grasp this second point without misreading, though, we need, first of all, to puzzle over the following question: what does the law have to do with Luther's reconceptualization of love? This is the subject of our next investigation.

The Christ-Given Law of Love

Luther explicates the relation of the law to Christians who have been made righteous by faith in Christ in the dimension of proper, active, and progressing righteousness and holiness: "Once we have been

geistliches Leben) to indicate the essence of what it means to be Christian, rejecting as essential to the Christian life the external forms of devotion of late medieval piety. Hendrix, "Martin Luther's Reformation of Spirituality," 256.

Focusing on the discontinuity of Luther's Reformation spirituality from the external religious activities in medieval Christianity, especially those of professionally religious people, Hendrix clearly recaptures how radical Luther's reformation of spirituality was. According to Hendrix, Luther's conception of the new spirituality, piety, and landscape of the evangelical life are characterized in the following facets: (1) At the center of Luther's notion of spirituality lies the connectedness of Christians to Christ; (2) The natural or spontaneous flow of Christian life has both external and internal components; (3) The Holy Spirit plays an essential role in Christian spirituality and, accordingly, Luther's spirituality is Christo-centric, but it is not Christo-monist; and (4) The connectedness to Christ is not so much a state of mystical union as it is the actual ongoing life of Christians with Christ through the Spirit in a new reality. Hendrix, "Martin Luther's Reformation of Spirituality," 254–63. In "Luther's reformation of spirituality, the Christian lives in the world neither as a mystic nor as a monk, but as a guest"; hence, Hendrix calls Luther's outlook of spirituality "guestly spirituality." Ibid., 262.

justified by faith, we enter the active life" that "should be sought from the Law, which does not grasp Christ but exercises itself in works of love toward one's neighbor."[27] This seemingly perplexing pronouncement raises the question: why is Luther, after all his fierce rejection of the law and works of the law, returning to the law in his treatment of love? Is he attempting to revive a legalistic system based on justification by faith? This question is legitimate and, in fact, is bound up with another: why does Luther talk predominantly about works when love is the subject under discussion in the dimension of active righteousness and holiness?

Bearing these questions in mind, we must remember that Luther sought to replace the scholastic terminologies such as *fides caritate formata*, unformed faith, and the merits of congruity and condignity with biblical language and concepts. Luther does not abandon love itself in his theology, but the scholastic concept of love. He now begins to unfold his biblically derived understanding of love.

It is no surprise that Luther (musing on Galatians 6:2: "Bear one another's burdens, and in this way you will fulfill the Law of Christ") exalts Paul's commendation to the Galatians of mutual love, in resonance with Jesus Christ's commandment to love one's neighbor or one another (Matthew 22:39; John 13:34-35; 15:12, 17). Soliciting Paul, who in turn invokes Christ as the source of the authority of his exhortation, Luther seizes a timely moment to demonstrate the will of Christ. Christians come into being through Christ. They also get their name from Christ. Now Christians are to live up to their identity and name, that is, to follow the will of Christ, which is love: *"The Law of Christ is the law of love."*[28] This is the leitmotif in Luther's

---

27. *LW* 26:287; *WA* 40/1. 447. 22–28: "Fide autem nobis iustificatis, egredimur in vitam activam . . . . . Activam vero vitam debere peti ex lege, quae Christum non apprehendit, sed exercet sese operibus charitatis erga proximum."

28. *LW* 27:113 (italics mine); *WA* 40/2. 144. 16: "*Lex Christi est lex charitis.*" This law and its function in the dimension of proper, active, and progressing righteousness and holiness can

reconceptualization of love and will continuously come into sight in a set of variations—namely, how Christians bear the fruits of faith in Christ by performing acts of love in the trichotomous direction: toward God, neighbor, and self.

Again, in reference to Leviticus 19:18[29] and John 13:34-35,[30] Luther declares that "[a]fter redeeming and regenerating us and constituting us as His church, Christ did not give us any new law except the law of mutual love."[31] By the "Law of Christ," Luther, of

be discussed in connection with the issue of *tertius usus legis* (the third use of the law). This discussion will be taken up in the Conclusion. See Johannes Heckel, *Lex Charitatis: A Juristic Disquisition on Law in the Theology of Martin Luther*, trans. and ed. Gottfried G. Krodel (Grand Rapids: Eerdmans, 2010), 84–93.

29. "You shall not take vengeance or bear a grudge against any of your people, but you shall love your neighbor as yourself; I am the Lord." (NRSV) See also Matthew 19:19: "Honor your father and mother; also, You shall love your neighbor as yourself."

30. "I give you a new commandment, that you love one another. Just as I have loved you, you also should love one another. By this everyone will know that you are my disciples, if you have love for one another." (NRSV)

31. *LW* 27:113; *WA* 40/2. 144. 16–18: "Christus postquam redemit, renovavit et constituit nos suam Ecclesiam, nullam nobis legem dedit praeterquam illam de mutua charitate."

This argument also appears in one of Luther's 1529 Holy Week and Easter Sermons: "The footwashing follows [John 13:1-11]. There you see that the Lord speaks as one who will depart and commands them with word and deeds to love and to serve one another. For this is the nature of love that it serves. For this reason he says, 'By this everyone will know that you are my disciples' [John 13:35]. This was his final command. It is therefore true that one serves what one loves, as Christ himself did . . . . Therefore Christ has thrown down all commands and given love alone as the final command: O dear disciples, I will not give you many commands, laws, and books. Love alone will teach you well what you should do. 'Love one another just as I have loved you' [John 13:34]. I am your servant. This is the 'example' [John 13:15], that he washes their feet. This is to be 'the new commandment.'" Martin Luther, "Maundy Thursday Afternoon March 25, 1529, The Passion: Anointing in Bethany, Last Supper, and Footwashing," in *The 1529 Holy Week and Easter Sermons of Dr. Martin Luther*, trans. Irving L. Sandberg [from "Predigten D. Martin Luthers auf Grund von Nachschriften Georg Rörers und Anton Lauterbachs," ed. Georg Buchwald (Gütersloh: Bertelsmann, 1925)] (Saint Louis: Concordia Publishing House, 1999), 84.

See also his gloss on John 14:15 ("If you love me, you will keep my commandments"): "These are the brief commandments which Christ calls 'My commandments.' 'And these,' He says, 'I impose on you only if you love Me and gladly keep them for My sake. For I do not want to be a Moses, who drives and plagues you with menace and terror; but I give you commands which you can and will surely observe without coercion if you love Me at all. If love is wanting, it is useless for Me to give you many commandments; for they would not be observed anyhow. Therefore if you want to keep My commandments, see that you love Me, and think of what I have done for you. It is proper that you should love Me, who am about to give My life for you and to shed My blood for you. Do this for My sake. Live in harmony and friendship with one

course, has in mind not legalistic stipulations or regulations but the most far-reaching guiding principle by which Christ, present in the heart through faith, operates in Christians. The law of Christ signifies the substance of the will of Christ, which he wants Christians to internalize and then act upon in every estate of their lives. When Christ is really present in a Christian's heart through faith, then Christ brings his law of love into force, so that the Christian's motives and actions reflect his loving will. The Christian's whole being and life will be active in compliance with this law of love. This love is certainly not prescribed for the justification of the unrighteous. Nonetheless, it is to be implemented as the will of Christ by justified Christians who love, respect, and follow him.[32]

Indeed, it is not a new law because it supersedes or is added to the old law, that is, the Mosaic law; rather, it is a new law because it presents itself to Christians with an entirely new thrust and substance. When Christ admonishes and encourages Christians to love, he has already empowered them to do so. For this reason, Christ's commandment to love is not a "law" as reckoned before

another. At the same time adhere steadfastly to Me in your preaching, bear with one another in love, and do not introduce schisms and factions." *LW* 24:102; *WA* 45. 553. 28–554. 3.

    In fact, when we read Luther's exposition of this biblical passage, it is not difficult to perceive that he seems to be speaking to his own people through the mouth of Jesus Christ who was about to depart from his disciples and from this world. This seems to be highly possible because his sermonic exposition of John 14–16 was written shortly after he returned to Wittenberg from Schmalkalden on March 14, 1537, after a serious and extremely painful illness. He might have put himself in Jesus' shoes, predicting schisms and factions and thereby championing again Jesus' commandment to love to his own people.

32. See, for instance, Luther's exposition of Matthew 5:17, bringing together Christ's claim that he has not come to abolish the law with Paul's claim (Rom. 3:31) that he does not intend to abolish the law through his teaching of justification by faith in Christ. Luther compares the accusation of the "papists" against him to those who misunderstood Christ and Paul. *LW* 21:69–70; *WA* 32. 356. 15–357. 12. See also Luther's gloss of Romans 3:31, where Luther accents that only when the law is truly fulfilled through faith and grace can it be said to be ratified and confirmed. *LW* 25:34; *WA* 56. 40. 4–5. He also mentions that "[t]his Law is established only through the spirit of faith; for what is impossible for the Law is possible for faith, and the Law is established, ratified, and grounded on that which is possible, as he [Paul] says above in ch. 3:31: 'But we establish the Law through faith.'" It is clear that "through faith" is Luther's addition. *LW* 25:67; *WA* 56. 74. 17–20.

Christians obtained their freedom through faith. In the state of Christian freedom, Christ's commandment contains the gospel within itself.

The Christian freedom that has been procured by Christ and freely bestowed upon Christians through faith in Christ accompanies a liberated will, which—now purified, illumined, and suitably activated—can discern and willingly submit to God's own will. Christians are enabled to keep the divine will prescribed in the divine commandments; in their new competence, both alien and proper, they now find genuine delight in abiding by the divine commandments.[33] To borrow Luther's words, it is as if Christ were speaking: "I have given you power to love. Just let it out."

In similar fashion, Luther (in his exposition of Galatians 3:12: "But the Law does not rest on faith") refers to the biblical passages in which love is portrayed as that which encompasses the whole of the law in a nutshell. Although the primary subject of this exposition is justification, the following passage containing those references

33. See Eric W. Gritsch, "Martin Luther's Commentary on Gal 5, 2–24, 1519 (WA 2, 574–597) and Sermon on Gal 4, 1–7, 1522 (WA 10 I 1, 325–378)," in *Freiheit als Liebe bei Martin Luther, Freedom as Love in Martin Luther: 8th International Congress for Luther Research in St. Paul, Minnesota, 1993, Seminar 1 Referate/Papers*, edited by Dennis D. Bielfeldt and Klaus Schwarzwäller (Frankfurt am Main: Peter Lang, 1995), 105–11. In terms of the tight connections between Luther's concepts of freedom and love and performing what Christians *ought to do* with willingness and spontaneity, see Dennis Bielfeldt's "Freedom, Love, and Righteousness in Luther's Sermo de Duplici Iustitia," in *Freiheit als Liebe bei Martin Luther*, 19–34.

Respecting the relationship between freedom, love, and adhering to the divine commandments, see Tuomo Mannermaa, "Freiheit als Liebe: Einführung in das Thema," in *Freiheit als Liebe bei Martin Luther*, 9–18, esp. 11–12, where he shows that, when Luther treats the problem of free will, it is a matter of the capacity of a person to fulfill the divine commandments, namely, the twofold commandment of the love of God and the love of neighbor out of a pure heart, abandoning perverse self-love. Mannermaa shows that only when we participate in the divine nature or name of freedom in union with Christ through justifying faith does the commandment or admonition "Tu, was in dir ist" (*facere quod in se est*) make sense. Mannermaa states, however, that this freedom bestowed on us through participation in God's nature or name can never be claimed as our *own* property. We have it or rather *participate in* this freedom only insofar as the divine freedom is present in us through the word of the gospel or the sacraments. Ibid., 11.

promotes our understanding of the connection between love and law in Luther's thought:

> *But what is the Law? Is it not also a commandment of love? In fact, the Law commands nothing else but love,* as the text says (Matt. 22:37): 'You shall love the Lord your God with all your heart, etc.' Again (Deut. 5:10): 'Showing steadfast love to thousands of those who love Me.' And again (Matt. 22:40): 'On these two commandments depend all the Law and the prophets.'[34]

With respect to this association between love and law, Luther appeals to Paul again as "an outstanding interpreter of the commandments of God" (using Galatians 5:14: "For the whole Law is fulfilled in one word: You shall love your neighbor as yourself.").[35] Luther takes Paul's statement to mean that "[t]he whole Law is completely

---

34. *LW* 26:270 (italics mine); *WA* 40/1. 423. 34–424. 15: "*Quid autem est Lex? An non est etiam charitatis praeceptum? Imo Lex nihil aliud praecipit quam charitatem,* ut textus ipse habet: 'Diliges dominum Deum tuum ex toto corde tuo'; Item: 'Faciens misericordiam in multa milia his qui diligunt me'; Item: 'In his duobus mandatis tota Lex et Prophetae pendent.'"

35. *LW* 27:56; *WA* 40/2. 70. 24: "Paulus optimus est interpres praeceptorum Dei." Luther also affirms that Paul's teaching confirms love as the fulfillment of the law, referring to Romans 13:8-10 ("Owe no one anything, except to love one another; for the one who loves another has fulfilled the law. The commandments, 'You shall not commit adultery; You shall not murder; You shall not steal; You shall not covet'; and any other commandment, are summed up in this word. 'Love your neighbor as yourself.' Love does no wrong to a neighbor; therefore, love is the fulfilling of the law").

    For instance, in *Wider die himmlischen Propheten, von den Bildern und Sakrament* (*Against the Heavenly Prophets in the Matter of Images and Sacraments,* 1525), Luther says that "Paul . . . in Rom. 13[:9] . . . sums up all the commandments of Moses in the love which also the natural law teaches in the words, 'Love your neighbor as yourself.' Otherwise, were it not naturally written in the heart, one would have to teach and preach the law for a long time before it became a concern of conscience. The heart must also find and feel the law in itself. Otherwise it would become a matter of conscience for no one." *LW* 40:97; *WA* 18:80.

    Another example appears in his *Betbüchlein* (*Personal Prayer Book*): "In all of these deeds we can see the same thing: love of self which seeks its own advantage, robs both God and one's neighbor of their due, and concedes neither to God nor man anything they have, or are, or could do or become. Augustine expressed this succinctly when he said, 'Self-love is the beginning of every sin.' The conclusion of all this is that the commandments demand or forbid nothing other than 'love.' Only 'love' fulfills and only 'love' breaks the commandments. Therefore St. Paul declares that 'love is the fulfilling of the law' [Rom. 13:8-10], just as an 'evil love' breaks all the commandments." *LW* 43:21; *WA* 10/2. 385. 14–386. 2. See also *LW* 43:23; *WA* 10/2. 387. 25–388. 7.

summarized in 'You shall love your neighbor as yourself.'"[36] Consequently, in Luther's reconceptualization of love, we find the following five propositions: (1) Christian life is the life of Christ, not of the flesh. (2) The life of Christ is regulated by the law of Christ. (3) The law of Christ is the law of love. (4) Christ's commandment to love is the encapsulation of the entire law. (5) Christian life in love springing from faith in Christ is the fulfillment of the law of Christ, namely, the law of love.

The fourth proposition is especially true as to the Decalogue, which is construed as a compact summary of the law and simultaneously an extended instruction on Christ's commandment to love. Luther mentions that, when Paul builds truly good works on the foundation of Jesus Christ or the righteousness of Christ, the apostle includes all truly good works in the brief commandment to serve one's neighbor through love ("You shall love your neighbor, etc.") and shows "on the basis of the Decalog what it means to be a servant through love."[37]

This aspect is important—particularly because, although the Decalogue (as the ceremonial and context-bound law originally given to the Jews in a specific historical setting) has lost its power with the first advent of Christ, it is still valid for Christians, yet with ever-new meanings by virtue of Christ. Only in this line of reasoning can we correctly appreciate the following statement: "Apart from the matter of justification, on the other hand, we, like Paul, should think

---

36. *LW* 27:55–56; *WA* 40/2. 70. 16–17: "Tota lex plenissime comprehenditur in uno illo verbo: 'Diliges proximum tuum sicut teipsum.'" Luther is certainly not omitting the first part of the commandment to love, namely, love of God. Luther's emphasis on neighbor-love in this context is understood in that Paul is exhorting the Galatians to be servants of one another through love. Luther makes it clear that neighbor-love is the highest virtue when the neighbor is designated as the worthiest object of love among creatures. See *LW* 27:58; *WA* 40/2. 72. 27–36. This issue will be taken up in chapter 5.

37. *LW* 27:51; *WA* 40/2. 64. 22–29: "Paulus iam pulcherrime declarabit [Paulus] ex decalogo, quid sit servire per charitatem etc . . . bona opera et vere bona, quae omnia includit brevi praecepto: 'Diliges proximum tuum' etc."

reverently of the Law. We should endow it with the highest praises and call it holy, righteous, good, spiritual, divine, etc."[38]

In his redefined love, Luther strives to convey his view that the law, for justified Christians, recapitulates the Christ-given law of love and that Christ empowers Christians to observe the law. Christ grasped by faith in one's heart not only lets love overflow purely and freely but also imparts that love in his followers as his will. What is noticeable here is that Luther highlights the spontaneity of Christian love but at the same time he does not forget to mention that Christian love is obligatory. This love given by Christ must be done. In this context, Luther presents the paradoxical characteristics of Christian love as follows: because of Jesus Christ, Christian love is spontaneous but it is also imperative. The spontaneity of Christian love does not mean that it is a matter of choice. This discussion on the law of love takes us to Luther's view of the twofold way of fulfilling the law.

Twofold Way of Fulfilling the Law

What, then, does it mean to live a Christian life pursuant to the law of Christ, that is, what does it mean to love? A suitable entry point to this question is Luther's definition of a "saint," which discloses the core of his theological anthropology and revolves around two connected questions: who can be considered genuine saints? What sort of life can be called saintly or holy?

Luther's answers appear in his explication of the two dimensions of the definition of a saint: "If they, first of all, declare that Christ is their wisdom, righteousness, sanctification, and redemption (1 Cor. 1:30), and if, in the second place, they all do their duty in their callings on the basis of the command of the Word of God, abstaining

---

38. *LW* 26:365; *WA* 40/1. 558. 24–26: "Caeterum extra locum iustificationis debemus cum Paulo reverenter sentire de lege et eam summis laudibus vehere, appellare sanctam, iustam, bonam, spiritualem, divinam etc."

from the desires and vices of the flesh for the sake of Christ."[39] The first of these dimensions corresponds to the Christian's alien, passive, and perfect righteousness and holiness; the second, to the Christian's proper, active, and progressing righteousness and holiness.

As to the first dimension, Luther emphasizes that Christ grants eternal righteousness and holiness to those who have faith in him. So Luther warns, "Let anyone be accursed who does not give Christ the honor of believing that he has been justified and sanctified by His death, the Word, and the sacraments, etc."[40] On the basis of this conviction, Luther declares that everyone who has grasped Christ in the heart through faith is entitled to be dubbed holy, that is, a saint, as well as justified.

Since *being* a Christian—Christian identity—is predicated solely upon *believing*, everyone who has faith in Christ is a Christian and a saint. Discrepancies in biological, social, political, and economic identity are irrelevant to identity as a Christian and a saint. By the same token, where a saint pursues her vocation is irrelevant to her becoming and being a saint. Based on this principle, Luther states that "[s]uch genuine saints include ministers of the Word, political magistrates, parents, children, masters, servants, etc."[41]

As to the second dimension of the definition of a saint, Luther says that, imputing Christ's righteousness and holiness to those grasping Christ through faith, God not only declares them righteous and holy but also initiates God's work to render them truly righteous and holy.

---

39. *LW* 27:82; *WA* 40/2. 103. 30–104. 7: "si primum omnium certo statuant, Christum esse suam sapientiam, iusticiam, sanctificationem et redemptionem, Deinde si unusquisque ex praescripto verbi Dei faciat officium in vocatione sua et propter Christum abstineat a desideriis et vitiis carnis."

40. *LW* 27:83; *WA* 40/2. 104. 24–26: "Anathema sit, quicunque hunc honorem Christo non habuerit, ut credat, quod eius morte, verbo, Sacramentis etc. iustificatus et sanctificatus sit etc."

41. *LW* 27:82; *WA* 40/2. 103. 29–30: "Sic vere Sancti sunt ministri verbi, Magistratus politici, parentes, liberi, heri, familia etc."

This work of God is not a natural or moral doing but a theological doing, which originates from faith in Christ.

According to Luther, what characterizes these two dimensions of the definition of a saint is discerned in a biblical concept: new creation. For Luther, faith has to do not only with justification—acquittal, imputation, declaration, and acceptance—but with a new creation as well. In the beginning, God brought human beings into existence as an original creation *ex nihilo*. After the fall, God continues to bring human beings into new existence as new creation. In Luther's mind, there is no doubt that justification, as the work of the divine Son in the incarnate man, is a new creation out of sinners, whose own capacity for salvation is as good as nothing (*nihil*). Hence, justification as a new creation is another divine creation *ex nihilo*. Justification, in particular, is designated as a spiritual birth and "spiritual birth is nothing other than faith."[42] The new creation, "by which the image of God is renewed,"[43] signifies the work of the Spirit of Christ bestowed through faith. It is "not a sham or merely a new outward appearance, but something really happens."[44]

---

42. *LW* 26:445; *WA* 40/1. 668. 35–669. 14: "Spiritualis enim nativitas nihil aliud est nisi fides." Seeing this new creation as a spiritual new birth, Luther expounds, "Therefore just as in society a son becomes an heir merely by being born, so here faith alone makes men sons of God, born of the Word, which is the divine womb in which we are conceived, carried, born, reared, etc. By this birth and this patience or passivity which makes us Christians we also become sons and heirs. But being heirs, we are free of death and the devil, and we have righteousness and eternal life. This comes to us in a purely passive way; for we do not do anything, but we let ourselves be made and formed as a new creation through faith in the Word." *LW* 26:392; *WA* 40/1. 597. 23–29: "Sicut ergo filius in politia tantum nascendo fit haeres, Sic hic sola fides efficit filios Dei, natos ex verbo, quod est uterus divinus, in quo concipimur, gestamur, nascimur educamur etc. Hac ergo nativitate, hac patientia seu passione, qua fimus Christiani, fimus etiam filii et haeredes. Existentes autem haeredes liberi sumus a morte, diabolo etc. et habemus iustitiam et vitam aeternam. Verum ista mere passive nobis obvenit, nihil enim facimus, sed patimur nos fieri et formari novam creaturam per fidem in verbum."
43. *LW* 27:139; *WA* 40/2. 178. 16: "Nova autem creatura, qua reparatur imago Dei."
44. *LW* 27:140; *WA* 40/2. 178. 24–25: "Hic non est fucus aut tantum nova externa species, sed res ipsa geritur."

Certainly, it is not the substance of human nature that is transformed as the scholastic theologians avow. Nevertheless, it is also more than an outward change expressed through outward works; it is "a renewal of the mind by the Holy Spirit."[45] It engenders a new attitude, new spiritual judgment, and new motivation. This real, internal change is "followed by an outward change in the flesh, in the parts of the body, and in the senses."[46] Indubitably, Luther, in principle, is considering an internal renewal of the heart in the dimension of passive righteousness and holiness and an external renewal of the flesh in the dimension of active righteousness and holiness.

This claim is correlated with Luther's notion of a twofold fulfillment of the law: "'to do' is first to believe and so, through faith, to keep the Law."[47] Luther argues that "we must receive the Holy Spirit; illumined and renewed by Him, we begin to keep the Law, to love God and our neighbor."[48] Only then, Luther argues, is it true that "God and our neighbor are loved, good works are performed, and the cross is borne. This is really keeping the Law; otherwise the Law remains permanently unkept."[49] "'To do' is simply to believe in Jesus Christ, and when the Holy Spirit has been received through faith in Christ, to do the things that are in the Law."[50] Therefore, "a true doer of the Law" is the one "who receives the Holy Spirit

---

45. *LW* 27:140; *WA* 40/2. 178. 31: ". . . est nova creatura . . . renovatio mentis per Spiritum sanctum."
46. *LW* 27:140; *WA* 40/2. 178. 32: "sequitur postea etiam mutatio carnis, membrorum et sensuum externa."
47. *LW* 26:255; *WA* 40/1. 400. 31: "Quare facere est primum credere et sic per fidem praestare legem."
48. *LW* 26:255; *WA* 40/1. 400. 31–33: "Oportet enim nos accipere Spiritum sanctum, quo illuminati et renovati incipimus facere legem, diligere Deum et proximum."
49. *LW* 26:255; *WA* 40/1. 401. 18–20: "Tum diligitur Deus et proximus, bona opera fiunt, fertur crux. Hoc tandem est vere Legem facere, alioqui lex perpetuo manet infecta."
50. *LW* 26:255; *WA* 40/1. 401. 20–22: "'Facere' simpliciter est credere in Iesum Christum et accepto per fidem in Christum Spiritu sancto operari ea quae sunt in Lege."

through faith in Christ and then begins to love God and to do good to his neighbor."[51]

Christians, having possessed the alien righteousness and holiness of Christ in his fulfillment of the entire law, are also admonished and empowered for their fulfillment of the law or, more precisely, the law of love, in the dimension of active righteousness and holiness. As to this twofold way in which Christians fulfill the law, Luther states, "A Christian fulfills the Law inwardly by faith—for Christ is the consummation of the Law for righteousness to everyone who has faith (Rom. 10:4)—and outwardly by works and by the forgiveness of sins."[52]

Now we have reached a better position from which to tackle our original question: what, then, does it mean to live a Christian life pursuant to the law of Christ, that is, to love, in the dimension of active righteousness and holiness? Luther's answer is: God continues to work through the Spirit of Christ to render Christians, who are already perfectly righteous and holy in Christ, righteous and holy in and through themselves.[53]

The Spirit of Christ bears fruit in the acts of love, particularly in three directions: towards God, one's neighbors, and oneself. In terms of the Christian's relation to self, daily mortification of the old self and daily vivification of the new self are vital. The daily advance of the Christian's proper righteousness is especially crucial from the viewpoint of Luther's concept of sin. Although he never gets tired of emphasizing that Christians already enjoy perfect righteousness,

---

51. *LW* 26:255; *WA* 40/1. 401. 30–402. 13: "Quare is verus est factor Legis qui accepto Spiritu sancto per fidem Christi incipit diligere Deum et benefacere proximo."

52. *LW* 27:96; *WA* 40/2. 121. 21–23: "Sic Christianus intus implet legem fide, Christus enim perfectio legis est ad iusticiam omni credenti, foris operibus et remissione peccatorum."

53. Regarding this idea of renewal in Luther, Lohse states, "For a long time, the fact that for Luther justification involved not merely forgiveness of sins or acquittal but also renewal has not been sufficiently appreciated. Melanchthon restricted the doctrine entirely to the imputation of Christ's righteousness. Following him, Lutheran theology long advocated merely the 'forensic' view of justification." Lohse, *Luthers Theologie*, 278–79; ET *Martin Luther's Theology*, 262.

holiness, eternal life, and freedom from sin and death in Christ, Luther is nevertheless fully aware of the fact that the remnants of sin remain as long as the body is alive. These residual sins exist, of course, not because there is any defect in Christ, but rather one in human beings.[54]

That being so, Christians have two antipodal guides in themselves: the Spirit and the flesh.[55] "The Spirit is whatever is done in us through the Spirit; the flesh is whatever is done in us in accordance with the flesh and apart from the Spirit."[56] The Christian's life is a persistent battle against the flesh's resistance to and interruption of the works of the Spirit. The Spirit of Christ assists saints in their daily battle against the flesh so that they will grow increasingly righteous and holy. In this process, the guiding principle is the law of Christ, that is, the law of love.

Proper, active, and progressing righteousness and holiness gradually increase in each Christian through industrious performance in compliance with the law of love. The Christian's alien

---

54. *LW* 26:349; *WA* 40/1. 535. 30–536. 11: "Defectus igitur non est in Christo, sed in nobis, qui nondum exuimus carnem, in qua, donec vivimus, haeret peccatum." Luther also mentions as follows: "After baptism original sin is like a wound which has begun to heal. It is really a wound, yet it is becoming better and is constantly in the process of healing, although it is still festering, is painful, etc. So original sin remains in the baptized until their death, although it is in the process of being rooted out. It is rendered harmless, and so it cannot accuse or damn us." *LW* 54:20 (no. 138, dated 30 November–14 December 1531); *WA*, *TR* 1:60.

55. *LW* 27:65; *WA* 40/2. 82. 15: "duo contrarii Duces sunt in vobis, Spiritus et Caro."

56. *LW* 26:217; *WA* 40/1. 348. 15–17: "Spiritus est, quicquid in nobis geritur per spiritum; Caro, quidquid in nobis geritur secundum carnem extra spiritum." In the matter of alien, passive, and perfect righteousness and holiness, the "flesh" does not merely mean "sexual lust, animal passions, or the sensual appetite" but "the very righteousness and wisdom of the flesh and the judgment of reason, which wants to be justified through the Law." *LW* 26:216; *WA* 40/1. 347. 21–29: "Paulus hic [Gal 3:3] opponit spiritum et carnem. Neque appellat carnem libidinem, passiones beluinas seu appetitum sensitivum . . . . Itaque caro est ipsa iustitia, sapientia carnis ac cogitatio rationis, quae per legem vult iustificari. Quidquid ergo optimum ac praestantissimum est in homine, Paulus vocat Carnem, scilicet summam sapientiam rationis et ipsam iustitiam legis." On the other hand, as to proper, active, and progressing righteousness and holiness, the "flesh" is used in a broader sense, obviously including whatever hinders vivification of a new creation in Christians (saints). This issue will be taken up toward the end of chapter 5, under the subtitle of "Daily Mortification of the Old Self."

righteousness is gratuitously bestowed by God in the passive reception of God's grace; her proper righteousness is brought to greater fruition day by day. Faith is genuine in its receptivity while "love is sweet, kind, and patient—not in receiving but in performing; for it is obliged to overlook many things and to bear with them."[57] These words get at the core of Luther's reconceptualization of faith and love: faith believes in Christ passively, receiving from God perfect righteousness and holiness; love performs actively, achieving daily growth in yet-imperfect righteousness and holiness.

This train of thought leads to the core of Luther's theological anthropology: the twofold meaning of *simul iustus et peccator*. On the one hand, the faith that brings about the Christian's alien, passive, and perfect righteousness and holiness shows that Christians are both totally sinners and totally righteous, because Christ's perfect righteousness makes a sinner righteous. Being both totally sinners and righteous points to the paradoxical identity of Christians: "Thus a Christian man is righteous and a sinner at the same time, holy and profane, an enemy of God and a child of God. None of the sophists will admit this paradox."[58] On the other hand, the love that increases the proper, active, and progressing righteousness and holiness demonstrates that Christians are both "partly sinners and partly righteous."[59]

---

57. *LW* 27:113; *WA* 40/2. 144. 25–26: "Charitas ergo dulcis, benigna, paciens est, non in recipiendo, sed exhibendo, cogitur enim ad multa connivere et ea portare."

58. *LW* 26:232; *WA* 40/1. 368. 26–27: "Sic homo Christianus simul iustus et peccator, Sanctus, prophanus, inimicus et filius Dei est. Haec contraria nulli Sophistae admittunt."

59. *LW* 27:68; *WA* 40/2. 86. 14–15: "Atque ita partim peccatores, partim iusti sumus." See also *LW* 27:74: "they [the faithful] have partly flesh and partly Spirit."; *WA* 40/2. 93. 19–20: "pii . . . quod norint se *partim* carnem *partim* Spiritum habere."

Lohse explains that it was chiefly Wilfried Joest who clarified the dynamics of the "total" and the "partial aspect" in Luther's theological anthropology: "The Christian in a total sense is both sinner and righteous, but likewise through the divine justifying and making righteous is in a 'partial' sense still sinner and in a 'partial' sense already righteous." Lohse, *Luthers Theologie*, 280; ET *Martin Luther's Theology*, 264.

Allowing for these subtle and multifarious distinctions, it becomes evident that Luther's discussion of love—whether against his opponents or in defense of his own ideas, in opposition to faith or in harmony with faith—always ushers in and is intricately tied to questions of works: works of the law and works of love. Careful scrutiny of the discourse on love exposes two presuppositions: living inevitably involves law, and observing the law is tantamount to performing works in compliance with the requirements of the law. This requirement, however, also raises questions: What kind of law are Christians obliged to keep as an expression of Christian living? Who is able to keep the law? How can Christians fulfill the law? What produces truly good works in genuine observance of the law?

Luther's answers are lucid. The kind of law that Christians are commanded to observe is the law of Christ, which is reformulated and reconditioned by the historical and spiritual significance of Christ. None except those who grasp Christ in their hearts through faith can truly keep the law. Christians can fulfill the law solely by and in Christ. In sum: Christians come into being by virtue not of their doing but their believing. Living a Christian life means living up to the name, that is, living up to the law of Christ. The law of Christ is the law of love. Living a Christian life is loving. This loving is nothing less than the fruit of believing.

As a corollary, the whole of the Christian life is compressed again into the following two commandments: "Believe in Christ" and "You shall love your neighbor as yourself."[60] Luther deciphers Paul's admonishment in Galatians 5:14 as signifying "above all persevere in the doctrine of faith . . . . Afterwards, if you want to do good works, I will show you in one word the highest and greatest works, and the way to keep all the laws: Be devoted to one another through

---

60. *LW* 27:56; *WA* 40/2. 70. 28–29: "'Crede in Christum', Item: 'Dilige proximum tuum sicut teipsum.'"

love."[61] "This is the perfect doctrine of both faith and love. It is also the shortest and the longest kind of theology—the shortest so far as words and sentences are concerned; but in practice and in fact it is wider, longer, deeper, and higher than the whole world."[62]

After we have observed faith and love as two conflicting theses in the dynamics of Christ and the law in the first chapter, we can see now that faith and love also emerge as two compatible theses in the dynamics of Christ and the law of love. In conjunction with his redefined faith, Luther's reconceptualized love amends the existing structure of relations among Christ, faith, law, and love. Justification and eternal life no longer depend upon the scholastic notion of a love or the notion of merits earned through works done by the infused love or grace. Justification no longer relies on a love that forms an unformed faith. Still less can one's own meritorious works of the law procure the infusion of a supernatural love or grace from God. All the scholastic logic is turned upside down and inside out. Faith grasps Christ. Christ is in action through the love that is his law. The law is observed and obeyed not for the sake of gaining God's grace or a greater portion of it but because Christians are empowered and set free from the captivity of sin to serve God and neighbors gratefully and willingly.

The relationships among faith, love, Christ, and the law never remain stagnant but undergo dynamic changes and reorientations. Unless this dynamic reconstruction gains the appreciation it deserves, Luther's theology will fall into the danger of being accused of inconsistency or self-contradiction. Only when our attention is

---

61. *LW* 27:59; *WA* 40/2. 74. 20–23: "ante omnia perseverate in fidei doctrina, quam a me accepistis. Post, si vultis bene operari, Ego uno verbo ostendam vobis summa et maxima opera et quomodo omnes leges impleatis: Diligite vos mutuo per charitatem."

62. *LW* 27:59; *WA* 40/2. 74. 25–27: "Haec absoluta est doctrina de fide et charitate et Theologia brevissima et longissima, Brevissima, quod ad verba et sententias attinet, sed usu et reipsa latior, longior, profundior et sublimior est toto mundo."

precisely focused on these internal theological dynamics can we accurately appreciate Luther's radical reordering and reconstruction of the entire conceptual and practical system of salvation and Christian life.

As for the Christian use of the law, Luther's confrontation with Johann Agricola's antinomianism is indispensable for comprehending the reformer's strident advocacy of the importance of the law for justified Christians.[63] As one of the controversial intra-Reformation disputes, the conflict centers on the following question: in what sense and to what extent is the preaching of the law the church's abiding task? Agricola, a pupil and friend of Luther, emphasizes that the law cannot lead to faith and that repentance is a fruit of the gospel. Christ fulfilled the law; as a consequence, the law had been abolished completely. Furthermore, the law by itself works wrath.[64] Agricola rebuts the idea that the church must preach the law, claiming that it may not even be called God's Word.[65] Dissenting from Agricola, Luther contends, "Whoever abolishes the law abolishes the gospel also."[66] Even if the law does not justify, it does not follow that it is to be rejected. As previously depicted concerning the necessity of the law for justification, a differentiation is required: "In one sense the question is to be answered in the negative, but in another, in the affirmative."[67] Agricola features a dichotomy between Christ's coming and fulfilling the law and a consequent nullification of the

63. *LW* 54:309 (no. 4007, dated 12 September 1538); *WA, TR* 4:72–73, *LW* 54:314 (no. 4050, dated 11 October 1538); *WA, TR* 4:101, *LW* 54:314–15 (no. 4057, dated 13 October 1538); *WA, TR* 4:105. In the second Antinomian Disputation, Luther had this to say: "tam diabolus, quam Christus utitur lege in terrendis hominibus, sed fines sunt dissimillimi et prorsus contrarii." ("Both the devil and Christ use the law to terrify, but the goals are quite different, entirely opposed.") *WA* 39/1. 426. 31–427. 21.

64. Lohse, *Luthers Theologie*, 197; ET *Martin Luther's Theology*, 179.

65. Lohse, *Luthers Theologie*, 199; ET *Martin Luther's Theology*, 181.

66. Cited in Lohse, *Luthers Theologie*, 200; ET *Martin Luther's Theology*, 181. See *WA, TR* 3:483 (no. 3650c, dated 21 December, 1537): "Qui tollit legem, et evangelium tollit."

67. Lohse, *Luthers Theologie*, 200; ET *Martin Luther's Theology*, 182.

law for Christians; Luther brings to the fore the ongoing internal dynamics between the gospel and the law. Luther's stance on the necessity of the law in Christian life stands out, in similar fashion, in his fight against those who prompted the Peasants' Revolt, proclaiming that the freedom of the gospel absolves people from all law of any kind.

Throughout the disputes with his opponents regarding the law, Luther discerns two fallacious outlooks: "Both groups sin against the Law: those on the right, who want to be justified through the Law, and those on the left, who want to be altogether free of the Law."[68] Neither groups do justice to the law, Luther insists, claiming "[t]herefore we must travel the royal road, so that we neither reject the Law altogether nor attribute more to it than we should."[69] The debate reveals that there are three groups of people who abuse the law: (1) the self-righteous and the hypocrites who seek justification by means of the law; (2) those who want to excuse Christians from the law altogether; (3) those who feel terrified by the law yet do not flee to Christ. For the first group of people, the misuse of the law is "a cause for despair"; for the second, the misuse of the law is a cause for antinomianism; for the third, the misuse of the law is "a cause for pride and presumption."[70] Therefore, Luther argues that, in order not to fall into any of these three groups, Christians not only need to have an accurate knowledge and definition of the law but also need to use it.

In opposition to crediting the law with justification, annihilating it, or living in fear because of it, Luther accents divergent ways to discuss the law or, more precisely, the functions thereof, according

---

68. *LW* 26:343; *WA* 40/1. 528. 2–3: "Utrique enim in legem peccant, in dextra qui per legem iustificari, in sinistra qui prorsus a lege liberi esse volunt."

69. *LW* 26:343; *WA* 40/1. 528. 4–5: "Ingrediendum est igitur regia via, ut neque legem plane reiiciamus, neque plus ei tribuamus, quam oportet."

70. *LW* 26:344–45; *WA* 40/1. 528. 21–34. See also *LW* 26:348; *WA* 40/1. 534. 14–17.

to different contexts. Notwithstanding, in Luther's mind the roles of the law share a common core. It stands out in sharp contrast to the character of God's promise: "The Law demands: 'Do this!' The promise grants: 'Accept this!'"[71] The law orders but does not provide the capacity to fulfill the order.

In contrast, faith instructs people to accept Christ, who has the power to enable them to observe the law. Luther says, "Faith . . . does not perform works; it believes in Christ, the Justifier. And so a man does not live because of his doing; he lives because of his believing. Yet a believer does keep the Law."[72] In this way, Luther shows his conviction that he does not advocate abolishing the law but truly upholds it. So Luther's depiction of the twofold way of fulfilling the law vindicates the claim that his redefined faith and love are not mutually exclusive but compatible in the dimension of proper, active, and progressing righteousness and holiness. This compatibility is also observed in Luther's application of christological terminologies and concepts, which is our next topic.

Christological Terminologies and Concepts

Absolute Faith versus Incarnate Faith

Among Luther's explanations of the relationship between faith and love in the dimension of proper, active, and progressing righteousness and holiness, his application of christological terminologies and concepts are particularly compelling. What is most engaging is the christological analogy applied to the two relations—the relation between Christ in terms of his divine nature and Christ in terms of his divine nature united with his human nature

---

71. *LW* 26:303; *WA* 40/1. 472. 18: "Lex enim exigit: Fac hoc! Promissio donat: Accipe hoc!"
72. *LW* 26:274; *WA* 40/1. 428. 20–22: "Fides vero non facit, sed credit in Christum iustificatorem; et sic homo vivit non propter facere, sed credere. Credens autem facit legem."

and the relation between an "abstract, bare, and simple faith" and "concrete, composite, and incarnate faith."[73] In order to elucidate the rationale for the utilization of this christological analogy, Luther calls attention to the twofold portrayal of Christ in Scripture.

> Why should Holy Scripture not speak in these different ways about faith when it speaks in different ways about Christ as God and man? That is, sometimes it [Scripture] speaks about His whole Person, sometimes about His two natures separately, either the divine or the human nature. If it speaks about the natures separately, it is speaking of Him absolutely; but if it speaks about the divine nature united with the human in one Person, then it is speaking of Christ as composite and incarnate.[74]

Even though Luther never forgets to deal with Christ in the context of his incarnation in a human body, he also clarifies that, just as the divinity alone created all things without the cooperation of the humanity, so the justification or the new creation has fundamentally become available to sinners because of his divinity, joined with his humanity. Luther explains,

> The kingly authority of the divinity is given to Christ the man, not because of His humanity but because of His divinity. For the divinity alone created all things, without the cooperation of the humanity. Nor did the humanity conquer sin and death . . . . Therefore the humanity would not have accomplished anything by itself; but the divinity, joined with the humanity, did it alone, and the humanity did it on account of the divinity.[75]

---

73. *LW* 26:266; *WA* 40/1. 417. 12–13: "loquatur [Spiritus] in Scripturis vel de fide abstracta, nuda, simplici, vel de concreta, composita, incarnata."

74. *LW* 26:265; *WA* 40/1. 415. 26–31: "Quidni ita varie loqueretur Scriptura de fide, cum etiam de Christo Deo et himine varie loquatur, scilicet iam de tota persona, iam de duabus naturis ipsius seorsim, aut divina aut humana. Si de naturis seorsim loquitur, de eo absolute loquitur. Si vero de divina unita humanae in una persona loquitur, de Christo composito et incarnato loquitur."

75. *LW* 26:267; *WA* 40/1. 417. 29–418. 10: "Ut regnum divinitatis traditur Christo homini non propter humanitatem sed divinitatem. Sola enim divinitas creavit omnia humanitate nihil cooperante; Sicut neque peccatum et mortem humanitas vicit . . . . Itaque sola humanitas nihil effecisset, sed divinitas humanitati coniuncta sola fecit et humanitas propter divinitatem."

With regard to this christological analogy, we should not rush to assume that humanity is minimized in Luther's Christology. His point is that Christ is true God by nature. "Just as

Just as Christ can be spoken of sometimes in terms of his absolute divine nature and sometimes in terms of his incarnate divine nature, so too faith is analogically spoken of sometimes as an absolute faith and sometimes as an incarnate faith. In other words, faith can be understood sometimes "apart from the work and sometimes with the work."[76] Luther elaborates,

> Faith is absolute or abstract when Scripture speaks absolutely about justification or about those who are justified . . . . But when Scripture speaks about rewards and works, then it is speaking about faith as something compound, concrete, or incarnate.[77]

By the same token, Luther analogically connects the relation between faith and works of love with the relation between Christ's divine

the Jews boast only about an Abraham who does works, so the pope sets forth only a Christ who does works or is an example." *LW* 26:246; *WA* 40/1. 389. 12–13: "Quemadmodum autem Iudaei gloriantur tantum de Abraham operante, ita Papa solum proponit Christum operantem seu exemplum." Luther also mentions: "For it belongs exclusively to the divine power to destroy sin and abolish death, to create righteousness and grant life. This divine power they have attributed to our own works" and thereby make human beings "true God by nature!" *LW* 26:283; *WA* 40/1. 442. 21–24: "Nam solius devinae potentiae est peccatum destruere, mortem abolere etc., creare iustitiam et vitam donare. Hanc divinam virtutem tribuerunt operibus nostris . . . ac fecerunt nos vere et naturaliter Deum."

    In dealing with this issue, it may be useful to look into the difference between Luther and Andreas Osiander regarding the manner of Christ's indwelling in Christians or the manner of the unity between Christ and Christians in conjunction with the question of a sinner's justification. Attempting to avoid the appearance that Christians may not really be justified and are only seen by God "as if" they were justified, Osiander contends that the righteousness of faith is not *extra nos*, but *in nobis* by virtue of the dwelling of the righteous Christ in us. One of the major problems in this argument is that the indwelling Christ has nothing to do with the divine–human Jesus of Nazareth. The inner-Christ is the divine Logos, stripped of his humanity, who instills in us with him God the Father and the Holy Spirit. It is this undifferentiated Godhead who infuses the divine essence and quality into us, effecting essential righteousness in us and making us substantially righteous. On the basis of our research on Luther's concept of faith that grasps the divine–human Jesus Christ in one's heart, we must clearly differentiate Luther's position from Osiander's. For further details on Osiander's notion, see John Calvin, *Institutes of the Christian Religion I*, 1559, ed. John T. McNeill and trans. Ford L. Battles (Philadelphia: Westminster, 1960), III. 11. 5–12; Julie Canlis, "Calvin, Osiander and Participation in God," *International Journal of Systematic Theology* 6, no. 2 (2004): 169–84.

76. *LW* 26:264; *WA* 40/1. 414. 24–25: "fides aliquando accipitur extra opus, aliquando cum opere."
77. *LW* 26:264–65; *WA* 40/1. 415. 13–17: "Fides absoluta seu abstracta est, quando Scriptura absolute loquitur de iustificatione seu de iustificatis . . . . Quando vero Scriptura loquitur de praemiis et operibus, tunc de fide composita, concreta seu incarnata loquitur."

nature and human nature in the following way: "In theology let faith always be the divinity of works, diffused throughout the works in the same way that the divinity is throughout the humanity of Christ . . . . Therefore faith is the 'do-all' in works."[78] Luther also states as follows: "Thus faith is universally the divinity in the work, the person, and the members of the body, as the one and only cause of justification; afterwards this is attributed to the matter on account of the form, to the work on account of the faith."[79] "So here faith alone justifies and does everything; nevertheless, it is attributed to works on account of faith."[80] On the basis of this christological analogy, Luther contends that "when faith is preexistent, a beautiful incarnation can take place."[81]

In this line of argument, a significant correlation emerges between God's initial creation *ex nihilo* and God's new creation of justified Christians out of sinners. Just as the power of initial creation is attributed solely to God, so the power of new creation is attributed to the deity of Christ in the incarnate man. On these grounds, "justification belongs to faith alone, just as creation belongs to the divinity [alone]; nevertheless, just as it is true to say about Christ the man that He created all things, so justification is attributed to incarnate faith or to faithful 'doing.'"[82]

---

78. *LW* 26:266; *WA* 40/1. 417. 15–19: "Sit ergo in Theologia fides perpetuo divinitas operum et sic perfusa per opera, ut divinitas per humanitatem in Christo . . . . Est ergo fides Fac totum . . . in operibus." With regard to the term *fac totum*, see also *LW* 3:90: "Christ is the Do-all: 'In Him the whole fullness of deity dwells bodily' (Col. 2:9); and 'From His fullness have we all received, grace upon grace' (John 1:16)."; *WA* 42. 612. 29–30: "Christus enim est fac totum. 'In eo est plenitude divinitatis.' 'Per eum habemus gratiam pro gratia: ac accipimus omnes de eius plenitudine.'"
79. *LW* 26:267; *WA* 40/1. 417. 26–29: "Ut fides in universum sit divinitas in opere, persona et membris, ut unica causa iustificationis quae postea etiam tribuitur materiae propter formam, hoc est, operi propter fidem."
80. *LW* 26:267; *WA* 40/1. 418. 10–11: "Sic hic sola fides iustificat et facit omnia; Et tamen operibus idem tribuitur propter fidem."
81. *LW* 26:272; *WA* 40/1. 426. 31–32: "quo [fide] praeexistente, tunc fiat pulchra incarnatio."

"New and Theological Grammar"

Here, Luther classifies "doing" and "working" in three fundamentally different ways: the essential or natural, the moral, and the theological.[83] In the first and second cases, these words are taken in their usual way. In theology, however, they achieve a completely new meaning. Whoever wants to be justified on the basis of the law and human works is performing a moral, not a theological action that must include faith. On that account, Luther contends that, since everything that is attributed to works au fond belongs to faith, love or works of love as the fruit of faith must not be looked at in a "moral sense" but in a "theological and faithful sense."[84] "Thus our opponents are forced to concede that in all the works of the saints the faith in virtue of which the works are pleasing is presupposed. In theology, therefore, there is a new 'doing,' one that is different from moral 'doing.'"[85] He emphatically inculcates these things because there are people who "confuse philosophy and theology and make theological works into moral works. A theological work is a work done in faith; thus a theological man is a man of faith."[86]

On the basis of this stance, Luther presents a very important and intriguing expression. In reference to Hebrews 11,[87] Luther argues

---

82. *LW* 26:266; *WA* 40/1. 416. 23–25: "Ita iustificatio solius fidei est ut Creatio divinitatis. Et tamen ut vere dicitur de Christo homine, quod creavit omnia, ita tribuitur etiam iustificatio fidei incarnatae seu fideli facere."

83. *LW* 26:267; *WA* 40/1. 418. 12–14: "Sunt igitur ista vocabula: 'Facere', 'operari', tripliciter accipienda, Substantialiter seu naturaliter . . . . moraliter et Theologice."

84. *LW* 26:266; *WA* 40/1. 417. 15–16: "Non enim moraliter, sed Theologice et fideliter sunt opera inspicienda."

85. *LW* 26:264; *WA* 40/1. 414. 20–23: "Sic coguntur adversarii concedere, quod in omnibus operibus Sanctorum praesupponitur fides propter quam opera placent. Ergo in Theologia est novum 'facere' et diversum a morali."

86. *LW* 26:266; *WA* 40/1. 417. 23–26: "commiscent Philosophiam et Theologiam et ex moralibus operibus Theologica faciunt, recte et facile respondere possitis. Theologicum opus est fidele opus. Sic homo Theologicus est fidelis."

87. For instance, Luther enumerates Abel's offering up by faith a better sacrifice to God than Cain (Heb. 11:4), Enoch's being taken up to heaven by faith (Heb. 11:5), and Abraham's obedience

that the actions (including offerings and sacrifices) of the patriarchs, prophets, and kings—whom Scripture portrays as working righteousness, raising the dead, and conquering kingdoms—must be interpreted according to "a new and theological grammar,"[88] that is, "a doing in faith."[89]

This new grammar replaces "the moral grammar" in the domain of theology.[90] People should not confuse true "doing" and hypocritical "doing"—theological "doing" and moral "doing." Those who apply the moral grammar to theology are employing "human will and reason," without "a theological right reason" illumined by faith and "good will" purified by faith as the necessary condition for true doing and working.[91] Once they have become accustomed to this new theological grammar, Luther argues, "they can easily explain all those passages that seem to assert a righteousness of works."[92]

Luther actually employs this "new and theological grammar" as the principle of interpretation for some biblical passages in the controversy between him and his opponents over the doctrine of faith and love: "faith working through love" (Galatians 5:6); "To the pure all things are pure" (Titus 1:15); "If you would enter life, keep the Commandments" (Matthew 19:17); "He who does them shall live by them" (Galatians 3:12); and "Depart from evil, and do good" (Psalm 37:27).[93] Likewise, Luther unswervingly affirms that scriptural injunctions to "do this, and you will live" (Luke 10:28 and similar

in faith (Heb. 11:8). On the basis of these examples, Luther underscores that only those who have faith can please God (Heb. 11:6). *LW* 26:267; *WA* 40/1. 418. 24–27.

88. *LW* 26:267; *WA* 40/1. 418. 24: "secundum novam et Theologicam Grammaticam."
89. *LW* 26:263; *WA* 40/1. 413. 19–20: "Itaque facere . . . non est naturale aut morale, sed fidele."
90. *LW* 26:268; *WA* 40/1. 419. 18: "Grammaticam morale."
91. *LW* 26:268; *WA* 40/1. 419. 14–20: "voluntatem et rationem humanam . . . . sine recta ratione et bona voluntate Theologica."
92. *LW* 26:268; *WA* 40/1. 419. 10–11: "facile explicare poterunt omnes locos qui iustitiam operum statuere videntur."
93. *LW* 26:265; *WA* 40/1. 415. 17–20: "'Fides per dilectionem efficax'; 'Omnia munda mundis'; 'Si vis in vitam ingredi, serva mandata Dei'; 'Qui fecerit haec, vivet in eis'; 'Declina a malo et fac bonum' etc."

passages) speak of "doing in faith";[94] namely, "faith in the concrete rather than in the abstract, in a composite sense rather than in a bare or simple sense."[95] The accurate deciphering of such a passage is "[t]ake care first that you be faithful, that you have right reason and a good will, that is, faith in Christ. When you have this, you can do works."[96] When Scripture speaks about rewards and works, then it is speaking about faith as incarnate. So, it is fallacious to think that "merits and rewards are promised to moral works rather than solely to works done in faith."[97]

The deliberate employment of this christological analogy in his doctrine of faith and love testifies to one of the ways Luther goes beyond Paul. This christological analogy reveals that Luther's reconceptualization of faith, love, and their relationship fundamentally hinges on Christ. His concept of faith exposes Christ as the living heart and centripetal force of his theology. In turn, his understanding of Christ reveals the absolute necessity of and legitimate space for a doctrine of love in his theology, and it throws light on his doctrine of faith and love as a coupled theme with a specific order.[98]

On the basis of this christological analogy, it may be possible to analyze the relationship between faith and love by borrowing the following three cardinal concepts of the Chalcedonian formula:

---

94. *LW* 26:265; *WA* 40/1. 415. 21: "de fideli 'facere'" ("faithful doing").

95. *LW* 26:266; *WA* 40/1. 416. 20–21: "de fide concreta, non abstracta; composita, non nuda aut simplici."

96. *LW* 26:265; *WA* 40/1. 415. 22–24: "cogita primum, ut sis fidelis, habeas rectam rationem et bonam voluntatem, id est, fidem in Christum et ea habita opereris."

97. *LW* 26:266; *WA* 40/1. 416. 25–28: "Ideo non est sentiendum . . . quod opera absolute et simpliciter iustificent quodque illis moralibus operibus promittantur merita et praemia, sed fidelibus."

98. A. Andrew Das elucidates the indissoluble connection (*nexus indivulsus*) between justification and sanctification in Paul's Epistle to the Galatians by focusing on the theme of "oneness in Christ (Gal. 3:28). A. Andrew Das, "*Oneness in Christ*: The *Nexus Indivulsus* between Justification and Sanctification in Paul's Letter to the Galatians," *Concordia Journal* 21, no. 2 (1995): 173–86.

unity, distinction, and order. There is a unity between faith and love. They are not separated from each other. However, faith and love are distinguished from each other without confusion. There is also a certain order between faith and love. Faith logically takes priority over love. The priority of faith over love can be understood in the following senses: (1) faith is the sole means by which sinners can become righteous and love is the fruit of faith that the righteous bear; (2) faith is directly linked with being and love, with doing which is rooted in being; (3) "in theology the work does not amount to anything without faith, but that faith must precede before you can do works";[99] (4) things associated with love must be guided by things affiliated with faith, as in the case of the Decalogue.[100]

This prioritization suggests the right ordering in the relation among God, neighbor, and self. The vertical relationship comprising the relation of God toward human beings should always be first. Without God's initiative, there would be no possibility of establishing right relations between human beings and God. We can respond to this initiative of God by faith in Christ alone. Only when these two

99. *LW* 26:264; *WA* 40/1. 414. 13: "In Theologia opus nihil valere sine fide, sed oportere praecedere fidem, antequam opereris." Luther's interpretation of the Decalogue in his *Small Catechism* is one of the most obvious examples showing the logical priority of faith to love. He repeats faith (in the form of loving and fearing God) before every commandment: "We are to fear and love God, so that . . . ." Martin Luther, "The Ten Commandments," *The Small Catechism*, trans. James Schaaf et al., in *The Book of Concord*, ed. Robert Kolb and Timothy J. Wengert (Minneapolis: Fortress Press, 2000), 352–54. "Wir sollen Gott fürchten und lieben, daß . . . ." ("Debemus Deum timere et diligere, ut ne/ne . . . .") *Die Bekenntnisschriften der evangelisch-lutherischen Kirche*, 12th ed. (Göttingen: Vandenhoeck & Ruprecht, 1998), 508–509. See also *LW* 26:255–56; *WA* 40/1. 400. 31–402. 28.

100. An aspect of Luther's confrontation with the sacramentarians reveals his position on the priority of faith over love, which he substantiates from the relationship between the Two Tables of the Decalogue: "In their books and writings the sacramentarians have pestered us with 'love.' They say to us, 'You Wittenbergers have no love.' But if one asks, 'What is love?' we are told that it means to be united in doctrine and to stop religious controversies. Yes, do you hear? There are two tables [of the Decalogue], the first and the second. Love belongs in the second table. It's superior to all other works there. On the other hand, [in the first table] it is commanded: 'Fear God. Listen to his Word.' The sacramentarians don't bother with this. 'He who loves father and mother more than me is not worthy of me' [Matt. 10:37], said Christ." *LW* 54:463 (no. 5601, dated Spring 1543); *WA, TR* 5:273.

vertical actions—God's initiative and our response—have occurred can Christians correctly approach their neighbors in a horizontal relationship of genuine love. This order signifies a further logical order: proper, active, and progressing righteousness and holiness consistently depend upon alien, passive, and perfect righteousness and holiness. The latter is not contingent on the former, however. Accordingly, Luther proclaims that "this love or the works that follow faith do not form or adorn my faith, but my faith forms and adorns love."[101]

The predominance of Christ in Luther's concepts of faith and love as well as the compatibility between faith and love in the dimension of active righteousness and holiness are also evident in his use of several other twofold formulas. For example, Luther speaks of: (1) a twofold way of Christ's being given to human beings; (2) a twofold way of Christ's coming; and (3) a twofold way of putting on Christ.[102]

---

101. *LW* 26:161; *WA* 40/1. 275. 15–16: "illa charitas vel sequentia opera nec informant meam fidem nec ornant, sed fides mea informat et ornat charitatem."

102. With regard to the christological explanations of his teaching on faith and love, Luther contemplates the twofold significance of the death and resurrection of Christ in conjunction with the death and resurrection of the inner and outward person: as a sacrament for the inner person and an example for the outward person. On this subject, see Luther's exposition of Rom. 6:3, in which he refers to Augustine's *De trinitate*, IV. 3. 6: "Blessed Augustine in Book 4, chapter 3, of *On the Trinity* says: 'For our twofold death the Savior pays with His single death, and in order to achieve a twofold resurrection for us, He has set before us and offered us His own single resurrection in His sacrament and example. For having put on our mortal flesh and dying only in it and rising only in it, now only in it He joins these things together for us, for in this flesh He became a sacrament for the inner man and an example for the outward man. With regard to the sacrament for the inner man we have this word: 'We know that our old self was crucified with Him, so that the body of sin might be destroyed' (v. 6). But to the example for the outward man this statement is pertinent: 'And do not fear those who kill the body' (Matt. 10:28). He most strongly encouraged His followers to this course through His own death, which was of this kind.' The resurrection of the body of the Lord is shown to pertain to the sacrament of the inner man through this statement of the apostle in Col. 3:1: 'If then you have been raised with Christ, seek the things that are above.' But to the example for the outward man this statement applies: 'Not a hair of your head will perish' (Luke 21:18), along with the fact that He showed His body to His disciples after His resurrection." *LW* 25:310; *WA* 56. 321. 23–322. 9. See St. Augustine, *De trinitate* in *Patrologiae cursus completes*, Series Latina,

Twofold Way of Christ's Being Given to Human Beings

As already indicated above, Luther draws on Scripture to explain that Christ is given as "a gift" and "an example for us to imitate."[103] Christ is, for all, "the divine and inestimable gift that the Father has given to us to be our Justifier, Lifegiver, and Redeemer."[104] Christ "has been made by God my wisdom, righteousness, sanctification, and redemption."[105] Moreover, Christ, who is the divine gift itself, brings other gifts of his own to those who grasp him in their hearts through faith. Hence, Luther contends that Christ "must be grasped by faith as a gift, not as an example."[106] He explains, "It pleases God to grant this inexpressible gift to us freely—to us who are unworthy."[107] This Christ given as a gift demands nothing but faith.

Christ the gift is differentiated from Christ the example whom all Christians are admonished to imitate.[108] "Thus it is a laudable and happy thing to imitate the example of Christ in His deeds, to love one's neighbors, to do good to those who deserve evil, to pray for one's enemies, and to bear with patience the ingratitude of those who require good with evil."[109] One of the ways to imitate Christ is "being crucified with Him—which is a crucifixion that

42–43, ed. Jacques-Paul Migne (Paris, 1865), IV. 3. 6; ET *The Trinity*, trans. Edmund Hill, O.P., ed. John E. Rotelle, O.S.A. (Brooklyn, NY: New City Press, 2000), IV. 3. 6.

103. *LW* 27:34; *WA* 40/2. 42. 19–25: "Scriptura proponit Christum dupliciter, Primum ut donum . . . . Deinde scriptura proponit etiam eum ut exemplum nobis imitandum." See Bengt Hoffman, "Lutheran Spirituality," in *Spiritual Traditions for the Contemporary Church*, ed. Robin Maas and Gabriel O'Donnell, O.P. (Nashville: Abingdon, 1990), 156–57.

104. *LW* 26:353; *WA* 40/1. 541. 16–17: "[Christus est] divinum et inenarrabile donum quod donavit nobis Pater, ut esset Iustificator, Vivificator et Redemptor noster."

105. *LW* 27:34; *WA* 40/2. 42. 22: "a Deo mihi factus est [Christus] sapientia, iusticia, sanctificatio et redemptio."

106. *LW* 26:247; *WA* 40/1. 389. 20: "fide apprehendendus est ut donum, non ut exemplum."

107. *LW* 26:214; *WA* 40/1. 344. 14–15: "Deo placeat hoc inenarrabile donum gratis et indignis nobis dare."

108. *LW* 26:352; *WA* 40/1. 539. 35–540. 11.

109. *LW* 26:247; *WA* 40/1. 389. 29–31: "magna laus et felicitas est, imitari exemplum Christi operantis, diligere proximos, benefacere male merentibus, orare pro inimicis, patienter ferre ingratitudinem eorum qui bonum malo rependunt."

pertains to the flesh."[110] However, Luther does not fail to articulate that the crucifixion of the Christian is a matter of proper, active, and progressing righteousness and holiness that must not be confused with Christ's crucifixion in the matter of alien, passive, and perfect righteousness and holiness. The latter is about "that sublime crucifixion by which sin, the devil, and death are crucified in Christ, not in me" because "here Christ does everything alone."[111]

Christ, who is given to human beings in a twofold way, bestows innumerable benefits upon them. Luther lays particular stress on a twofold benefit: passive and perfect righteousness and holiness and active and progressing righteousness and holiness. So, when Luther says "new creation," it conveys two significances: a new creation already complete and perfect in its givenness and a new creation still in progress.

Twofold Way of Christ's Coming

Luther emphasizes that, even if Adam and all the faithful prior to Christ had the gospel and faith in forms efficient for salvation, everything pertinent to justification is predicated on Christ's coming once for all at a set time. Likewise, "faith came once for all when the apostles preached the Gospel throughout the world."[112] Christ, however, also "comes spiritually every day," "as we gradually acknowledge and understand more and more what has been granted to us by Him," and "through the Word of the Gospel faith also comes every day."[113]

---

110. *LW* 26:165; *WA* 40/1. 280. 25–281. 16: "imitari exemplum Christi est etiam cum eo crucifigi, quae concrucifixio pertinet ad carnem."

111. *LW* 26:165; *WA* 40/1. 281. 18–19: "de illa sublimi concrucifixione qua peccatum, Diabolus, mors crucifigitur in Christo, non in me. Hic Christus solus omnia facit."

112. *LW* 26:351; *WA* 40/1. 538. 29–30: "semel Christus venit praefinito tempore, semel venit et fides, cum Apostoli Evangelium per totum mundum praedicaverunt." See also *LW* 26:360; *WA* 40/1. 550. 20–24.

The daily coming of Christ and its significance are always contingent upon the coming of Christ at a set time in history and its import. As previously mentioned, even after justification, the remnants of sin still adhere to the flesh. For this reason, Christians are still troubled by the remnants of sin in the flesh, especially in their conscience and feelings, and by the law that, mirroring the remnants of sin, continues to accuse and afflict them. After the resurrection of Christ, Christians are not left alone in this struggle. Christ comes daily and spiritually to assist them in proper, active, and progressing righteousness and holiness:

> But it [conscience] is always encouraged by the daily coming of Christ. Just as He once came into the world at a specific time to redeem us from the harsh dominion of our custodian, so He comes to us spiritually every day, causing us to grow in faith and in our knowledge of Him. Thus the conscience takes hold of Christ more perfectly day by day; and day by day the law of flesh and sin, the fear of death, and whatever other evils the Law brings with it are diminishing.[114]

---

113. *LW* 26:351; *WA* 40/1. 538. 30–34: "Deinde quotidie etiam venit spiritualiter Christus, Venit et per verbum Evangelii quotidie fides . . . . Christus spiritualiter venit, quando subinde magis magisque agnoscimus et intelligimus, quae ab ipso donata sint nobis." Concerning the daily coming of Christ, see also *LW* 26:349; *WA* 40/1. 536. 25–26 (*quotidiano adventu Christi*; by the daily coming of Christ), *LW* 26:360; *WA* 40/1. 550. 24–29.

114. *LW* 26:349–50; *WA* 40/1. 536. 25–537. 16: "Ipsa [conscientia] tamen semper iterum erigitur quotidiano adventu Christi qui, ut semel certo tempore venit in mundum redempturus nos a durissimo imperio paedagogi nostri, ita quotidie spiritualiter ad nos venit hoc agens, ut in fide et cognitione ipsius crescamus, ut conscientia de die in diem perfectius se, Christum, apprehendat et in dies magis magisque minuatur Lex carnis et peccati, pavor mortis et quidquid malorum Lex secum affert." Luther also mentions Christ's coming in a different way for unbelievers: "Today Christ is still present to some, but to others He is still to come. To believers He is present and has come; to unbelievers He has not yet come and does not help them. But if they hear His Word and believe, Christ becomes present to them, justifies and saves them." *LW* 26:240; *WA* 40/1. 379. 14–17: "Et hodie Christus quibusdam est praesens, quibusdam est futurus. Credentibus praesens est seu venit, Incredulis nondum venit neque eis prodest. Hi si audiunt ipsius verbum et credunt, fit ipsis Christus praesens, iustificat et salvat eos."

Twofold Way of Putting on Christ

In relation to these previously mentioned twofold formulas, Luther (drawing on Galatians 3:27) mentions a twofold way of putting on Christ: "according to the Law and according to the Gospel."[115] The gospel teaches that "putting on" Christ signifies grasping him through faith in the heart as the sole savior and justifier without any human involvement or collaboration. It is a matter "not of imitation but of a new birth and a new creation, namely, that I put on Christ Himself, that is, His innocence, righteousness, wisdom, power, salvation, life, and Spirit."[116] When we were dressed in "the leather garment of Adam, which is a deadly garment and the clothing of sin" which Paul calls "the old man," we put on a new garment, Christ, through baptism.[117]

On the basis of Romans 13:14, Luther also explains that putting on Christ means imitating the example and virtues of Christ: "In Christ we see the height of patience, gentleness, and love, and an admirable moderation in all things. We ought to put on this adornment of Christ, that is, imitate these virtues of His."[118] In a similar fashion, the difference is highlighted in the metaphor of two kinds of garments: "the garment of our righteousness and salvation" that Christians put on by a new birth in baptism and "the garment of imitation" that Christians put on by imitating Christ.[119] While these christological terminologies and concepts clarify the way faith correlates with love,

---

115. *LW* 26:352; *WA* 40/1. 539. 34: "Induere Christum dupliciter intelligitur, Legaliter et Evangelice."

116. *LW* 26:352; *WA* 40/1. 540. 17–19: "Induere vero Christum Evangelice non est imitationis, sed nativitatis et creationis novae, Quod videlicet ego induor ipso Christo, hoc est, ipsius innocentia, iustitia, sapientia, potentia, salute, vita, Spiritu etc."

117. *LW* 26:352–53; *WA* 40/1. 540. 19–541. 20.

118. *LW* 26:352; *WA* 40/1. 540. 13–16: "Videmus autem in Christo summam patientiam, summam lenitatem et charitatem et admirabilem in omnibus rebus moderationem. Hunc ornatum Christi induere, id est, has eius virtutes imitari debemus."

119. *LW* 26:353; *WA* 40/1. 541. 32–35: "Docet ergo Paulus baptismum non sginum, sed indumentum Christi, imo ipsum Christum indumentum nostrum esse. Quare baptismus

there is a simile and two metaphors that shed additional light on the tight and dynamic interconnectedness between faith and love, which will be examined in the following section.

Metaphors

In the dimension of active righteousness and holiness, Luther employs specific similes and metaphors to portray his conceptions of the relationship between faith and love—linking Christ and Christians, a doer and deeds, and a tree and fruits.

Christians like Christ

Just as Christ plays a decisive role in Luther's reconceptualization of faith, so he does in Luther's reconceptualization of love. In particular, two facets characterize Christ's role in Luther's delineation of love in the dimension of active righteousness and holiness. The first facet is a logical corollary of Luther's doctrine of justification by faith in Christ alone: insofar as the sole demand, object, content, and form of faith is Christ (especially reckoned from the standpoint of his proper function) and a genuine Christian love flows out of this faith, Christ remains the true initiator, activator, and actor in such a love.

The second facet of Christ's role is found in the fact that he is the example for his followers. Luther calls this role Christ's "accidental" function. Though it is not as determining as his proper function, it can scarcely be overestimated for Christians, from the vantage point of a Christian's life and love in the dimension of active righteousness and holiness. Christ is not only the justifier but also the example for his followers. Faith believes in Christ the justifier; love imitates Christ the example. Of course, this statement must be made with a clear

---

potentissima ac efficacissima res est. Ubi vero induti sumus Christum, indumentum iustitiae et salutis nostrae, tum etiam induemus Christum vestimentum imitationis."

qualification: no law, no human work of the law, no human sinner can be Christ in terms of Christ's proper function. When Luther portrays Christians, passively and completely justified and sanctified, as "Christs" to their neighbors, Christ's accidental function, not his proper function, is germane.

The implication of this connection exposes two of the pivotal characteristics of Luther's concept of love in the dimension of active righteousness and holiness. First, genuine Christian love is an imitation of Christ. This imitation is active, incessant, and committed and sees every place as full of opportunities to practice following in Christ's footsteps. Second, this imitation is, in any event, never an imitation of Christ's proper function but of his accidental function. If one attempts to imitate Christ in his proper function, then one is, in truth, attempting to usurp Christ's divine power for the justification and salvation of sinners. The expressions related to "as Christ . . . Christians . . . too" pinpoints very precisely the relationship between Christ, the example, and Christians, the imitators.[120]

In dealing with the relation of faith to love, Luther makes repeated use of the expression "as Christ . . . Christians . . . too." This expression illustrates the relationship between a referential person or thing as an example and Christians being exhorted to faithful imitation of the example. The prototype for imitation is found in how God handles human beings in and through Jesus Christ. That

---

120. Luther's sermons demonstrate these ideas very clearly: "love must deal with our neighbor in the same manner as God has dealt with us." *LW* 51:75; *WA* 10/3. 14. 20–23. "Then a person, after he has given all glory to Christ, is always remembering to do to his neighbor as Christ has done to him, in order that he may help him and everyone else." *LW* 51:116; *WA* 10/3. 351. 22–24. In his *Treatise on Good Works*, Luther also says, "Therefore, a Christian man must rise higher, letting his kindness serve even those who do not deserve it: evil-doers, enemies, and the ungrateful, even as his heavenly Father makes his sun to rise on good and evil alike, and his rain to fall on the grateful and the ungrateful [Matt. 5:45]." *LW* 44:109; *WA* 6. 272. 31–35. "Just as on the cross Christ prayed not for himself alone but rather for us when he said, 'Father, forgive them, for they know not what they do' [Luke 23:34], so we must also pray for one another." *LW* 44:71; *WA* 6. 242. 30–33.

is, what is revealed in the vertical relation, which is actively initiated by God and passively responded to by human beings through faith in Christ, becomes the paradigm for Christians in their horizontal acts of love.

When we dive into this thought of Luther's that Christ is the example for Christians and that God's way of dealing with human beings in the vertical relation is paradigmatic for Christians dealing with other human beings in the horizontal relation, we are challenged with two kinds of spatial movements, which are symbolic as well as literal. One of them is an outward movement and the other is a downward movement. This experience evokes an imitation of Christ in exactly same pattern of an outward and downward spatial movement.

The term "outward" encapsulates Luther's thought about Christian freedom: the theologically momentous movement from "freedom from" to "freedom for." Christian freedom means a liberation of the human free will from its captivity to sin and the self-centeredness of fallen human nature. When Christians are set free from the bound will, their liberation reverses the hereditary propensity of human nature to turn inward to itself. It is "so deeply curved in upon itself."[121]

Bearing in mind Luther's belief that the self-centeredness of fallen human nature is the source of all actual sins, we cannot overstate the seriousness of the transition from inward to outward. The outward

---

121. "Our nature has been so deeply curved in upon itself because of the viciousness of original sin that it not only turns the finest gifts of God in upon itself and enjoys them (as is evident in the case of legalists and hypocrites), indeed, it even uses God Himself to achieve these aims, but it also seems to be ignorant of this very fact, that in acting so iniquitously, so perversely, and in such a depraved way, it is even seeking God for its own sake." *LW* 25:291; *WA* 56. 304. 24–29: "Ratio est, Quia Natura nostra vitio primi peccati tam profunda est in seipsam incurua, vt non solum optima dona Dei sibi inflectat ipsisque fruatur (vt patet in Institiariis et hipocritis), immo et ipso Deo vtatur ad illa consequenda, Verum etiam hoc ipsum ignoret, Quod tam inique, curue et praue omnia, etiam Deum, propter seipsam querat." See also *LW* 25:313; *WA* 56. 325. 19–21, *LW* 25:513; *WA* 56. 518. 6–7.

movement of God the Son shows that the being and living of Christians, who have the holy duty of imitating Christ, should be fundamentally reoriented from *inward* to self to *outward* to neighbors. Just as Christ, out of his complete freedom, made an outward movement in service to human beings, so Christians make the same outward movement in their gratuitously bestowed Christian freedom in service to neighbors.

The term "downward" is no less crucial in the Christian's imitation of Christ. The eternal Son took on human flesh, living among human beings or, more precisely, sinners, and serving them.[122] He did not cling to his divine status, but became instead the foremost of sinners and willingly immersed himself in the lives of sinners. This downward movement and involvement with sinners were not necessary for him; it did not bring about any fulfillment in the immanent Trinity. It was the Son's free decision for the sake of sinners, who stand at the crossroads of eternal life and death but either do not know which way to choose or even take the way of eternal death without hesitation.

The same downward movement is perceived in Jesus' earthly ministry. In the stories about Jesus, what irrefutably stands out is his special inclination and service to social outcasts. He never failed those in need; furthermore, he developed friendships with the socially

---

122. Luther, for instance, states in one of his sermons as follows: "Christ, the Son of God, was also high and noble, and yet he made himself equal to us poor men, indeed, he humbled himself beneath everybody." *LW* 51:352; *WA* 49. 612. 21–22: "Christus, Gottes Son, ist ja auch hoch und Edel gewest und hat sich doch uns armen menschen gleich gemacht, ja sich unter alle gedemütigt." He also describes: "No one has ever been humbled so deeply, no one has made himself smaller than did Christ, and for this reason, too, he alone may say: 'Learn of me, I am meek and lowly in heart.' Such words no saints have ever said or been able to say, nor could they compare themselves to his perfect lowliness and meekness. All of them remain pupils of this teacher." *LW* 52:4; *WA* 10^1/1. 3. 2–7: "der selb kleinist ist allein Christus. Niemant ist ihe so tieff ernidrigt, Niemant hatt sich selb so seher vorkleinet als Christus, daher auch er allein thar sagen: Lernet von mir, ich bin sanfftmutig und demutig von herzen, wilchs wort hatt noch mag kein heilige immer mehr sagen, noch die meisterschafft der demut und sanfftmutickeit ihm zu messen. Die bleiben alle sampt schuler unter disem meister."

excluded. In this service, he made a double downward movement: a movement from heaven to earth and, on earth, a movement to the lowest among human beings.

From Luther's understanding of the outward and downward movement of Christ, we can deduce two summary instructions: just as Christ, the Son, made an outward and downward movement to reach out to human beings in his unconditional love, so justified Christians make the same outward and downward movement to reach out to neighbors in altruistic and unconditional love. Just as Christ, the incarnate man, made an outward and downward movement, extending his sympathetic heart and caring hands to embrace those socially ostracized, so justified Christians make the same outward and downward movement to their neighbors. Christians are exhorted to be industrious in serving their neighbors with hospitable and humble hearts, without prejudging anyone or, more precisely, with a special intention to imitate Christ in the service of the poorest and the lowest in society.[123]

Among the many connotations of this literal and symbolic concept of outward and downward movement, one is humility. This attitude and practice of Christians is well exposed in Luther's theology of the cross, which he advances in opposition to the theology of glory. By the theology of the cross, Luther points to the dangers of pursuing an upward movement and suggests instead a downward movement, which can also be called humility. It can be divided as follows into epistemological humility, soteriological humility, and ethical humility.

First, in the matter of theological epistemology, Luther holds that Christians, and especially theologians, must not attempt to scrutinize the being and nature of God, which would be an upward movement.

---

123. This will be more concretely treated in chapter 5, under the subtitle of "Love in Relation to Neighbors: Vocation."

This theological exaltation as speculation wrongly attempts to fathom knowledge of God.[124] Christ's downward movement evidences God's decision to reveal who God is and what God intends for human salvation in and through Jesus Christ, the incarnate man, down on this earth—not up in heaven.[125]

Second, Luther's theology of the cross, which features the significance of a downward movement as a necessary epistemological humility in Christian faith, accompanies another kind of humility, namely, soteriological humility. It is characterized by an affective

124. Luther, for instance, states as follows: "I avoid all speculations about the Divine Majesty and take my stand in the humanity of Christ." *LW* 26:39; *WA* 40/1. 93. 24–25. In his exposition of Galatians 1:3 ("Grace to you and peace from God the Father and our Lord Jesus Christ"), Luther draws out two significant aspects of Paul's wishing grace and peace not only from God the Father but also from Jesus Christ. First, Luther argues that "[t]his is why Paul makes such a frequent practice of linking Jesus Christ with God the Father, to teach us what is the true Christian religion. It does not begin at the top, as all other religions do; it begins at the bottom. It bids us climb up by Jacob's ladder; God Himself leans on it, and its feet touch the earth, right by Jacob's head (Gen. 28:12). Therefore whenever you are concerned to think and act about your salvation, you must put away all speculations about the Majesty, all thoughts of works . . . . And you must run directly to the manger and the mother's womb, embrace this Infant and Virgin's Child in your arms, and look at Him." *LW* 26:30; *WA* 40/1. 79. 24–31.

On this theme, Paul Althaus provides an insightful statement: "For Luther, concern for the true knowledge of God and concern for the right ethical attitude are not separate and distinct but ultimately one and the same. The theology of glory and the theology of the cross each have implications for both. Natural theology and speculative metaphysics which seek to learn to know God from the works of creation are in the same category as the work righteousness of the moralist." Paul Althaus, *Die Theologie Martin Luthers*, 4th ed. (Gütersloh: Gerd Mohn, 1975), 35–36; ET *The Theology of Martin Luther*, trans. Robert C. Schultz (Philadelphia: Fortress Press, 1966), 27. Nygren also draws attention to the critical function of Luther's theology of the cross which opposes a theology of glory in its "upward tendency or ascent" through the metaphoric heavenly ladders. Anders Nygren, *Agape and Eros*, trans. Philip S. Watson (New York: Harper & Row, 1969), 700–709.

125. According to Luther, "Christ came into the world so that He might take hold of us and so that we, by gazing upon Christ, might be drawn and carried directly to the Father. As we have warned you before, there is no hope that any saving knowledge of God can come by speculating about the majesty of God; this can come only by taking hold of Christ, who, by the will of the Father, has given Himself into death for our sins. When you have grasped this, then all wrath stops, and fear and trembling disappear; and God appears as nothing but the merciful One who did not spare His own Son but gave Him up for us all (Rom. 8:32). It is extremely dangerous to speculate about the majesty of God and His dreadful judgments—how He destroyed the whole world with the Flood, how He destroyed Sodom, etc,; for this brings men to the brink of despair and plunges them into total destruction, as I have shown before." *LW* 26:42–43; *WA* 40/1. 98. 26–99. 20.

and volitional humility of trusting in Christ. Through surrendering themselves entirely to God in their daily lives, Christians give up trusting in humanly constructed ways.

Third, the Christian's imitation of Christ in his downward movement in connection with the theology of the cross also sheds light on the ethical humility required in the Christian's active life of love. God's love, which the theology of the cross reveals, teaches Christians how to make an intentional downward movement to the socially underprivileged by following in Jesus' footsteps.[126] God's love, according to Luther, also teaches Christians to put aside their natural predilection to regard themselves as better than others. Additionally, it is a matter of arduously eradicating their intrinsic proclivity to gather around people and things associated with fame, wealth, power, and authority.[127] In the sense that Christians do not seek self- or works-righteousness by doing these works of love, it is a genuine humility. They reach out to their neighbors with a pure heart and spontaneous love, becoming humble Christs to those in need.[128]

---

126. This position of Luther's is well noted when, in his *Heidelberg Disputation*, he designates the love of God as "the love of the cross, born of the cross.": "The love of God which lives in man loves sinners, evil persons, fools, and weaklings in order to make them righteous, good, wise, and strong. Rather than seeking its own good, the love of God flows forth and bestows good . . . . This is the love of the cross, born of the cross, which turns in the direction where it does not find good which it may enjoy, but where it may confer good upon the bad and needy person." *LW* 31:57; *WA* 1. 365. 9–15: "Amor Dei in homine vivens diligit peccatores, malos, stultos, infirmos, ut faciat iustos, bonos, sapientes, robustos et sic effluit potius et bonum tribuit . . . . Et iste est amor crucis ex cruce natus, qui illuc sese transfert, non ubi invenit bonum quo fruatur, sed ubi bonum conferat malo et egeno."

127. "Humility means that they are not interested in all those things which are high and mighty in the world and that they associate with lowly, poor, despised people." *LW* 52:35; *WA* 10¹/1. 133. 7–9: "Die demutt bringt den mit sich, das sie nichts fragen nach allem, das da groß und hoch ist inn der wellt, und hallten sich zu den geringen, armen, vorachten menschen."

128. On the subject of Luther's theology of the cross and its socio-ethical ramifications, one persuasive effort is Mary Solberg's. Drawing on her personal experience with the poor of El Salvador, Solberg essays to display affinities between Luther's theology of the cross and feminist epistemologies in order to suggest grounds for an epistemology of the cross. According to Solberg's analysis of the affinities between Luther's theology of the cross and feminist epistemologies, an epistemology of the cross emerges with four broad characteristics: power,

Doer and Deeds

Luther's thought on the relationship of faith to love is also well encapsulated in the metaphorical relationship of a doer to deeds (person to work).[129] The relationship between a doer and deeds can be approached from two angles: (1) deeds make a doer and (2) a doer produces deeds. Luther employs the second approach in order to explain the relationship of faith to love. He contends that "once there is the person or doer who comes into being through faith in Christ, then works follow. For there must be a doer before deeds, not deeds before the doer."[130]

This premise must be interpreted theologically. Luther provides a further explication:

> Christians do not become righteous by doing righteous works; but once they have been justified by faith in Christ, they do righteous works. In civil life the situation is different; here one becomes a doer on the basis of deeds . . . as Aristotle says. But in theology one does not become a doer on the basis of works of the Law; first there must be the doer, and then the deeds follow.[131]

---

experience, objectivity, and accountability. (1) An epistemology of the cross entails a critique of power dynamics between knowers and knowledge. (2) It accepts mundane, interpreted experience as the context and ground of knowledge. (3) Its "objectivity" arises at the foot of the cross and in solidarity with the poor and the victimized. (4) It is profoundly relational and calls for accountability in the knowing relationship. An epistemology of the cross thus has three parts: (1) perceiving what is going on (or that something is going on); (2) recognizing and comprehending one's own relation to or involvement in what is going on; and (3) doing something about what is going on. Mary M. Solberg, *Compelling Knowledge: A Feminist Proposal for an Epistemology of the Cross* (New York: State University of New York Press, 1997).

129. On the basis of this distinction between person and work to indicate the distinctive relationship between faith and love in Luther's doctrine of faith and love, Helmar Junghans argues that what is demanded by the law is not the person but the works and love. Helmar Junghans, "Martin Luther über die Nächstenliebe," *Luther: Zeitschrift der Luther-Gesellschaft* 62, no. 1 (1991): 5, 6.

130. *LW* 26:255–56; *WA* 40/1. 402. 19–21: "Posita . . . persona seu factore qui fit per fidem in Christum, sequuntur opera. Oportet enim factorem esse ante facta, non facta ante factorem."

131. *LW* 26:256; *WA* 40/1. 402. 24–28: "Quia Christiani non fiunt iusti operando iusta, sed iam fide in Christum iustificati operantur iusta. Illud alterum politicum est, scilicet ex factis fieri factorem . . . ut ait Aristoteles . . . . Sed in Theologia factor non fit ex operibus legis, Sed oportet prius esse factorem, postea sequuntur facta."

This statement indicates that Luther possesses a clear understanding of Aristotelian virtue theory: just as continuous practices of carpentry (deeds) make a carpenter (a doer), so persistent practices of virtue (deeds) make a virtuous person (a doer). The one practicing a habit obtains what she is practicing or making a habit of. According to this Aristotelian logic, a person becomes righteous by strenuously practicing righteous things. External works produce, form, and define internal being. In diametrical opposition to this philosophical logic, Luther's theological logic of the relationship of deeds to doer operates differently.

A "doer" in the theological meaning of the word must be a new creature. Only God can create and re-create. Justified persons as new creations, therefore, are God's deeds. That means that only God's deeds, not human deeds, can create a doer (a righteous person) who is capable of performing righteous deeds. Internal being produces, forms, and defines external doing.[132]

This reasoning also entails interpreting the semantic relationship of the adjective "righteous" to the noun "works" in a completely different way. The adjective "righteous" can be put in front of "works" because the works are the results of a righteous person, not because those works possess righteousness in themselves. Accordingly, even though the same works are performed by those who are justified by faith in Christ and by those who seek self- or works-righteousness, the works of the former are judged as truly righteous works, while the works of the latter as unrighteous. In

---

132. See *LW* 25:151–52; *WA* 56. 171. 26–172. 15. Regarding the difference between Luther and Aristotle in the matter of the relationship of a doer to deeds, see Theodor Dieter, *Der junge Luther und Aristoteles: Eine historisch-systematische Untersuchung zum Verhältnis von Theologie und Philosophie* (Berlin: Walter de Gruyter, 2001), 149–75. However, it must be remembered that Luther is not nullifying the necessity of practice to enhance human skills, such as baking, hunting, studying, building, and so forth. For instance, Luther confesses that his theological knowledge did not develop all at once and claims that learning requires practice. *LW* 54:50–51 (no. 352, dated Fall 1532); *WA, TR* 1:146.

other words, the "righteousness" of works is defined by God through righteously remade human agents, not by the nature of the works themselves.[133]

Furthermore, Luther's theological logic underlying the relationship of doer to deeds concerns acknowledgement or judgment in the sight of God, not in the sight of other human beings. As sketched above, from the standpoint of proper, active, and progressing righteousness and holiness, Christians are not yet totally perfect. Consequently, their works do not in fact deserve to be called truly "righteous" works. Nonetheless, their works are still deemed righteous because of Christ. By virtue of Christ grasped by faith in the heart, their being as righteous ones never changes in the sight of God. On this account, their works are consistently assessed as righteous in the sight of God.

Tree with Fruits

The core of Luther's thought on the relationship of faith to love is also clearly elucidated in his favorite horticultural image: the relationship

---

133. Due to this theological logic, the sacredness of a life lived in faith is credited not to human activity but to the fact that it is a gift from God (its givenness). Luther makes a sharp distinction between Christian holiness and other kinds of holiness. Whereas others claim to be holy on the basis of an agent's active attempt to be holy by way of good works, Christian holiness is passive. People, the church, and the city are holy "not on the basis of their own holiness but on the basis of a holiness not their own, not by an active holiness, but by a passive holiness. They are holy because they possess something that is divine and holy, namely, the calling of the ministry, the Gospel, Baptism, etc." *LW* 26:25; *WA* 40/1. 70. 20–22: "non sua sed aliena, non activa sed passiva sanctitate, Quia res habet divinas et sanctas, scilicet vocationem ministerii, Evangelium, Baptisma etc."

of tree to fruits.[134] When Luther explicates the true meanings of "to do," "to keep the law," and doer of the law, he says,

> "To do" includes faith at the same time. Faith takes the doer himself and makes him into a tree, and his deeds become fruit. First, there must be a tree, then the fruit. For apples do not make a tree, but a tree makes apples. So faith first makes the person, who afterwards performs works.[135]

According to this theological logic, "[t]o keep the Law without faith, therefore, is to make apples without a tree, out of wood or mud."[136] Good works "should be done as fruits of righteousness, not in order to bring righteousness into being. Having been made righteous, we must do them; but it is not the other way around: that when we are unrighteous, we become righteous by doing them. The tree produces fruit; the fruit does not produce the tree."[137]

The logical significance of this metaphor of tree and fruits is the inner necessity of every tree to bear fruits—namely, the external

---

134. This horticultural image comes from Luther's favorite biblical passage, John 15:4-6 ("Abide in me as I abide in you. Just as the branch cannot bear fruit by itself unless it abides in the vine, neither can you unless you abide in me. I am the vine, you are the branches. Those who abide in me and I in them much fruit, because apart from me you can do nothing. Whoever does not abide in me is thrown away like a branch and withers; such branches are gathered, thrown into the fire, and burned.") See Matt 7:16-20 ("You will know them by their fruits . . . . In the same way, every good tree bears good fruit, but the bad tree bears bad fruit. A good tree cannot bear bad fruit, nor can a bad tree bear good fruit. Every tree that does not bear good fruit is cut down and thrown into the fire. Thus you will know them by their fruits."); Matt 12:33 ("Either make the tree good, and its fruit good; or make the tree bad, and its fruit bad; for the tree is known by its fruit."); Luke 6:43 ("No good tree bears bad fruit, nor again does a bad tree bear good fruit.") For Luther's exposition of John 15:4-6, see *LW* 24:213–38; *WA* 45. 655. 9–678. 32, and for that of Matt 7:16-20, see *LW* 21:259–68; *WA* 32. 514. 21–522. 2.

135. *LW* 26:255; *WA* 40/1. 402. 13–17: "facere includat simul fidem, quae fides habet ipsum facientem et facit arborem, qua facta fiunt fructus. Oportet enim prius esse arborem, deinde fructus. Poma enim non faciunt arborem, sed arbor poma facit. Sic fides primum personam facit quae postea facit opera."

136. *LW* 26:255; *WA* 40/1. 402. 17–18: "facere Legem absque fide est facere poma sine arbore ex ligno et luto."

137. *LW* 26:169; *WA* 40/1. 287. 20–23. Luther also states that Paul "did reject circumcision in the sense of something necessary for righteousness; for the fathers themselves had not been justified by it but had it merely as a sign or a seal of righteousness (Rom. 4:11), by which they gave witness and expression to their faith." *LW* 26:83–84; *WA* 40/1. 157. 17–20.

evidence of its being internally alive. In the same way, those who grasp Christ by faith in their hearts are like "trees planted by streams of water, which yield their fruit in its season" (Psalm 1:3). Concentrating on the inner necessity of a tree bearing fruits, Luther articulates: a person who has Christ by faith in his heart requires no external command to work, since he has an internal driving force originating from Christ in his heart. Therefore, a Christian "will certainly not be idle but, like a sound tree, will bear good fruit (Matt. 7:17)." The Spirit of Christ "does not permit a man to be idle but drives him to all the exercises of devotion, to the love of God, to patience in affliction, to prayer, to thanksgiving, and to the practice of love toward all men."[138] Although fruits do not make a tree but are produced by a tree, they are sure evidence of its being either alive or lifeless. Fruits are external signs of the identity and internal health of a tree. Righteous works likewise distinguish an authentic Christian from a fake and bear witness to the spiritual health of a person.

Stressing Luther's reconceptualization of love as the fruit that authenticates one's faith, chapter 4 chiefly endeavored to find the theological reasoning behind Luther's reintroduction of love in harmony with faith. Thereby, it focused on Luther's concepts of Christian freedom, the Christ-given law of love, the twofold way of fulfilling the law, and several christological terminologies and concepts as the logical rationale behind his reintroduction of love as compatible with faith. These concepts reveal that when Luther constructs the relation of faith to love that is the fruit of faith and the sign that betrays whether faith is authentic or forged, he does so with special deliberation.

---

138. *LW* 26:155; *WA* 40/1. 265. 31–36: "certe non erit [homo] otiosus sed ut bona arbor proferet bonos fructus, Quia credens habet Spiritum sanctum; ubi is est, non sinit hominem esse otiosum, sed impellit eum ad omnia exercitia pietatis, ad dilectionem Dei, ad patientiam in afflictionibus, ad invocationem, gratiarum actionem, ad exhibendam charitatem erga omnes."

This chapter also strived to demonstrate that the relationship between faith and love emerges diversely depending on whether it is dealt with in the dimension of the alien, passive, and perfect righteousness and holiness or in the dimension of proper, active, and progressing righteousness and holiness. The reason why this endeavor is critical is that it will aid us in avoiding the wrongful argument that Luther is self-contradictory in his statements about faith and love when we approach those statements with the interpretive framework comprising the two dimensions of righteousness and holiness. In addition, through an analysis of the relationship between faith and love, it was argued that the relationship cannot be fittingly comprehended if it is construed as a mere juxtaposition between two things of equal import or as parallel lines that never intersect. Furthermore, in order to capture the nature of Luther's concept of the relationship between faith and love, Luther's favorite expression ("as Christ . . . Christians . . . too") and two metaphors (doer and deeds and tree with fruits) were furnished. In chapter 5, we will dig into the concrete content of Luther's redefined love.

5

Love: Means of Authenticating Faith

Luther's reconfiguration designates faith as the only means of grasping Christ in the heart. It is characterized by accurate knowledge of God, Christ, and self, and by firm trust in God's promise and Christ's soteriological significance. Luther's reconceptualized faith is also identified by the bearing of its fruit, that is, by being spontaneously and imperatively active in love. Love does not form faith as the scholastics maintain, but faith that is formed by Christ manifests itself in the outpouring of love. In Luther's reconfiguration, faith is not idle, nor is it private, individualistic, or egocentric. Faith propels Christians to act outwardly. This love overflows, in particular, in three distinctive but interrelated relations to God, neighbor, and self.

Love in Three Major Relations

Love in Relation to God

Luther unreservedly denounces the opinion that human beings can, out of their own nature, love God above all other things. Human beings can neither love God out of their own nature nor take the initiative in loving God. Human depravity precludes a pure and true love for God, which is different from an acquisitive and egocentric love toward God. Such love degrades the idea of God to a mere means of satisfying one's own selfish desires. This is why Luther so emphatically advocates faith as the first thing that human beings need in order to love God. Faith grasps Christ; then he, giving himself "out of sheer love to redeem" them, purifies their hearts as well as consciences and brings about a new reality of Christian freedom.[1] Christ thereby enables them to love God with a pure heart. So, love "must follow faith as a kind of gratitude" for what God has done for human beings in and through Christ.[2] Unless the Spirit of Christ purifies the heart, no pure love can come out of depraved human nature. This is the reason Luther persistently employs faith first, prior to love, when he discusses the relationship of a human being to God.[3]

1. *LW* 26:177; *WA* 40/1. 297. 32–33: "ex mera charitate tradidit [Christus] seipsum pro me redimendo."
2. *LW* 26:138; *WA* 40/1. 241. 21: "quae [charitas] quidem fidem sequi debet, sed ut gratitudo quaedam."
3. Concerning this aspect, Berndt Hamm argues that Luther arrives at a distinctly new Reformation theology when he realizes that justification does not depend on a human love for God that produces the necessary contrition, but rather on faith in God that focuses on the forgiving word first offered by God. Hamm recognizes that Luther can also speak of this faith as a joyful and confident love of God and can sing the praises of God's abundant love for us. However, he perceives that, instead of love, Luther chooses faith to express our response to God, even though faith was that dimension of being Christian [in the Middle Ages] "that was weakest in affect and the most distant from piety and devotion." Berndt Hamm, "Von der Gottesliebe des Mittelalters zum Glauben Luthers: Ein Beitrag zur Bußgeschichte," *Lutherjahrbuch* 65 (1998): 42–43. Luther chooses faith because justification does not come through our love for God and our contrition, but through our passive reception of the righteousness of Christ. According to Hamm, Luther's own experience showed him that

In addition to engendering the new reality of Christian freedom, by which Christians are capable of genuinely loving God, Christ has a further role in the Christian's love for God. In his descent from heaven to earth and in his death and resurrection, Christ heralds the "great depth and burning passion of divine love toward" human beings.[4] The love of God made manifest to them in and through Christ sheds light on the immensity of the divine love, especially revealing God's soteriological concern for them.[5]

---

salvation cannot depend on the human capacity for love or on any virtue or power that we possess. Instead, the purpose of selecting faith over love is to preclude linking justification to any such intrinsic quality and to make it "only a relationship of letting oneself be given a gift (*eine Beziehung des Sich-Beschenken-Lassens*)." Hamm concludes, "Thus faith justifies and saves not through its loving but through its receiving; the sinful person rather than the loving person is declared to be free." Ibid., 43. See also Berndt Hamm, *The Early Luther: Stages in a Reformation Reorientation*, trans. Martin J. Lohrmann (Grand Rapids: Eerdmans, 2014), 1–25, 59–84.

4. *LW* 26:292; *WA* 40/1. 455. 17–18: "illam abyssum profundissimam et Zelum ardentissimum divinae charitatis erga nos."

5. Luther portrays God as "a glowing furnace of love." *LW* 51:95; *WA* 10/3. 56. 2–3. God's love is out of "sheer, pure love, of which his heart is full to overflowing, and which he pours out freely over every one without exception, be he good or bad, worthy or unworthy. This is a real, divine, total, and perfect love, which does not single out one person nor cut and divide itself, but goes out freely to all." *LW* 51:267; *WA* 36. 358. 30–32. This love is specifically and unreservedly manifest when the eternal Son made an outward and downward movement from the Trinity "by stepping down so deep into flesh and blood." *LW* 52:12; *WA* 10¹/1. 68. 11–12. This love of God revealed in and through Christ has a particular significance for human beings in virtue of its saving power: "purely through his love and goodness that we are saved through Christ." *LW* 52:19; *WA* 10¹/1. 77. 7–8. So Luther identifies this love of God as "Christ's love, which has covered my sins" and designates this love of Christ as "another's love." *LW* 51:297; *WA* 47. 769. 15. Luther repeatedly underscores that it is not our own works of love but "another's love" that merits forgiveness of sins and therewith the alien righteousness (of Christ).

With regard to the question of how to perform the law, Luther states, "You must have the love that flows and issues from a pure heart and a good conscience and sincere faith. You just stick to that! All right preaching starts from there and remains there, which is something none of these rabble-rousers and stated spirits can do. He does not do it, Paul is saying, with a doctrine of all kinds of works, in which everything is cut into pieces and peddled. What must be there is what the law really requires, and that is love, and the kind of love that flows like a rivulet, a stream, or a spring from a heart which is pure and a good conscience and sincere, unfeigned faith. If that's the way it goes, it's right; if not, then the meaning and sense of the whole law is missed." *LW* 51:266–67; *WA* 36. 357. 37–358. 7. "True love flows from a pure heart. God has commanded me to let my love out to my neighbor and to be kindly disposed to all, whether they be my friends or enemies, just as our heavenly Father himself does." *LW* 51:267; *WA* 36. 358. 23–26.

==If God's love is not approached in and through Christ, human beings will miss the essential message of God's self-emptying (*kenotic*) love for them.==[6] Believers in Christ, bearing in mind all the things God has done for them, though they are undeserving of the divine love, feel their hearts enflamed with the enthusiasm of a respondent love. ==So Christ mediates between God and Christians in the divine-human love affair by revealing God's unconditional love and filling them with love and gratitude.==[7]

6. On Luther's portrayal of God's love, see the twenty-eighth thesis in his *Heidelberg Disputation*. God's love is not the kind of love that loves what is worthy of love or that delights the eye, but the kind of love that loves what is altogether hateful in its sin and which becomes worthy of love only through being loved by God: "The love of God does not find, but creates, that which is pleasing to it." *LW* 31:57; *WA* 1. 365. 2: "Amor Dei non invenit sed creat suum diligibile." "Therefore sinners are attractive because they are loved; they are not loved because they are attractive." *LW* 31:57; *WA* 1. 365. 11–12: "Ideo enim peccatores sunt pulchri, quia diliguntur, non ideo diliguntur, quia sunt pulchri."

   Drawing a parallel between the twentieth and twenty-eighth theses in the *Heidelberg Disputation*, Jüngel deals with the relation between God's visibility and invisibility. Jüngel aptly underscores that just as God becomes visible as the One hidden in suffering and knowable as the God hidden in the humiliation and shame of the cross, so God is related through love to human beings. Jüngel explains that Luther's theology of the cross, in contrast to the theology of glory, locates the distinctive trait of true theology and knowledge of God in the crucified Christ as "the event of love." Eberhard Jüngel, *Zur Freiheit eines Christenmenschen: eine Erinnerung an Luthers Schrift* (Munich: Kaiser, 1991), 38; ET *The Freedom of a Christian: Luther's Significance for Contemporary Theology*, trans. Roy A. Harrisville (Minneapolis: Augsburg Publishing House, 1988), 36.

   According to Jüngel, Luther puts God's love (*amor dei*) and love of the cross (*amor crucis*) that corresponds to God's love in diametrical opposition to the structure of human love, which arises from the appearance and visible value of its object. Jüngel, *Zur Freiheit eines Christenmenschen*, 38; ET *The Freedom of a Christian*, 36. "Accordingly, within what is created, God's sight observes what is defined more by nothing than by being, more by absence than the total possession of possibilities. This divine sighting of the eye is superior, because *creative* love is at work in it, love which first creates its beloved counterpart by making it beautiful and worthy of love. Thus, wherever the gaze of the divine love is directed, an object of this love *arises* which is worthy of it. There, in God's eyes, and on this account also in actuality, the sinner, totally unworthy of love, crooked and ugly, becomes upright in a new righteousness and conformable to God. This creative power gives to the divine seeing its definitive character which passes sentence on whatever exists." Jüngel, *Zur Freiheit eines Christenmenschen*, 39; ET *The Freedom of a Christian*, 37.

7. In addition, distinguishing God's gift of salvation from God's incitement to active Christian love, Luther adds that God rewards a Christian's acts of love and calls this God's pedagogy for Christians. Although God freely bestows eternal life to those who believe in Christ, God also finds it necessary to coax Christians into more active love "with promises of spiritual and physical things." Therefore, "it ought to be taught in the church that God will repay good

Moreover, Christ as God and human exemplifies Christian love by personifying God's love toward sinners and setting the paradigm for human love for God. His obedient love for God the Father teaches a purely doxological, non-acquisitive love for God. That being so, Luther declares: "Because you have taken hold of Christ by faith, through whom you are righteous, you should now go and love God and your neighbor. Call upon God, give thanks to Him, preach Him, praise Him, confess Him."[8]

Incontestably, while Christians await the consummation of righteousness and holiness through the resurrection of the human body, their love for God always falls short of the divine standard. Yet God is no less pleased with their human love, by virtue of Christ's intercession. He makes imperfect human love perfect in the sight of God and assures Christians that their love is gratifying to God.

Having firmly established love for God in response to God's love (the vertical relationship) as the bedrock of Christian love, Luther turns his attention toward love for neighbors (the horizontal relationship). Luther maintains that human love for God is not confined to genuine worship of God. It constitutes the basic disposition of Christians in all activities. No matter where they are or what they do, that disposition is a fundamental expression of love.

Love in Relation to Neighbors: Vocation

Though love for God is the foundation of Christian love, Luther's writings mention love for neighbors more frequently.[9] Indeed, this

works, save in the article of justification which is the origin and source of all other promises . . . . Accordingly we should remember that those promises and rewards are the *pedagogy* by which God, as a very gentle father, invites and entices us to do good, serve our neighbor." *LW* 54:240 (no. 3600, dated 18 June 1537); *WA, TR* 3:443–44.
8. *LW* 26:133; *WA* 40/1. 234. 19–21: "Quia apprehendisti fide Christum per quem iustus es, nunc eas et diligas Deum et proximum, Invoca, Gratias age, praedica, lauda, confitere Deum."
9. See chapter 1, "Previous Research," in this book.

finding should not surprise us. Luther appeals all the time to Paul (and to Christ through Paul) as the recognized authority on love. He turns to Matthew 22:36-40 and the second table of the Decalogue in these discourses. Paul's exaltation of love occurs predominantly within the context of equipping other Christians with spiritual armaments and virtues in the interest of improving the harmony of Christian communal life. As a professor, pastor, and reformer in the vanguard of the sixteenth-century Reformation, Luther was daily surrounded by people looking to him for leadership—though for different reasons. Many people found themselves in the middle of chaos, confusion, destruction, disputes, and discord. Luther responded by assimilating and applying Paul's authoritative teaching on love to his ecclesiastical and socio-political context. Considering this special pastoral concern, it is to be expected that Luther's handling of neighbor-love should occupy a large space in his teaching on love.

From this standpoint, we must be cautious not to misconstrue Luther's teaching on love as concerned primarily with neighbor-love, reducing love for God merely to neighbor-love or even according neighbor-love greater weight than love for God. When Luther seems to elevate neighbor-love, he is not placing it above love for God. Rather, he is elaborating on neighbor-love against the backdrop of love for creatures. Luther's explanation is as follows:

> No creature toward which you should practice love [*charitatem*] is nobler than your neighbor . . . . There is nothing living on earth that is more pleasant, more lovable, more helpful, kinder, more comforting, or more necessary. Besides, he is naturally suited for a civilized and social existence. Thus nothing could be regarded as worthier of love [*amore*] in the whole universe than our neighbor.[10]

10. *LW* 27:58; *WA* 40/2. 72. 31–36: "nullum animal, erga quod exercere debes charitatem, nobilius est proximo tuo . . . . nullum vivit in terris iucundius, amabilius, utilius, benignius, magis consolatorium et necessarium, quodque naturaliter conditum est ad civilitatem et societatem. Ideo nihil in tota rerum natura potuit constitui magis dignum amore, quam proximus noster."

No love is nobler than neighbor-love, when all creatures are taken into consideration as possible objects of love. For all that, without love for God in response to God's love as the source of neighbor-love, neighbor-love cannot be genuine. Luther's position that love for God in response to God's love is far more fundamental than love for neighbors patently presents itself in his understanding of the relation between the first and second tables of the Decalogue. According to Luther, there is an ordering principle between them: the first table should always be given primacy over the second. The priority of the first table over the second is also detected in Jesus' commandment, which encapsulates the entire Decalogue, to love God "with all your heart, with all your soul, and with all your mind." This is the first and great commandment. The second follows: love your neighbor as yourself (Matthew 22:37-38). Nothing can take the place of God as the focus of the first table of the Decalogue, especially the first commandment.

When we ponder the hierarchy between the first and second tables of the Decalogue and the first and second parts of Jesus' commandment to love, we can perceive a salient difference in what constitutes love for God and neighbor-love. God is the Creator. Neighbors are creatures, and no creature can replace the Creator as the primary object of a Christian's love.[11] Love for God embodies gratitude, highest esteem, utter submission, undivided trust, reverential fear, and awe at who God is and what God does. Neighbor-love is an expression of love for God.

Nevertheless, the significance of neighbor-love does not diminish. For none other than Christ, the Son of God, descended from heaven

---

11. For instance, in his treatment of the circumcision controversy in Paul's Epistle to the Galatians, Luther claims that God's creatures, such as bread, wine, clothing, possessions, and gold are given not to be served or worshiped or trusted, but to be used. God alone is "to be loved, feared, and honored." *LW* 26:96; *WA* 40/1. 176. 19: "Is [Deus] solus amandus, metuendus, colendus est."

and took human form to express his divine love for all human beings, without condition and without exception. Even though neighbors are not commensurate with God, they are objects of the divine love, and they are created in the image of God. Moreover, Jesus commands human beings to love their neighbors as he himself loves them.

At the center of Luther's concept of neighbor-love, his thought on Christian freedom *from* moves to freedom *for*.[12] Only through faith in Christ—and the freedom this brings—can Christians genuinely love their neighbors. This kind of neighbor-love, flowing out of faith in Christ as a pure love, contrasts starkly with "fanatical and superstitious works."[13] In addition, confirming Paul's assertion that the law of Christ is the law of love, Luther demonstrates that Christ not only enforces the commandment to love but also sets the example of how it is to be obeyed.

He illustrates Christ's living example of love in two paramount ways. The first is exposed in his descent from heaven to earth in order to rescue the whole of humanity, which had set itself against

12. This thought is clearly presented in *The Freedom of a Christian*. Without accurate comprehension of Luther's teaching on faith and love, we will fail to grasp the dialectic determined by the contrast between freedom and servitude portrayed in this treatise. Oswald Bayer contends that the whole of Luther's work could be "summed up in the statement that Luther endorses Paul's call to freedom contained in his letter to the Galatians: 'For freedom Christ has set us free; stand fast therefore, and do not submit again to a yoke of slavery' (Gal 5:1). Luther took this call to freedom, as articulated in the New Testament and especially by St. Paul, and gave it a powerful new thrust: You are called to freedom." Bayer stresses Luther's notion that justified Christians are called to freedom, not to serve one's own flesh but to be one another's servants in love. Bayer's main argument lies in the claim that this call to the freedom to serve embraces and permeates the whole of Christian life in all its individual and social dimensions. Bayer explicates Luther's concern for Christian pastoral care based on sin and forgiveness is indispensable to Luther's ethics, which hinge on the calling to freedom. According to Bayer, this feature is exposed in Luther's treatment of the three monastic vows (poverty, chastity, and obedience) as encapsulating the three estates—family life, economic life, and political life. Oswald Bayer, "Luther's Ethics as Pastoral Care," *Lutheran Quarterly* 4, no. 2 (1990): 125–42. Forell's *Faith Active in Love* is a good resource for grasping this aspect of Luther's ethics. George Wolfgang Forell, *Faith Active in Love: An Investigation of the Principles Underlying Luther's Social Ethics* (Eugene, OR: Wipf & Stock, 1999; Minneapolis: Augsburg Publishing House, 1954). See especially the section "The Practical Principle," 112–55.

13. *LW* 27:55; *WA* 40/2. 69. 20: "phanatica et supersticiosa opera."

God and did not deserve the divine sublime love. The second way is evidenced in his humble service during his earthly ministry to his followers and to those who were socially despised and estranged. The two ways in which Luther finds the substance of neighbor-love display a conceptual link between the core of his concept of neighbor-love and his theology of the cross.[14] Luther also adds that, when Christians strive to imitate Christ, it is critical that they not try to coerce others into doing something. God never forces human beings into complying with God's will. This is well exemplified through Christ, who liberates human free will, and the Holy Spirit, who inspires, but does not force.

What is striking in Luther's conception of love is its radical activity. Loving goes far beyond passively wishing someone else well. The Son of God did not remain in heaven wishing sinners well from afar. He took action and evinced his love, occupying himself with divergent and powerful ministries during his time on earth. The law of Christ as the law of love operates in the Christian's heart—but not only there. It must find external expression. Christians are to take Christ as the prototype, keeping the law of love in action, not simply in passive good wishes. So Luther avers,

> The notion that the sophists have about the word "love" is completely cold and vain. They say that "to love" means nothing else than to wish someone well, or that love is a quality inhering in the mind by which a person elicits the motivation in his heart or the action which they call "wishing well." This is a completely bare, meager, and mathematical love, which does not become incarnate, so to speak, and does not go to work. By contrast, Paul says that love should be a servant, and that unless it is in the position of a servant, it is not love.[15]

---

14. This was treated in chapter 4 under the subtitle of "Christians like Christ." With regard to this interconnection, see Helmar Junghans, "Martin Luther über die Nächstenliebe," *Luther: Zeitschrift der Luther-Gesellschaft* 62, no. 1 (1991): 7; Veli-Matti Kärkkäinen, "'The Christian as Christ to the Neighbor,'" *International Journal of Systematic Theology* 6, no. 2 (2004): 108–109.

Genuine love is "to bear someone else's burdens, that is, to bear what is burdensome to you and what you would rather not bear. Therefore a Christian must have broad shoulders and husky bones to carry the flesh, that is, the weakness, of the brethren," Luther advances.[16] Neighbor-love must be an active love, performed in visible and tangible activities as God's love for human beings was personified by the incarnation of the eternal Son.[17]

---

15. *LW* 27: 51–52; *WA* 40/2. 64. 32–65. 22: "Cogitatio Sophistarum, quam habent de verbo diligendi, prorsus frigida ac vana est, dicunt enim diligere nihil aliud esse nisi velle alicui bonum, Aut charitatem esse qualitatem inhaerentem animo, qua homo elicit motum cordis vel actum, qui vocatur bene velle. Illa est plane nuda, macilenta et Mathematica charitas, quae non est, ut ita dicam, incarnata neque procedit in opus. Paulus contra dicit charitatem debere esse servam, et nisi sit in officio servitutis, non esse charitatem."

16. *LW* 27:113; *WA* 40/2. 144. 21–24: "ferre alterius onera, hoc est, illa ferre, quae tibi molesta sunt et non libenter fers. Oportet igitur Christianum habere fortes humeros et robusta ossa, quae possint ferre carnem, hoc est, infirmitatem fratrum."

17. This declaration is not merely in empty words. Expanding on the social-ethical ramifications of the principle of love flowing out of faith in Luther's theology, Forell points to some actual institutional changes that took place during Luther's time, thanks to this principle, such as the reform of schools and Protestant churches, the implementation of restraints on usury, the counseling of people regarding fair trade practices, and the organization of rehabilitation efforts for the poor. Forell's depiction of Luther's treatment of beggars and the church-sponsored perpetuation of the begging system is noteworthy. As Forell describes, Luther acutely nails down the possible circumstances under which a genuine concern for the suffering of one's neighbor might contradict the selfish interests of the Christian individual. For instance, if there were no beggars, the opportunities of obtaining merits by giving alms to beggars might be eliminated. Underscoring love flowing out of faith and condemning halfway measures contrived to assist beggars temporarily while keeping them begging, Luther concerns himself with abolishing the underlying cause of begging. Forell explains that, for Luther, "it is at least as useful a service to help a person to avoid becoming a beggar as to give him alms after he has become one." Forell, *Faith Active in Love*, 106.

Forell continues that Luther also "insisted that all organized begging on the part of the church-sponsored orders who supported themselves by begging be discontinued. He suggested that the institutions that had harbored these ecclesiastical beggars be turned into shelters for the sick and needy. This was an indication of the very concrete application of his ethical principle. For Luther the neighbor was no longer a means to an end, but a most real and important end in himself. Therefore, even in the dissolution of these monastic institutions which Luther personally despised, he felt that love should prevail." Ibid., 107. On this issue, see also Carter Lindberg, *Beyond Charity: Reformation Initiatives for the Poor* (Minneapolis: Fortress Press, 1993), 161–69; Lindberg, "Luther on Poverty," in *Harvesting Martin Luther's Reflections on Theology, Ethics, and the Church*, ed. Timothy J. Wengert (Grand Rapids: Eerdmans, 2004), 134–51; Samuel Torvend, *Luther and the Hungry Poor: Gathered Fragments* (Minneapolis: Fortress Press, 2008).

Another aspect of the radicality of Luther's thought on love can be detected in his definition of neighbor. In reference to Luke 10:30-37, Luther clarifies that "neighbor" means "any human being, especially one who needs our help . . . . Even one who has done me some sort of injury or harm . . . does not stop being my neighbor."[18] Luther's definition is radical in its inclusion of everyone who needs help, that is, it is not confined to those in need of special or emergency assistance. In his mind, every single person has some form of need; hence, the world is crowded with neighbors.[19]

Luther's neighbor-love is a versatile concept with numerous ramifications. In particular, it relates to his convictions on Christian vocation. Luther's idea of vocation captures the quintessence of his vision for the Christian life consisting in faith and love.[20] Luther's sixteenth-century mindset views the whole of human society as revolving around three primary estates: the family, the state, and the church.[21] Vocational settings fundamentally comprise two parties:

---

18. *LW* 27:58; *WA* 40/2. 73. 25–28: "proximus est quilibet homo, praesertim qui ope nostra indigent . . . . Qui etiamsi me aliqua iniuria affecit aut nocuit . . . non desinit esse proximus meus."

19. "You will not lack for people to help, for the world is full of people who need the help of others." *LW* 27:59; *WA* 40/2. 74. 23–25: "Non deerunt, quibus benefacere poteritis, mundus enim plenus est hominibus, qui ope aliorum egent."

20. See *LW* 27:119–20; *WA* 40/2. 152. 38–153. 29.

21. *LW* 27:113; *WA* 40/2. 144. 26–30: "In Ecclesia . . . . In Politia . . . . In Oeconomia . . . ." "According to the plan of creation every man is either a domestic or a political or an ecclesiastical person. Outside of these ordinances he is not a man, unless he is miraculously exempted." *LW* 54:268 (no. 3754, dated 18 February 1538); *WA, TR* 3:593: "Nam hominem quemlibet iuxta creationem aut oeconomicum aut politicum aut ecclesiasticum esse: Extra has conditiones non est homo, nisi ipse sit exemptus mirabiliter."

Luther makes it clear that the mention of father in the fourth commandment includes everyone who is called "father." So there are four kinds of fathers: fathers/parents by birth, masters as fathers of the household (*patres familias*), princes as fathers of the land (*patres patriae*), and bishops as ecclesiastical fathers. "Ten Sermons on the Catechism, 1528," *LW* 51:148–49; *WA* 30/1. 69–71. Oswald Bayer insightfully describes how Luther's understanding of faith and love functions in conjunction with his teaching on the three orders, which are the household (*oeconomiam*), the government (*politiam*), and the church (*ecclesiam*). See Oswald Bayer, "Nature and Institution: Luther's Doctrine of the Three Orders," *Lutheran Quarterly* 14, no. 2 (1998): 125–59, esp. 132–41.

those who are in need and those who meet needs. This means that vocational settings are the concrete loci in which Christians take opportunities to serve others, that is to say, in which they practice their love for neighbor. Faithful and sincere performance of one's vocation is tantamount to neighbor-love. Regardless of the specific conditions of this work—the kind of vocation, amount of salary, level of personal satisfaction, or treatment by one's master or mistress—the principal ethos of vocation always remains the same: Christians are loving God and neighbors in their vocational services.[22] Accordingly, neighbor-love operates across the vocational spectrum in every domain of human life. Whenever and wherever Christians are carrying out their duties, they should be fulfilling the commandment to love neighbors and thereby to love God. In sum, Luther articulates,

> When I have this righteousness within me, I *descend* from heaven like the rain that makes the earth fertile. That is, I come forth into another kingdom, and I perform good works whenever the opportunity arises. If I am a minister of the Word, I preach, I comfort the saddened, I administer the sacraments. If I am a father, I rule my household and family, I train my children in piety and honesty.[23]

There is no discrepancy in value before God among various performances of neighbor-love. No matter how cheap and meager in appearance, anything done in faith, with a joyful spirit, obedience, and gratitude toward God is good, pleasing, and acceptable to God.[24]

---

22. Martin Luther, "Eighteenth Sunday after Trinity, Matthew 22:34-46, 1532," in *The Complete Sermons of Martin Luther*, vol. 7, ed. Eugene F. A. Klug (Grand Rapids: Baker Books, 2000), 51–60. See Gustaf Wingren's *Luther on Vocation*, which is a classic examination of Luther's teaching on vocation. Gustaf Wingren, *Luther on Vocation*, trans. C. C. Rasmussen (Eugene, OR: Wipf & Stock, 2004; 1957). See also Karlfried Froehlich, "Luther on Vocation," in *Harvesting Martin Luther's Reflections on Theology, Ethics, and the Church*, 121–33; Robert Kolb, *Martin Luther: Confessor of the Faith* (Oxford: Oxford University Press, 2009), 172–96.
23. *LW* 26:11 (italics mine); *WA* 40/1. 51. 21–25: "Hanc cum intus habeo, *descendo* de coelo tanquam pluvia foecundans terram, hoc est: prodeo foras in aliud Regnum et facio bona opera quaecumque mihi occurrunt. Si sum minister verbi, praedico, consolor pusillanimes, administro sacramenta; Si paterfamilias, rego domum, familiam, educo liberos ad pietatem et honestatem."

Standing firmly on this conviction, Luther draws our attention to Galatians 3:3, where Paul juxtaposes the spirit to the flesh.[25] In his exposition of this passage, Luther explains that the "papists" use it to criticize him and his followers, contending that Luther and his followers began with the Spirit, but, having taken wives, are now living according to the flesh. To this accusation, Luther responds by interpreting the passage with an entirely different thrust: "All the duties of Christians—such as loving one's wife, rearing one's children, governing one's family, honoring one's parents, obeying the magistrate, etc., which they [the papists] regard as secular and fleshly—are fruits of the Spirit."[26]

Notwithstanding the fact that every vocation has equal value in the eyes of God, Luther adds that not every work is the same, in that some works more immediately serve the spiritual welfare of neighbors than others. For this reason, the Christian's primary works of neighbor-love are practiced in preaching, forgiving, and comforting the consciences of their neighbors, by lightening their consciences through proclaiming the word and exercising mutual forgiveness.[27] Even though physical care and material benevolence

---

24. *LW* 26:376; *WA* 40/1. 573. 21–574. 22.

25. Gal. 3:3. "Are you so foolish? Having started with the Spirit, are you now ending with the flesh?" (NRSV)

26. *LW* 26:217; *WA* 40/1. 348. 17–19: "Quare omnia officia Christianorum, ut diligere uxorem, alere liberos, regere familiam, honore afficere parentes, obedire Magistratui etc., quae ipsis saecularia et carnalia sunt, sunt fructus spiritus." Luther's marriage and his commitment to his family evince how he lived out his own theological convictions.

27. *LW* 27:111; *WA* 40/2. 141. 16–142. 26. As the place where the Word of God is proclaimed and the sacrament is administered, the church takes an essential role in Luther's teaching on faith and love. For Luther, the church is an assembly of all believers. Luther portrays the believers as those who "are pregnant and fruitful by the Holy Spirit, give Christian birth, and lead a Christian life." *LW* 52:275–76; *WA* 10¹/1. 712. 2–3. This figurative characterization of Christians is powerful because Luther views Christ as the ultimate one who gives a new spiritual birth to all believers. Following Christ's footsteps, Christians, individually or corporately, give birth spiritually to other Christians. This takes place especially in and through the church—"a dwelling" in which not only is God loved and heard but also Christians "increase in faith daily through hearing the Word of God and the right and perfect use of the blessed sacraments" and therefore there "is strengthening and comfort in this church." *LW* 51:310; *WA* 47. 778.

are also indispensable in neighbor-love, spiritual and pastoral stewardship is preeminent in Luther's understanding of neighbor-love.

Insofar as genuine Christian love is esteemed as the fruit of faith, there is another noticeable feature in Luther's concept of love: faith is not only the point of departure for love in that love always flows from faith; it is also the destination in that love ultimately aims at it. In love, Christians do their utmost to bring others to faith and grow continuously together in faith. They nourish and build each other up, encouraging one another in the strenuous journey to God through faith in Christ.[28] Furthermore, in this endeavor, Christians are never

3–7. When people come together as a congregation, in this dwelling place of God, Christ, the Word, preaching, and baptism, all these are "the common possession of all Christians. So also they all pray and sing and give thanks together; here there is nothing that one possesses or does for himself alone; but what each one has also belongs to the other." *LW* 51:343; *WA* 49. 600. 17–21.

In this preaching and listening to the proclamation of the Word, Luther's emphasis lies on faith; while in this community of the Word and the Sacrament, Christian sisters and brothers also have "love and keep it and forsake everything for the sake of love." *LW* 51:311; *WA* 47. 778. 17–20. On preaching, Luther designates proclaiming the word about Jesus Christ as "the greatest work in the Christian life." *LW* 52:37; *WA* 10^1/1. 136. 20–21. The "greatest divine service is the preaching [of the Word of God]." *LW* 51:232; *WA* 36. 237. 29. "The Word is the cause, foundation, ground, fountain, and spring of love from the heart and of all good works, if they are to please God, for they cannot do so unless the heart first be pure." *LW* 51:272; *WA* 36. 362. 11–13. God requires "a heart which does everything for the sake of the Word." *LW* 51:272; *WA* 36. 362. 16–17. "That is why he causes his Word to be preached, in order that we conform ourselves to it in all our life and action." *LW* 51:272; *WA* 36. 362. 17–18. In the matter of Christian forgiveness, he states, "'One ought to love one's neighbor with a love as chaste as that of a bridegroom for his bride. In this case all faults are concealed and covered over and only the virtues are seen.'" *LW* 54:28 (no. 217, dated April 1532); *WA, TR* 1:92–93.

28. This imagery of the Christian's journey originally from God and ultimately back to God through faith in Christ is most eloquently articulated in Luther's "golden ring" metaphor. Luther urges Christians to stay firm in faith and not to lapse back into works by discarding faith, saying that "in this way we come back at last to our homeland, from which we set out, that is, to God, by whom we were created. So the end and the beginning are reunited, like a golden ring." *LW* 52:286; *WA* 10^1/1. 727. 20–728. 2: "Aber man muß heraußkommen ynn den lauttern glawben, und darnach nit widderumb ynn die werck auß dem glawben fallen. Alßo kommen wyr recht ynn unßer vatterland, da wyr herkommen sind, das ist: zu gott, von dem wyr geschaffen sind, und kompt das ende mitt dem ursprung widder zusamen, wie eyn guldener rinck."

Furthermore, Luther asserts that this faith is never concerned solely with one's own salvation. Faith has the inner necessity of reaching out to others in order to share the word of

left alone because Christ, who has come once for all, comes daily and spiritually to guide Christians back to God:

> [In many passages in the Gospel of John] Christ, in asserting His commission, calls us back to the will of the Father, so that in His words and works we are to look, not at Him but at the Father. For Christ came into the world so that He might take hold of us and so that we, by gazing upon Christ, might be drawn and carried directly to the Father.[29]

In neighbor-love, Christians participate in this mission of Christ by imitating him. Just as Luther's reconceptualization of love is manifest in relation to God and neighbor, so is it in relation to self. Bearing fruit through the persistent mortification of the old self and vivification of the new self is a sure sign of genuine faith and love. This brings us to the next topic.

God, which is a communal possession, not a private one. So Luther admonishes Christians to accompany their neighbors in their journey to God: "What does a mother do to her child? First she gives it milk, then gruel, then eggs and soft food, whereas if she turned about and gave it solid food, the child would never thrive [cf. I Cor. 3:2; Heb. 5:12-13]. So we should also deal with our brother, have patience with him for a time, have patience with his weakness and help him bear it; we should also give him milk-food, too [I Pet. 2:2; cf. Rom. 14:1-3], as was done with us, until, he, too, grows strong, and thus we do not travel heavenward alone, but bring our brethren, who are not now our friends, with us." *LW* 51:72; *WA* 10/3. 6. 4–7. 2: "Was thut die mutter yrem kinde? Zum ersten gibt sie ym milch, darnach ein brey, darnach eyr und weyche speyß: wo sie es zum ersten gewendte unnd herte speyß gebe, würde auß dem kinde nichts guts. Also sollen wir auch thun unserm bruder, gedult mit ym tragen ein zeyt lang und seine schwacheit gedulden und helffen tragen, ym auch milchspeyß geben, wie uns geschehen ist, biß er auch starck werde, und nit allein gen hymel fare, sonder unser brüder, die yezt nit unser freünd sein, mit pringen."

29. *LW* 26:42; *WA* 40/1. 98. 23–99. 11: "Est et alia causa, cur de voluntate patris dicat, quae etiam passim in Evangelio Ioannis indicatur. Illic Christus suum officium commendans revocat nos ad voluntatem Patris, ut in suis verbis et operibus non tam Se quam Patrem intelligamus. Ideo Chrsitus venit, ut nos apprehendat nosque vicissim eum apprehendamus et sic fixis oculis in eum recta trahamur et rapiamur ad Patrem."

Love in Relation to Self: *simul iustus et peccator*

Three Meanings of Self-Love

In appreciating Luther's reconceptualization of love, the theme of self-love may escape our attention. There is a prevailing opinion that Luther condemns self-love. Even though this opinion is not completely incorrect, it oversimplifies the complexity of Luther's notion of self-love and, as a result, hinders further inquiry into it.

Luther's handling of self-love can be investigated in three distinct, though not entirely separate, usages: (1) in his unqualified rejection of perverted self-love, (2) in his treatment of self-love as a plausible pattern of neighbor-love, and (3) in his reconceptualization of Christian love in relation to self as the fruit of faith.[30]

30. With regard to this classification, John Burnaby's presentation of Augustine's three different types of self-love is also relevant to our comprehension of the usages of self-love in Luther. By referring to *De doctrina christiana*, Burnaby tries to show how Augustine develops the idea of an *ordo amoris* that distinguishes true from perverted self-love and indicates that true self-love is founded on the denial of perverted self-love. Furthermore, the love we have for God and our neighbor is not egocentric but the gift of the Holy Spirit or the Holy Spirit itself. Augustine understands the communion between the Father and the Son in the Trinity as the love that the Father and the Son commonly share, which is none other than the Spirit. The Holy Spirit as love binds the Father as the lover and the Son as the beloved. St. Augustine, *De trinitate* in *Patrologiae cursus completes*, Series Latina, 42–43, ed. Jacques-Paul Migne (Paris, 1865), VI. 1. 7; VIII. 5. 14; XV. 5. 27, 28, 29, 31, 32, 37; ET *The Trinity*, trans. Edmund Hill, O.P., ed. John E. Rotelle, O.S.A. (Brooklyn, NY: New City Press, 2000), VI. 1. 7; VIII. 5. 14; XV. 5. 27, 28, 29, 31, 32, 37. The Spirit as love motivates us to love our neighbor and God in the bond of unity.

Burnaby recognizes that Anders Nygren's main criticism of Augustine comes from his conclusion that Augustine's concept of love is grounded in an egocentric and acquisitive love. Burnaby contends that Nygren overlooked the fact that Augustine's conception of self-love is differentiated into three separate types: (1) a natural and morally neutral love for self, (2) a morally wrong love for self, and (3) a morally right love for self. A natural and morally neutral self-love is implanted in human nature. Augustine understands it as the instinct for self-preservation. A morally perverted self-love pursues its own advantage in every object of love. It seeks to put the lover in the place of God, not acknowledging the Creator but attempting to be its own master. A morally proper self-love is one that assures its own advantage only by not pursuing it. According to Burnaby, this third type of self-love is that which Augustine emphasizes as genuine self-love. When a person pursues a private, individual, and personal will, this is perverted, not true, self-love. In true self-love, a person loves God for the glory of God. When self-love is not love of God, it is better called self-hatred. This inappropriate self-love is injurious, bringing forth self-destruction. John Burnaby, *Amor Dei: A Study of the Religion of St. Augustine* (Norwich: Canterbury, 1991), 116–26. With respect to Luther's

(1) Perverted Self-Love

An advantageous point of departure for our inquiry into Luther's rejection of self-love is his interpretation of the second portion of Christ's love commandment: love your neighbor as yourself. Luther's exegesis diverges from the traditional one prevalent among his contemporaries, which asserts that self-love is one of three components of the love commandment. It must logically precede neighbor-love, because we are to love our neighbors as we love ourselves. In the context of choosing not to ratify this position, Luther ventures an alternative: Christ's love commandment does not call on self-love.[31]

Luther's repudiation of self-love according to the traditional explication consists in the following train of reasoning. First, self-love does not necessitate an extra commandment in practice, since it is an inherent proclivity of human nature. Second, making allowances for the gravity of the fallenness of human nature, self-love, from a theological perspective, is perverse. This perverse self-love exposes human free will in its captivity to sin. Third, in its depravity, self-love is tantamount to self-interest, that is, egocentricity, self-worship, self-centeredness, and self-contentment. Always looking to one's own interests, one takes advantage of God and neighbor for one's own profit instead of serving them. Luther condemns this kind of self-

understanding of self-love, see also Mary Gaebler, *The Courage of Faith: Martin Luther and the Theonomous Self* (Minneapolis: Fortress Press, 2013), 117–54; Raymond Canning, *The Unity of Love for God and Neighbour in St. Augustine* (Heverlee-Leuven: Augustinian Historical Institute, 1993), 117–35; Anders Nygren, *Agape and Eros*, trans. Philip S. Watson (New York: Harper & Row, 1969), 709–16; Jüngel, *Zur Freiheit eines Christenmenschen*, 80–83; ET *The Freedom of a Christian*, 63–65. On self-love, see Gene Outka, *Agape: An Ethical Analysis* (New Haven, CT: Yale University Press, 1972), 56–63.

31. This position of Luther, for instance, is found in his Scholiaon Romans 13:10 ("Love is the fulfilling of the Law"). *LW* 25:475; *WA* 56. 482. 20–27. Luther, to take another example, explicates his position on this issue in his exposition on Romans 15:2. *LW* 25:513; *WA* 56. 518. 4–12. These expositions will be dealt with in more detail later, in "Self-love as a Pattern of Neighbor-Love."

love as follows: "self-love is something wicked by which I love myself in opposition to God."[32] On these grounds, self-love cannot be construed as a part of Christ's commandment to love. The phrase "as yourself" in Jesus' statement of the love-command cannot be interpreted as authorizing self-love as an independent commandment.

One more thing must be clarified in conjunction with Luther's denunciation of perverse self-love. Luther's concept of faith cannot be private and individualistic, considering his argument that a distorted self-love is the source of all evils in human life. Luther characterizes perverted self-love as self-centeredness. It is not extroverted; it is introverted. It destroys human relationships. It blinds a person to the concerns of God and the outside world. Luther's faith cannot coexist with such self-love in a justified Christian, nor can such a self-love be construed as part of Christ's commandment to love.

(2) Self-Love as a Pattern of Neighbor-Love

There are some cases in which Luther portrays self-love as if it could be used as a pattern for neighbor-love. Indeed, Luther does not entirely dismiss self-love when he mentions that human beings have self-love as a form of the natural law inscribed in their hearts for the sake of self-preservation and self-protection.[33] Thus, the way

---

32. *LW* 26:297; *WA* 40/1. 461. 23–24: "Quia amor mei est viciosus, quo diligo meipsum contra Deum." Arthur Skevington Wood, "Theology of Luther's Lectures on Romans, I," *Scottish Journal of Theology* 3, no. 1 (1950): 5–7.

33. Bayer's article on "Luther's Ethics as Pastoral Care" addresses something relevant to this aspect. For instance, Bayer refers to *Die Zirkulardisputation über das Recht des Widerstands gegen den Kaiser* (*Circular disputation on the right of resistance against the Emperor*, 1539), especially Theses 11–13 (*WA* 39/2. 39. 23–28), Thesis 14 (39/2. 40. 1–3), Thesis 17 (39/2. 40. 8–9), and Theses 18–19 (39/2. 40. 10–13). In these theses, according to Bayer, Luther points to the irony that the mendicant monks maintain that they have sold their possessions and left everything behind, but then they live on the goods of others. Further, Luther claims that, if they truly wish to absolve themselves of all material possessions, they must leave this world. From this perspective,

one takes care of oneself out of self-preservation might be deemed a conceivable paradigm for neighbor-love. A good example of such an assessment of this type of self-love is observed in Luther's exposition of the Golden Rule. Luther states that even though human beings do not truly fathom and carry out the intent of the commandment to love, "they have it written in their hearts, of course, because by nature they judge that one should do to others what one wants done to oneself (Matt 7:12)."[34] He further expounds on this love commandment ("You shall love your neighbor as yourself"):

> No one can find a better, surer, or more available *pattern than himself*; nor can there be a nobler or more profound attitude of the mind than love; nor is there a more excellent object than one's neighbor. Therefore the pattern, the attitude, and the object are all superb. Thus if you want to know how the neighbor is to be loved and want to have an outstanding pattern of this, *consider carefully how you love yourself*. In need or in danger you would certainly want desperately to be loved and assisted with all the counsels, resources, and powers not only of all men but of all creation. And so you do not need any book to instruct and admonish you how you should love your neighbor, for you have the loveliest and best of books about all laws *right in your own heart*. You do not need any professor to tell you about this matter; merely *consult your own heart*, and it will give you abundant instruction that you should love your neighbor as you love yourself.[35]

---

to take responsible care of oneself in terms of living, eating, drinking, and clothing as self-preservation and self-protection is not at all condemned but rather appraised as a responsible Christian attitude. See also *WA* 47. 353. 10–354. 15. In this sermon on Matthew 19, Bayer explains, Luther clarifies that Christian discipleship does not coerce Christians to kill themselves and deny everything God has given them. Luther rather urges them to be held accountable for their own lives and to stay with their own families and possessions unless the things of God are at stake. Oswald Bayer, "Luther's Ethics as Pastoral Care," *Lutheran Quarterly* 4, no. 2 (1990): 125–42, esp. 134–39.

34. *LW* 27:56; *WA* 40/2. 71. 22–24: "Toto igitur coelo errant homines, quando somniant se belle intelligere praeceptum charitatis; habent quidem illud scriptum in corde, quia naturaliter iudicant Alteri faciendum, quod sibi quis cupit fieri." However, Luther immediately adds that "But it does not follow that they understand this." *LW* 27:56; *WA* 40/1. 71. 24–25: "sed hinc non sequitur, quod illud intelligant."

35. *LW* 27:57–58 (italics mine); *WA* 40/2. 72. 16–27: "Nemo potest dare melius, certius et propius *exemplum* quam *Seipsum*. Neque dari potest nobilior et profundior habitus quam charitas,

The natural need for preserving one's own welfare could provide a person with an awareness of how she wants to be treated by others. In this context, Luther exhorts Christians to consult their hearts to derive a pattern for neighbor-love based on the way they cherish and shelter themselves. Luther also shows that the phrase "as yourself" urges us to love our neighbors with the same zeal and committedness as that with which we attend to ourselves.[36] Notwithstanding, Luther is certainly not ignorant of the fact that this kind of self-love may

Neque excellentius obiectum quam proximus. Exemplum ergo, habitus et obiectum sunt nobilissima. Itaque si cupis scire, quo modo diligendus sit proximus, et habere exemplum illustre huius rei, *considera diligenter, quo modo Tu teipsum diligas*. Certe cuperes anxie in necessitate aut periculo te amari et iuvari omnibus consiliis, facultatibus et viribus non solum omnium hominum sed etiam omnium creaturarum. Quare nullo libro indiges, qui te erudiat et admoneat, quomodo proximum diligere debeas, habes enim pulcherrimum et optimum librum omnium legum *in corde tuo*. Non eges ullo doctore hac in re, *tantum consule tuum proprium cor*, hoc satis abunde docebit te, ita diligendum esse tuum proximum, ut Teipsum." Luther draws our attention to the Golden Rule as the summary of the Decalogue. In his *Betbüchlein* (*Personal Prayer Book*) Luther describes how "In Matthew 7 [:12] Christ himself summarizes the Ten Commandments briefly, saying 'Whatever you want others to do to you, do the same to them; this is the whole Law and the Prophets.'" *LW* 43:16; *WA* 10/2. 380. 4–6. See also *LW* 25:476–78; *WA* 56. 484. 3–485. 15.

36. Luther departs from the traditional idea that claims a commandment of self-love in the commandment of love to one's neighbor. Luther's position on this comes into view in his Scholia on Romans 13:10 ("Love is the fulfilling of the Law."). In the matter of Christ's love commandment, "You shall love your neighbor as yourself" (Matt. 19:19 or Lev. 19:18), Luther is aware of two possible interpretations. It may mean that both the neighbor and one's own self are to be loved. It may signify that only love to our neighbor is commanded, whilst the way in which we love ourselves in obedience to our selfish nature is set forth as a pattern. Luther judges that the latter interpretation is better than the former, not because he endorses a self-love originating from human natural sinfulness, but because he considers that, when one loves one's neighbor as intensively as oneself, then such a love will exclude every pretentious love. *LW* 25:475; *WA* 56. 482. 20–21.

In the Scholia on Romans 15:2 ("Let each of us please his neighbor"), Luther returns to the question of how to interpret the commandment "as yourself" and makes this point: "Therefore I believe that with this commandment 'as yourself' man is not commanded to love himself but rather is shown the sinful love with which he does in fact love himself, as if to say: 'You are completely curved in upon yourself and pointed toward love of yourself, a condition from which you will not be delivered unless you altogether cease loving yourself and, forgetting yourself, love your neighbor.['] For it is a perversity that we want to be loved by all and want to seek our interests in all people; but it is uprightness that if you do to everyone else what in your perverseness you want done to yourself, you will do good *with the same zeal* as you used to do evil. *In this we surely are not commanded to do evil, but the zeal should be the same.*" *LW* 25:513 (italics mine); *WA* 56. 518. 4–12.

be subject to the selfish or egocentric propensity of depraved human nature, because a person does not possess discrepant types of self-love, such that a morally neutral self-love exists independently from a perverted self-love.

(3) Self-love as the Fruit of Faith in Relation to Self

Another aspect of Luther's thought on self-love can be examined in conjunction with his concept of faith in Christ. We must put aside the negative connotations embedded in some interpretations of "self-love," so that they do not hinder an accurate perception of Luther's intention. In connection with his reconceptualization of faith, love is best designated as the fruits of faith in Christ. Love is a visible sign of Christ's presence in a Christian's heart and an *a posteriori* verification of the authenticity of faith.

It follows, then, that self-love can be conceived of as the evidential fruits of faith in Christ that a Christian bears and must bear in her relation to herself—namely, managing her life in compliance with the law of Christ in the dimension of proper, active, and progressing righteousness and holiness. Strictly in this sense, it can and must be said that Luther acknowledges and discusses a Christian's self-love.[37]

---

37. In relation to the issue of self-love, Arthur S. Wood insists that Luther, in the Lectures on Romans, breaks free from the Augustinian conception that had dominated the Middle Ages and that Luther knows no justifiable self-love. Arthur S. Wood, "Theology of Luther's Lectures on Romans," *Scottish Journal of Theology* 3, no. 1 (1950): 5–6. These claims must be made with due qualification. First, considering the fact that Augustine did not endorse any kind of connatural perverse self-love, we must reassess Luther's own comment on Augustine before we make an oversimplified comparison between them. It is also worth noting that the Augustinian conception prevalent during the Middle Ages likely digressed from Augustine's original teaching. Second, insofar as love is interpreted strictly as the fruit of faith and self-love is reckoned as the fruit of faith in relation to self, then "self-love" with its new meaning is not entirely foreign to Luther's teaching on faith and love.

Love as the Fruit of Faith in Relation to Self

(1) Daily Mortification of the Old Self

In compliance with the law of Christ—pursuant to the law of love, in imitation of Christ, and with the daily assistance of Christ—Christians bear the fruits of faith in Christ in themselves in two ways: mortification of the old self (or the old Adam) and vivification of the new self (or the new creation).[38] Luther mentions these two ways in his Galatians commentary, for instance, when he explains that, in the practice of daily mortification and vivification, the law has its own legitimate role as a disciplinarian and instructor providing suitable guidance:

> As long as we live in a flesh that is not free of sin, so long the Law keeps coming back and performing its function, more in one person and less in another, not to harm but to save. *This discipline of the Law is the daily mortification of the flesh, the reason, and our powers, and "the renewal of our mind"* (2 Cor. 4:16).[39]

---

38. See *LW* 51:19: "God's alien work, therefore, is the suffering of Christ and sufferings in Christ, the crucifixion of the old man and the mortification of Adam. God's proper works, however, is the resurrection of Christ, justification in the Spirit, and the vivification of the new man." *WA* 1. 112. 37–113. 1: "Igitur opus Dei alienum sunt passiones Christi et in Christo, crucifixio veteris hominis et mortificatio Adae, Opus autem Dei proprium resurrectio Christi et justificatio in spiritu, vivificatio novi hominis." See also *LW* 41:165: "These are the true seven principal parts of the great holy possession whereby the Holy Spirit effects in us a daily sanctification and vivification in Christ, according to the first table of Moses." *WA* 50. 642. 32–36: "Dis sind nu die rechten sieben heubtstück des hohen heilthumbs, da durch der Heilige geist in uns eine tegliche heiligung und vivification ubet in Christo, und das nach der ersten tafeln Mosi."

39. *LW* 26:350 (italics mine); *WA* 40/1. 537. 16–20: "Quamdiu igitur in carne quae sine peccato non est, vivimus, subinde redit lex et facit suum officium, in uno plus, in alio minus, Non tamen ad perniciem, sed salutem. *Hoc enim exercitium legis est quotidiana mortificatio carnis, rationis et virium nostrarum et 'innovatio mentis nostrae'*, 2 Corin. 4." Luther also states, "Meanwhile, as long as the body is alive, the flesh must be disciplined by laws and vexed by the requirements and punishments of laws, as I [Luther] have often admonished." *LW* 26:164; *WA* 40/1. 279. 33–34: "Interim tamen, donec corpus vivit, ut saepe iam admonui, debet caro exerceri legibus et vexari exactionibus ac poenis legum." Luther also highlights that, even though love is the fulfillment of the law, "this fulfillment (namely, love) is weak in our flesh, that we must struggle daily against the flesh with the help of the Spirit, and this belongs under the law." *LW* 54:234 (no. 3554, dated 21 March 1537); *WA, TR* 3:405.

In inquiring into Luther's ideas on these two ways, the concept of *simul iustus et peccator* is useful. This twofold Christian identity is unveiled in two senses: totally and partly. On the one hand, in the dimension of alien, passive, and perfect righteousness and holiness, all Christians are totally sinners and totally righteous. On the other hand, in the dimension of proper, active, and progressing righteousness and holiness, different Christians stand at multifarious levels of righteousness and holiness, as each is engaged in diverse stages of battling against the remnants of sin that so tenaciously adhere to the flesh.

By faith in Christ, Christians are completely righteous, holy, and pure. Nevertheless, they are subject to greed, inordinate sexual desire, anger, pride, the fear of death, sadness, anxiety, hate, grumbling, and impatience against God. Christ present in faith certainly cannot coexist with these vestiges of sin clinging to the flesh. Christians must bear the fruits of faith in their relation to themselves through a determined and persevering eradication of all residual sin. So Luther explicates:

> This whole discussion of works shows that true believers are not hypocrites . . . . Whoever belongs to Christ . . . crucifies the flesh with all its diseases and faults. For because the saints have not yet completely shed their corrupt flesh, they are inclined toward sinning. They do not fear and love God enough, etc. They are aroused to anger, envy, impatience, sexual desire, and similar feelings; nevertheless, they do not carry out these feelings, because . . . they crucify their flesh with its passions and faults.[40]

---

40. *LW* 27:96; *WA* 40/2. 121. 27–122. 11: "Ille totus locus de operibus ostendit, vere credentes non esse hypocritas . . . . Quicunque, inquit, ad Christum pertinent, crucifigunt carnem cum morbis et vitiis. Sancti enim, quia nondum exuerunt prorsus carnem viciatam, propensi sunt ad peccandum, non satis timent et diligunt Deum etc., Item solicitantur ad iram, invidiam, impatientiam, libidinem et similes motus, quos tamen non perficiunt, quia . . . crucifigunt carnem cum passionibus et vitiis." See also *LW* 27:109; *WA* 40/2. 138. 21–139. 22.

Christians are involved in a lifelong task of mortification of the old self—a continuous battle against the wages of sin lodged in the flesh: "We also discipline ourselves in piety and avoid sin as much as we can."[41] Christians undergo this daily mortification when they "repress the wantonness of the flesh by fasting or other kinds of discipline," but most importantly when they "walk by the Spirit."[42] For this reason, Luther (in reference to Romans 8:23) states, "We have the first fruits of the Spirit and have begun to be leavened, but . . . we shall be completely leavened when this sinful body is destroyed and we arise new with Christ."[43]

(2) Daily Vivification of the New Self

The other side of Luther's thought on love in relation to self as the fruits of faith is daily vivification of the new self. Vivification is the work of the Spirit of Christ grasped by faith in one's heart. It involves daily exercises of faith whereby Christians grow more and more in conformity with Christ. When Luther explicates vivification of the new self in contrast to mortification of the old, he categorically denies the old while affirming the new. Luther advocates the continuous growth of every new self in matters of self-control, self-discipline, and self-cultivation as various aspects of the daily renewal of a Christian. In this context, Luther strongly values love in relation to self, that is, the bearing of more and more fruits of faith in the daily progress of vivification. Luther describes how God continues to sustain Christians through daily practices of faith:

---

41. *LW* 26:375–76; *WA* 40/1. 573. 21–22: "Exercemus deinde nos ad pietatem et vitamus peccata, quantum possumus."

42. *LW* 27: 96; *WA* 40/2. 122. 11–13: "Quod fit, cum non solum ieiuniis aut aliis exercitiis petulantiam carnis deprimunt, sed . . . cum Spiritu ambulant."

43. *LW* 26:351; *WA* 40/1. 538. 24–26: "primitias Spiritus habentes incepimus fermentari, fermentabimur autem toti, cum corpus hoc peccati dissolvetur et novi cum Christo resurgemus."

As God creates faith, so He preserves us in it. And just as He initially gives us faith through the Word, so later on He exercises, increases, strengthens, and perfects it in us by that Word. Therefore the supreme worship of God that a man can offer, the Sabbath of Sabbaths, is to practice true godliness, to hear and read the Word.[44]

What catches our attention in this statement is the notion of relativized faith, namely, that a Christian may go through various levels of faith throughout her life and that different Christians may represent different levels of faith. The faith by which sinners are justified through God's imputation of Christ's righteousness in the dimension of alien, passive, and perfect righteousness and holiness is an absolute faith. Although it is imperfect, God regards it as an absolute faith in that God imputes Christ's own righteousness because that faith, though imperfect, nonetheless grasps Christ fully in the heart.

In contrast to this absolute faith, the faith of individual Christians will be measured in multiple degrees in the dimension of proper, active, and progressing righteousness and holiness. Faith must be constantly exercised, increased, strengthened, and perfected. Reliable indicators of steady growth in faith are procured, in particular, in three domains: (1) knowing the truth about God, Christ, and self, (2) trusting in God and Christ, and (3) being active in love. For instance, Luther relates Christ's daily spiritual coming to a Christian's daily improvement in the knowledge of Christ: "Christ comes spiritually as we gradually acknowledge and understand more and more what has been granted to us by Him. 2 Peter 3:18 says: 'Grow in the grace and knowledge of our Lord and Savior Jesus Christ.'"[45]

---

44. *LW* 26:64; *WA* 40/1. 130. 13–17: "Qui [Deus] ut creat, ita conservat fidem in nobis. Sicut autem per verbum fidem primum donat, ita deinceps per verbum exercet, auget, confirmat et perficit eam. Itaque summus Dei cultus et sabbatum sabbatorum est exercere sese ad pietatem, tractare et audire verbum."

In addition, Luther states that, in the matter of daily vivification of the new self, the law functions as a disciplinarian and instructor. However, he qualifies, this function of the law should not torment the Christian's conscience in the dimension of active righteousness and holiness. A Christian should "permit the Law to rule his body and its members," but "not [his] conscience."[46] This dictum is critical. It singles out one of the central facets of Luther's idea of the law in the dimension of active righteousness and holiness. In this dimension, when justified Christians embrace the law or, more precisely, the God-given commandments, the law functions differently from its spiritual and theological function. This is a fine distinction, but critical for the Christian life as well as theology.

Examining love in conjunction with faith in Christ, we must remember that the three primary relations (to God, neighbor, and self) in which love is practiced are not separated from each other. Love in each relation has unique qualities because the fruits of faith in Christ vary in each relation. Yet, as Luther repeatedly emphasizes, love in all three of these relations originates from a single source: faith in Christ or Christ in faith.

On the one hand, practicing love in relation to one's neighbors and oneself is radically expressing love to God in divergent forms. Love actively expressed for one's neighbors and oneself finds its ultimate goal in God. On the other hand, Christian love for God is destined to be embodied as love for neighbors and oneself. In this sense, Luther sees that bearing the fruits of faith in relation to oneself, namely, daily mortification of the old self and daily vivification of the new self, is inseparable from producing better and more abundant fruits of faith

---

45. *LW* 26:351; *WA* 40/1. 538. 33–35: "Tunc autem Christus spiritualiter venit, quando subinde magis magisque agnoscimus et intelligimus, quae ab ipso donata sint nobis, 2. Pet. 3: 'Crescite in gratia et cognitione Domini nostri et Salvatoris Iesu Christi.'"

46. *LW* 26:120; *WA* 40/1. 213. 30–31: "Patiatur sane legem dominari corpori et membris ipsius, non item conscientiae."

in relation to God and to neighbors as well. Bearing the fruits of faith in a purer and more genuine love for God and neighbor also stimulates the production of greater fruits of faith in oneself. In this way, there is an inextricable mutual interdependence among the love in relation to God, neighbor, and self. Each love requires the others for stimulus and inspiration and as evidence of their own existence and growth.

In the context of this conversation about the love in relation to God, neighbor, and self, Luther's appeal to the law of mutual love (by pointing to John 13:34)[47] is worthy of special notice: "After redeeming and regenerating us and constituting us as His church, Christ did not give us any new law except the law of mutual love."[48] Turning to this "law of mutual love," Luther exhorts Christians to engage in reciprocal encouragement and provision of care. All Christians await the consummation of the freely bestowed righteousness and holiness of Christ in the resurrection of their bodies: "For His sake this body of mine will be raised from the dead and delivered from the slavery of the Law and sin, and will be sanctified together with the spirit."[49] Until then, without exception, every Christian is to undergo the trials and temptations by residual sin in the flesh, whether at a personal or communal level.

Love in relation to neighbor and self inspires all to persevere through the daily battle against the lingering influence of sin until the promised perfection of righteousness and holiness is fully revealed in eternal life. Seen from this perspective, each Christian's vigilant attention to herself and honest expectation of being strengthened and

---

47. John 13:34: "A new commandment I give to you, that you love one another, even as I have loved you." (NRSV)
48. *LW* 27:113; *WA* 40/2. 144. 16–19: "Christus postquam redemit, renovavit et constituit nos suam Ecclesiam, nullam nobis legem dedit praeterquam illam de mutua charitate, Ioan. 13.: 'Mandatum novum do vobis, ut diligatis invicem, sicut dilexi vos.'"
49. *LW* 26:9; *WA* 40/1. 48. 19–20: "propter quem [Christum] etiam hoc corpus meum mortuum resuscitabitur et liberabitur a servitute legis et peccati, simulque cum spiritu sanctificabitur."

inspired by other Christians is not at all incongruous with Luther's redefinition of love in conjunction with faith in Christ alone. By its own nature, the concept of mutual love stands above an unnecessarily sharp breach between neighbor-love and self-love, especially when "self-love" is falsely loaded with one-sided negative connotations. When this contrast is intensified, neighbor-love is elevated at the expense of self-love. Luther's accentuation of the biblical theme of mutual love and his reconceptualization of love as the fruits of faith in Christ clarify the appropriateness and necessity of endorsing proper Christian self-love as a valid expression of faith in Christ.

Taking into account all of these essential qualities of Luther's redefined love, we can proclaim that his vigorous condemnation of self-love in the form of self-worship, self-interest, egocentrism, and failure to oppose works of the flesh should not be misapprehended as a tragic advocacy of anything like a pathological self-contempt or destruction. It has nothing in common with the psychological or physical mistreatment of self. Heeding the variant contexts of Luther's handling of self-love helps avoid such a misreading and discern how to attend to self in order to make it wholesome. We can also declare that Luther's reconceptualized love covers the entire breadth, width, and height of the Christian life. This life is built upon the solid foundation of faith in Christ and manifest in love exercised by the newly created beings under the new reality of Christian freedom, that is, the reign of Christ. There is no space or time in the Christian life that escapes the outpouring of love from faith in Christ alone. Now we are in a better position to appreciate Luther's claim that the whole of the Christian life consists in both faith and love. Being is believing; living is loving.[50]

---

50. In view of the features of Luther's redefined love, especially in its threefold relation to God, neighbor, and self, Luther's statement that a Christian is a vessel through which the stream of divine blessings flows to other people must be discreetly translated. See *WA* 10/1. 100 (Kirchenpostille, 1522, Titus 3:4–7). In this analogy, the point is not that a Christian functions

For all that, Luther is undoubtedly cognizant of the tribulations that life's journey so continually entails. While Christians are performing genuine good works through incarnate love with divine empowerment and inspiration, the spiritual trials and temptations never end this side of heaven. On the one hand, Christians may suspect that the accomplishment of their acts of love is insignificant and their faith is rather sterile. On the other hand, Christians may begin to misjudge, as the momentum of faith in Christ alone fades from memory, that they are now self-sufficient and self-contained, no longer needing the assistance of the Holy Spirit. This is the precise reason why we have to return to the theme of faith in Christ alone and to the theme of the theological or spiritual function of the law, our next subject. The major dissimilitude between our discourse on these themes in chapters 2 and 3 and the following section is that now we will address those themes in reference to already justified Christians. Therefore, this discussion is pertinent to the dimension of active righteousness and holiness. Yet it will also consider the way in which this dimension is predicated on and interrelated to the dimension of passive righteousness and holiness.

merely as a materialistic medium, but that a Christian actively mediates God's love to others, just as Jesus Christ mediated and manifested the unfathomable divine love. It does not do justice, therefore, to Luther's concept of love simply to designate it as "emanationism." See George Hunsinger, *Disruptive Grace: Studies in the Theology of Karl Barth* (Grand Rapids: Eerdmans, 2000), 163 and n. 17; Karl Barth, *Church Dogmatics*, IV/2, *The Doctrine of Reconciliation*, trans. G. W. Bromiley (Bloomsbury: T & T Clark, 1958), 752.

Insofar as such an allegation concerns us, when George Forell describes how "he [Luther] considered man *merely* the tube or channel through which God's love flows. . . . Luther spoke of faith and love as 'placing man between God and his neighbor,' as a medium which receives from above and gives out again below, and which is like 'a vessel or tube through which the stream of divine blessings must flow without intermission to other people,'" the term "merely" seems to be unbefitting in this sentence. Forell, *Faith Active in Love*, 100.

The Law and Christ in the Dimension of Active Righteousness and Holiness

In the dimension of alien, passive, and perfect righteousness and holiness, Luther opposes the law if it attempts to usurp Christ's proper authority and power in the matter of justification. In this dimension, he keeps the law within the limits of its spiritual and theological function. On the other hand, in the dimension of proper, active, and progressing righteousness and holiness, Luther recognizes another function for the law in its redefined form—as the law of Christ, the law of love.

Luther now concentrates on the matter of how a justified Christian should live in the dimension of active righteousness and holiness, that is, in a way befitting the name "Christian." Then, what does it mean to live a life that is worthy of being called "Christian"? It entails nothing less than the imitation of Christ and obedience to his will. A Christian's ontological identity is formed by faith in Christ. Those who are bestowed with this new ontological identity bear fruits befitting their new identity just as a living tree bears its fruits and a well-trained craftsperson produces quality articles of craftwork. What, then, is the will and primary example he left to his followers? Luther's answer to this question is that Christ's law is the law of love. Since this answer was already dealt with in chapter 4, it will not be repeated here. What needs to be reiterated is that this answer provides an important clue to Luther's idea on the function of the law in the dimension of active righteousness and holiness. Luther demonstrates how Christ, faith, love, and the law are harmonized in a Christian's life. This function of the law in a Christian's life can be discussed under the topic of the third use of the law, which will be dealt with in more detail in the Conclusion.[51]

Into this picture of the distinctive uses of the law, Luther brings another complexity: the continual validity of the spiritual and theological function of the law in the life of justified Christians. This function of the law is still applicable in the dimension of active righteousness and holiness for two reasons.

First, when Christians feel strong and capable in their performances of love in virtue of the empowerment and assistance of the Spirit of Christ, they can easily be tempted to believe that they are capable of exercising love self-sufficiently. They may also begin to deceive themselves, believing that they are contributing in some way to their justification. The law interrupts this miscalculation, exhibiting to them the profundity of its requirements. It crushes the resurging arrogance of the flesh so that Christians may rely again only on Jesus Christ, the manifestation of God's promise and its fulfillment, with undivided confidence in the matter of their justification and salvation.

Second, throughout daily battle against residual influence of sin, the law continues to unveil imperfections, revealing repeatedly the sinfulness that clings to the flesh and leaves them conscience-stricken. Christians constantly experience this spiritual and theological function of the law until the flesh's warfare against the spirit terminates.[52] Hence, Luther states that "[a]ccording to our feelings, however, sin still clings to the flesh and continually accuses and troubles the conscience"[53] and that Christians undergo "the time of Law and the time of grace in constant alternation" in their daily experiences.[54]

---

51. Sun-young Kim, "The Third Use of the Law in Luther?," *Korean Journal of Christian Studies* 73 (2011): 119–51.

52. *LW* 26:341; *WA* 40/1. 524. 32–525. 10: "Est igitur in Christiano utrumque tempus legis et gratiae in affect . . . . Ibi tum lex est in vero suo usu quem Christianus subinde sentit, donec vivit."

53. *LW* 26:349; *WA* 40/1. 536. 21–23: "Secundum affectum tamen haeret adhuc in carne peccatum quod subinde accusat et perturbat conscientiam."

As a consequence, in the daily process of struggling against the flesh, Christians may plunge into despair and become vulnerable to the incessant accusations of the law. Under the great burden of guilt, Christians can easily lose their trust in God's mercy and their belief that God wants to forgive sins for the sake of Christ. To tackle this existential and spiritual predicament, Luther adjures Christians to not only hold fast to their faith in Christ but also develop practical strategies in anticipation of these spiritual and psychological challenges. Such strategies, for instance, involve "a constant gaze that looks at nothing except Christ, the Victor over sin and death and the Dispenser of righteousness, salvation, and eternal life."[55] This gaze looks only at Christ with eyes of faith, as demonstrated by the story of the bronze serpent, a figure of Christ (John 3:14), so that Christians will not lose sight of him and all the blessings he has promised them.[56]

According to Luther, when the law afflicts the Christian's conscience and reminds them of sin and imperfection in the dimension of active righteousness and holiness, presenting Jesus Christ as a lawgiver and condemning judge, and causing to feel fear and doubt about salvation, these are the devil's tricks:[57] "This temptation is not human; it is diabolical."[58] In this context, whoever falls from a true definition of Christ is conceiving of the devil, not

---

54. *LW* 26:340; *WA* 40/1. 524. 15–16: "in quolibet Christiano, in quo subinde invenitur per vices tempus legis et gratiae."

55. *LW* 26:356; *WA* 40/1. 545. 30–32: "Quare fides est pertinacissimus intutus qui nihil aspicit praeter Christum victorem peccati et mortis et largitorem iustitiae, salutis et vitae aeternae." According to the meaning of this sentence, "intutus" (adj. "defenseless," "unsafe") is rather to be replaced by "intuitus" (m. "a look," "gaze"), and this is what the editors of the American edition did. However, it seems that we cannot simply say that it is a mistake to have "intutus" in this sentence, since the same word reappears in its ablative form, "intutu," in *LW* 26:166–67; *WA* 40/1. 282. 33–283. 15. Furthermore, an infinitive form, "intueri," of "intueor" (a deponent verb, "gaze at") appears in a correct form in *LW* 26:343, "the Christian should . . . gaze at Christ Himself."; *WA* 40/1. 527. 15–16: "Debet . . . Christianus . . . intueri in ipsum Christum."

56. *LW* 26:357; *WA* 40/1. 546. 11–21.

57. *LW* 26:37; *WA* 40/1. 90. 14–24.

58. *LW* 26:196; *WA* 40/1. 321. 12–13: "Atque illa tentatio non est humana, sed diabolica."

Christ: "This is not really Christ but the devil," because "Scripture portrays Christ as our Propitiator, Mediator, and Comforter."[59] So, guarding against the law's presentation of Christ as a furious judge or a minister of sin and death, Christians must never be deprived of the "sweet definition of Christ"[60]—the unadulterated "true and correct definition of Christ."[61] Christians must remind themselves that Christ is the "sweet Savior and High Priest"[62] and "our High Priest, interceding for us and reigning over us and in us through grace."[63] In addition, Luther, out of pastoral consideration, recommends that to those "who are afraid and have already been terrified by the burden of their sins," "Christ the Savior and the gift should be announced, not Christ the example and the lawgiver."[64]

Christians must flee to this Christ, remembering that they are already in a state of grace and once again claiming assurance of their status as justified and adopted children of God.[65] So, in despairing

---

59. *LW* 27:11; *WA* 40/2. 13. 15–16: "Christum enim Scriptura depingit nostrum esse propiciatorem, interpellatorem et consolatorem." Christ is portrayed by Luther in more detail, as the sweet Savior with variations: (1) as the blessed Offspring as God's promised one—who is promised to Abraham (*LW* 26:334; *WA* 40/1. 515. 30, *LW* 26:374; *WA* 40/1. 570. 25–31, *LW* 26:396; *WA* 40/1. 602. 19); (2) as victor (*LW* 26:21–22; *WA* 40/1. 10–18, *LW* 26:41; *WA* 40/1. 96. 12–25, *LW* 26:134; *WA* 40/1. 235. 23–25, *LW* 26:283; *WA* 40/1. 441. 32); (3) as High Priest (*pontifex*) (*LW* 26:8; *WA* 40/1. 47. 20); (4) as the Lamb of God (*Agnus Dei*) (*LW* 26:278; *WA* 40/1. 435. 13–16); and (5) as Mediator (*LW* 26:235; *WA* 40/1. 325–26).

60. *LW* 26:38; *WA* 40/1. 91. 23–24: "dulcissima definitione Christi."

61. *LW* 26:39; *WA* 40/1. 93. 18–19: "bene et proprie Christum definire."

62. *LW* 26:38; *WA* 40/1. 92. 13: "dulcissimum Salvatorem ac Pontificem."

63. *LW* 26:8; *WA* 40/1. 47. 20–21: "noster pontifex, intercedens pro nobis, et regnans super nos et in nobis per gratiam."

64. *LW* 27:35; *WA* 40/2. 43. 15–16: "Pavidis igitur et iam antea conterritis mole peccatorum suorum Christus Salvator et donum, non exemplum et legislator inculcandus est."

65. As to a continuous clinging to Christ and forgiveness, Luther explains, "'But the Christian says: I believe and cling to him who is in heaven as a Savior. If I fall into sin I rise again but don't continue to sin. I rise up and become the enemy of sin. Thus the Christian faith differs from other religions in this, that the Christian hopes even in the midst of evils and sins. Without the Holy Spirit natural man can't do this.'" *LW* 54:70 (no. 437, dated early in the year 1533); *WA*, TR 1:190. "'But a Christian remains firmly attached to Christ and says, 'If I'm not good, Peter wasn't either, but Christ is good.' Such are the elect . . . . To him will I cling, even if I sin.' It is thus that one has assurance.'" *LW* 54:87 (no. 501, dated Spring 1533); *WA*, TR 1:225.

circumstances, Christians must find a haven of peace in Christ in his proper function, being assured that they are already in Christ.

This pattern of the accusation and torment of the law and subsequent flight to Christ unmistakably resonates with the sequence analyzed in the spiritual and theological function of the law in the matter of justification. Does this ostensible similarity, then, indicate that nothing has changed for justified Christians from the perspective of their relation to the law? Or, worse still, do Christians need to undergo justification again and again?

In response to these questions, Luther's position is that the reality for justified Christians, which is invisible to physical eyes and visible only to the eyes of faith, is substantially different than it is for unjustified sinners. In principle, Christians need not fight against original sin and its power, since the power of sin and death has already been nullified by Christ through his once-and-for-all coming, death, and resurrection. They live in Christian freedom by faith in Christ. Their daily struggle is only with the remnants of sin still adhering to the flesh, and through that struggle, they are daily sustained and empowered by Christ.

On this account, in the new reality, the interaction of Christians with the law is in principle different from that of unjustified sinners with the law. For Christians, the root of sin and eternal death is completely eradicated; but the radical power of sin is still deeply rooted in the nature of the unjustified. Thereby, Christians encounter conflict with the law through their conscience and feelings in practical life situations, but unjustified sinners encounter conflict with the law even in their very being. This topic is deliberately expounded in Luther's discussion of the duration of the law.

Luther cautions that the spiritual and theological function of the law is still effective even for the justified: "The spiritual duration of the Law clings very tenaciously to the conscience; therefore a man who is applying the theological use of the Law has great difficulty reaching the end of the Law."[66] Touching on Paul's notion of the fulfillment of the law in the once-and-for-all coming of Christ, Luther asserts that the fulfillment of the law is relevant not only in regard to the absolute point in history when Christ was incarnate, but also for an extended period of time. The abrogation of the law that has occurred "historically and temporally" with the once-and-for-all coming of Christ also happens "personally and spiritually every day in any Christian."[67]

The proposition that justification is unaffected by works of the law is kept intact after justification as firmly as before justification. Christ alone is the fulfillment of the law; accordingly, when Christians stand in front of the judgment seat, they attain eternal life only by virtue of Christ's righteousness. This is the reason the dimension of proper, active, and progressing righteousness and holiness hinges on the dimension of alien, passive, and perfect righteousness and holiness, and the latter unconditionally remains the primary point of reference in a Christian's life.

Just as works of the law do not justify sinners before justification, so even after justification (in a state of grace) they do not contribute to securing or maintaining their justification:[68]

> But the works of the Law can be performed either before justification or after justification. Before justification many good men even among the pagans . . . performed the works of the Law and accomplished great things . . . but these men were not justified by these works. After justification, moreover, Peter, Paul, and all other Christians have done

66. *LW* 26:317–18; *WA* 40/1. 493. 11–13: "Sed ista legis duratio spiritualis tenacissime haeret in conscientia; ideo difficillimum est homini qui Theologico usu legis exercetur, finem legis attingere."

67. *LW* 26:340; *WA* 40/1. 523. 31–524. 15: "Hoc Paulus dicit pro tempore plenitudinis, quo Christus venit. Tu vero accommoda non solum ad tempus illud, sed etiam ad affectum. Quia, quod gestum est historice et temporaliter, quando Christus venit: legem abrogavit . . . . Hoc privatim quotidie fit Spiritualiter in quolibet Christiano."

68. *LW* 26:380; *WA* 40/1. 579. 20: "in gratia."

and still do the works of the Law; but they are not justified by them either.[69]

The act of striving to fulfill the law in the dimension of active righteousness and holiness (no matter how noble and dignified) must not be imagined or practiced apart from Christ's fulfillment of the law. The Christian's daily endeavor to fulfill the law is entirely contingent on Christ's once-and-for-all fulfillment of the law. That is, the Christian's active expression of love always flows from faith in Christ, who is the sole source of justification and eternal life. For the final judgment of salvation will be made according to the alien, passive, and perfect righteousness and holiness of Christ, not the Christian's own proper, active, and progressing righteousness and holiness.

This consistent dependence of justification and salvation on faith in Christ explains why faith always (in both active and passive dimensions) takes priority over love and is the foundation and source of love. To those who succumb to self-confidence and vainglory and to those who fall into despair, Luther seems to proclaim: let it not be so. The ultimate criterion for our justification and eternal life is our faith in Christ alone, not the degree or amount of our works of love.

This insight helps put into perspective the dynamics between the active and passive dimensions of Christian existence. In the dimension of active righteousness and holiness, an appraisal of who Christians are and what they do falls into the category of "partial"—somewhere between no righteousness and holiness and perfect righteousness and holiness, which is never to be achievable in this life. In the dimension of passive righteousness and holiness,

---

69. *LW* 26:123–24; *WA* 40/1. 219. 22–30: "Possunt autem opera legis fieri aut ante iustificationem aut post iustificationem. Ante iustificationem multi boni viri etiam inter gentiles . . . praestiterunt legem et fecerunt egregia opera . . . . et tamen per ea non sunt iustificati. Post iustificationem faciunt opera legis Petrus, Paulus et omnes Christiani, sed per ea non iustificantur."

an appraisal of who Christians are and what they do falls in the category of "total." In the sight of God, they are both totally sinners and totally righteous, by virtue of their faith in Christ who possesses perfect righteousness and holiness: "Thus a Christian man is righteous and a sinner at the same time, holy and profane, an enemy of God and a child of God."[70] The verdict bestowing total righteousness "in the sight of God" by virtue of faith in Christ must invalidate the judgment of being partly righteous and holy according to one's own merits. Even amidst the Christian's daily sufferings, temptations, and inevitable relapses, the cause, source, and principle of their assurance for justification and eternal life remains unchanging and secure, since it hinges on Christ.

As Luther clarifies, "the defects [of our active faith] lie not in the fact [of what we believe] itself, which is completely true, but in our incredulity."[71] The flaw is detected not in what Christians believe—namely, who God is and what God has fulfilled in and through Jesus Christ—but in how they believe—namely, the degree to which they hold fast to their faith in Christ in the dimension of active righteousness and holiness.

Thus, the Christian's life operates in two dimensions that require unending attention to faith in Christ: "As long as we live here, both remain. The flesh is accused, exercised, saddened, and crushed by the

---

70. *LW* 26:232; *WA* 40/1. 368. 26–27: "Sic homo Christianus simul iustus et peccator, Sanctus, prophanus, inimicus et filius Dei est."

71. *LW* 26:285; *WA* 40/1. 444. 23: "defectus est in re, cum sit verissima, sed in incredulitate nostra." Luther also explains, "The question of justification is an elusive thing—not in itself, for in itself it is firm and sure, but so far as we are concerned." *LW* 26:63; *WA* 40/1. 128. 34–129. 12: "Deinde quoque causa iustificationis lubrica est, non quidem per se—per se enim est firmissima ac certissima—sed quoad nos." Luther knows this from his own experience. He is describing the conflicts of faith and doubt that he usually calls *Anfechtungen*. Again he explains that the reason lies in the instability of human beings: The flesh resists the spirit, refusing to believe the truth of God's promise. *LW* 26:64; *WA* 40/1. 129. 27–30: "Ideo quantum ad nos attinet, res valde lubrica est, quia nos lubrici sumus. Deinde dimidium nostri, nempe ipsam rationem et vires rationis habemus contrarias nobis. Resistit insuper spiritui caro quae non potest certo statuere promissa Dei vera esse."

active righteousness of the Law. But the spirit rules, rejoices, and is saved by passive righteousness."[72] Luther continues,

> I am indeed a sinner according to the present life and its righteousness, as a son of Adam where the Law accuses me, death reigns and devours me. But above this life I have another righteousness, another life, which is Christ, the Son of God, who does not know sin and death but is righteousness and eternal life.[73]

Because Christians are living simultaneously in these two inseverable dimensions, Luther insists that they must remain vigilant at all times not to mingle them: "Consciences should be carefully taught to understand the doctrine of the distinction between the righteousness of the Law and that of grace."[74] Amidst their experiences of trials and feelings that seem to oppose the promised reality, Christians must "not judge according to the feeling" of their heart. Instead, they "must judge according to the Word of God, which teaches that the Holy Spirit is granted to the afflicted, the terrified, and the despairing in such a way that He encourages and comforts them, so that they do not succumb in their trials and other evils but conquer them."[75]

Luther stresses that this matter is understood accurately only when the strategies are "transferred to practice," for without experience they are never learned.[76] To talk about Christian freedom is easy,

---

72. *LW* 26:9; *WA* 40/1. 48. 21–23: "Ita utrumque manet dum hic vivimus: Caro accusatur, exercetur, contristatur et conteritur iustitia activa legis, Sed spiritus regnat, laetatur et salvatur passiva iustitia."

73. *LW* 26:9; *WA* 40/1. 48. 15–19: "Sum quidem peccator secundum praesentem vitam et eius iustitiam, ut filius Adae, ubi accusat me lex, regnat mors et devorabit me, Sed supra hanc vitam habeo aliam iustitiam, aliam vitam quae est Christus, filius Dei, qui nescit peccatum et mortem, sed est iustitia et vita aeterna."

74. *LW* 26:158; *WA* 40/1. 270. 28–29: "Conscientiae diligenter sunt docendae, ut Locum de discrimine iustitiae legis et gratiae bene discant."

75. *LW* 26:383; *WA* 40/1. 584. 14–17: "Itaque non debemus iudicare secundum sensum cordis nostri, sed secundum verbum Dei, quod docet Spiritumssanctum ideo donari afflictis, conterritis, desperabundis etc., ut eos erigat ac consoletur, ne in tentationibus et omnibus malis succumbant, sed ea vincant."

76. *LW* 26:379; *WA* 40/1. 578. 23–24: "Ideo res ista tum demum recte intelligitur, cum ad usum transfertur, sine experientia enim nunquam discitur."

but "to feel the greatness of this freedom and to apply its results to oneself in a struggle, in the agony of conscience, and in practice—this is more difficult than anyone can say. Therefore one's spirit must be trained."[77] If a Christian should "sense that he is in doubt, let him exercise his faith, struggle against the doubt, and strive for certainty," securing a safe haven in the doctrine of justification by faith in Christ alone.[78]

Christian life involves ongoing movement from uncertainty to certainty: "Therefore we should strive daily to move more and more from uncertainty to certainty; and we should make an effort to wipe out completely that wicked idea, namely, that a man does not know whether he is in a state of grace."[79] For if Christians are in doubt about their being in a state of grace and about their being pleasing to God for the sake of Christ, they are, in fact, denying the fact that Christ has redeemed them and spurning all his benefits.

In faith, "we must by all means believe for a certainty that we are in a state of grace, that we are pleasing to God for the sake of Christ, and that we have the Holy Spirit."[80] Irrespective of the

77. *LW* 27:5; *WA* 40/2. 4. 22–26: "Verba quidem illa: libertas ab ira Dei, lege, peccato, morte etc., dictu facialia sunt, sed magnitudinem huius libertatis sentire et fructum eius in certamine, in agone conscientiae, in praxi applicare sibi, hoc plus, quam dici potest, difficile est. Ideo imbuendus est animus."

78. *LW* 26:379; *WA* 40/1. 578. 26–27: "Si autem sentit se dubitare, exerceat fidem et luctetur contra dubitationem ac nitatur ad certitudinem."

79. *LW* 26:380; *WA* 40/1. 579. 17–20: "Debemus igitur quotidie magis magisque luctari ab incertitudine ad certitudinem et operam dare, ut istam pestilentissimam opinionem (Quod homo nescit, utrum in gratia sit), quae totum mundum devoravit, funditus extirpemus."

80. *LW* 26:377–78; *WA* 40/1. 575. 32–33: "Omnino autem nos certo statuere oportet, quod simus in gratia, quod placeamus Deo propter Christum, quod habeamus spiritumsanctum." "As far as we are concerned, we now have God's Word, and so we ought not have any doubt about our salvation. It's in this way that we should dispute about predestination, for it has already been settled: I have been baptized and I have the Word, and so I have no doubt about my salvation as long as I continue to cling to the Word. When we take our eyes off Christ we come upon predestination and start to dispute. Our Lord God says, 'Why don't you believe me? Yet you hear me when I say that you are beloved by me and your sins are forgiven." *LW* 54:57–58 (no. 365, dated Fall 1532); *WA, TR* 1:156–57. "He [Martin Luther] spoke at length about the idle people who occupy themselves with disputation about predestination beyond the limits of Scripture. It is the most ungodly and dangerous business to abandon the certain and revealed

degree of achievement in the dimension of active righteousness and holiness, justified Christians should never doubt their already being in God's grace. Indeed, active defiance to the devil's tricks already shows the presence of the Holy Spirit: "These things certainly testify that the Holy Spirit is present."[81] Such exercise of faith is not a human work, but the work of the Spirit of Christ in Christians. God provides Christians with not only internal testimony of their assurance through the proclamation of the word accepted by faith in their hearts, but also external signs, by which they "are assured and confirmed a posteriori that" they "are in a state of grace."[82]

Indeed, the heart of these strategies for the Christian's daily spiritual struggle has nothing to do with subjectivizing or psychologizing his doctrine of justification by faith in Christ alone. Luther railed against such a propensity in his dispute with the "fanatics." The issue of assurance in one's conscience and feelings in the dimension of active righteousness and holiness is a matter of eternal life and death. When Christians do not succeed in holding fast to Christ in faith, the potential arises for a relapse from total confidence in Christ to dependence on the law: "For human nature and reason does not hold Christ firmly in its embrace but is quickly drawn down into thoughts

will of God in order to search into the hidden mysteries of God." *LW* 54:249 (no. 3655b, dated 25 December 1537); *WA, TR* 3:492. See also *LW* 26:8–9; *WA* 40/1. 47. 26–29: "But if there is any conscience or fear present, this is a sign that this righteousness has been withdrawn, that grace has been lost sight of, and that Christ is hidden and out of sight. But where Christ is truly seen, there must be full and perfect joy in the Lord and peace of heart."

81. *LW* 26:379; *WA* 40/1. 578. 34: "Haec certo testantur Spiritumsanctum adesse."

82. *LW* 26:379; *WA* 40/1. 577. 29–30: "Istis signis certi reddimur et confirmamur a posteriori nos esse in gratia." "But the external signs, as I have said earlier, are these: to enjoy hearing about Christ; to teach, give thanks, praise, and confess Him, even at the cost of property and life; to do one's duty according to one's calling in a manly way, in faith and joy; not to take delight in sin; not to invade someone else's calling but to serve one's own; to help a needy brother, comfort the sorrowful, etc." *LW* 26:379; *WA* 40/1. 577. 25–29. Luther blasts the scholastics and the monks who teach that "no one can know for a certainty whether he is in a state of grace, even if he does good works according to his ability and lives a blameless life." *LW* 26:377; *WA* 40/1. 575. 14–15: "Neminem certo posse scire, etiamsi pro viribus suis bene operetur et inculpate vivat, Utrum in gratia sit." See "The Decrees and Canons of the Council of Trent," Session VI, Canons 13, 15, 16. *LW* 26:377, n. 15.

about the Law and sin."[83] Christians may then feel that they are obliged to procure by works their own justification and eternal life. This is a natural human tendency, Luther believes. When a person loses Christ, he "must fall into a trust in his own works."[84] When this happens, anguish and futility ensue, as when Sisyphus endlessly rolled the rock from the bottom of the mountain to the top, only to have it roll down again each time.[85] In this case, what is worse is that Christ's death is in vain, and Christians may lose their justification and eternal life.

Furthermore, adhesion to Christ in faith even in the dimension of active righteousness and holiness turns out to be critical, especially because Luther's concept of faith has a strong eschatological character. The daily warfare against the remnants of sin will subside only after the end of earthly life. What Christians have been promised and even granted through faith in Christ will be revealed in its entirety only upon entering into eternal life. For this reason, Luther's concept of faith cannot be fully appreciated without recognizing the role of eschatological hope therein. Alien, passive, and perfect righteousness and holiness are invisible to our physical eyes. They are only visible through hope to the eyes of faith: "For we are alive in Christ, in whom and through whom we are kings and lords over sin, death, the flesh, the world, hell, and every evil . . . . How? In faith. For our blessing has not yet been revealed. But meanwhile we await it in patience and yet already possess it certainly through faith."[86]

---

83. *LW* 26:120; *WA* 40/1. 214. 21–23: "Ratio enim et natura humana non haeret Christo firmiter in amplexibus, sed subinde relabitur ad cogitationes de lege et de peccato."

84. *LW* 26:9; *WA* 40/1. 48. 32–33: "oportet eum amisso Christo ruere in fiduciam operum."

85. *LW* 26:406; *WA* 40/1. 616. 32– 617. 23. Luther uses Aesop's fable of the dog that snaps at its shadow and loses the meat to illustrate the futility of efforts "to appease the wrath of God and to justify" oneself. *LW* 26:405; *WA* 40/1. 616. 15–31.

86. *LW* 26:453; *WA* 40/1. 679. 14–19: "In Christo enim vivimus, in quo et per quem Reges sumus et domini supra peccatum, mortem, carnem, mundum, infernum et omnia mala . . . . Quomodo? in fide, nondum enim revelatum est bonum nostrum, quod per patientiam interim expectamus, et tamen certo iam tenemus illud per fidem." Luther also says, "He must not enjoy

In his definition of a Christian as a saint, Luther repeatedly underscores that "a Christian is not someone who has no sin or feels no sin; he is someone to whom, because of his faith in Christ, God does not impute his sin."[87] As saints, Christians are not immune to fallibility in this life. Saints "are not all of equal firmness of character, and many weaknesses and offenses are discernible in every one of them; it is also true that many of them fall into sin."[88] Stressing that saints "are not stumps and stones" who remain unaffected by anything and never experience the desires of the flesh,[89] Luther draws our attention to Peter: "No man has ever fallen so grievously that he could not have stood up again. On the other hand, no one has such a sure footing that he cannot fall. If Peter fell, I, too, may fall; if he stood up again, so can I."[90] Luther explains, "Such errors and sins of the

the freedom of the sprit or of grace unless he has first put on the new man by faith in Christ, but this does not happen fully in this life." *LW* 26:7; *WA* 40/1. 45. 29–31. Eternal life "has been given to us by Christ and . . . it is ours even now because we have faith, [but] it won't be made known to us until hereafter. It isn't given to us here to know what that creation of the next world is like." *LW* 54:297 (no. 3951, dated 7 August 1538); *WA, TR* 4:30. A perfectly righteous and holy and blameless life "would be a life of angels and it will not be ours except in the future life . . . . In the meantime we are content with that righteousness which exists in hope through faith in Jesus Christ. Amen.'" *LW* 54:374–75 (no. 4991, dated 21 May–11 June 1540); *WA, TR* 4:602–603.

    In eternity, faith will be replaced by glory: "But in the life to come believing will cease, and there will be a correct and perfect keeping and loving. For when faith ceases, it will be replaced by glory, by means of which we shall see God as He is (1 John 3:2). There will be a true and perfect knowledge of God, a right reason, and a good will, neither moral nor theological but heavenly, divine, and eternal. Meanwhile we must persevere here in faith that has the forgiveness of sins and the imputation of righteousness through Christ." *LW* 26:274; *WA* 40/1. 428. 29–429. 16. "Then, in the conflicts and fears that continually return to plague you, you should patiently look with hope for the righteousness that you have only by faith, though only in an incipient and imperfect form, until it is revealed perfectly and eternally in due time." *LW* 27:26; *WA* 40/2. 31. 30–32. 16: "Deinde in istis pugnis et terroribus, qui subinde redeunt et exercent te, per spem patienter expecta iusticiam, quam modo fide habes, sed tantum inceptam et imperfectam, donec ea suo tempore reveletur perfecta et aeterna."

87. *LW* 26:133; *WA* 40/1. 235. 15–17: "Definimus ergo hunc esse Christianum, non qui non habet aut non sentit peccatum, sed cui illud a Deo propter fidem in Christum non imputatur."

88. *LW* 27:82; *WA* 40/2. 104. 7–9: "Quod omnes aeque non sunt firmi, sed multae adhuc imbecillitates et offensiones cernuntur in quibusdam, Item quod plerique etiam ruunt in peccat."

89. *LW* 27:76; *WA* 40/2. 96. 17–19: "Sunt [veri Sancti] autem non trunci et lapides . . . qui prorsus nulla re afficiantur aut nunquam concupiscentiam carnis sentiant."

saints are set forth in order that those who are troubled and desperate may find comfort and that those who are proud may be afraid."[91]

From the perspective of active righteousness and holiness, Luther claims that saints are those who maximize their love to live up to their name as followers of Christ. Saints "do not manage all at once

90. *LW* 26:109; *WA* 40/1. 197. 9–12: "Nemo unquam tam graviter lapsus est, qui non possit resurgere. Econtra nemo tam firmiter fixit pedem qui non possit labi. Si Petrus lapsus est, et ego labi possum; si resurrexit, possum et ego resurgere."

Apropos of Luther's stance that even so-called saints undergo struggles between the spirit and the flesh, Luther's comment starting from Romans 7:7 to the end of the chapter is noteworthy. Referring to Paul's description of the battle between the spirit and the flesh, Luther, in line with Augustine, argues that Paul himself is depicting the conflict of a spiritual person, not of a carnal person. Luther contends that there are people who "plunged into this false and injurious opinion, that the apostle was not speaking in his own person but in the person of carnal man, for they chatter the nonsense that the apostle had absolutely no sin." *LW* 25:338; *WA* 56. 349. 27–29. Luther continues, "This foolish opinion has led to the most injurious deception, such as, that people who have been baptized or absolved think that they are immediately without any sin; they become smug in that they have obtained righteousness and are at rest and relaxed." *LW* 25:338; *WA* 56. 350. 1–3.

On Augustine's changed interpretation of Romans 7:7, Luther delineates, "St. Augustine first asserted this extensively and repeatedly in his book against the Pelagians. Hence in his *Retractations*, I, 23, taking back a former explanation of this passage, he says: 'When the apostle says: 'We know that the Law is spiritual; but I am carnal' (v. 14), I was absolutely unwilling to understand this passage as referring to the person of the apostle who was already spiritual, but I wanted to refer it to him as a man placed under the Law and not yet under grace. This is the way I first understood these words, but later, after I had read certain interpretations of the divine words by men whose authority impressed me, I considered the matter more carefully and saw that the passage could also be understood of the apostle himself.' And in Book 2 of his *Contra Julianum*: 'Note that it is not, as you think, some Jew who is speaking, but according to most blessed Ambrose, the apostle Paul is speaking of himself when he says, 'I see in my members another law at war with the law of my mind, etc.' (v. 23). And a little later he cited these words of blessed Ambrose from his *De sacramento regenerationis*: 'We must struggle against our flesh. Paul struggled against his flesh. He finally says: 'I see in my members another law at war with the law of my mind.' Are you stronger than Paul? Do not put your trust in the zeal of your flesh and do not put your confidence in it, for even Paul cries out: 'For I know that nothing good dwells within me, that is, in my flesh. I can will what is right, but I cannot do it' (v. 18) . . . . And he makes the clearest explanation of all in book six of the same work, from chapter 11 to the end." *LW* 25:327–28; *WA* 56. 339. 7–340. 4.

Luther's concern for this aspect of a spiritual person's lifelong struggle between the spirit and the flesh comes into clear view in his exposition of Romans 7:7, then 7:14–25, eventually going back to 7:8, and so on. Luther meticulously follows Paul's statements from Romans 7:14 through verse 25 and illustrates twelve various expositions to substantiate his theological position on a spiritual person's persistent struggle.

91. *LW* 26:109; *WA* 40/1. 196. 24–197. 8: "Proponuntur ergo errores et peccata Sanctorum, ut afflicti et desperabundi consolationem inde accipiant et superbi terreantur."

to divest themselves of the old Adam with all his activities; but throughout their life the desires of the flesh remain with them."[92] However, insofar as they subject the desires of the flesh to the Spirit, sinning only out of weakness and not deliberate wickedness, their sin does not bar them from eternal salvation. When they fall unexpectedly into sin, they obtain forgiveness by returning to Christ through faith, and God does not count their sin against them. Seen from this perspective, Luther's interpretation of the interaction between faith and love and between active and passive righteousness and holiness explains why he declares that the doctrine of justification by faith in Christ alone is the sweetest doctrine, bringing "firm consolation to troubled consciences amid genuine terrors."[93]

---

92. *LW* 27:84; *WA* 40/2. 105. 105. 27–28: "non semel exuunt veterem hominem cum actibus suis, sed durante vita manet in eis concupiscentia." Luther also says, "Let Christians strive to avoid the works of the flesh; they cannot avoid its desires." *LW* 27:85; *WA* 40/2. 107. 21: "Opera igitur carnis studeant vitare Christiani, desideria non possunt."

93. *LW* 26:133; *WA* 40/1. 235. 17–18: "Ista doctrina affert firmam consolationem conscientiis in veris pavoribus." See also *LW* 26:231–32; *WA* 40/1. 366. 27–367. 21, *LW* 26:285; *WA* 40/1. 444. 30–445. 22, *LW* 27:33–35; *WA* 40/2. 41. 18–44. 13.

Conclusion

Paul Althaus has stated that an intensive study of Luther's theology is rewarding on the strength of the originality of his theological methodology, which is firmly rooted in his conviction of the authority of Scripture. Althaus claims that all Luther's theological thinking is nothing more than an attempt to interpret Scripture and almost every single step in Luther's theology receives its basis and direction from Scripture.[1] Luther's reconceptualization of faith and love supports this claim in that it is consequent upon his devoted exegesis of Paul's teaching on faith and love.

Calling into question any inclination to play down Luther's teaching on love and the relationship of faith to love through a disproportionate stress on his teaching of justification by faith alone, this dissertation proposed that Luther's teaching on faith and love functions as the overriding structural and conceptual pair undergirding the 1535 Galatians commentary. Furthermore, this dissertation advanced the argument that this feature is laid bare in full measure when it is seen from the vantage point of Luther's understanding of the functions of Christ and the law.

---

1. Paul Althaus, *Die Theologie Martin Luthers*, 4th ed. (Gütersloh: Gerd Mohn, 1975), 17; ET *The Theology of Martin Luther*, trans. Robert C. Schultz (Philadelphia: Fortress Press, 1966), 3–4.

Allying himself with Paul, Luther advocates sound, biblically based, Christian teaching on faith and love in a specific manner and in a certain order. However, Luther does not merely emulate what Paul argued in his own context. In Luther's exegesis of Paul, intended to bring the ancient truth of the Apostle out of obscurity and into the light, the ancient truth becomes new through Luther's vigorous interaction with his polemical opponents.

While developing and honing his teaching on faith and love, for instance, Luther does not merely juxtapose his redefined faith and love as two independent theological themes. Instead, he intentionally molds their relationship into a certain configuration that is not detected in Paul. To demonstrate the significance Luther attributes to this relationship, this dissertation highlighted how Luther heeds Paul's instructions on faith and love as the definitive structural division of Paul's Epistle to the Galatians.[2] Luther's elaboration on the structural division, in turn, gives rise to his teaching on faith and love as a thematic pair in the two dimensions of righteousness and holiness. Taking advantage of the emergence of Luther's teaching on faith and love as a thematic pair in those two dimensions, this dissertation utilized them as an interpretive framework.

In this framework, Luther's teaching on faith and love was explored as two conflicting theses in the dimension of alien, passive, and perfect righteousness and holiness, on the one hand, and as two harmoniously coordinated theses in the dimension of proper, active, and progressing righteousness and holiness, on the other. This aspect was demonstrated at the outset of chapter 2 from the standpoint

---

2. Accordingly, in this dissertation, the relationship between faith and love is underscored not only conceptually and ideologically but also structurally, namely, as a unique literary device. This reveals the significance Luther attributes to his teaching on faith and love. However, it is not a matter of Luther's own convenience but, according to Luther, is substantially derived from the authoritative teaching of the apostle Paul, and validated by its conformity to Paul's teaching.

of the literary structure and logical cohesion of the 1535 Galatians commentary.

Chapter 2 then proceeded to explore Luther's redefined faith that excludes love in the dimension of alien, passive, and perfect righteousness and holiness. This concept of faith was described in consideration of Luther's polemical engagement with the medieval Roman Church and the intra-Reformation Radicals. Throughout the course of those controversies, irrespective of the varying identities of his polemists, Luther consistently declares Christ as the sole savior of the unrighteous and faith as the sole means to grasp Christ in one's heart. Defying the scholastic doctrines of *fides caritate formata* and merit, Luther upholds Christ as the only demand, object, content, and form of faith. Faith is not only necessary but also sufficient for justification of the unrighteous. Christ, faith, and imputation are, thus, the three inseverable constituents needed for justification.

In our continuing investigation of Luther's view of faith as antithetical to love in the dimension of passive righteousness and holiness, chapter 3 laid out three cardinal facets of Luther's redefined faith, namely, justifying faith. Knowing the truth of the heart about God, Christ, and self, as revealed in the gospel, faith discerns God as a loving Father, Christ as the only savior, and the self as a sinner unworthy of justification and eternal life. As a full-hearted trust, faith has confidence in God's promise and faithfulness and in Christ, in and through whom God's promise has been fulfilled. In addition, although faith is incompatible with love in the dimension of passive righteousness and holiness, Luther's redefined faith does entail love that is active in the dimension of active righteousness and holiness. This redefined love was the guiding topic in chapters 4 and 5, whereas Luther's redefined faith was the defining topic in chapters 2 and 3.

Chapter 3 also called attention to how Luther's reconceptualization of faith cautiously re-institutes the law with a duly qualified role in the dimension of alien, passive, and perfect righteousness and holiness. Luther designates this as the theological or spiritual function of the law. Luther's faith unreservedly excludes the law as long as it claims jurisdiction over the justification of sinners. Nonetheless, Luther maintains that, insofar as the law does not transgress Christ's jurisdiction in the matter of justification, the law works as a stimulus to faith in Christ.

The framework of chapter 4 exhibited how Luther reintroduces love as concordant with faith. When his teaching on faith in the dimension of alien, passive, and perfect righteousness and holiness is correctly comprehended, Luther stretches us to the next level: his teaching on love in the dimension of proper, active, and progressing righteousness and holiness. As regards Luther's redefined faith and love, while this dissertation predominantly characterized faith as the sole means of grasping Christ and thereby justifying faith, it designated love as faith incarnate and thereby a determining means of authenticating faith. This chapter concentrated on Luther's purposeful reconstruction of the relationship of faith to love. The rationale upholding Luther's reintroduction of love as compatible with faith was illustrated in light of the twofold nature of Christian freedom, the Christ-given law of love, the twofold way of fulfilling the law, and christological premises.

A noteworthy reason for Luther's harmonizing of love and faith was identified in his conviction that Christian freedom, in faith, from the law, sin, and death is intertwined with Christian freedom, in love, for service. The interconnection of "freedom from" with "freedom for" in Luther's thought challenges us to contemplate what the assurance of justification and the attainment of eternal life signify to Christians. The question of how sinners are justified is not separated from the question why they are justified. An answer to the question of why is not satisfactorily offered, according to Luther, if it is searched for in an individualistic and private mode. Although the gratuitously bestowed justification through faith in Christ alone makes a justified Christian a "lord," God calls the "lord" to servanthood for the sake of others. A justified Christian as a "lord" can become complacent about the divine promise of her salvation and her personal spiritual well-being and safety. This should not be, Luther interrupts. God liberates a justified Christian from self-centeredness. If freedom for serving others and communal sharing does not ensue from "freedom from," such a freedom is not what Luther esteems as genuine Christian freedom.

We also studied Luther's outlook on the twofold fulfillment of the law as another logical reason for his reintroduction of love in harmony with faith. On the one hand, there is complete fulfillment of the law through participation in Christ by faith in the dimension of passive righteousness and holiness. On the other hand, we see the gradual fulfillment of the law by performing acts of love that flow out of faith in Christ in the dimension of active righteousness and holiness. Since Christ is the fulfillment of the law, in Christ we also fulfill the law. At the same time, God empowers and motivates us to fulfill the law in ourselves.

To fathom Luther's stance on the Christian's own way of fulfilling the law, which is pertinent to his teaching on love, two essential points need to be mentioned. First, the law that Christians are admonished to observe is not any kind of humanly contrived law, but the law of Christ, namely, the law of love, and the Decalogue that is illuminated with a new spiritual thrust from the vantage point of the Christ-given commandment to love. According to Luther, the Decalogue is fundamentally a collection of detailed stipulations of the Christ's commandment to love. Second, Christ has left his followers with the will that they keep his commandment. Christ commands and inspires justified Christians to keep the law of love. The Christian's love that springs from faith in Christ is measured in view of the fulfillment of the law in the dimension of active righteousness and holiness.

This dissertation also brought to the fore Luther's elaboration on the relationship between faith and love by setting it alongside his analysis of Christ's twofold function: proper and accidental. Christ's proper function is his unique soteriological work accomplished in his person for the justification of human sinners, while Christ's accidental function is to be an example for justified Christians. After identifying the relationship of Christ's proper function to his accidental one as analogous to that of faith to love, this dissertation cautiously touched on how Luther portrays Christ's two natures in his discussion of Christ's two functions. Therein Luther primarily emphasizes Christ's divinity in his concept of Christ's proper function and Christ's humanity in his concept of Christ's accidental function.

In this context, faith analogously corresponds to Christ's divinity, and love to Christ's humanity. In order to avoid any docetic implications in Luther's christological analogy, this dissertation emphasized that the motive of Luther's christological analogy is not to diminish the soteriological significance of Christ's humanity in conjunction with his divinity. Just as Christ's humanity is not the sufficient cause of the justification of the unrighteous, so love does not cause the justification of sinners. The justification of the unrighteous as a new creation is brought about primarily by virtue of Christ's divinity and it is likewise affected by faith.

Dwelling on this christological analogy as a defining concept for the relationship of faith to love, this dissertation argued that the analogy alludes to a specific scheme to designate the way faith is interlinked with love: the Chalcedonian formula. Just as there is unity between Christ's divinity and humanity, so there is unity between faith and love because Christ is the content of faith and love. However, since unity does not mean a mingling or confusion of Christ's divinity with his humanity, faith and love are not to be mingled or confused with each other. In addition, just as Christ's divinity and humanity are distinct but not separate, so are faith and love. Furthermore, just as Christ's divinity always takes priority over Christ's humanity, so does faith over love.

In exploring the christological analogy for the relationship between faith and love, this dissertation argues that it is Christ who stands not only between God and sinners through faith but also between a Christian and her neighbors through love. Christ is the one who corrects sinners' erroneous approach to God and their neighbors. While a perverse human self is turned inward, cutting off both the vertical and the horizontal relationship, Christ eradicates the depravity of human nature and creates a pure heart by faith, establishing channels between God and human beings and between Christians and their neighbors. Via a matrix of such channels, Christ lets the unfathomable and unwavering divine love issuing from the eternal Trinity overflow into and among human beings.

From this perspective, it can be said that Luther's reconceptualization of faith and love involves the issue of right-ness, namely, how to put all relations, vertical and horizontal, in proper order and mode. Only when a sinner has a right relationship with God through faith solely in Christ can she as a justified Christian rightly bear multifarious fruits of faith in every estate of her life. When Christ is appropriately recognized as the one who is standing at the center of the vertical and horizontal relations, it becomes clear that Christ calls us to both faith and love and that the whole of Christian life revolves around only one center: Christ.

Bearing all these features in mind, we are not surprised at Luther's contention that the whole of Christian life consists in both faith and love. Having said that, if love is omitted or overlooked from Luther's theology, we are missing half the picture. His teaching on love is far from being merely an afterthought or an appendix added to his teaching on faith.

Rather than neglecting or underestimating Luther's teaching on love, we are challenged to apply his proposal for "a new and theological grammar" as explained in chapter 4. There is an appropriate time, space, and manner in which to converse about faith and love, respectively or together, as a guiding theme or themes. The new theological grammar instructs us to always presuppose justifying faith when the issue at hand is love. On the other hand, when the discourse is about faith, it is assumed that we are talking about a genuine faith, not a counterfeit faith that is not manifest in love. As the relationships between a doer and deed and between a tree and its fruits indicate, the order between faith and love follows a particular sequence. Expanding on this facet, chapters 4 and 5 also laid out the relationship between the two dimensions of righteousness and holiness—alien, passive, and perfect vis-à-vis proper, active, and progressing.

Chapter 5 then gave prominence to the trichotomous relation, in which the fruits of faith are borne in the performance of love for God, neighbor, and self. Chapter 5 also endeavored to clarify that the theological or spiritual function of the law remains in the dimension of active righteousness and holiness. In Luther's teaching on faith and love with respect to the functions of the law, we found, first, that Luther categorically rejects the law when it competes with Christ the Savior over the matter of justification of the unrighteous. We then learned that Luther assigns a theological or spiritual function to the law as a stimulus to faith in Christ in the dimension of passive righteousness and holiness. In the dimension of active righteousness and holiness, the law or, more precisely, the law of Christ is introduced into the life of justified Christians. While always guarding against relapse into a legalistic inclination toward self- or works-righteousness, Luther holds the theological function to be legitimate even for justified Christians as an impetus for their continual dependence on Christ and not their own performances of the law.

In reference to the functions of the law, what attracts our special attention is the question of the presence of *tertius usus legis* (the third use of the law) in Luther's theology. Even though I am not going to investigate this issue in depth, I want to touch on it briefly here on the basis of my research on Luther's reconceptualization of faith and love.

Apropos the third use of the law, Bernhard Lohse contends that Luther "never advocated any such use, whether in terminology or subject matter."[3] Lohse's explanation is as follows: there is a mention of the third use of the law in the *Kirchenpostille* of 1522.[4] However, Lohse argues that this mention cannot be attributed to Luther because it appears there rather in order to exclude the expression and concept of the third use of the law employed in Melanchthon's sense. In this case, Lohse points out that if we discount Luther's remark about the third use of the law in the *Kirchenpostille* of 1522, there is only one other instance in which Luther spoke of such a use, namely, at the conclusion of *The Second Disputation against the Antinomians* (1538). With regard to this passage, however, Lohse, referring to Gerhard Ebeling and an Erlangen Luther scholar, Werner Elert, insists that "modern research has made clear that this passage is an interpolation

---

3. Bernhard Lohse, *Luthers Theologie in ihrer historischen Entwicklung und in ihrem systematischen Zusammenhang* (Göttingen: Vandenhoeck & Ruprecht, 1995), 281; ET *Martin Luther's Theology: Its Historical and Systematic Development*, trans. and ed. Roy A. Harrisville (Minneapolis: Fortress Press, 1999), 275.
4. *WA* 10^1/1. 456. 8–457. 14.

on the part of a pupil of Melanchthon, who in transcribing it assigned to Luther what his teacher had said."[5] So, according to Lohse's conclusion, the expression of the third use of the law was never actually penned by Luther himself.

However, Lohse admits that this argument does not necessarily mean that "Luther believed the law had no meaning for the 'justified.'" It is notable that Lohse rules out Luther's employment of the third use of the law, on the one hand, and cautiously acknowledges Luther's use of the law or, more precisely, the commandment, in terms of *paraenesis* (admonition), on the other. Lohse describes how, for the justified, the law "retains its accusing function" and then "has an educative function, in which case it is better to speak of a commandment rather than of a law. In any event, the function of the law in this sense is not identical with its accusing function. Particularly in his sermons, Luther continually adverted to the law in terms of *paraenesis*."[6] Regrettably, Lohse does not specify what exactly differentiates *tertius usus legis* from *paraenesis*. He also does not provide substantial or persuasive reasons for his disapproval of any conceptual presence of *tertius usus legis* in Luther's theology.

William H. Lazareth emphasizes the contrast between Luther and Philip Melanchthon, too. According to Lazareth, in order to "protect Christian freedom from the continual threats of moralism and legalism," Luther "consistently taught only two uses of the law since 1517."[7] He even claims that the "third function of the law [was] specifically rejected by Luther," who insisted that we must not make Christ a new Moses.[8]

5. Lohse, *Luthers Theologie*, 202; ET *Martin Luther's Theology*, 183.
6. Lohse, *Luthers Theologie*, 281; ET *Martin Luther's Theology*, 275.
7. William H. Lazareth, "Love and Law in Christian Life," in *Piety, Politics, and Ethics: Reformation Studies in Honor of George Wolfgang Forell*, ed. Carter Lindberg (Kirksville, MO: Sixteenth Century Journal Publishers, 1984), 110, 112.
8. Ibid., 111.

Lazareth further adds that "Melanchthon introduced a 'threefold function of the law' (*triplex usus legis*) for the first time on Lutheran soil in the 1533 edition of his *Christian Doctrine* (*Loci Communes*). In addition, and therefore in contradiction, to its civil and theological functions, the law is now acknowledged to have also a 'didactic use' (*usus didacticus*) for moral instruction in the sanctification of the regenerate."[9] In addition, referring to *The Second Disputation against the Antinomians* in the Weimar edition, Lazareth states that Luther "suddenly—and totally inconsistently—apparently also teaches the law's *three*-fold use."[10]

With regard to this seemingly sudden change of position, Lazareth, like Lohse, draws on Werner Elert's explanation. The conclusion of Elert's literary analysis of this text is that this sole exception in the Luther corpus is a forgery. According to Lazareth, Elert's main argument is as follows. Luther's *Disputation* is extant in nine manuscripts; only two however contain the closing sentences in question. One of these manuscripts is undated; the other is presumably attributed to Israel Alekriander, a student who was not matriculated at Wittenberg until 1550 and therefore could not himself have heard the *Disputation* (1538). He took these sentences almost verbatim from Melanchthon's *Loci* in 1533 and ascribed them to Luther in 1538. "In this way the Melanchthonian view of the law's didactic function also came traditionally to be ascribed erroneously to Luther as well."[11]

Consenting to Elert's position, Lazareth raises and answers the following question: "What, then, is the relation of Luther and Calvin to each other in their ethical thinking on the law? For Luther, the law plays only a negative and regulative role for the Christian insofar as

9. Ibid.
10. Ibid.
11. Ibid., 113.

one is still sinful. For Calvin (and for the Melanchthonian Crypto-Calvinists), however, the law also plays a positive and normative role for the Christian insofar as one is already righteous."[12]

Lazareth continues: "After decades of controversy on this crucial point, the *Formula of Concord* (1577) finally sided with the followers of Luther against those of Melanchthon. The freedom of the Christian was undergirded by confessional authority against the unevangelical alternatives of antinomianism (license) and legalism."[13] Lazareth understands Article VI ("The Third Use of the Law") in the *Formula of Concord* as follows: "insofar as Christians remain sinful, they are still completely subject to the civil and theological demands of God's law (vs. Neander's antinomianism). But insofar as Christians are already righteous, they are completely free from the bondage of the law to live in God's will of love under the guidance of the indwelling Holy Spirit (vs. Calvin's legalism)."[14]

In comparison with those who insists that neither the terminology nor the concept of the third use of the law appears in Luther's theology, Althaus maintains his position as follows:

> Luther does not use the expression 'the third function of the law [*tertius usus legis*].' Melanchthon did use this expression and it was then adopted in the *Formula of Concord*, in Lutheran orthodoxy, and by nineteenth century theology. In substance, however, it also occurs in Luther . . . . Since he [Luther] knows of a law of God before man's fall into sin, why should he not also recognize it in the life of a Christian—not only in its theological function and thus not only intended to lead the old man to know his sin and cleanse him of it, but also in its function of training the Christian in good works.[15]

---

12. Ibid.
13. Ibid.
14. Ibid.
15. Althaus, *Die Theologie Martin Luthers*, 238; ET *The Theology of Martin Luther*, 273. On this issue of Luther's application of the third use of the law, see further, among many, Paul Althaus, "Gebot und Gesetz," in *Gesetz und Evangelium: Beiträge zur Gegenwärtigen Theologischen Diskussion*, ed. Ernst Kinder and Klaus Haendler (Darmstadt: Wissenschaftliche

In dealing with the law, Luther indeed walks a fine line. He strives to avoid both legalism and antinomianism. However, while heedfully maneuvering his stance on the law away from those fallacies, Luther makes it clear that, insofar as the law is taken into account in light of the Christ-given law of love and the God-given Decalogue, it has a positive function for justified Christians. Luther holds that this law of love should be practiced by justified Christians, and indeed, they are bound by it, though not for justification. Considering this aspect, Althaus's exposition of the issue of the third use of the law in Luther's theology seems to be more nuanced and appropriate than that of those who deny the presence of any concept of the third use.[16]

Buchgesellschaft, 1968), 201–38, esp. 226–38; Edmund von Schlink, "Gesetz und Paraklese," in *Gesetz und Evangelium*, 239–59; Werner Elert, "The Third Use of the Law," *The Lutheran World View* 2 (1949): 38–48; Edward A. Dowey, "Law in Luther and Calvin," *Theology Today* 41, no. 2 (1984): 146–53.

    In relation to the issue of Luther's treatment of the law, it is worth considering Stephen Westerholm's *Perspectives Old and New on Paul: The "Lutheran" Paul and His Critics* (Grand Rapids: Eerdmans, 2004), 22–41. Although Westerholm's portrayal of Luther's reading of Paul delivers the essence of Luther's teaching on the law in its conciseness, some additional issues should be mentioned here. First, though he addresses the relationship between faith and love, the relationship is stated only in his explanation of the features of faith, and Luther's doctrine of love is not fully delineated in regard to the life of justified Christians. Second, he points out that the law must be banished from the minds of believers when their relationship with God is the issue, though the identifying and judging function of the law for believers is still maintained. Westerholm neglects the positive function of the law as guidance for believers in Luther's teaching. Third, though it is true that Luther makes it clear that the Mosaic law is not applicable to Christians, he qualifies that it is applicable to Christians in its *spiritual* meaning. Westerholm misses this point. It seems that if a new interpretation is necessary for Paul, the necessity is no less true for Luther.

16. See also Scott R., *Law, Life, and the Living God: The Third Use of the Law in Modern American Lutheranism* (Saint Louis: Concordia Publishing House, 2002); Gerhard Ebeling, "Zur Lehre vom triplex usus legis in der reformatorischen Theologie," *Theologische Literaturzeitung* 75 (1950): 236–46. Its English translation can be found in Ebeling, *Word and Faith* (Philadelphia: Fortress Press, 1963), 62–78 ("On the Doctrine of the *Triplex usus legis* in the Theology of the Reformation").

    In relation to the controversial discourse on Luther's employment of the third use of the law, there is a description of a fourfold use of the law in Heinrich Schmid's book. It is a compilation of theological statements, drawn from the writings of fourteen prominent Lutheran theologians who lived during the sixteenth and seventeenth centuries, in order to support and clarify the Christian faith after the pattern of presentation developed in the early Lutheran tradition. It states: "According to these different designs for which the Law was given, the use of it is divided into *political, elenchtical, pedagogical,* and *didactic.*" Heinrich Schmid, *Die Dogmatik der evangelisch-*

Before my dissertation draws to an end, I would like to make several observations on the Finnish scholars' identification of Luther's doctrine of justification with *theosis*. Other Luther scholars have already expressed some reservations or outright opposition to the Finnish scholars' argument about *theosis* in Luther. For instance, Dennis Bielfeldt finds a type of *theosis* in Luther's *Sermo de Duplici Iustitia*, but warns that it may differ from the Eastern Orthodox understanding of *theosis*. He cautions against the temptation to identify Luther's concept of union between Christ and Christians with the Orthodox notion of *theosis*.

One of the most critical questions is how to construe Luther's statements about the presence of the divine properties in a Christian

---

lutherischen Kirche, ed. Horst Georg Pöhlmann (Gütersloh: Gerd Mohn, 1979), 325: "Nach diesen verschiedenen Endzwecken, um deretwillen das Gesetz gegeben ist, unterscheidet man einen vierfachen *usum legis*, nämlich usum *politicum, elenchticum, paedagogicum* und *didacticum*."; ET *The Doctrinal Theology of the Evangelical Lutheran Church*, 3rd ed. rev. and, trans. Charles A. Hay and Henry E. Jacobs (Minneapolis: Augsburg Publishing House, 1961), 510.

A detailed explanation of this fourfold use of the law goes as follows: "[Hollazius] (1) *The political use of the Law* consists in the preservation of external discipline, that wicked and licentious men may be turned away from heinous offences, by presenting before them the penalties and rewards. According to this use, the Law is a bridle or barrier by which sinners are restrained. (2) *The elenchtical use* consists in the manifestation and reproof of sins . . . . (3) *The pedagogic use* of the Law consists in indirectly compelling the sinner to go to Christ. Although the Law formally and directly neither knows nor teaches Christ, yet by accusing, convincing, and alarming the sinner, it indirectly compels him to seek for solace and help in Christ the Redeemer. Wherefore the Law is our schoolmaster, to bring us unto Christ. Gal. 3:24. (4) *The didactic use* consists in the instruction and direction of all internal and external moral actions. Thus the Law is a perpetual rule of life. Matt. 5:17." "[Quenstedt] The first use pertains to unregenerate and obstinate sinners; the second and third to men about to be justified; the fourth to those who are justified and regenerate." Schmid, *Die Dogmatik der evangelisch-lutherischen Kirche*, 328–29; ET *The Doctrinal Theology of the Evangelical Lutheran Church*, 515–16.

This account is noteworthy on four accounts. First, it unequivocally posits a *didactic use* of the law for justified Christians as the guidance of moral behaviors. Even though the depiction does not employ the term *third use of the law*, it seems that the *didactic use* is, in substance, tantamount to the *third use*. Second, the explication also distinguishes the *elenchtical use* from the *pedagogic use* of the law. In Luther's analysis, both of these uses fall into the same category of the theological or spiritual use of the law. Third, it conceptually differentiates the *didactic use* from the *pedagogic use* of the law, though those two words can be regarded as synonyms. Fourth, it does not clarify whether the *elenchtical* and *pedagogic* uses of the law are pertinent not only for those about to be justified but also for those who are already justified.

as the presence of God. Drawing attention to Orthodoxy's careful distinction between *energeia* and *ousia*—for instance, in Gregory Palamas—Bielfeldt suggests that, when Luther identifies God with God's properties, he may mean something somewhat different from the Orthodox theologians. He continues, "[w]hile the *energeia/ousia* distinction tries to clarify the metaphysics of participation *in se*, Luther's identification of the divine essence and properties seems chiefly concerned with God's availability *pro me*."[17]

Klaus Schwarzwäller claims that the thematic method of the Finnish school of Luther research predetermines its conclusions and, moreover, that its concept of divinization obscures the distinction between Creator and creature.[18] Albrecht Beutel maintains that

17. Dennis Bielfeldt, "Freedom, Love, and Righteousness in Luther's *Sermo de Duplici Iustitia*," in *Freiheit als Liebe bei Martin Luther, Freedom as Love in Martin Luther: 8th International Congress for Luther Research in St. Paul, Minnesota, 1993, Seminar 1 Referate/Papers*, edited by Dennis D. Bielfeldt and Klaus Schwarzwäller (Frankfurt am Main: Peter Lang, 1995), 33. For a critique of this concept in Lutheran studies, see also Bielfeldt, "The Ontology of Deification," in *Caritas Dei: Beiträge zum Verständnis Luthers und der gegenwärtigen Ökumene, Festschrift für Tuomo Mannermaa zum 60. Geburtstag*, ed. Oswald Bayer, Robert W. Jenson, and Simo Knuuttila (Helsinki: Luther-Agricola-Gesellschaft, 1997), 90–113; Bielfeldt, "Response" [to Luther and Metaphysics: What is the Structure of Being according to Luther? by Sammeli Juntunen], in *Union with Christ*, 161–66. Bielfeldt offers and critically scrutinizes several complementary models used to describe the presence of Christ in the believer in Luther's theology. Lohse also cautions that "[s]imilarly, we should not adopt the thesis recently defended by a few Finnish Luther scholars that Luther gave great weight to the ancient church's idea of 'deification.' Though we cannot dispute a deification motif alongside others, we must be cautioned against overestimating this line of the tradition." Lohse, *Luthers Theologie*, 239; ET *Martin Luther's Theology*, 220–21. Scott Hendrix also cautiously states that the Finnish scholars' notion of *theosis* or divinization is not to be taken to mean that baptized Christians are unencumbered by sin or that no forensic language whatsoever is appropriate. Underscoring that Christians never become Christ in the sense of losing their humanity in a union with the divine, Hendrix states that he prefers to speak of "the believer's connectedness to Christ instead of the believer's union with Christ." Scott H. Hendrix, "Martin Luther's Reformation of Spirituality," *Lutheran Quarterly* 13, no. 3 (1999): 258.

18. Klaus Schwarzwäller, "Verantwortung des Glaubens Freiheit und Liebe nach der Dekalogauslegung Martin Luthers," in *Freiheit als Liebe bei Martin Luther*, 144–48. See also a Roman Catholic theologian's evaluation of the Finnish Luther research from the perspective of the ecumentical endeavor to resolve all church-dividing differences on justification through the "Joint Declaration on Justification" signed by Catholics and Lutherans in 1999. Christopher J. Malloy, *Engrafted into Christ: A Critique of the Joint Declaration* (New York: Peter Lang, 2005), 145–67.

"Luther uses the terms *deificare* and its derivatives sparingly and does not engage in speculation about the divinization of humanity."[19]

To these comments, the following observations can be added. First, Luther's use of a "Hebrew way of speaking" plays a vital role in the Finnish scholars' argument on the Christian's participation in God's nature through union with Christ in faith. According to their interpretation, a "Hebrew way of speaking" evinces Luther's identification between God's properties and God's nature. When Christians participate in Christ and the happy exchange occurs, they in fact participate in God's nature because Christ is God. This interpretation, however, seems to overlook Luther's point in his treatment of a Hebrew way of speaking.

As displayed in chapter 3, it is well known that Luther was struggling with the concept of the righteousness of God. The so-called "tower experience" stands for Luther's hermeneutical breakthrough, which enables him to correlate "the righteousness of God" with "the righteous" and discern the righteousness of God that makes unrighteous sinners righteous. Through this experience, Luther is freed from his anxiety, caused by the absolute righteousness of God that is unfathomable to human minds. Luther elucidates this insight in terms of how a Hebrew way of speaking works in the Scripture. In this context, Luther's usage of a Hebrew way of speaking rather speaks against an immediate identification between what God bestows to Christians and what God possesses as God's immanent nature and properties.

In addition, Luther semantically presses home a passive tense and thereby sense of human passivity in his interpretation of "the

---

19. Albrecht Beutel, "Antwort und Wort," in *Luther und Ontologie: Das Sein Christi im Glauben als strukturierendes Prinzip der Theologie Luthers*, ed. A. Ghiselli, K. Kopperi, and R. Vinke (Helsinki and Erlangen: Luther-Agricola-Gesellschaft and Martin-Luther-Verlag, 1993), 76, n. 27. See also Anna Briskina, "An Orthodox View of Finnish Luther Research," trans. Dennis Bielfeldt, *Lutheran Quarterly* 22, no. 1 (2008): 16.

righteousness of God" by "the Hebrew way of speaking." According to this interpretation, the righteousness of God is that by which God makes unrighteous sinners righteous. That being so, Luther's point in his interpretation of the righteousness of God according to the Hebrew way of speaking is that the status of sinners can be transformed into that of the righteous only by the righteousness of God.[20]

Furthermore, Luther declares that he would rather not think about the righteousness of God in terms of God's own nature because of his notion of the hidden God (*absconditus Deus*): "Take hold of Him [Jesus Christ, the incarnate man]; cling to Him with all your heart, and spurn all speculation about the Divine Majesty; for whoever investigates the majesty of God will be consumed by His glory."[21]

20. With regard to this interpretation, consider the following of Luther's table talks: "'For a long time I went astray [in the monastery] and didn't know what I was about. To be sure, I knew something, but I didn't know what it was until I came to the text in Romans 1[:17], 'He who through faith is righteous shall live.' That text helped me. There I saw what righteousness Paul was talking about. Earlier in the text I read 'righteousness.' I related the abstract ['righteousness'] with the concrete ['the righteous One'] and became sure of my cause. I learned to distinguish between the righteousness of the law and the righteousness of the gospel. I lacked nothing before this except that I made no distinction between the law and the gospel. I regarded both as the same thing and held that there was no difference between Christ and Moses except the times in which they lived and their degree of perfection. But when I discovered the proper distinction—namely, that the law is one thing and the gospel is another—I made myself free.' Then Dr. Pomeranus said, 'I began to experience a change when I read about the love of God and what it signifies passively, namely, that by which we are loved by God. Before I had always taken love actively [namely, that by which we love God.]' The doctor [Martin Luther] said, 'Yes, it is clear—by charity or by love!—that it's often understood [in the Scriptures] of that by which God loves us. However, in Hebrew the genitives of 'love' are difficult.'" *LW* 54:442–43 (no. 5518, dated Winter of 1542–1543); *WA, TR* 5:210.

21. *LW* 26:29; *WA* 40/1. 78. 17–18. Luther also expresses: "He [Jesus Christ] wanted us to fix the gaze of our hearts upon Himself and thus to prevent us from clambering into heaven and speculating about the Divine Majesty." *LW* 26:29; *WA* 40/1. 78. 10–13. "Therefore whenever you consider the doctrine of justification and wonder how or where in what condition to find a God who justifies or accepts sinners, then you must know that there is no other God than this Man Jesus Christ." *LW* 26:29; *WA* 40/1. 78. 14–16. Then Luther mentions that "I know from experience what I am talking about. But these fanatics, who deal with God apart from this Man, will not believe me." *LW* 26:29; *WA* 40/1. 78. 18–20. "Take note, therefore, in the doctrine of justification, or grace that when we all must struggle with the Law, sin, death, and the devil, we must look at no other God than this incarnate and human God." *LW* 26:29; *WA* 40/1. 78. 24–26.

Second, as mentioned in chapter 1, the Finnish scholars frequently refer to Luther's statement that faith "takes hold of Christ in such a way that Christ is the object of faith, or rather not the object but, so to speak, the One who is present in the faith itself."[22] Employing this statement, they claim that Luther's idea of Christ's being present in faith is the structuring principle of his theology and informs the Christian's participation in Christ through faith; hence, this idea reveals that Luther's view of justification can also be considered to be *theosis*.

Although consenting to the Finns' accentuation of Luther's notion of Christ who is present in Christians through faith, I would suggest that the move from an appropriate appreciation of Luther's notion of Christ who is present in faith to the contention that Luther's doctrine of justification is identical to *theosis* is a conceptual-logical jump. I would underscore instead that, although he fervently insists on the real presence of Christ, Luther shies away from putting any specific label on the way Christ is present in a Christian through faith. In fact, right after the statement cited above, Luther himself acknowledges that he does not know how Christ is really present: "Therefore faith justifies because it takes hold of and possesses this treasure, the present Christ. But how He is present—this is beyond our thought; for there is darkness, as I have said. Where the confidence of the heart is present, therefore, there Christ is present, in that very cloud and faith."[23] When Luther himself does not specifically define the

---

22. *LW* 26:129; *WA* 40/1. 228. 33–229. 15.

23. *LW* 26:130; *WA* 40/1. 229. 22–25: "Iustificat ergo fides, quia apprehendit et possidet istum thesaurum, scilicet Christum praesentem. Sed quo modo praesens sit, non est cogitabile, quia sunt tenebrae, ut dixi. Ubi ergo vera fiducia cordis est, ibi adest Christus in ipsa nebula et fide."

To spotlight the unique characteristic of the relationship between faith and Christ, which allows no interruption, especially from law and reason, Luther employs the following figure of speech: To have Christ in faith is like ascending "into the darkness, where neither the Law nor reason shines, but only the dimness of faith (1 Cor. 13:12), which assures us that we are saved by Christ alone, without any Law. Thus the Gospel leads us above and beyond the light of the Law and reason into the darkness of faith, where the Law and reason have no business"

presence of Christ in Christians, conflating Luther's notion of justification with *theosis* seems to be a logical leap and remains disputable.

With respect to the issue of *theosis*, I want to call attention to what Eberhard Jüngel says. He refers to Luther's *Disputation against Scholastic Theology* (1517), in which Luther states: Thesis 17 "Man is by nature unable to want God to be God. Indeed, he himself wants to be God, and does not want God to be God."[24] Jüngel elucidates that "the chief thing in Christian theology is that an end is put to this self-deception, and thus the proper distinction between God and humanity is reached. This is the fundamental distinction of Christian theology." He also highlights Luther's focal points in his exposition of Ps. 5:3: "The very reason for God's becoming man in Jesus Christ is that humans become human." Drawing the

---

LW 26:113–14; *WA* 40/1. 204. 24–27. Insofar as faith grasps Christ, it transcends the frame of reference available to human reason. Here we find an intriguing expression of traditional mysticism in Luther. The editors comment: "Both the affinities and the contrasts of Luther's thought with traditional mysticism are evident in his use of 'darkness' in passages like this." *LW* 26:113, n. 32. Luther also says that faith "takes hold of Christ in such a way that Christ is the object of faith, or rather not the object but, so to speak, the One who is present in the faith itself." He continues to mention as follows: "Thus faith is a sort of knowledge or darkness that nothing can see. Yet the Christ of whom faith takes hold is sitting in this darkness as God sat in the midst of darkness on Sinai and in the temple. Therefore our 'formal righteousness' is not a love that informs faith; but it is faith itself, a cloud in our hearts, that is, trust in a thing we do not see, in Christ, who is present especially when He cannot be seen. Therefore faith justifies because it takes hold of and possesses this treasure, the present Christ. But how He is present—this is beyond our thought; for there is darkness, as I have said. Where the confidence of the heart is present, therefore, there Christ is present, in that very cloud and faith." *LW* 26:129–30; *WA* 40/1. 229. 15–22. See also *LW* 26:228; *WA* 40/1. 362. 23–24.

   In addition, Luther's attitude to so-called mystical theology needs to be considered. "The speculative learning of the theologians is altogether worthless. I have read Bonaventure on this, and he almost drove me mad because I desired to experience the union of God with my soul (about which he babbles) through a union of intellect and will. Such theologians are nothing but fanatics. This is the true speculative theology (and it's practical too): Believe in Christ and do what you ought. Likewise, the mystical theology of Dionysius is nothing but trumpery, and Plato prattles that everything is non-being and everything is being, and he leaves it at that. This is what mystical theology declares: Abandon your intellect and senses and rise up above being and non-being.'" *LW* 54:112 (no. 644, dated Fall 1533); *WA, TR* 1:302–303.

24. *LW* 31:10; *WA* 1. 225. 1–2: "Non potest homo naturaliter velle deum esse deum, Immo vellet se esse deum et deum non esse deum."

proper distinction between God and humanity is done for humanity's own good. According to Jüngel, this distinction between God and humanity is given "in the event of justification by faith alone" and "to be justified means to be unconditionally distinguished from God for one's own good."[25] Additionally, Jüngel quotes a passage from Luther's *Operationes in Psalmos, 1519–1521*: "For as in Adam we have risen to the image of God, so he has descended to our image, that he might lead us back to a knowledge of ourselves. And this takes place in the sacrament of his incarnation. This is the kingdom of faith, in which the cross of Christ reigns, which hurls pretended divinity down and summons perversely deserted humanity and the despised infirmity of the flesh to honor again."[26] On the basis of my understanding of Luther, I ardently agree with what Jüngel is trying to express. From this perspective, the following questions arise: why do we as human beings desire to become like God when we have not become truly human? Must we not desire to become genuine human beings? I think that Luther endeavors to tackle these questions in his teachings on faith and love.

Being fully aware of the complexity of Luther's teaching on faith and love, I did not intend to offer any exhaustive presentation of it in this dissertation. By demonstrating Luther's teaching on faith and love as the overriding thematic pair, structurally and conceptually, I hope that this dissertation has proposed a constructive and positive

---

25. Eberhard Jüngel, *Zur Freiheit eines Christenmenschen: eine Erinnerung an Luthers Schrift* (Munich: Kaiser, 1991), 23–27; ET *The Freedom of a Christian: Luther's Significance for Contemporary Theology*, trans. Roy A. Harrisville (Minneapolis: Augsburg Publishing House, 1988), 24–27.

26. WA 5. 128. 39–129. 4: "Quia enim ascendimus in Adam ad similitudinem dei, ideo descendit ille in similitudinem nostram, ut reduceret nos ad nostri cognitionem. Atque hoc agitur sacramento incarnationis. Hoc est regnum fidei, in quo Crux Christi dominatur, divinitatem perverse petitam deiiciens et humanitatem carnisque contemptam infirmitatem perverse desertam revocans."). Jüngel, *Zur Freiheit eines Christenmenschen*, 24–25; ET *The Freedom of a Christian*, 25.

direction in which the subject might be fruitfully pursued for continuous discussion and further research.

Bibliography

Primary Literature

Aquinas, Thomas. *Summa Theologiæ: Complete Set*. Latin-English Edition, vols. 13–20. Translated by Fr. Laurence Shapcote, O.P. Edited by John Mortensen and Enrique Alarcón. Lander, WY: Aquinas Institute, 2012.

Aristotle. *Nicomachean Ethics*. In *The Basic Works of Aristotle*, 935–1112. Edited by Richard McKeon. New York: Modern Library, 2001.

Augustine. *De doctrina Christiana* in *Patrologiae cursus completus*. Series Latina, 34–35. Edited by Jacques-Paul Migne. Paris, 1865; ET *Teaching Christianity*. Translated by Edmund Hill, O.P. Edited by John E. Rotelle, O.S.A. Brooklyn, NY: New City Press, 1997.

_____. *De spiritu et littera* in *Patrologiae cursus completus*. Series Latina, 44–45. Edited by Jacques-Paul Migne. Paris, 1865.

_____. *De trinitate* in *Patrologiae cursus completus*. Series Latina, 42–43. Edited by Jacques-Paul Migne. Paris, 1865; ET *The Trinity*. Translated by Edmund Hill, O.P. Edited by John E. Rotelle, O.S.A. Brooklyn, NY: New City Press, 2000.

Barth, Karl. *Church Dogmatics, IV/2: The Doctrine of Reconciliation*. Translated by G. W. Bromiley. Bloomsbury: T & T Clark, 1958.

Calvin, John. *Institutes of the Christian Religion I*, 1559. Edited by John T. McNeill. Translated by Ford L. Battles. Philadelphia: Westminster, 1960.

Die Bekenntnisschriften der evangelisch-lutherischen Kirche. 12th ed. Göttingen: Vandenhoeck & Ruprecht, 1998.

Luther, Martin. "A Sermon on the Strength and Increase of Faith and Love, October 1, 1525 (?) Sixteenth Sunday after Trinity." In *Sermons of Martin Luther*, vol. 8, edited by John Nicholas Lenker, 259–80. Grand Rapids: Baker Book House, 1988.

_____. "Eighteenth Sunday after Trinity, Matthew 22:34-46, 1532." In *The Complete Sermons of Martin Luther*, vol. 7, edited by Eugene F. A. Klug, 51–60. Grand Rapids: Baker Books, 2000.

Luther's Works, American Edition. 75 vols. Edited by Jaroslav Pelikan, Helmut T. Lehmann, and Christopher Boyd Brown. Saint Louis: Concordia Publishing House, 1955ff.; Philadelphia: Fortress Press, 1955–86.

Vol. 2. *Lectures on Genesis Chapters 6–14*. Edited by Jaroslav Pelikan. Translated by George V. Schick.

Vol. 3. *Lectures on Genesis Chapters 15–20*. Edited by Jaroslav Pelikan. Translated by George V. Schick.

Vol. 4. *Lectures on Genesis Chapters 21–25*. Edited by Jaroslav Pelikan. Translated by George V. Schick.

Vol. 13. *Selections from the Psalms*. Edited by Jaroslav Pelikan.
Psalm 90. Translated by Paul M. Bretscher, 75–141.

Vol. 17. *Lectures on Isaiah Chapters 40–66*. Edited by Hilton C. Oswald. Translated by Herbert J. A. Bouman.

Vol. 21. *The Sermon on the Mount and the Magnificat*. Edited by Jaroslav Pelikan.
The Sermon on the Mount. Translated by Jaroslav Pelikan, 3–294.

Vol. 24. *Sermons on the Gospel of St. John Chapters 14–16*. Edited by Jaroslav Pelikan. Translated by Martin H. Bertram.

Vol. 25. *Lectures on Romans*. Edited by Hilton C. Oswald. Chapters 1–2. Translated by Walter G. Tillmanns. Chapters 3–16. Translated by Jacob A. O. Preus.

Vol. 26. *Lectures on Galatians, 1535, Chapters 1–4*. Edited by Jaroslav Pelikan and Walter A. Hansen. Translated by Jaroslav Pelikan.

Vol. 27. *Lectures on Galatians, 1535, Chapters 5–6* and *Lectures on Galatians 1519, Chapters 1–6*. Edited by Jaroslav Pelikan and Walter A. Hansen. *Lectures on Galatians, 1535, Chapters 5–6*. Translated by Jaroslav Pelikan.

Vol. 31. *Career of the Reformer I*. Edited by Harold J. Grimm. *Disputation against Scholastic Theology*, 1517. Translated by Harold J. Grimm, 9–16.

Heidelberg Disputation, 1518. Translated by Harold J. Grimm, 39–70.

Explanations of the Ninety-Five Theses, 1518. Translated by Carl W. Folkemer, 83–252.

The Freedom of a Christian, 1520. Translated by W. A. Lambert. Revised by Harold J. Grimm, 333–77.

Vol. 33. *Career of the Reformer III*. Edited by Philip S. Watson. *The Bondage of the Will*, 1526. Translated by Philip S. Watson and Benjamin Drewery.

Vol. 34. *Career of the Reformer IV*. Edited by Lewis W. Spitz. *The Disputation Concerning Justification*, 1536. Translated by Lewis W. Spitz, 151–96.

Preface to the Complete Edition of Luther's Latin Writings, 1545. Translated by Lewis W. Spitz, 327–38.

Vol. 35. *Word and Sacrament I*. Edited by E. Theodore Bachmann. "The Holy and Blessed Sacrament of Baptism." Translated by Charles M. Jacobs. Revised by E. Theodore Bachmann, 29–43.

"The Blessed Sacrament of the Holy and True Body of Christ, and the Brotherhoods." Translated by Jeremiah J. Schindel. Revised by E. Theodore Bachmann, 49–73.

Preface to the Epistle of St. Paul to the Romans, 1546 (1522). Translated by Charles M. Jacobs. Revised by E. Theodore Bachmann, 365–80.

Preface to the Old Testament, 1545 (1523). Translated by Charles M. Jacobs. Revised by E. Theodore Bachmann, 235–51.

Vol. 40. *Church and Ministry II*. Edited by Conrad Bergendoff.

Against the Heavenly Prophets in the Matter of Images and Sacraments, 1525. Translated by Bernhard Erling and Conrad Bergendoff, 79–223.

Vol. 43. *Devotional Writings II*. Edited by Gustav. K. Wiencke.

Personal Prayer Book, 1522. Translated by Martin H. Bertram, 5–45.

Vol. 44. *The Christian in Society I*. Edited by James Atkinson.

Treatise on Good Works, 1520. Translated by W. A. Lambert, 15–114.

Vol. 51. *Sermons I*. Translated and edited by John W. Doberstein.

"Sermon Preached in the Castle at Leipzig on the Day of St. Peter and St. Paul, Matt. 16:13–19, June 29, 1519," 53–60.

"Eight Sermons by Dr. M. Luther, Preached by him at Wittenberg in Lent, dealing briefly with the masses, images, both kinds in the sacrament, eating [of meats], and private confession, etc." March 9–16, 1522, 69–100.

"Two Sermons," Matt. 22:37–39, October 19, 1522, Preached at Weimar in the Parish Church, 111–17.

"Ten Sermons on the Catechism" before the Publication of the Large and Small Catechisms, November 30 to December 18, 1528, 135–93.

"[First] Sermon at the Funeral of the Elector, Duke John of Saxony, I Thess. 4:13–14, August 18, 1532," 231–43.

"Sermon on the Sum of the Christian Life, I Tim. 1:5–7, Preached in Wörlitz, November 24, 1532," 259–87.

"Sermon on Soberness and Moderation against Gluttony and Drunkenness, I Pet. 4:7–11, May 18, 1539," 291–99.

"Sermon Preached in Castle Pleissenburg on the Occasion of the Inauguration of the Reformation in Leipzig, John 14:23–31, May 24, 1539," 303–12.

"Sermon on Matt. 3:13–17 at the Baptism of Bernhard von Anhalt, Preached in Dessau, April 2, 1540," 315–29.

"Sermon at the Dedication of the Castle Church in Torgau, Luke 14:1–11, October 5, 1544," 333–54.

"The Last Sermon in Wittenberg, Rom. 12:3, January 17, 1546," 371–80.

Vol. 52. *Sermons II.* Edited by Hans J. Hillerbrand.

"The Gospel for Christmas Eve, Luke 2[:1–14]." Translated by John G. Kunstmann, 7–31.

"The Gospel for the Early Christmas Service, Luke 2[:15–20]." Translated by John G. Kunstmann, 32–40.

"The Gospel for the Festival of the Epiphany, Matthew 2[:1–12]." Translated by S. P. Hebart, 159–286.

Vol. 53. *Liturgy and Hymns.* Edited by Ulrich S. Leupold.

"The German Mass and Order of Service." Translated by Augustus Steimle. Revised by Ulrich S. Leupold, 61–90.

Vol. 54. *Table Talk.* Translated and edited by Theodore G. Tappert.

Luthers Werke, Kritische Gesamtausgabe. 72 vols. Edited by J. K. F. Knaake et al. Weimar: Hermann Böhlau, 1883–2009.

Vol. 1. Edited by J. K. F. Knaake.

Disputatio contra scholasticam theologiam, 1517, 221–28.

Disputatio Heidelbergae habita. 1518, 353–74.

Resolutiones disputationum de indulgentiarum virtute. 1518, 525–628.

Vol. 2. Edited by J. K. F. Knaake.

"Ein Sermon gepredigt zu Leipzig auf dem Schloß am Tage Petri und
Pauli. 1519," 244–49.

Ein Sermon von dem heiligen hochwürdigen Sakrament der Taufe. 1519,
724–37.

*Ein Sermon von dem hochwürdigen Sakrament des heiligen wahren
Leichnams Christi und von den Brüderschaften. 1519,* 738–58.

Vol. 6. Edited by D. Knaake.

Von den guten werckenn, 202–76.

Vol. 7. Edited by Paul Pietsch.

*Von der Freiheit eines Christenmenschen. 1520/ Tractatus de libertate
christiana. 1520.* Edited by J. K. F. Knaake, 20–73.

Vol. 10^{1}/1. Edited by Karl Drescher.

"Evangelium in der Christmeß, Luk. 2, 1–14," 58–95.

"Evangelium in der Früh-Christmeß. Luk. 2, 15–20," 128–41.

"Das Evangelium am Tage der Heiligen drei Könige. Matth. 2,
1–12," 555–728.

Vol. 10/2. Edited by Karl Drescher.

Betbüchlein. 1522. Edited by F. Cohrs and A. Göze, 375–406.

Vol. 10/3. Edited by Paul Pietsch.

"Acht Sermon D. M. Luthers von jm geprediget zu Wittemberg in
der Fasten, 1522," 1–64.

"Reisepredigten in Weimar und Erfurt, 1522," 341–52.

Vol. 18. Edited by Karl Drescher.

Wider die himmlischen Propheten, von den Bildern und Sakrament. 1525.
Edited by O. Brenner and H. Barge, 62–214.

De servo arbitrio. 1525. Edited by A. Freitag, 600–787.

Vol. 19. Edited by Paul Pietsch.

Deutsche Messe und Ordnung Gottesdiensts. 1526, 72–113.

Vol. 30/1. Edited by Karl Drescher.

"Katechismuspredigten, 1528." Edited by Georg Buchwald, 57–122.

Vol. 31/2. Edited by Karl Drescher.

Vorlesung über Jesaias (1527–1530). Edited by G. Buchwald and O. Brenner, 1–585.

Vol. 32. Edited by Paul Pietsch.

Wochenpredigten über Matth. 5–7. 1530/2, 299–544.

Vol. 36. Edited by Karl Drescher.

"Die erste Predigt" in "Zwo Predigt uber der Leiche des Kurfürsten Herzog Johans zu Sachsen, 1532." Edited by G. Buchwald and O. Brenner, 237–70.

"Summa des christlichen Lebens, 1. Timoth. 1." Edited by G. Buchwald and O. Brenner, 352–75.

Vol. 39/1. Edited by Karl Drescher.

Die Disputation de iustificatione, 1536, 82–126.

Vol. 39/2. Edited by G. Bebermeyer.

"Die Zirkulardisputation über das Recht des Widerstands gegen den Kaiser (Matth. 19, 21). 9. Mai 1539," 34–91.

Vol. 40/1. Edited by Karl Drescher.

In epistolam S. Pauli ad Galatas Commentarius ex praelectione D. Martini Lutheri (1531) collectus 1535. Edited by A. Freitag.

Vol. 40/2. Edited by Karl Drescher.

In Epistolam S. Pauli ad Galatas Commentarius 1531 (1535). Edited by A. Freitag, 1–184.

Vol. 40/3. Edited by G. Bebermeyer and A. Freitag.

Enarratio Psalmi XC, 1534/35. [1541], 476–594.

Vol. 42. Edited by Karl Drescher.

Vorlesung über 1. Mose. Edited by G. Koffmane and O. Reichert.

Vol. 43. Edited by Karl Drescher.

Vorlesung über 1. Mose. Edited by O. Reichert.

Vol. 45. Edited by Karl Drescher and Oskar Brenner.

Das XIV. und XV. Capitel S. Johannis, Edited by G. Buchwald and O. Brenner, 465–733.

Vol. 46. Edited by Karl Drescher.

Das XVI. Kapitel S. Johannis. Edited by G. Buchwald and O. Brenner, 1–111.

Vol. 47. Edited by Karl Drescher.

"Ein Predig von Rüchterkait und Mässigkait, 1 Pet. 4," 1539. Edited by G. Buchwald, 757–71.

"Predigt auf dem Schloß Pleißenburg zu Leipzig, S. Johannis am 14. Capitel, 1539." Edited by G. Buchwald, 772–79.

Vol. 49. Edited by Karl Drescher.

"Predigt am Freitag nach Ostern, 1540." Edited by G. Buchwald, 124–35.

"Predigt am 17. Sonntag nach Trinitatis, bei der Einweihung der Schloßkirche zu Torgau gehalten, 1544." Edited by G. Buchwald, 588–615.

Vol. 51. Edited by Karl Drescher.

"Die lezte predigt Doctoris Martini Lutheri zu Wittenberg 17. Januar 1546 (Rom. 12, 3)." Edited by G. Buchwald, 123–34.

Vol. 54. Edited by Karl Drescher.

Vorrede zum ersten Bande der Gesamtausgaben seiner lateinischen Schriften, Wittenberg 1545, 179–87.

Vol. 56. Edited by G. Bebermeyer and J. Ficker. *Divi Pauli apostoli ad Romanos Epistola, 1515–1516.*

Luthers Werke, Kritische Gesamtausgabe, *Die Deutsche Bibel*. 15 vols. Edited by Paul Pietsch et al. Weimar: Hermann Böhlau, 1906-61.

Vol. 7. Edited by G. Bebermeyer.

Vorrede auf die Epistel S. Pauli an die Römer. 3–27.

Luthers Werke, Kritische Gesamtausgabe, *Tischreden*. 6 vols. Edited by J. F. K. Knaake et al. Weimar: Hermann Böhlau, 1912–21.

The 1529 Holy Week and Easter Sermons of Dr. Martin Luther. Translated by Irving L. Sandberg (from "Predigten D. Martin Luthers auf Grund von Nachschriften Georg Rörers und Anton Lauterbachs." Edited by Georg Buchwald. Gütersloh:

Bertelsmann, 1925). Saint Louis: Concordia Publishing House, 1999.

The Book of Concord. Edited by Robert Kolb and Timothy J. Wengert. Minneapolis: Fortress Press, 2000.

Wesley, John. *The Works of John Wesley.* Vol. 1, *Sermons I: 1–33.* Edited by Albert C. Outler. The Bicentennial Edition of the Works of John Wesley. Nashville: Abingdon, 1984.

_____. *The Works of John Wesley.* Vol. 3, *Sermons III: 71–114.* Edited by Albert C. Outler. The Bicentennial Edition of the Works of John Wesley. Nashville: Abingdon, 1986.

_____. *The Works of John Wesley.* Vol. 19, *Journal and Diaries II (1738–1743).* Edited by W. Reginald Ward and Richard P. Heitzenrater. Nashville: Abingdon, 1990.

Secondary Literature

Althaus, Paul. *Die Ethik Martin Luthers.* Gütersloh: Gerd Mohn, 1965.

_____. *Die Theologie Martin Luthers.* 4th ed. Gütersloh: Gerd Mohn, 1975.

_____. "Gebot und Gesetz." In *Gesetz und Evangelium: Beiträge zur Gegenwärtigen Theologischen Diskussion,* edited by Ernst Kinder and Klaus Haendler, 201–38. Darmstadt: Wissenschaftliche Buchgesellschaft, 1968.

_____. *The Ethics of Martin Luther.* Translated by Robert C. Schultz. Philadelphia: Fortress Press, 1972.

_____. *The Theology of Martin Luther.* Translated by Robert C. Schultz. Philadelphia: Fortress Press, 1966.

Andersen, Svend. "Lutheran Ethics and Political Liberalism." In *Philosophical Studies in Religion, Metaphysics, and Ethics: Essays in Honour of Heikki Kirjavainen. Schriften der Luther-Agricola-Gesellschaft* 38, edited by Timo Koistinen and Tommi Lehtonen, 292–302. Helsinki: Luther-Agricola-Society, 1997.

Bainton, Roland H. *Studies on the Reformation: Collected Papers.* Boston: Beacon, 1963.

Bayer, Oswald. *Aus Glauben leben: Über Rechtfertigung und Heiligung.* Stuttgart: Calver Verlag, 1990.

_____. *Living by Faith: Justification and Sanctification.* Translated by Geoffrey W. Bromiley. Grand Rapids: Eerdmans, 2003.

_____. "Luther's Ethics as Pastoral Care." *Lutheran Quarterly* 4, no. 2 (1990): 125–42.

_____. "Nature and Institution: Luther's Doctrine of the Three Orders." *Lutheran Quarterly* 12, no. 2(1998): 125–59.

_____. "The Being of Christ in Faith." *Lutheran Quarterly* 10, no. 2 (1996): 135–50.

Bayer, Oswald, Robert W. Jenson, and Simo Knuuttila, eds. *Caritas Dei: Beiträge zum Verständnis Luthers und der gegenwärtigen Ökumene. Festschrift für Tuomo Mannermaa zum 60. Geburtstag. Schriften der Luther-Agricola-Gesellschaft* 39. Helsinki: Luther-Agricola-Gesellschaft, 1997.

Beutel, Albrecht. "Antwort und Wort." In *Luther und Ontologie: Das Sein Christi im Glauben als strukturierendes Prinzip der Theologie Luthers,* edited by A. Ghiselli, K. Kopperi, and R. Vinke, 70–93. Helsinki and Erlangen: Luther-Agricola-Gesellschaft and Martin-Luther-Verlag, 1993.

Bielfeldt, Dennis. "Freedom, Love, and Righteousness in Luther's Sermo de Duplici Iustitia." In *Freiheit als Liebe bei Martin Luther, Freedom as Love in Martin Luther: 8th International Congress for Luther Research in St. Paul, Minnesota, 1993, Seminar 1 Referate/Papers,* edited by Dennis D. Bielfeldt and Klaus Schwarzwäller, 19–34. Frankfurt am Main: Peter Lang, 1995.

_____. "Response" [to "Luther and Metaphysics: What is the Structure of Being according to Luther?" by Sammeli Juntunen]. In *Union with Christ: The New Finnish Interpretation of Luther,* edited by Carl E. Braaten and Robert W. Jenson, 161–66. Grand Rapids: Eerdmans, 1998.

_____. "The Ontology of Deification." In *Caritas Dei: Beiträge zum Verständnis Luthers und der gegenwärtigen Ökumene, Festschrift für Tuomo Mannermaa zum 60. Geburtstag*, edited by Oswald Bayer, Robert W. Jenson, and Simo Knuuttila, 90–113. Helsinki: Luther-Agricola-Gesellschaft, 1997.

Braaten, Carl E. *Justification: The Article by Which the Church Stands or Falls*. Minneapolis: Fortress Press, 1990.

Brecht, Martin. *Martin Luther*. Vol. 1, *His Road to Reformation*. Translated by James L. Schaaf. Philadelphia: Fortress Press, 1985.

Briskina, Anna. "An Orthodox View of Finnish Luther Research." Translated by Dennis Bielfeldt. *Lutheran Quarterly* 22, no. 1 (2008): 16–39.

Brondos, David A. "*Sola fide* and Luther's 'Analytic' Understanding of Justification: A Fresh Look at Some Old Questions." *Pro Ecclesia* 13, no. 1 (2004): 39–57.

Burger, Christoph. "Gottesliebe, Erstes Gebot und menschliche Autonomie bei spätmittelalterlichen Theologen und bei Martin Luther." *Zeitschrift für Theologie und Kirche* 89, no. 3 (1992): 280–301.

Burgess, Joseph A. and Marc Kolden, eds. *By Faith Alone: Essays on Justification in Honor of Gerhard O. Forde*. Grand Rapids: Eerdmans, 2004.

Burnaby, John. *Amor Dei: A Study of the Religion of St. Augustine*. Norwich: Canterbury, 1991.

Canlis, Julie. "Calvin, Osiander and Participation in God." *International Journal of Systematic Theology* 6, no. 2 (2004): 169–84.

Canning, Raymond. *The Unity of Love for God and Neighbour in St. Augustine*. Heverlee-Leuven: Augustinian Historical Institute, 1993.

Clark, R. Scott. "*Iustitia Imputata Christi*: Alien or Proper to Luther's Doctrine of Justification." *Concordia Theological Quarterly* 70 (2006): 269–301.

Crouse, R. D. "Recurrens in te unum: The Pattern of St. Augustine's *Confessions*." *Studia Patristica* 14 (1976): 389–92.

Das, A. Andrew. "*Oneness in Christ*: The *Nexus Indivulsus* between Justification and Sanctification in Paul's Letter to the Galatians." *Concordia Journal* 21, no. 2 (1995): 173–86.

Dieter, Theodor. "Justification and Sanctification in Luther." In *Justification and Sanctification: In the Traditions of the Reformation*. The Fifth Consultation on the First and Second Reformations Geneva, 13 to 17 February 1998, edited by Milan Opočenský and Páraic Réamonn, 87–96. Geneva: World Alliance of Reformed Churches, 1999.

_____. *Der junge Luther und Aristoteles: Eine historisch-systematische Untersuchung zum Verhältnis von Theologie und Philosophie*. Berlin: Walter de Gruyter, 2001.

Ebeling, Gerhard. "Faith and Love." In *Martinus Luther: 450ᵗʰ Anniversary of the Reformation*, edited by Helmut Gollwitzer, 69–79. Bad Godesberg: Inter Nationes, 1967.

_____. *Luther: An Introduction to His Thought*. Translated by R. A. Wilson. Philadelphia: Fortress Press, 1977.

_____. *Luther–Einführung in sein Denken*. 2nd ed., with Epilogue by Albrecht Beutel. Tübingen: Mohr Siebeck, 2006; Tübingen: J. C. B. Mohr (Paul Siebeck), 1964.

_____. *Lutherstudien III*. Tübingen: J. C. B. Mohr (Paul Siebeck), 1985.

_____. *Word and Faith*. Philadelphia: Fortress Press, 1963.

_____. "Zur Lehre vom triplex usus legis in der reformatorischen Theologie." *Theologische Literaturzeitung* 75 (1950): 236–46.

Elert, Werner. "The Third Use of the Law." *The Lutheran World View* 2 (1949): 38–48.

Erling, Bernhard. "The Role of Law in How a Christian Becomes what He/She is." In *Freiheit als Liebe bei Martin Luther, Freedom as Love in Martin Luther: 8th International Congress for Luther Research in St. Paul, Minnesota, 1993, Seminar 1 Referate/Papers*, edited by Dennis D. Bielfeldt and Klaus Schwarzwäller, 63–78. Frankfurt am Main: Peter Lang, 1995.

Fitzgerald, Allan D., O.S.A., ed. *Augustine through the Ages: An Encyclopedia.* Grand Rapids: Eerdmans, 1999.

Forde, Gerhard O. *Justification by Faith—A Matter of Death and Life.* Mifflintown, PA: Sigler Press, 1999.

_____. "The Lutheran View of Sanctification." In *The Preached God: Proclamation in Word and Sacrament,* edited by Mark C. Mattes and Steven D. Paulson, 226–44. Grand Rapids: Eerdmans, 2007.

Forell, George W. *Faith Active in Love: An Investigation of the Principles Underlying Luther's Social Ethics.* Eugene, OR: Wipf & Stock, 1999; Minneapolis: Augsburg Publishing House, 1954.

_____. "Freedom as Love: Luther's *Treatise on Good Works.*" In *Freiheit als Liebe bei Martin Luther, Freedom as Love in Martin Luther: 8th International Congress for Luther Research in St. Paul, Minnesota, 1993, Seminar 1 Referate/Papers,* edited by Dennis D. Bielfeldt and Klaus Schwarzwäller, 79–83. Frankfurt am Main: Peter Lang, 1995.

Froehlich, Karlfried. "Luther on Vocation." In *Harvesting Martin Luther's Reflections on Theology, Ethics, and the Church,* edited by Timothy J. Wengert, 121–33. Grand Rapids: Eerdmans, 2004.

Gaebler, Mary. *The Courage of Faith: Martin Luther and the Theonomous Self.* Minneapolis: Fortress Press, 2013.

Gollwitzer, Helmut, ed. *Martinus Luther: 450th Anniversary of the Reformation.* Bad Godesberg: Inter Nationes, 1967.

Grislis, Egil. "The Foundation of Creative Freedom in Martin Luther's 'Von den Guten Werken' (1520)." In *Freiheit als Liebe bei Martin Luther, Freedom as Love in Martin Luther: 8th International Congress for Luther Research in St. Paul, Minnesota, 1993, Seminar 1 Referate/Papers,* edited by Dennis D. Bielfeldt and Klaus Schwarzwäller, 85–103. Frankfurt am Main: Peter Lang, 1995.

Gritsch, Eric W. "Martin Luther's Commentary on Gal 5, 2–24, 1519 (WA 2, 574–597) and Sermon on Gal 4, 1–7, 1522 (WA 10 I 1, 325–378)."

In *Freiheit als Liebe bei Martin Luther, Freedom as Love in Martin Luther: 8th International Congress for Luther Research in St. Paul, Minnesota, 1993, Seminar 1 Referate/Papers*, edited by Dennis D. Bielfeldt and Klaus Schwarzwäller, 105–111. Frankfurt am Main: Peter Lang, 1995.

Hamm, Berndt. *The Early Luther: Stages in a Reformation Reorientation.* Translated by Martin J. Lohrmann. Grand Rapids, MI: William B. Eerdmans, 2014.

_____. "Von der Gottesliebe des Mittelalters zum Glauben Luthers: Ein Beitrag zur Bußgeschichte." *Lutherjahrbuch* 65 (1998): 19–44.

Heckel, Johannes. *Lex Charitatis: A Juristic Disquisition on Law in the Theology of Martin Luther.* Translated and edited by Gottfried G. Krodel. Grand Rapids: Eerdmans, 2010.

Heinz, Johann. *Justification and Merit: Luther vs. Catholicism.* Eugene, OR: Wipf & Stock, 2002.

Hendrix, Scott H., ed. *Early Protestant Spirituality.* Mahwah, NJ: Paulist, 2009.

_____. "Martin Luther's Reformation of Spirituality." *Lutheran Quarterly* 13, no. 3 (1999): 249–70.

_____. "The Reformer of Faith and Love: Luther's Lectures on Genesis." Paper presented at Luther als Theologe des Glaubens und der Liebe, Helsinki, September 2000.

Hendrix, Scott H. and Günther Gassmann. *Fortress Introduction to the Lutheran Confessions.* Minneapolis: Fortress Press, 1999.

Hoffman, Bengt. "Lutheran Spirituality." In *Spiritual Traditions for the Contemporary Church*, edited by Robin Maas and Gabriel O'Donnell, O.P., 145–61. Nashville: Abingdon, 1990.

Holl, Karl. *Die Rechtfertigungslehre in Licht der Geschichte des Protestantismus.* Tübingen: T. G. B. Mohr (Paul Siebeck), 1906.

Hunsinger, George. *Disruptive Grace: Studies in the Theology of Karl Barth.* Grand Rapids: Eerdmans, 2000.

_____. *"Fides Christo Formata*: Luther, Barth and the Joint Declaration." In *The Gospel of Justification in Christ: Where Does the Church Stand Today?*, edited by Wayne C. Stumme, 69–84. Grand Rapids: Eerdmans, 2006.

Jenson, Robert W. "An Ontology of Freedom in the 'De Servo Arbitrio' of Luther." In *Freiheit als Liebe bei Martin Luther, Freedom as Love in Martin Luther: 8th International Congress for Luther Research in St. Paul, Minnesota, 1993, Seminar 1 Referate/Papers*, edited by Dennis D. Bielfeldt and Klaus Schwarzwäller, 113–18. Frankfurt am Main: Peter Lang, 1995.

Joint Declaration on the Doctrine of Justification: The Lutheran World Federation and the Roman Catholic Church. Grand Rapids: Eerdmans, 2000.

Jüngel, Eberhard. *Das Evangelium von der Rechtfertigung des Gottlosen als Zentrum des christlichen Glaubens: Eine theologische Studie in ökumenischer Absicht*. Tübingen: J. C. B. Mohr (Paul Siebeck), 1998.

_____. *Justification: The Heart of the Christian Faith—A Theological Study with an Ecumenical Purpose*. 3rd ed. Translated by Jeffrey F. Cayzer. Edinburgh: T & T Clark, 2001.

_____. *The Freedom of a Christian: Luther's Significance for Contemporary Theology*. Translated by Roy A. Harrisville. Minneapolis: Augsburg Publishing House, 1988.

_____. *Zur Freiheit eines Christenmenschen: eine Erinnerung an Luthers Schrift*. Munich: Kaiser, 1991.

Junghans, Helmar. "Martin Luther über die Nächstenliebe: Auszug aus seiner Auslegung der Epistel zum 4. Sonntag nach Epiphanias (Röm. 13, 8–10) in der 'Fastenpostille' von 1525. " *Luther: Zeitschrift der Luther-Gesellschaft* 62, no. 1 (1991): 3–11.

_____. "The Center of the Theology of Martin Luther." Translated by Gerald S. Krispin. In *And Every Tongue Confess: Essays in Honor of Norman Nagel on the Occasion of His Sixty-fifth Birthday*, edited by Gerald

S. Krispin and Jon D. Vieker, 179–94. Dearborn, MI: Nagel Festschrift Committee, 1990.

Juntunen, Sammeli. "Luther and Metaphysics: What is the Structure of Being according to Luther?" In *Union with Christ: The New Finnish Interpretation of Luther*, edited by Carl E. Braaten and Robert W. Jenson, 129–60. Grand Rapids: Eerdmans, 1998.

Kärkkäinen, Veli-Matti. "'Drinking from the Same Wells with Orthodox and Catholics': Insights from the Finnish Interpretation of Luther's Theology." *Currents in Theology and Mission* 34, no. 2 (2007): 85–96.

_____. "'The Christian as Christ to the Neighbor': On Luther's Theology of love." *International Journal of Systematic Theology* 6, no. 2 (2004): 101–17.

Kim, Sun-young. "Faith and Love as the Overriding Thematic Pair in Luther's Exposition of the Lord's Prayer." *Korean Journal of Christian Studies* 72 (2010): 87–107.

_____. "Faith and Love in Luther's Sacramental Theology: Its Theological Significance and Ethical Ramifications." *Korean Journal of Christian Studies* 84 (2012): 127–47.

_____. "Luther on 'Sabbatical Observance': Faith and Love." *Korean Journal of Christian Studies* 87 (2013): 81–102.

_____. "Luther on Women: The Dualism of Flesh and Spirit versus the Logic of Faith and Love." Paper presented at the Conference of the Church History Society in Korea, Pyungtaek, South Korea, May 24, 2014. *Source Book*, 90-108.

_____. "Luther's Principles of Biblical Interpretation: Jesus Christ, Law & Gospel, and Faith & Love." Paper presented at the Conference of Korea Association of Christian Studies, Asan, South Korea, October 18, 2013. *Source Book*, 99–116.

_____. "The Third Use of the Law in Luther?" *Korean Journal of Christian Studies* 73 (2011): 119–51.

Kolb, Robert. "Luther on the Two Kinds of Righteousness: Reflections on His Two-Dimensional Definition of Humanity at the Heart of His Theology." *Lutheran Quarterly* 13, no. 4 (1999): 449–66.

_____. *Martin Luther: Confessor of the Faith*. Oxford: Oxford University Press, 2009.

Krodel, Gottfried G. "The Lord's Supper in the Theology of the Young Luther." *Lutheran Quarterly* 13, no. 1 (1961): 19–33.

Laato, Timo. "Justification: The Stumbling Block of the Finnish Luther School." *Concordia Theological Quarterly* 72 (2008): 327–46.

Lazareth, William H. "Love and Law in Christian Life." In *Piety, Politics, and Ethics: Reformation Studies in Honor of George Wolfgang Forell*, edited by Carter Lindberg, 103–17. Kirksville, MO: Sixteenth Century Journal Publishers, 1984.

_____. *Christians in Society: Luther, the Bible, and Social Ethics*. Minneapolis: Fortress Press, 2001.

Leroux, Neil R. *Luther's Rhetoric: Strategies and Style from the Invocavit Sermons*. Saint Louis: Concordia Publishing House, 2002.

Lindberg, Carter. *Beyond Charity: Reformation Initiatives for the Poor*. Minneapolis: Fortress Press, 1993.

_____. "Do Lutherans Shout Justification but Whisper Sanctification? Justification and Sanctification in the Lutheran Tradition." In *Justification and Sanctification: In the Traditions of the Reformation*. The Fifth Consultation on the First and Second Reformations Geneva, 13 to 17 February 1998, edited by Milan Opočenský and Páraic Réamonn, 97–112. Geneva: World Alliance of Reformed Churches, 1999.

_____. *Love: A Brief History through Western Christianity*. Malden, MA: Blackwell, 2008.

_____. "Luther on Poverty." In *Harvesting Martin Luther's Reflections on Theology, Ethics, and the Church*, edited by Timothy J. Wengert, 134–51. Grand Rapids: Eerdmans, 2004.

Lohse, Bernhard. *Luthers Theologie in ihrer historischen Entwicklung und in ihrem systematischen Zusammenhang.* Göttingen: Vandenhoeck & Ruprecht, 1995.

_____. *Martin Luther: An Introduction to His Life and Work.* Translated and edited by Robert C. Schultz. Philadelphia: Fortress Press, 1986.

_____. *Martin Luther: Eine Einführung in sein Leben und sein Werk.* Munich: C. H. Beck, 1981.

_____. *Martin Luther's Theology: Its Historical and Systematic Development.* Translated and edited by Roy A. Harrisville. Minneapolis: Fortress Press, 1999.

Loofs, Friedrich. "Der 'articulus stantis et cadentis ecclesiae'." *Theologische Studien und Kritiken* 90 (1917): 323–420.

Mahlmann, T. "Articulus stantis et [vel] cadentis ecclesiae." In *Die Religion in Geschichte und Gegenwart*, vol. 1. 4th ed. Tübingen: Mohr Siebeck, 1998.

Malloy, Christopher J. *Engrafted into Christ: A Critique of the Joint Declaration.* New York: Peter Lang, 2005.

Malysz, Piotr J. "*Nemo iudex in causa sua* as the Basis of Law, Justice, and Justification in Luther's Thought." *Harvard Theological Review* 100, no. 3 (2007): 363–86.

Mannermaa, Tuomo. "Das Verhältnis von Glaube und Liebe in der Theologie Luthers." In *Luther in Finnland—Der Einfluß der Theologie Martin Luthers in Finnland und finnische Beiträge zur Lutherforschung*, edited by Miikka Ruokanen, 99–110. Schriften der Luther-Agricola-Gesellschaft, no. A 23. Helsinki: Luther-Agricola-Gesellschaft, 1986. See (duplicated) also, "Das Verhältnis von Glaube und Nächstenliebe in der Theologie Luthers." In *Der im Glauben gegenwärtige Christus: Rechtfertigung und Vergottung zum ökumenischen Dialog*, 95–105. Arbeiten zur Geschichte und Theologie des Luthertums, Neue Folge Bd. 8. Hannover: Lutherisches Verlagshaus, 1989.

_____. *Der im Glauben gegenwärtige Christus: Rechtfertigung und Vergottung zum ökumenischen Dialog.* Arbeiten zur Geschichte und Theologie des Luthertums, Neue Folge Bd. 8. Hannover: Luthersches Verlagshaus, 1989.

_____. "Doctrine of Justification and Trinitarian Ontology." In *Trinity, Time, and Church: A Response to the Theology of Robert W. Jenson,* edited by Colin E. Gunton, 139–45. Grand Rapids, MI: Eerdmans, 2000.

_____. "Freiheit als Liebe: Einführung in das Thema." In *Freiheit als Liebe bei Martin Luther, Freedom as Love in Martin Luther: 8th International Congress for Luther Research in St. Paul, Minnesota, 1993, Seminar 1 Referate/Papers,* edited by Dennis D. Bielfeldt and Klaus Schwarzwäller, 9–18. Frankfurt am Main: Peter Lang, 1995.

_____. "Grundlagenforschung der Theologie Martin Luthers und die Ökumene." In *Der im Glauben gegenwärtige Christus: Rechtfertigung und Vergottung zum ökumenischen Dialog,* 183–200. Arbeiten zur Geschichte und Theologie des Luthertums, Neue Folge Bd. 8. Hannover: Lutherisches Verlagshaus, 1989; In *Thesaurus Lutheri: Auf der Suche nach neuen Paradigmen der Luther-Forschung, Referate des Luther-Symposiums in Finnland 11. –12. November 1986,* edited by Tuomo Mannermaa, Anja Ghiselli, and Simo Peura, 17–35. Veröffentlichungen der Finnischen Theologischen Literaturgesellschaft, no. 153 (Jahrbuch 1987) and Luther-Agricola-Gesellschaft, no. A 24. Helsinki: Finnische Theologische Literaturgesellschaft and Luther-Agricola-Gesellschaft, 1987.

_____. "Hat Luther eine trinitarische Ontologie?" In *Luther und Ontology: Das Sein Christi im Glauben als strukturierendes Prinzip der Theologie Luthers.* Schriften der Luther-Agricola-Gesellschaft 31. Referate der Fachtagung des Instituts für Systematische Theologie der Universität Helsinki in Zusammenarbeit mit der Luther-Akademie Ratzeburg in Helsinki 1.–5. 4. 1992, edited by Anja Ghiselli, Kari Kopperi, and Rainer

Vinke, 9–27. Helsinki: Luther-Agricola-Gesellschaft, 1993. See (duplicated) also, "Hat Luther eine trinitarische Ontologie?" In *Luther und die trinitarische Tradition. Ökumenische und philosophische Perspektiven,* Veröffentlichungen der Luther-Akademie Ratzeburg, Bd. 23, edited by Joachim Heubach, 43–60. Erlangen: Martin-Luther-Verlag, 1994.

_____. "In ipsa fide Christus adest: Der Schnittpunkt zwischen lutherischer und orthodoxer Theologie." In *Der im Glauben gegenwärtige Christus: Rechtfertigung und Vergottung zum ökumenischen Dialog,* translated by Hans-Christian Daniel and Juhani Forsberg, 11–93. Arbeiten zur Geschichte und Theologie des Luthertums, Neue Folge Bd. 8. Hannover: Lutherisches Verlagshaus, 1989; *In ipsa fide Christus adest: Luterilaisen ja ortodoksisen kristinuskonkäsityksen leikkauspiste (In Faith Itself Christ Is Really Present: The Point of Intersection between Lutheran and Orthodox Theology),* Missiologian ja Ekumeniikan Seura R. Y., Missiologian ja Ekumeniikan Seuran julkaisuja, vol. 30. Vammala: Vammalan Kirjapaino, 1979; ET *Christ Present in Faith: Luther's View of Justification.* Edited by Kirsi Stjerna. Minneapolis: Fortress Press, 2005.

_____. "Justification and *Theosis* in Lutheran-Orthodox Perspective." In *Union with Christ: The New Finnish Interpretation of Luther,* edited by Carl E. Braaten and Robert W. Jenson, 25–41. Grand Rapids: Eerdmans, 1998.

_____. "Participation and Love in the Theology of Martin Luther." In *Philosophical Studies in Religion, Metaphysics, and Ethics: Essays in Honour of Heikki Kirjavainen. Schriften der Luther-Agricola-Gesellschaft* 38, edited by Timo Koistinen and Tommi Lehtonen, 303–11. Helsinki: Luther-Agricola-Society, 1997.

_____. "Theosis als Thema der finnischen Lutherforschung." In *Luther und Theosis: Vergöttlichung als Thema der abendländischen Theologie.* Referate der Fachtagung der Luther-Akademie Ratzeburg in Helsinki 30.3–2.4. 1989. Schriften der Luther-Agricola-Gesellschaft A 25, edited by Simo Peura and Antti Raunio, 11–26. Helsinki: Luther-Agricola-Gesellschaft; Erlangen: Luther- Akademie Ratzebrug, 1990.

_____. "Theosis as a Subject of Finnish Luther Research." *Pro Ecclesia* 4 (1995): 37–48.

_____. *Von Preussen nach Leuenberg: Hintergrund und Entwicklung der theologischen Methode in der Leuenberger Konkordie*. Arbeiten zur Geschichte und Theologie Luthertums. Hamburg: Lutherisches Verlagshaus, 1981.

_____. "Why Is Luther So Fascinating? Modern Finnish Luther Research." In *Union with Christ: The New Finnish Interpretation of Luther*, edited by Carl E. Braaten and Robert W. Jenson, 1–20. Grand Rapids: Eerdmans, 1998.

Martikainen, Eeva. "Die Unio im Brennpunkt der theologischen Forschung." In *Unio: Gott und Mensch in der nachreformatorischen Theologie*, edited by Eeva Martikainen, 13–18. Helsinki: Luther-Agricola-Gesellschaft, 1996.

Marty, Martin. "Luther on Ethics: Man Free and Slave." In *Accents in Luther's Theology: Essays in Commemoration of the 450th Anniversary of the Reformation*, edited by Heino O. Kadai, 199–227. Saint Louis: Concordia Publishing House, 1967.

Maschke, Timothy. "Contemporaneity: A Hermeneutical Perspective in Martin Luther's Work." In *Ad Fontes Lutheri: Toward the Recovery of the Real Luther-Essays in Honor of Kenneth Hagen's Sixty-Birthday*, edited by Timothy Maschke, Franz Posset, and Joan Skocir, 165–82. Milwaukee: Marquette University Press, 2001.

Mattes, Mark C. *The Role of Justification in Contemporary Theology*. Grand Rapids: Eerdmans, 2004.

Mau, Rudolf. "Liebe als gelebte Freiheit der Christen: Luthers Auslegung von G 5, 13–24 im Kommentar von 1519." *Lutherjahrbuch* 59 (1992): 11–37.

McCormack, Bruce L., ed. *Justification in Perspective: Historical Developments and Contemporary Challenges.* Grand Rapids: Baker Academic, 2006.

McGrath, Alister E. *Iustitia Dei: A History of the Christian Doctrine of Justification*, 3rd ed. Cambridge: Cambridge University Press, 2005.

_____. *Luther's Theology of the Cross: Martin Luther's Theological Breakthrough.* Malden, MA: Blackwell, 2004.

Meinhold, Peter. *Die Genesisvorlesung Luthers und ihre Herausgeber.* Stuttgart: W. Kohlhammer, 1936.

Murray, Scott R. *Law, Life, and the Living God: The Third Use of the Law in Modern American Lutheranism.* Saint Louis: Concordia Publishing House, 2002.

Niebuhr, Reinhold. *Christian Realism and Political Problems: Essays on Political, Social, Ethical and Theological Themes.* New York: Charles Scribner's Sons, 1953.

_____. *The Nature and Destiny of Man.* Vol. 2, *Human Destiny.* Louisville: Westminster John Knox, 1964.

Nygren, Anders. *Agape and Eros.* Translated by Philip S. Watson. New York: Harper & Row, 1969.

O'Donovan, Oliver. *The Problem of Self-Love in St. Augustine.* New Haven, CT: Yale University Press, 1980.

Oberman, Heiko A. "*Facientibus quod in se est Deus non denegat gratiam*: Robert Holcot O.P. and the Beginnings of Luther's Theology." In *The Reformation in Medieval Perspective*, edited by Steven E. Ozment, 119–41. Chicago: Quadrangle Books, 1971; *Harvard Theological Review* 55 (1962): 317–42.

_____. *Forerunners of the Reformation: The Shape of Late Medieval Thought.* Translated by Paul L. Nyhus. Cambridge: James Clarke & Co., 2002; Lutterworth, 1967.

_____. "'Iustitia Christi' and 'Iustitia Dei': Luther and the Scholastic Doctrines of Justification." *Harvard Theological Review* 59 (1966): 1–26.

_____. *Luther: Man between God and the Devil*. Translated by Eileen Walliser-Schwarzbart. New York: Image Books, 1992.

_____. *The Dawn of the Reformation: Essays in Late Medieval and Early Reformation Thought*. Grand Rapids: Eerdmans, 1992.

_____. *The Harvest of Medieval Theology: Gabriel Biel and Late Medieval Nominalism*. Grand Rapids: Baker Academic, 2000.

Oberman, Heiko A., ed. *Luther and the Dawn of the Modern Era: Papers for the Fourth International Congress for Luther Research*. Leiden: Brill, 1974.

Outka, Gene H. *Agape: An Ethical Analysis*. New Haven, CT: Yale University Press, 1972.

Ozment, Steven E. "*Homo Viator*: Luther and Late Medieval Theology." In *The Reformation in Medieval Perspective*, edited by Steven E. Ozment, 142–54. Chicago: Quadrangle Books, 1971; *Harvard Theological Review* 62 (1969): 275–87.

Pelikan, Jaroslav. "Luther Comes to the New World." In *Luther and the Dawn of the Modern Era: Papers for the Fourth International Congress for Luther Research*, edited by Heiko A. Oberman, 1–10. Leiden: Brill, 1974.

Peura, Simo. "Christ as Favor and Gift (*donum*): The Challenge of Luther's Understanding of Justification." In *Union with Christ: The New Finnish Interpretation of Luther*, edited by Carl E. Braaten and Robert W. Jenson, 42–69. Grand Rapids: Eerdmans, 1998.

_____. "Christus als Gunst und Gabe: Luthers Verständnis der Rechtfertigung als Herausforderung an den ökumenischen Dialog mit der Römisch-katholischen Kirche." In *Caritas Dei: Beitrage zum Verständnis Luthers und der gegenwärtigen Okumene: Festschrift für Tuomo Mannermaa zum 60. Geburtstag*, edited by Oswald Bayer, Robert W. Jenson, and Simo Knuuttila, 340–63. Helsinki: Luther-Agricola-Gesellschaft, 1997.

_____. "Die Teilhabe an Christus bei Luther." In *Luther und Theosis: Vergöttlichung als Thema der abendländischen Theologie*. Referate der

Fachtagung der Luther-Akademie Ratzeburg in Helsinki 30.3–2.4. 1989. Schriften der Luther-Agricola-Gesellschaft A 25, edited by Simo Peura and Antti Raunio, 121–61. Helsinki: Luther-Agricola-Gesellschaft; Erlangen: Luther-Akademie Ratzebrug, 1990.

_____. *Mehr als ein Mensch? Die Vergöttlichung als Thema der Theologie Martin Luthers von 1513 bis 1519.* Veröffentlichungen des Instituts für Europäische Geschichte, Mainz, Band 152. Mainz: Philipp von Zabern, 1994.

_____. "What God Gives Man Receives: Luther on Salvation." In *Union with Christ: The New Finnish Interpretation of Luther,* edited by Carl E. Braaten and Robert W. Jenson, 76–95. Grand Rapids: Eerdmans, 1998.

Raunio, Antti. "Die Goldene Regel als Gesetz der göttlichen Natur: Das natürliche Gesetz und das göttliche Gesetz in Luthers Theologie 1522–1523." In *Luther und Theosis: Vergöttlichung als Thema der abendländischen Theologie.* Referate der Fachtagung der Luther-Akademie Ratzeburg in Helsinki 30. 3–2. 4. 1989. Schriften der Luther-Agricola-Gesellschaft A 25, edited by Simo Peura and Antti Raunio, 163–86. Helsinki: Luther-Agricola-Gesellschaft; Erlangen: Luther-Akademie Ratzebrug, 1990.

_____. "Die 'Goldene Regel' als theologisches Prinzip beim jungen Luther." In *Thesaurus Lutheri: Auf der Suche nach neuen Paradigmen der Luther-Forschung, Referate des Luther-Symposiums in Finnland 11. –12. November 1986,* edited by Tuomo Mannermaa, Anja Ghiselli, and Simo Peura, 309–27. Veröffentlichungen der Finnischen Theologischen Literaturgesellschaft, no. 153 (Jahrbuch 1987) and Luther-Agricola-Gesellschaft, no. A 24. Helsinki: Finnische Theologische Literaturgesellschaft and Luther-Agricola-Gesellschaft, 1987.

_____. "Natural Law and Faith: The Forgotten Foundations of Ethics in Luther's Theology." In *Union with Christ: The New Finnish Interpretation of Luther,* edited by Carl E. Braaten and Robert W. Jenson, 96–124. Grand Rapids: Eerdmans, 1998.

_____. *Summe des christlichen Lebens: die "Goldene Regel" als Gesetz der Liebe in der Tehologie Martin Luthers von 1510–1527*. Mainz: Verlag Philipp von Zabern, 2001.

Ritschl, Albrecht. *The Christian Doctrine of Justification and Reconciliation*. Edited by H. R. Mackintosh and A. B. Macaulay. Eugene, OR: Wipf & Stock, 2002; 1966.

Root, Michael. "The Implications of the *Joint Declaration on Justification* and its Wider Impact for Lutheran Participation in the Ecumenical Movement." In *Justification and the Future of the Ecumenical Movement: The Joint Declaration on the Doctrine of Justification*, edited by William G. Rusch, 47–60. Collegeville, MN: Liturgical Press, 2003.

Rousselot, Pierre. *The Problem of Love in the Middle Ages: A Historical Contribution*. Translated by Alan Vincelette. Reviewed and corrected by Pol Vandevelde. Milwaukee: Marquette University Press, 2001; 1908.

Rusch, William G., ed. *Justification and the Future of the Ecumenical Movement: The Joint Declaration on the Doctrine of Justification*. Collegeville, MN: Liturgical Press, 2003.

Saarinen, Risto. *Faith and Holiness: Lutheran-Orthodox Dialogue, 1959–1994 (Kirche und Konfession)*. Göttingen: Vandenhoeck & Ruprecht, 1997.

_____. *Gottes Wirken auf uns: Die transzendentale Deutung des Gegenwart-Christ-Motivs in der Lutherforschung*. Veröffentlichungen des Instituts für europäische Geschichte, Mainz 137. Wiesbaden: Steiner, 1989.

_____. "The Presence of God in Luther's Theology." *Lutheran Quarterly* 3 (1994): 3–13.

_____. "Salvation in the Lutheran-Orthodox Dialogue: A Comparative Perspective." In *Union with Christ: The New Finnish Interpretation of Luther*, edited by Carl E. Braaten and Robert W. Jenson, 167–81. Grand Rapids: Eerdmans, 1998.

Sauter, Gerhard. "Rechtfertigung." *Theologische Realenzyklopädie*, vol. 28. Berlin: Walter de Gruyter, 1997; ET "God Creating Faith: The Doctrine of Justification from the Reformation to the Present." Translated by Arthur Sutherland and Stephan Kläs. *Lutheran Quarterly* 11, no. 1 (1997): 17–102.

Schmid, Heinrich. *Die Dogmatik der evangelisch-lutherischen Kirche*. Edited by Horst Georg Pöhlmann. Gütersloh: Gerd Mohn, 1979.

_____. *The Doctrinal Theology of the Evangelical Lutheran Church*. 3rd ed. Revised and translated by Charles A. Hay and Henry E. Jacobs. Minneapolis: Augsburg Publishing House, 1961.

Schwarz, Reinhard. *Fides, spes und caritas beim jungen Luther, unter besonderer Berücksichtigung der mittelalterlichen Tradition*. Berlin: Walter de Gruyter, 1962.

Schwarzwäller, Klaus. "Verantwortung des Glaubens Freiheit und Liebe nach der Dekalogauslegung Martin Luthers." In *Freiheit als Liebe bei Martin Luther, Freedom as Love in Martin Luther: 8th International Congress for Luther Research in St. Paul, Minnesota, 1993, Seminar 1 Referate/Papers*, edited by Dennis D. Bielfeldt and Klaus Schwarzwäller, 133–58. Frankfurt am Main: Peter Lang, 1995.

Singer, Irving. *The Nature of Love: Plato to Luther*. Vol. 1. New York: Random House, 1966.

Solberg, Mary M. *Compelling Knowledge: A Feminist Proposal for an Epistemology of the Cross*. New York: State University of New York Press, 1997.

Steinmetz, David C. *Luther in Context*. 2nd ed. Grand Rapids: Baker Academic, 2002.

Strohl, Jane E. "Luther's Invocavit Sermons." In *Freiheit als Liebe bei Martin Luther, Freedom as Love in Martin Luther: 8th International Congress for Luther Research in St. Paul, Minnesota, 1993, Seminar 1 Referate/Papers*, edited by Dennis D. Bielfeldt and Klaus Schwarzwäller, 159–66. Frankfurt am Main: Peter Lang, 1995.

Thompson, Virgil, ed. *Justification is for Preaching: Essays by Oswald Bayer, Gerhard O. Forde, and Others.* Eugene, OR: Pickwick, 2012.

Torvend, Sameul. *Luther and the Hungry Poor: Gathered Fragments.* Minneapolis: Fortress Press, 2008.

Totten, Mark T. "Luther on unio cum Christo: Toward a Model for Integrating Faith and Ethics." *Journal of Religious Ethics* 31, no. 3 (2003): 443–62.

Troeltsch, Ernst. *The Social Teaching of the Christian Churches*, vol. 2. Translated by Olive Wyon. Louisville: Westminster John Knox, 1992.

van Bavel, Tarsicius J. "Love." In *Augustine through the Ages: An Encyclopedia*, edited by Allan D. Fitzgerald, O.S.A., 509–16. Grand Rapids: Eerdmans, 1999.

Vinke, Rainer. "'…aber die Liebe ist die größte unter ihnen' Zu Luthers Auslegung von 1. Korinther 13." In *Freiheit als Liebe bei Martin Luther, Freedom as Love in Martin Luther: 8th International Congress for Luther Research in St. Paul, Minnesota, 1993, Seminar 1 Referate/Papers*, edited by Dennis D. Bielfeldt and Klaus Schwarzwäller, 167–80. Frankfurt am Main: Peter Lang, 1995.

von Schlink, Edmund. "Gesetz und Paraklese." In *Gesetz und Evangelium: Beiträge zur Gegenwärtigen Theologischen Diskussion*, edited by Ernst Kinder and Klaus Haendler, 239–59. Darmstadt: Wissenschaftliche Buchgesellschaft, 1968.

Wannenwetsch, Bernd. "Luther's Moral Theology." In *The Cambridge Companion to Martin Luther*, edited by Donald K. McKim, 120–35. Cambridge: Cambridge University Press, 2003.

Watson, Philip S. *Let God Be God!: An Interpretation of the Theology of Martin Luther.* Eugene, OR: Wipf & Stock, 2000.

Weber, Max. *The Protestant Ethic and the Spirit of Capitalism.* Translated by Talcott Parsons with an introduction by Anthony Giddens. London: Routledge, 2002.

Westerholm, Stephen. *Perspectives Old and New on Paul: The "Lutheran" Paul and His Critics.* Grand Rapids: Eerdmans, 2004.

Wicks, Jared, S. J. "Justification and Faith in Luther's Theology." *Theological Studies* 44, no. 1 (1983): 3–29.

_____. *Luther and His Spiritual Legacy.* Wilmington, DE: Michael Glazier, 1983.

Wingren, Gustaf. *Luther on Vocation.* Translated by C. C. Rasmussen. Eugene, OR: Wipf & Stock, 2004; 1957.

Wood, Arthur S. "Theology of Luther's Lectures on Romans, I." *Scottish Journal of Theology* 3, no. 1 (1950): 1–18.

_____. "Theology of Luther's Lectures on Romans, II." *Scottish Journal of Theology* 3, no. 1 (1950): 113–26.

Wriedt, Markus. "Luther's Theology." In *The Cambridge Companion to Martin Luther,* edited by Donald K. McKim, 86–119. Cambridge: Cambridge University Press, 2003.

Wright, David. "The Ethical Use of the Old Testament in Luther and Calvin: A Comparison." *Scottish Journal of Theology* 36 (1983): 463–85.

Ziemke, Donald C. *Love for the Neighbor in Luther's Theology: The Development of His Thought 1512–1529.* Minneapolis: Augsburg Publishing House, 1963.

_____. *The Hermeneutical Basis for Luther's Doctrine of Love for the Neighbor.* PhD diss., Princeton Theological Seminary, 1960.

Index of Subjects

Index of Names

Index of Biblical References

CPSIA information can be obtained at www.ICGtesting.com
Printed in the USA
LVOW04s1238230814

400579LV00003B/6/P